JOHN DEERE LIFE INSURANCE CO.
DAVE KING, DIV. MGR.
516 S. E. MORRISON, SUITE M8
PORTLAND, OREGON 97214

COMPLETE SALES CONFERENCE DESK HANDBOOK

COMPLETE SALES CONFERENCE DESK HANDBOOK

Herbert G. Schubert

PARKER PUBLISHING COMPANY, INC.   West Nyack, NY

© 1981 *by*
Sales Communications

All rights reserved. No part of this book may be reproduced in any form or by any means, without permission in writing from the publisher.

Library of Congress Cataloging in Publication Data

Schubert, Herbert G
  Complete sales conference desk handbook.

  Includes index.
  1. Sales meetings. 2. Meetings. I. Title.
HF5438.8.M4S38   658.8'106   79-25233
ISBN 0-13-162453-9

Printed in the United States of America

How the Complete Sales Conference Desk Handbook Can Help You

The date of the meeting has been set, and you wonder . . . "How am I going to produce an outstanding program?" You begin to think: "Wouldn't it be great to have a source to turn to for ideas on how to conduct a meeting that is lively, sparkling, enthusiastic, and resultful." Such an idea source is available in this desk book.

The book is the outgrowth of my needs when I was called upon to stage sales meetings and conferences. Over the years I had developed and refined checklists which became very useful under the pressure of time. Also especially important was my file of "ideas" pertaining to conferences. Every time I would hear or read of an interesting and profitable idea it would go into the file.

In talking with other meeting planners, I found that they, too, had the same need for an idea file, so I decided to organize my collected information into this manual. The result is a compendium of *tested ideas* which are useful to planners of both sales and association conferences of every size and type. The information is for all members of the meeting team—sales and association managers, advertising and promotion managers, seminar leaders, trainers, speakers, and personnel responsible for the production of conference material. In all, there are over 1,000 ideas.

The handbook contains "how to" information for every stage of the conference—for the planning, promoting, conducting, and evaluation of the meeting. In short, it is a library of ideas which can be turned to for suggestions on how to make that next meeting even more exciting, dramatic, stimulating, and rewarding.

There are no lengthy discussions, only the distillation of ideas. You will note that the manual essentially is an idea-starting device. The suggestions contained herein can, of course, be refined, changed, and embellished for your own particular requirements. The table of contents guides you in your search, and in addition the index is cross-referenced to provide still another means to locate the appropriate idea.

And in the narrative you will observe that the manual gives supplier addresses and approximate price. In addition, there is a handy "Buyer's Guide" of meeting and promotion supplies.

The handbook begins with a step-by-step planning outline—including "How to set objectives" and "How to set up the budget." Then there is a list of conference themes, tips on site selection, and instructions on how to negotiate with the hotel.

There is a chapter on "How to Stretch the Meeting Budget" which could pay for the manual many times over in your very first meeting. It gives tips on how to save hundreds (even thousands) of dollars on beverages. There are tips on how to cut down on those expensive hors d'oeuvre costs by 25 to 40%. The chapter tells you where to find dozens of free sources of supply—a real treasure in obtaining the most mileage from your budget.

You learn how to involve the audience in presentations, how to keep technical speeches from being dull. A "Three-Minute Communications Test" for the beginning of the program (Chapter 10) practically guarantees that your attendees will be paying close attention the rest of the meeting.

The manual tells how to charge your meeting with excitement. There are showmanship ideas, dramatic uses of charts and slides, hints on introducing the product, how to present sales campaigns, and tips for building esprit de corps. Most of these suggestions are simple, inexpensive-to-produce, but highly effective ideas which are used by the professionals.

Chapters tell you how to promote attendance, how to enliven the printed program, and how to plan, prepare, and use visual presentations. For the speakers and the MC, there are hundreds of jokes and one-liners indexed by subject.

There are ideas for making your guests welcome, on do-it-yourself entertainment, and suggestions for conducting the golf tournament. Also ideas for the banquet and for the hospitality suite, and much more.

Whether you are a full-time or a part-time conference planner, or a newcomer or an old pro, you will find this handbook a useful tool for making your next meeting outstanding, exciting, and different! It will be your handy reference source to turn to for many years to come.

Herbert G. Schubert

Contents

Chapter

How the Complete Sales Conference Desk Handbook Can Help You .   1

1. How to Plan a Successful Conference Program   7
2. 209 Themes for the Conference 21
3. How to Evaluate and Follow Up on the Conference 25
4. 214 Ways to Stretch the Meeting Budget 31
5. Conference Site Selection Tips 49
6. How to Create Interest, Enthusiasm, and Results 55
7. How to Make the Most Effective Use of Panels 75
8. 39 Tested Ideas to Secure Participation 79
9. Creative Techniques to Promote the Conference 89
10. Tested Ideas to Dramatize the Conference 111
11. 75 Proven Showmanship Techniques for Presentations and Speeches 121
12. Using Stunts and Gags to Enliven the Conference 137
13. How to Plan, Prepare, and Use Visual Presentations Effectively 149
14. How to Enliven the Conference Printed Program 167
15. Sales Conference Icebreaker and Welcome Ideas 173
16. Do-It-Yourself Ideas for the Reception, Banquet, and Theme Parties 191
17. How to Program the Ladies' Events 209
18. 31 Tips for Serving Liquid Refreshment 219
19. How to Plan Meal Functions and Menus 227

Chapter

20. 14 Imaginative Techniques for the Hospitality Suite 235
21. How to Plan, Promote, and Conduct the Golf Tournament 239
22. 12 Step-by-Step Conference Planning Checklists 253
Appendix 1 275
Appendix 2 326
Directory of Suppliers 356
Index 383

COMPLETE SALES CONFERENCE DESK HANDBOOK

Chapter 1

How to Plan a Successful Conference Program

Contents

1. Appoint and Brief Planning Committee
2. Determine the Purpose of the Meeting—the Information to Be Imparted and Changes and Improvements Required
3. List the Specific Objectives
4. Rank Objectives and Determine Time Allocations
5. Select a Theme to Fit Objectives
6. Decide on Type of Meeting to Be Held
7. Delegate Program Responsibilities
8. Set the Meeting Budget
9. Determine How to Get the Participants Involved
10. Decide on Presentation Methods
11. Plan the Program Timing
12. Insure That Action Takes Place After the Meeting
13. Hold Program Planning Review Meetings
14. Rehearse and Rehearse
15. Additional Planning Tips
16. Advance Bulletin Mailings
17. How to Plan the Budget

Program Planning Steps

1. Appoint and brief planning committee.
2. Determine the purpose of the meeting—the information to be imparted and the changes and improvements required.
3. List the specific objectives.
4. Rank objectives and determine time allocations.
5. Select a theme to fit objectives.
6. Decide on type of meeting to be held (training clinic, seminar, workshop, etc.)
7. Delegate program responsibilities.
8. Set the meeting budget.
9. Determine how to get the participants involved.
10. Decide on presentation methods.
11. Plan the program timing.
12. Insure that action takes place after the meeting.
13. Hold program planning review meetings.
14. Rehearse and rehearse.

1. APPOINT AND BRIEF PLANNING COMMITTEE.

Begin planning by appointing a "Program Planning Committee." Hold a briefing session and present a planning outline. In the briefing, point out that the committee's first and most important task is to determine what results the conference should produce.

The planning committee must ascertain what the needs of both the company and attendees are, and then decide what changes and improvements are needed to implement these needs.

In other words, start with the conclusion of the conference: (1) provide the attendees with information they can use, (2) see that they are instructed in using this information to best advantage, and (3) motivate them to use the information.

2. DETERMINE THE PURPOSE OF THE MEETING— THE INFORMATION TO BE IMPARTED AND CHANGES AND IMPROVEMENTS REQUIRED.

Information sources in determining the meeting's purpose can be a review of the company's yearly marketing plan, sales targets, input from product managers, field supervisors, market intelligence or market analysis group, and input from the attendees. Look for actual sales situations which call for improvement. Question managers who have attended previous meetings. Review the planning files of previous conferences. Send a questionnaire to prospective attendees.

Some typical purposes of a conference are:
(a) To impart information
(b) To obtain acceptance of a plan or proposal
(c) To motivate and enthuse
(d) To train
(e) To obtain solutions to a problem
(f) To uncover selling problems
(g) To change an attitude

As the conference's purpose is developed ask yourselves if a conference is the best way to achieve the stated objectives. Conferences are expensive in actual expenditures and in time away from work. Could the objectives be achieved by a telephone conference? Or by a policy memo? Or by a carefully prepared presentation which is mailed? Or by trips by staff members to groups in the field?

(a) Obtain Participation of Key Decision Makers in the Program Planning Process.

In most cases the program is evolved by the conference committee holding an initial meeting to discuss general ideas. At a later meeting the conference committee reviews a proposed program as submitted by the program planner. It is important that the planner consult with each committee member individually, not only to obtain ideas but, more importantly, to make sure that the committee member feels that he or she is involved in the planning process. Otherwise, the planner may find that a key member severely criticizes the proposed program and it must be redrawn completely.

(b) What do the Delegates Want Discussed at the Meeting?

What management wants is important, but equally important is what the audience wants discussed. So send out a questionnaire to both participants and management personnel soliciting their views concerning the program content. This will make participants feel involved and help make them feel favorable about the meeting content. They will perceive that management is concerned with their problems, thus resulting in a meeting where communication really takes place.

Better yet, instead of a mailed questionnaire, go out in the field to discuss and probe into the needs and desires of the typical attendee. And, if possible, go back into the field to observe the response to the program.

If it is an association meeting, it is necessary to obtain a profile of the typical attendee before planning the program. What is the average degree of knowledge in the subject matter? Are the attendees supervisors, owners, salesmen? What is the average age? How many years of experience? Are they from diversified departments or industries?

(c) Suggested Questionnaire Content:
- (a) Ask participants to list job problems that should be discussed and to rank the problems in importance.
- (b) Furnish a list of topics which management wishes to present and ask participants to rank them according to which they would like to have discussed.
- (c) Ask what topics are preferred for discussion groups.
- (d) What kind of product or sales demonstrations are preferred?
- (e) What information should be presented?
- (f) What topics would they prefer outside guest speakers to cover?
- (g) What can be done to improve over previous meetings?
- (h) Be sure to leave a space for additional suggestions.

You may want to consider stating that a copy of the meeting plan, based on the questionnaires, will be sent prior to the meeting. In the report give a tabulation or summary of the types of responses.

Instead of a questionnaire you may wish to consider making up a tentative program and asking prospective attendees to express their views on program improvements to meet their particular needs.

3. LIST THE SPECIFIC OBJECTIVES.

State what the meeting is to accomplish. State what corrective action is to be taken to solve problems which have been uncovered.

Make the objectives specific; and if at all possible, make the objectives measurable.

Make the meeting goals realistic, i.e., make sure that the meeting can meet the goals within the time frame, budget, and available manpower. Include in the objectives items which enable the participants to do their job better when they are back home.

Some specific objectives are:
- (a) To improve communications.
- (b) To impart full knowledge of a particular product or market.

(c) To change attitude on _____ .
(d) To introduce a new policy on _____ .
(e) To motivate the participants to _____ .
(f) To provide an idea exchange on _____ .
(g) To encourage creative thinking.
(h) To solve the problem relating to _____ .

4. RANK OBJECTIVES AND DETERMINE TIME ALLOCATIONS.

Select the main objectives and rank them. Then determine how much time to spend on each.

If the convention is composed of mixed groups, build a matrix of objectives and a time allocation for each group.

During initial planning, the committee should always be mindful of the objectives of the conference. The entire program and each portion of the program should be examined with these questions in mind:

(a) Will this help us sell the objective to our audience?
(b) How does the audience currently feel about the subject or item? "What will the presentation do for me" reaction be?
(c) How can we make this particular part of the program interesting so that attention is captured?
(d) Have we planned what action is to be taken by the audience to get them involved?
(e) Have plans been made for carrying out the objectives after the conference?

5. SELECT A THEME TO FIT OBJECTIVES.

Endeavor to tie in the meeting theme with the objectives.

See Chapter 2—"207 THEMES FOR THE CONFERENCE" for suggestions.

6. DECIDE ON TYPE OF MEETING TO BE HELD.

You now have listed the objectives or problems to be solved. Next, you plan the most practical type of meeting (or sessions within the conference) to achieve the objectives. Following is a description of format types:

General Session Meeting

This is a general meeting with the entire group in attendance. A General Session Meeting is excellent for imparting straight information.

Seminars

Experts with similar interests get together in discusssion groups and share opinions.

Clinic

These are training sessions conducted by expert staff leaders. Usually they are composed entirely of small group sessions, but may include some general sessions as well.

Workshop

Members of the group train each other through an exchange of knowledge, job skills, and sharing of solutions to mutual problems. These are generally followed by a report by each group to a general session.

Work Conference

Good for solving assigned problems and for making action plans. A Work Conference has a high degree of participation.

Skills Training

Small groups practice skills under the direction of a trainer.

Special Interest Sessions

Attendees break up into groups which have similar interests. Sometimes the sessions are headed by experts on a particular subject.

7. DELEGATE PROGRAM RESPONSIBILITIES.

Delegate major and minor responsibilities for the various areas. Put these responsibilities in writing. Assign fixed deadlines. Responsibilities can rest with an individual or committee (in which case a chairman should be appointed to head each committee). Suggested responsibilities are:

General Chairperson	Entertainment
Co-Chairperson	Publicity
Secretary	Promotion
Treasurer or Finance	Functions (Banquet, Dance)
Program Planning	Ladies Program
Housing & Registration	Transportation

Some responsibilities may be combined such as secretary and treasurer, or treasurer and finance, or publicity and promotion.

For a committee delegation checklist see Chapter 22.

8. SET THE MEETING BUDGET.

A member of the planning committee should be responsible for the budget. He should ask each committee chairman to provide him with an itemized budget. The amount of money available may dictate where the meeting will be held and the degree of lavishness. But conversely, the objectives decided upon and the planned-for results may make it advisable to increase the budget.

Develop a budget estimate using last year's expenditures as a guide. A suggested procedure is to develop a master binder with a page for each segment of the convention, such as transportation, rooms, audio visuals, banquet, cocktail party, golf tours, ladies entertainment, etc. On this page place the anticipated budget and in a column alongside record the actual expenditures as they occur. Have another column for cumulative costs. This lets you know exactly where you stand at any time.

Be sure to budget for unanticipated items. This saves having to cut out a part of the program.

For detailed instructions on budgeting see item number 17 in this section titled, "How to Plan the Budget."

Also see Chapter 4, "214 WAYS TO STRETCH THE MEETING BUDGET."

Also see "Budget Planning Checklist" in Chapter 22.

9. DETERMINE HOW TO GET THE PARTICIPANTS INVOLVED.

Getting participation should be one of the main objectives of the meeting. Involvement will spark interest and enthusiasm and will generally lead to greater sales results after the meeting. First and foremost, make sure the program relates to the participants' problems when they are back home on the job.

Consider giving the audience a briefing prior to the meeting by mailing information in advance. This creates a feeling of involvement. The mailing can consist of a general outline of the meeting and its purpose, or the background material for the workshops.

See Chapter 8 for detailed ideas on how to stimulate participation.

10. DECIDE ON PRESENTATION METHODS.

In planning the methods of presentation, keep in mind what the presentation is to accomplish (the objective) and what action the audience is to take.

Types of presentation are many and varied. Following is a description of the main categories:

Speech Without Visuals

This is good for leaders of the organization, for presenting a point of view, and for presenting subject matter which is not too complex. Also it can be used for establishing a give-and-take atmosphere in preparation for small group discussions.

Speech With Visuals

If the material is of a complex or abstruse nature and needs to get points across in a hurry, use visual presentations such as slides, Vu-graph, flip charts, pull-down chart, blackboard, flip-flop, flannel board, or other visual methods.

Film
Film is used for presenting a volume of information, for presenting in visual form items which cannot be brought to the stage, for inspiration, and for using skilled actors to demonstrate a situation.

Panel
An informal method of presenting the views of experts who hold discussions among themselves in front of an audience and who are guided by a moderator. Questions may be asked by the audience.

Role Playing
Role playing consists of live demonstration sketches for illustrating a situation such as a sales presentation. They may be followed by small group sessions which analyze the presentations.

Forum
A Forum is good for developing opposing points of view. It is more like a debate in that the two or more speakers address the audience. A moderator summarizes the views.

11. PLAN THE PROGRAM TIMING.

(a) Overall Time Planning.
Follow the fundamental sales approach in planning the sequence of the conference events: (a) Get attention, (b) maintain interest, (c) create desire, and (d) appeal for action. This means start with an interesting beginning, keep increasing the interest, and end with bell-ringing inspiration.

Plan for the heavy speeches in the morning and schedule the participation sessions and question-and-answer periods in the afternoons. This offsets the siesta inclination after lunch.

The traditional 8-to-5 schedule need not be adhered to each day. Break the routine with an afternoon off, and then hold an evening session. Consider a breakfast session with an afternoon off, or don't start until after lunch and follow with an evening meeting.

If the meeting is in a luxurious resort or exotic location, you will, of course, want to take advantage of the surroundings. Participants will willingly attend breakfast or evening sessions in order to have half a day free. And, if possible, get away from the confines of a room; hold some of the discussion sessions in a patio or porch.

Vary the routine by showing a motivational film. Avoid showing a film right after a meal. A full stomach and a dark room provide too much competition to the presentation. And instead of giving out awards traditionally at the end of the conference, give them out at various periods during the days, but save the main award until the end. Don't rush the lunch period for large groups. Plan on allowing an hour and a half for the meal. It may be desired to have planned seating during one or two lunches to ensure the mixing of the attendees.

Allow a cushion of time throughout the program for speakers who go past the time allowed, or for question and answer periods that are too good to stop. In fact, a good rule to follow during the actual program is to always cut speaker time in favor of stimulating question and answer periods.

(b) **Breakfast Program.**

This breaks up the routine. It makes up for some lost meeting time on a day with a free afternoon. Plan for the breakfast to be served buffet style.

(c) **Evening Meeting Scheduling.**

For voluntary attendance start the meetings at 7:00 or 7:30 p.m. This allows time for eating and relaxing after the afternoon session. Close the meeting between 9:00 and 9:30 p.m. Some registrants, thus, still have time to go out for dinner or entertainment. Don't schedule heavy subjects. Provide sufficient time for questions and answers or discussions which will prove to be the most popular part of the program.

(d) **"Last Day" Planning.**

If it is a three-day meeting, the last day (especially if attendance is voluntary) may end with light attendance. To avoid this, plan for presenting the most interesting subjects for this day, and plan to promote attendance for this event. If there are drawings, hold them at the last meeting. Recreational events should not be scheduled on the last day. Consider plane schedules; persons flying from one coast to another need to leave by mid-morning, so conclude the meeting by this time. If the convention site is in the Midwest, the meeting can conclude at noon. Consult with the hotel on arranging expedited check-out.

(e) **Sessions Between Individuals and Company Management.**

Determine if such sessions are to be held and the best time for these informal meetings. Also, decide if special suites are required for these meetings.

12. INSURE THAT ACTION TAKES PLACE AFTER THE MEETING.

This is a basic and important part of planning. Get down on paper what action should take place to ensure that the objectives of the meeting are accomplished.

For company meetings, give participants a plan of action to follow to implement the ideas received at the meeting. The plan may consist of making sure that the materials given out at the meeting are used.

Make sure that material is prepared for use by the stay-at-homes. Also prepare instructions for use by supervisors in the field.

For association meetings especially, arrange for summaries to be sent to the members.

13. HOLD PROGRAM PLANNING REVIEW MEETINGS.

Hold review meetings initially with all members of the program planning committee in attendance. Require oral and progress reports. Distribute notes of these progress-review meetings with appropriate indications of responsibility and new deadlines.

Hold review meetings with specialized committees as required. The full complement of the program planning committee may not be required here.

14. REHEARSE AND REHEARSE.

Plan for rehearsals for all company speakers. Keep in mind that the meeting which appears to flow along easily and spontaneously generally is one which has been much rehearsed.

15. ADDITIONAL PLANNING TIPS.

(a) Insurance.

Here is something which is seldom thought of. Check to see if your men and women are covered by insurance while attending your convention. Also, make sure that all entertainers, models, actors, etc. are hired as "independent contractors," thus generally absolving you of liability.

(b) Create a "Convention Workbook" for the Hotel and Convention Staff Members.

This guide consists of a daily minute-by-minute schedule of events and what is required for that event. The workbooks should be in loose-leaf form so that last-minute changes can be inserted. Indicate hotel personnel's areas of responsibility. List telephone numbers of key hotel employees. If there is an exhibit, give information on which company handles the set-up and dismantling services, the guard service, cleaning, the arrival of packages, etc. List who can sign for charges against the master hotel account. List the convention member in charge of each activity. Indicate the number of persons expected in each meeting room, the type of room set-up, hotel room, beginning/ending time, and a floor plan if required.

"At-Conference Workbook" for Conference Planner. Each conference planner has his own system for handling the mechanics of the conference when he arrives at the meeting site. The following is an idea which many conference planners use:

A notebook is prepared which contains a series of checklists for each element of the conference (accommodations, meals, banquet, the meetings, exhibit, reception, recreation, personnel transportation, items shipped, etc.). The notebook may be a three-ring binder or a Duo-Tang folder, or perhaps all the information may fit into a manila folder. In fact, some planners use a manila folder for each main element of the conference, or for each day's activities. The paper work is loose or stapled onto the folder.

If a binder is used, the checklists are filed under appropriate tabs. Back-up material is filed behind each checklist (bills of lading, list of attendees, pertinent hotel correspondence, list of props required for each room, names of tour guides, list of individuals at the head table, exhibit information, etc.). Not all of the paperwork accumulated in planning the conference is placed in the notebook—just the needed reference material. The workbook also contains a page which lists names of all key hotel personnel and their telephone numbers.

(c) Thoughtfulness for the Wives at Home.

If the meeting is held at a glamorous resort, and especially if it is a weekend meeting, it is good public relations to send a letter to the wives thanking them for sharing their husbands. A little gift can also be sent—flowers, a box of cookies, perfume, etc. Send the letter to arrive just as the conference begins.

(d) Post-Conference "Thank You's."

Needless to say, a "Thank you" note should be sent to all the individuals who worked on the conference. It is suggested that a copy be sent to the individual's supervisor and so indicated on the letter. As an extra gesture, provide certificates indicating that the individual was instrumental in helping make the meeting a success. And perhaps give an appreciation plaque to the one or two key organizers. Blank certificates may be obtained from Goes Lithographing Co., 42 W. 61st St., Chicago, Ill. 60621.

(e) Shipping Tips.

Allow for delays when using a truck shipper. Truckers generally wait until they have a full load before starting the trip. Also, there can be weather delays.

All shipments to hotels should be prepaid.

Shipments to hotels should be marked "Hold for Arrival" and should give the individual's name as well as company name. If "hold for arrival" is not on the shipping label and the guest has not checked in, hotels often refuse the shipment.

Air freight forwarders will handle the entire shipping process for you—pickup, the air shipment, and local delivery at the other end.

Where time is essential, it is best to arrange for pickup by one of your staff at the airport. Be sure to handle the shipment this way if the shipment is required on a weekend, as local delivery service may not be available at that time. Mark the shipment "Hold At Airport For Pickup."

Have only one person in your organization responsible for shipments.

All material should flow to your company from local suppliers rather than depending upon the supplier to make the shipment. Consolidated shipments save money, and more importantly there is only that one shipment to follow up.

Mark all cartons for easy identification—use colored marking pens, a colored container, large decals, bright labels, etc.

For insurance against foul-ups, notify the hotel's sales office or reservation office that a shipment is coming.

When tracing a shipment give the shipment's waybill number, air bill number, the carrier, and the date shipped.

(f) Other Program Events.

Consider inviting an industry speaker.

Think about inviting a customer to speak—a purchasing agent, dealer, engineer.

A sales consultant or sales psychologist can give an interesting talk.

Plan for an examination—and give awards for best scores.

If the meeting is held near your plant, consider a plant tour.

16. ADVANCE BULLETIN MAILINGS

Plan on sending an advance bulletin to the attendees, giving thoughts something like this:

"Probably one of the most valuable benefits of this gathering of marketeers from around the world will be the opportunity to exchange ideas. Here are suggestions that should assist you in making the most of this occasion:

(a) Jot down situations that now confront you in your work. Plan to find men at the meeting who can discuss them and help you find a solution.

(b) Check over the list of attendees. Are there any men whose experiences make them qualified to help steer you in the right direction? Ask if they have a similar situation and what they are doing to solve it. Contact in advance some of these men and make appointments to get together.

(c) Capitalize on mealtime hours. Ample time has purposely been made available for informal luncheon discussions. Luncheon seating has been arranged so that there will be a representative cross-section of men from all sections of the country. (The conference committee might want to make placards for the tables, giving suggested discussion topics.)

(d) Plan to spend at least some time with old and new friends in an old-fashioned bull session. Many a tip, more valuable than any in the best-planned program, can be dug out of such informal talks. A hospitality suite will be open in the evenings to serve as a gathering place for discussions."

17. HOW TO PLAN THE BUDGET.

(a) Budget Responsibility.

A conference planning committee member should be made responsible for the budget. The head of each working committee should be required to prepare a list of anticipated expenses and submit the planned expense budget for approval. Be sure to set up a reserve for unanticipated expenses and for inflation—otherwise, it may be necessary to cut a part of the program.

(b) Constructing the Budget.

There are two methods of constructing a conference budget:
  (1) "Cost per person" or a "total figure" based on an earlier conference. The conference is planned to fit within this budget. In other words, you start at the top with the amount allocated.
  (2) Budget to attain the objectives. An estimate is made of the various elements required to attain the objectives. In this method you start at the bottom and work up to what dollar amount is required.

(c) Organizing the Budget.

  (1) Determine what expenses, if any, will be paid by the guests, by representatives vs. company salesmen, and by advertisers and suppliers.
  (2) Determine specific numbers: The total number of guests, rooms (twin, double, or single), suites, meeting rooms, meals eaten in the hotel and at other locations, dances and banquets, cocktail parties and coffee breaks. Estimated number of participants in recreation programs, tours, etc.
  (3) Obtain costs of prior conferences as a starting point for estimating. Check these for extra expenses not commonly thought of.
  (4) In order to obtain uniform price quotations, set up a base such as price per hundred persons per day, or as required.

(d) First Rough Budget.

Using the previous conference costs as a starting point, draft a rough budget. Make telephone calls to obtain a quick survey of estimated ballpark costs of various considered locations and the larger meeting props.

Be sure to provide for unexpected extras and inflation. If the meeting is quite some time in the future, allow a larger margin for contingencies. Next, review the rough budget with the planning committee to ensure that there is a general agreement and understanding.

(e) Firm Budget.

Now you are ready to obtain detailed bids. Be very specific. State specific amounts and dates, the exact capacity of meeting rooms, number of rooms (twin, double, or single), number of meals, seating style, audio-visual requirements, etc.

(f) Notify the Hotel of the Budget.

If you have a tight conference budget, tell the hotel what kind of budget you have. To the hotel manager, a tight budget can be a blessing, for the hotel can suggest a period when it can offer reduced rates for rooms, meals, facilities, and services when the hotel needs the business. Additional complimentary services are often offered.

> *Site Selection Checklist.* See Chapter 22.
> *Hotel Inspection Checklist.* See Chapter 22.
> *Meeting Rooms Prop Checklist.* See Chapter 22.
> *Gratuity Checklist.* See Chapter 22.
> *Post Meeting Evaluation.* See Chapter 3.
> *Budget Planning Checklist.* See Chapter 22.
> *Budget Stretching.* See Chapter 4.

Chapter 2

209 Themes for the Conference

Contents

1. Accentuate the Positive
2. A-C-T-I-O-N!
3. Analyze—Dramatize
4. Be on Top with ———
5. Big Game Hunt
6. Big Payoff
7. Blueprint for Success
8. Break the ——— Barrier
9. Break Par
10. Building Stones for the Eighties
11. Buried Treasure
12. Caesar's Forum
13. Centsible Selling
14. Champions Conference
15. College of Sales Knowledge
16. Compete, Campaign, Capture
17. Conference of Champions
18. Cross Fertilization
19. Cultivating Customers
20. Customer Roundup
21. Developing Creative Imagination
22. Developing the Territory
23. Discover ———
24. Do-It-Yourself Conference
25. Down with Competition
26. Do Your Thing
27. Expansion
28. Experience Interchange
29. Explore the Great Values
30. Fame & Fortune
31. Fiesta in Spain
32. Fish for the Big Ones
33. For Men Only
34. Formula for More Sales
35. For Professionals Only
36. Fundamentals of Successful Selling
37. Get a Grip on Your Future
38. Getting the Most Out of Your Territory
39. Get Your Share
40. Go-Getters Conference
41. go Go GO
42. Gold Strike

43. Go Man . . . Go
44. GOYSAS (Get Off Your Seat and Sell)
45. Greenpower
46. Happiness Is
47. Happiness Is Beating Quota
48. Hawaii Getaway
49. Heads Up with _____
50. Hidden Treasure
51. Hit the Trail
52. H-O-W
53. How Can We Do It Better?
54. How to Increase Sales
55. How to Sell _____
56. How to Sell and Grow Rich
57. How to Succeed and Grow Rich
58. How to Succeed in Business
59. Hunting for Sales
60. _____ Happening
61. Idea Clinic
62. Idea Mint
63. Idea Workshop
64. Imaginative Marketing
65. Imagineering
66. Ingredients for Successful Selling
67. It's Your Move
68. Join the _____ Rebellion
69. Keys to Profits
70. Know-How Pow Wow
71. Know-How Roundup
72. Knowledge is Sales Power
73. Leadership Conference
74. Magic Carpet to the _____ Market
75. Make It Happen
76. Make Tracks
77. Mañana Today
78. Market Supremacy in the Eighties
79. Masters Conference
80. Measure the Difference
81. Measure Your Values
82. Mission Impossible
83. Mission Possible
84. Money for Everybody
85. More Feathers in Your Cap
86. More Productive Sales
87. Multiplying Your Effectiveness
88. New Horizons
89. Nice Guys Don't Win
90. Nothing Happens Until Somebody Sells Something
91. Number One
92. Open the Door and Travel
93. Operation _____
94. Operation Success
95. Organizing Your Total Effort
96. Pacesetters
97. Paris Getaway
98. Patience Hell! We'll Kill the Competition
99. Personal Turnaround
100. Planning for Success
101. Planning the Sales Story
102. Professional Salesmanship
103. Profitable Selling
104. Program for Action
105. Project Well Done

106. Prospecting for Bigger Sales
107. Putting the Pro in Profits and Promotion
108. Rendezvous in Rio
109. Room at the Top
110. Rope in Values
111. RYCDBSOYS (Remember, you can't do business sitting on your seat)
112. RX for success
113. _____ Roundup (Year)
114. Sail Through Selling
115. Sale Away to _____
116. Sales-A-Go-Go
117. Salesarama
118. Sales Fever
119. Sales Carnival
120. Sales Happening
121. Sales Magic
122. Sales Odyssey
123. Sales Power
124. Sales Rally
125. Sales Roundup
126. Sales Safari
127. Sales Secrets Seminar
128. Sales Sermons
129. Sales Success Secrets
130. Sales Turnaround
131. Salute to the Eighties
132. Second Effort
133. Seek, Seize, Sell
134. Select the Winners
135. Selective Selling
136. Sell & Score
137. Sell Benefits—Not Things
138. Sell In
139. Sell-O-Rama
140. Sell-O-Thon
141. Sell the Sizzle
142. Sellebration
143. Selling Against Competition
144. Selling Creatively
145. Selling Gems
146. Selling in the Computer Age
147. Shakedown and Shakeout
148. Shoot for the Green
149. Show, Tell & Sell
150. Speak Low—Sell LOUD
151. Spirit of ('80, '81, etc.)
152. Step High with _____
153. Straight Shooters Convention
154. Strike It Rich
155. Strive in ('80, '81, etc.)
156. Success Is
157. Take the _____ Route
158. The Anatomy of Selling
159. The Basic Ingredient of Sales Success—YOU
160. The Best Way _____
161. The Big Event
162. The Big Hunt
163. The Big Roundup
164. The Big Think
165. The Great Brain Robbery
166. The Great Race
167. The Magical _____
168. The _____ Magic Carpet
169. The Men From _____
170. The Money Men
171. The More You Tell, the More You Sell

172. The Science of Showing
173. The _____ Thing
174. There Is Nothing So Powerful As an Idea Whose Time Has Come
175. Think In
176. Think Sales
177. Think Smarter—Sell More
178. Think Smarter—Work Less
179. "Tops" (Total Organization to Promote Sales)
180. Tour de Paris
181. Trade in Tactics
182. _____ Treasure Hunt
183. Try It, You'll Like It
184. Turn On
185. Trips 'n Treasure
186. Upward in the Eighties
187. Vote _____
188. Wake Up and Live
189. Wake Up and Sell
190. We Can Do Better
191. We're in the Money
192. What Makes People Buy
193. What's The BIG IDEA
194. What's My Line?
195. What's New
196. Who Are Our Customers
197. Win, Place, Show
198. Win Power
199. Work Now—Retire Later
200. World Series
201. Write Your Own Check
202. Year of the Brass Knuckle
203. You Can Make It Happen
204. You Can't Make a Profit Without a Sale
205. You Can't Sell Goods From an Empty Wagon
206. Your Passport to _____
207. You've Got to Know the Territory
208. Open Forum
209. Meet with Success

Chapter 3

How to Evaluate and Follow Up on the Conference

Contents

1. Types of Evaluations
2. Timing of Questionnaire Distribution
3. Meeting Critique
4. Evaluating During the Meeting
5. Evaluating for Responses on Hotel Service
6. Evaluating for Response to Speakers Early in the Meeting
7. Evaluating the Meeting's Objectives
8. Questionnaire Format
9. Post-Conference Questionnaire—Sample
10. Another Post-Conference Questionnaire
11. Meeting Follow-Up Ideas

1. TYPES OF EVALUATIONS.

    There are several elements of the meeting which generally are evaluated. They are:
    a. The mechanics of conducting the conference.
    b. Checking with the sales force to see if the objectives of the meeting have been accomplished.
    c. Evaluating the effect of the meeting on association members, or on dealers and distributors.

    In setting up an evaluation program, first write down the objectives of the meeting. Then write the objectives of the evaluation. Is the purpose of the evaluation to provide help in planning better future programs? Is it to measure attendee attitude? Is it to determine if the sales force has absorbed the features and selling strategy of the new line? Have the desired results been obtained from particular sessions?

2. TIMING OF QUESTIONNAIRE DISTRIBUTION.

    Distribute the questionnaire at the beginning of the conference; the attendees thus have time to think about the questions which they will be asked to answer later.

    Most evaluators believe it is best to obtain answers to questionnaires at the end of the conference. If the conference is advertised as finishing at five, allow time before the ending to fill out the questionnaire. Provide adequate time so as not to invite brief answers.

    If it is a conference where attendance is voluntary, it might be wise to attach a ticket to each questionnaire. Then collect the tickets after the allocated time and hold a drawing for prizes.

How to Evaluate and Follow Up on the Conference

3. MEETING CRITIQUE.

Be sure to hold a post-conference meeting with the original meeting planning committee. Here the committee critiques its own performance. It analyzes the entire conference for the meeting of objectives, the choice of location, and meeting rooms, the speakers, the session lengths, the audio-visuals, the hotel service, etc.

All this is written down while memories are fresh. This data will provide valuable background material when planning the next meeting.

4. EVALUATING DURING THE MEETING.

Measurement cannot only be made after the meeting, but also during the meeting to determine if changes should be made as the meeting progresses.

5. EVALUATING FOR RESPONSES ON HOTEL SERVICE.

During the meeting it is suggested that $3'' \times 5''$ cards be handed out. Make the card simple, such as assigning ratings of "Excellent," "O.K.," and "Poor" to such items as the quality of breakfast, lunch, and dinner, the hotel service, the rooms, etc. Ask that comments be given on the reverse side. You may discover that sandwiches are preferred to a heavy luncheon.

6. EVALUATING FOR RESPONSE TO SPEAKERS EARLY IN THE MEETING.

Here is a suggested technique: Give out evaluation cards for a particular speaker to about 12 to 20 individuals. Assign another speaker to another group, and so on. Ask the respondent to give the three main points of the speech and to write in additional comments if desired. Give these cards to the speakers without anyone looking at them other than the speaker. The purpose is to assist the speaker in making his subsequent presentations. And you will find that it makes the attendees inclined to be better listeners.

In addition, here are other techniques to use to substantiate the written questionnaire:

(a) Ask informal questions during luncheons. Ask questions about the session program content, the seating, the hotel service, the food, the effectiveness of the speakers, etc.

(b) Listen in at evening bull sessions.

(c) The best method of conducting evaluations is by personal interviews conducted by professionals—attendees will be more prone to express their honest opinions to strangers. But professional interviews are generally expensive. An alternative method is to gather a small group of attendees whose opinions you respect and conduct an in-depth interview yourself.

7. EVALUATING THE MEETING'S OBJECTIVES.

The tendency of many managers who are charged with evaluating the meeting is to measure only the "feelings" of the attendees; that is, are the attendees happy about the meeting? But the chief item to concentrate on is what should be happening after the meeting. That is, *have the objectives of the meeting been accomplished*—have the planned changes taken place or will they take place?

A way to determine if the goals have been met is to check afterwards with the supervisors. Are their men doing what has been taught? Has the material been used? Are calls being made as planned?

8. QUESTIONNAIRE FORMAT.

Keep the questionnaires simple and short. Don't use long, involved forms. They won't get filled out.

And "make the questions easy to tabulate" as many an amateur will say after he has discovered that the tabulation has taken six times as long as expected.

Leave room for comments and suggestions.

Replies will be more honest if a signature is not required.

Provide space in the questionnaire to identify the type of person questioned. Is he a salesman, a new salesman, a factory representative, a dealer, distributor, a staff member, etc.?

9. POST-CONFERENCE QUESTIONNAIRE—SAMPLE.

(a) How would you sum up your feelings about the sales conference?
    ( ) Limited value ( ) All right, but not outstanding ( ) Good
    ( ) Excellent
(b) The sessions where I exchanged work experience with my fellow salesmen were:
    ( ) Poor ( ) Fair ( ) All right ( ) Good ( ) Excellent
(c) The sessions on improving my technical background were:
    ( ) Poor ( ) Fair ( ) All right ( ) Good ( ) Excellent
(d) What was the best session for you? Why?
(e) What was the poorest session? Why?
(f) What would you like to see done at the next meeting to make it more effective for you?
(g) Other Comments.

How to Evaluate and Follow Up on the Conference   29

The following questionnaire should provide a measurement of the objectives of the meeting. Add other questions as required to indicate if specific objectives were achieved.

10. ANOTHER POST-CONFERENCE QUESTIONNAIRE.
    (a) The most helpful speaker for me was _____ because _____.
    (b) The work session of most benefit to me was _____ because _____.
    (c) Time devoted to speakers: ( ) Too much ( ) Just right ( ) Not enough
    (d) Time devoted to work sessions: ( ) Too much ( ) Just right ( ) Not enough
    (e) What subjects should be emphasized more or added to the next meeting? _____
    (f) The greatest benefit I gained from attending the conference was _____.
    (g) The idea I obtained which will be of greatest profit to me was _____.
    (h) The main change which I will make when I get back out in the field will be _____.
    (i) What changes would I like to see in next year's conference? _____

Please note that the answers to a number of the above questions force the attendee to think about what he has learned, thus reinforcing the objectives of the meeting.

11. MEETING FOLLOW-UP IDEAS.
- Make duplicate slides for holding meetings at field sales offices or at dealers.
- Devise a call report on the presentation of new products to prospects.
- Make outlines for conducting field meetings.
- Require a report on dealer meetings held.
- Mail literature kits and new bulk literature during the meeting period so that the material is on hand in the field for immediate use.

Chapter 4

214 Ways to Stretch the Meeting Budget

Contents

1-17	Room Rates
18-22	Other Hotel Charges
23-34	Transportation Savings
35-37	Time Savings
38-59	Promotional Materials
60-69	Printing Savings
70-72	Publicity and Photographer
73-77	Coffee Breaks
78-93	Hors d'oeuvres
94-114	Beverages
115-142	Meals
143-154	Entertainment
155-157	Flowers
158-170	Speakers
171-180	Income Boosting Ideas
181-194	Hotel Finances and Auditing
195-197	Gratuities
198-214	Miscellaneous

Convention planners may obtain extra mileage from their budget and get more bang for the buck by taking a close look at the following areas:

Room Rates

1. Negotiate with the hotel *for a convention rate*.
2. Check for *complimentary sleeping rooms*. The general rule is one room free for every 50 rooms. A one-bedroom suite is often available with each 100 rooms.
3. *Hotel Low-Demand Periods*. Commercial travelers and large associations generally come in on a Sunday and leave on a Thursday. *So plan on a Thursday arrival* which permits departure Saturday or Sunday, and you will be in a good bargaining position, thus obtaining the best prices and better suites and meeting rooms.
4. Best rates are also obtainable on *holiday weeks*, and prior to or following holidays.
5. Hotels which cater to conventions will sometimes have dates on their calendar with quite a *number of empty rooms*. Ask about these dates. A little bargaining can save $5 to $8 per room.
6. For resort areas, prices are often only half the season rate if *an off-season time* is selected.
7. *Doubling up* not only saves money, but is generally preferred by the men. Pairing can be a device to help facilitate the exchange of ideas between persons with similar territories or positions.
8. *Guaranteed Group Rates* produce dollar savings. If attendance is voluntary, guarantee the number of rooms required on the low side.
9. Booking the group on the *American Plan* (room and meals) saves money.
10. If a series of small meetings are to be held in different cities, consider using *the same hotel chain* as a means of obtaining a better price.

11. *Request rooms with the best views.* The added cost is little or none at all and adds much toward making the meeting memorable.
12. *Negotiate for a "weekend special"* for those who wish to come early or stay over. Discounts up to 50% have been given.
13. *Older hotels* may give the best bargain on room rates.
14. Make a proviso in the contract that *if overbooked the hotel will pay for the rooms in the other hotel,* as well as taxis and tips.
15. Have the hotel agree to *late checkout on the last day.*
16. Ask the hotel to provide flowers, fruit, and other stock at no charge *for the presidential suite.*
17. Ask the hotel management, if you end the use of the meeting room at 4:00 or 4:30 p.m., can you obtain a better price as *the hotel can book that same room to another group* for an evening meeting?

Other Hotel Charges

18. *To avoid financial surprises be sure to check in advance if there is a charge for the use of meeting rooms.* Nowadays more and more hotels are charging for the use of public rooms. Get it in writing that there will be no charge.
19. When holding mealtime meetings during the convention find out if the hotel has *restaurant meeting rooms.* If there is a charge for converting a meeting room into smaller partitioned rooms for meal meetings, a switch to the restaurant may result in a free room.
20. Check the hotel to see if there will be *overtime charges for the bartenders, captains, and maids.*
21. *Get everything that has been promised by the hotel in writing* with a signature. This not only is your guarantee of the mutual understanding, but also helps both the hotel and yourself in case there is a personnel change.
22. *Check to see if the quoted room rate includes taxes.* Then you won't have a surprise which may place you over budget.

Transportation Savings

23. For large groups to other countries and within the U.S., *have the airlines submit bids.* Be sure to specify to each the type of meals to be served, the number of meals, wine, mixed drinks or champagne, flight bags, movies, etc.
24. *Schedule meetings for the off-season.* Both transportation and hotel rates may be lower. But be sure to check the type of weather to be expected.
25. Thirty-five to 40 attendees flying to the meeting site from the same city

can save money by going on a *group flight*. Include suppliers and exhibitors in your solicitation.

26. Generally, an airline will give a *complimentary "tour director"* seat with each 15 tickets purchased for a group.
27. *Travel agencies don't charge you for their services* (they work on commissions from the airlines), so utilize their expertise for advice on savings.
28. As you know, there are a number of different airline rates. As a refresher, here are some of the basic types. The types of special fares seem to change every few months. Check with the airlines for any changes.
    Charter—requires a minimum of 125 persons.
    Group Discounts—requires a minimum of 25 persons.
    Excursion Rates—generally the same as group discounts.
    Night Coach Flights—less than day rates, but these red-eye specials are not recommended unless absolutely necessary. Guests will not arrive refreshed.
    Family Plan—applicable to any class flight. Not available on Friday or Sunday afternoon. Typically a wife receives 25% off; children ages 12 to 21 one-third off; and no charge for anyone under two years of age.
29. *Most car rental agencies will provide group discounts.* Additionally, some will provide maps and other sightseeing literature. It has been noted that Avis will furnish folders imprinted with the convention name, date, and location. These folders contain rental rates, maps, and a car reservation card.
30. Wish you could afford the rental of a bus or buses, but don't have the money in your budget? *Let the guests subsidize part of the cost by putting money in the slot.* Most guests would prefer this to hiring a taxi.
31. For conventions held in Mexico, utilize the services of *"travel planners"* in that country, since the Mexican National Tourist Council and convention bureaus offer mainly promotional help only. They do not get involved with housing and travel. The services of the travel planners are free, as they obtain their revenue from commissions. They can provide considerable savings on travel fares, line up decorators, drayage firms, buses. Telephone the Mexico National Tourist Council in New York City (212) 757-7212 for suggested names of travel planners.
32. Check if *special low fares are available during certain days of the week*, then set the starting date of your meeting accordingly.
33. *Designate one car rental company as the official car rental firm* for your convention in exchange for courtesy cars. If a corporate discount is available, make this fact known to your guests.

34. Check airline fares when considering meeting sites as *the savings in transportation* may run into several thousands of dollars.

Time Savings

35. Ground travel time can be cut down by holding the convention at an *airport motor hotel.* A busy executive can also fly in, address the group, and ten minutes later be on his way. Usually, there is a cocktail lounge for after-dinner drinks and often entertainment.
36. *All costs* (rooms, meals, services) *are generally lower at an airport facility.* Airport hotel locations, however, are not recommended for holding meetings for customers as they lack varied entertainment facilities.
37. Holding the meeting *over a weekend* is a means of saving time. To compensate for weekends away from the family, think about inviting the wives. Special hotel weekend rates can be arranged, and the wives can fly at reduced rates.

Promotional Materials

38. *Obtain competitive prices* on all items to be produced, and on rentals.
39. *Use Local Sources of Supply.* Start by determining if there is a visitor's and convention bureau in the area. They can steer the planner to local sources of supply (such as audio-visuals, stage props, party decorations), thus saving on freight. An added bonus is that they know the reliable firms. A convention bureau will know the general costs of tours, nightclubs, recreation and, thus, make recommendations to fit your pocketbook.
40. Determine if the *hotel will print badges* for you.
41. Check *art schools for poster talent,* and music and acting schools for their talent.
42. Check the availability of *free audio-visual equipment* (mikes, projectors, etc.) from the hotel rather than renting, or try negotiating the rental of a complete audio-visual package through the hotel if this will produce a savings.
43. *Give accurate scheduling* on when and where rental equipment is required—and include time for meeting room set-up instructions. You may find you require less equipment than originally planned.
44. Keep a tab on the rental equipment which is being used to *ensure that it is returned promptly,* thus not being subject to rental charges for another day.
45. Have those *directional signs made on heavy cardboard* so they can be saved and reused at other meetings.

46. *Ship back to your home base all signs, banners, and promotional material* for use at regional meetings.
47. Require that local suppliers (in the city in which your company is located) *send their conference supplies to one central point* at your company rather than have each supplier individually ship his item to the conference location and charge you. Such a consolidated shipment will save money, and there is only one follow-up required.
48. If exhibits are a part of the meeting, advance planning will *keep down overtime set-up charges, extra handling, and storage costs.*
49. Check the phone book for "decorators." They may have suitable "leftover" items at low cost. Also check with *local adult high schools for classes on decorating for personnel and supplies.*
50. *Use films of the area's attractions* to promote the meeting. Contact the convention planning bureau of the meeting site and the airlines for the availability of such films. And check with other companies and associations which have used the site. Also talk to local audio-visual companies to determine if they have taken films of the site. You can customize the film by using slides of your convention or organization logo, of the convention theme, program highlights, dates, speaker photos, etc.
51. Companies and associations provide *free films* as a means of advertising (the credit line is usually low key). Hundreds are available on such subjects as travel, how to play golf, the space age, farming, education, etc.

   Some distributors of free films are:

Modern Talking Pictures	1212 Avenue of the Americas New York, N.Y. 10036
Sterling Movies, Inc.	375 Park Ave. New York, N.Y. 10022
Radiant Films	220 W. 42nd St. New York, N.Y. 10036
Association Films	600 Madison Ave. New York, N.Y. 10022

52. *Consult with the airline representative for other special free services.* For instance, the group may be seated together on the plane, allowed to board first, given personal welcomes from the stewardess or captain, given assistance on car, bus, and taxi arrangements, or have chits paid in advance by you for on-board drinks.
53. *Many airlines will furnish mailers* for promoting attendance. Some will even mail them to your prospective attendees. Some will make phone calls to local chapters soliciting attendance.
54. It has been heard that Continental Airlines *will provide an "800" phone*

to provide answers to questions on meeting starting times, exhibit hours, seminars, etc.

55. If you have an association magazine *the airlines may gladly pay for the cost of an ad* as an alternative to mailings.
56. *Ask if the following free promotional services are available from your airline:* Directional and welcome signs at the airport, imprinted "welcome" on menus, use of a VIP room at the airport, special speedy baggage handling, giveaways, baggage tags, local brochures, regional recipe booklets.
57. *When planning slides for a presentation, a storyboard will save hundreds of dollars.* A storyboard is simply the correct sequence of slides together with a sketch of the art required along with the key words. Use 3" × 5" or 4" × 5" cards. Artistic ability is not important. This preplanning saves money in that the audio-visual production company is not required to bill you for their research time in determining your needs.
58. *When making a mailing, use a plain envelope* and indicate the return address by means of the postage meter slug. This saves on envelope printing costs. And direct mail experts tell us that a plain envelope almost always gets opened first because of curiosity.
59. *Bring your own audio-visual equipment,* thus avoiding hotel charges.

Printing Savings

60. Make it a point to *inquire of the hotel and convention bureaus as to what printed material is available.* Often, they can furnish four-color program covers, badges, mailings to build up attendance, etc., all of which are added cost savings.
61. Check the *state tourism department* for colorful promotional mailing brochures.
62. When requesting a quote on an item *let the printer know that you will be bringing him more business.* If the printer thinks it's a one-time order, he may charge you more.
63. But be sure to *obtain a quote on subsequent printing jobs,* for the printer may have given you a low price on the first job with the expectation of charging a higher price on future jobs.
64. *Make sure the quote covers everything*—no extras for bleeds, photographs, etc.
65. Check if the *use of colored paper* instead of a second color of ink will save money.
66. Use *stock art or clip art* for illustrations. See the "Meeting Supplies & Sales Promotion Buyer's Guide" for addresses.
67. *Don't use photographs of speakers* on the printed program. Photographs add to the cost.

68. Many companies make it a practice *not to spend money on sales literature* especially produced for handout at the event. They feel that a large stock of take-home material will never get read. This policy not only saves printing money, but also saves in-house writing and production time.
69. *Watch the materials prepared for the speakers.* The department or outside agency preparing flip charts and slides should be made aware that the material is for one-time use (perhaps for a half a minute or a few seconds) and should be produced at a price accordingly.

Publicity and Photographer

70. *Send publicity to the trade press.* You thus obtain publicity equivalent to free ads. Also check about the possibility of articles being written up on your meeting either before or after the event.
71. *Photographer savings.* Provide a space for the photographer to display his pictures for sale to attendees. In exchange, he is to provide you with a set of these pictures for your use for news. If this is not possible, negotiate for *unlimited shots at a flat rate* rather than a charge for individual shots.
72. *Go to local TV and radio stations and newspapers* one or two weeks prior to the meeting if you have something newsworthy—such as a new product, a business forecast, something that lends itself to an unusual demonstration, etc.

Coffee Breaks

73. *Estimate the coffee quantity for the coffee break carefully.* You are paying from 50¢ to $1 per cup. Often, half of the coffee which has been paid for is returned. Also, estimate the pastries carefully.
74. Danish pastry is usually too large. *Ask for miniature Danish.* If this is not available, have the Danish cut into fours.
75. *Buy coffee by the gallon* instead of by the cup. The same for fruit juices.
76. Rather than let the hotel take away the coffee, rolls, and juices (which you have paid for), state that you wish these *leftovers left* on the table throughout the morning. Attendees can partake in these items during the meeting or during breaks in the program.
77. Obtain a credit on all unused soft drinks.

Hors d'oeuvres

78. When a cocktail party is held and a dinner does not follow, *serve hand-carved sandwiches, garnishes, wine, cheese, and fruit.* This will save the cost of going out to dinner afterwards and provide more time

for socializing. If hot roast beef sandwiches are served, you receive approximately twice as many trays of food for the money, the food value is worth more—the sandwiches take more time to eat.

79. You may not have realized it, but *beef is generally cheaper than turkey*. A round of beef provides from 200 to 240 sandwiches; a whole turkey provides only about 100 sandwiches. And watch out for inexpensive turkeys; they may weigh only half the usual 20-pound average weight.
80. An excellent lifesaver for small budgets is a *"Chip and Dip" reception*. Bowls of differnet dips placed about the room lead to talk and social mingling. Make sure the dip is the right consistency and that the chips are thick enough.
81. Here is an *hors d'oeuvre budget-saving idea* from the pros: Rather than place the hors d'oeuvres on a table, have *a waiter serve them as he passes through the crowd*. Since the snacks appear to be guarded, guests take only a few rather than a fistful. This calls for furnishing of finger foods. These two tips can cut down food costs by 25 to 40%!
82. *Serve only cheeses and crackers*, thus saving the appetite for the main meal.
83. *Serve nonsalty snacks* at cocktail parties. The amount of beverages consumed will go down substantially.
84. If your association has 500 guests for the meeting, *guarantee only half that amount* for reception, as hotels generally try to sell more food than is actually consumed.
85. *Do not use plates for hors d'oeuvres*. Make the guests use their fingers or napkins. Otherwise, the reception will turn into a dinner.
86. *Place the hors d'oeuvres* away from the bar.
87. *Start the party early*—before 7:00 p.m., otherwise the hors d'oeuvres become a substitute for dinner.
88. *Cold snacks* are usually much less expensive than hors d'oeuvres.
89. If you really want to save money, *stay away from serving shrimp*. Guests will eat shrimp as long as it is served; there is no consumption limit. However, if shrimp is a must, here are some tips: Order shrimp by the pound, not by the piece. Rather than having a shrimp bowl, have a waitress pass out the shrimp about 15 minutes after the party has started. Then about 15 minutes before the event ends, repeat the process. Guests will get the impression that the shrimp is being served continuously.
90. *Order hors d'oeuvres by the piece* rather than by the person.
91. *Spread out the hors d'oeuvres on the table,* don't line them up buffet style. And count the contents before the guests arrive, you may be surprised at the mistakes on quantity made in the kitchen.
92. *Under-guarantee* on the hors d'oeuvres.

93. Set your figures for hors d'oeuvres on the basis of starting with *six pieces per person.*

Beverages

94. *Provide a definite time* when beverage service is to begin and end. Last-minute drinks after closing can increase the bar bill considerably.
95. If this is a company convention, on free evenings, have an *"Open Bar."* Though at first glance the total bar charge may seem high, the total cost of this device is much less than the expense accounts of the men on the town.
96. Have the hotel charge on a *"per head" basis or by the bottle.* It is considerably cheaper than by the drink.
97. *Have drinks measured into glasses before the doors open.* When the bartender is in a rush, and when on a "liquor consumed" basis, the liquor is prone to be poured a quarter to a half as much over that of a measured glass.
98. Generally, it is much less expensive if *hotel house brands* of liquor are used for the hospitality suite and cocktail party.
99. *However, compare the prices and serve brand name liquors if there is little or no difference in cost.* It adds that touch of class.
100. *Serve wines instead of cocktails.* It's less expensive. Use domestic wines instead of imported wines.
101. *Place a time limit of 45 minutes for the cocktail party* if held before your dinner. Otherwise, your guests may be too full from the hors d'oeuvres and the drinks to want to eat.
102. On free evenings *set up a company hospitality suite* and announce that *expense account bar bills will not be honored* during convention time.
103. *Make sure the bartenders use jigger glasses* to measure the prescribed amount of liquor instead of pouring straight from the bottle.
104. *Appoint individuals from your organization to keep an eye on the bars.* Their job is to check the amount of liquor per drink, to keep a count of bottles, and, in general, to watch the bartenders.
105. Check with the catering manager; you may be able to obtain an *opening cocktail party sponsored by the hotel* if your group is large enough and will be spending a lot of money.
106. If you are an association, think about asking *a supplier or a group of suppliers to sponsor a cocktail party.* The same holds true for coffee breaks and recreational events. Even banquets are subject to sponsorship. And rather than negotiate for prices, have the supplier deal directly with the hotel as to what to serve. Your hotel can act as the middle man if you do not wish to deal directly with the sponsors about footing the bill. Just provide a list of prospective sponsors and let the hotel

contact the sponsors. The advantage to the hotel is that sponsored functions tend to be more lavish, hence more money for the hotel. In return, you allow small exhibits at the reception or other areas, or literature in the reception kit.

107. *Plan receptions so that they are hosted by the hotel.* Thus, should a guest who has been drinking get involved in an accident, it may eliminate or lessen your organization's liability.
108. Rather than having a hospitality suite open after the banquet, one company *rolled a bar into the dining area* after the meal. Attendees left earlier and drank less than at the hospitality suite the previous year.
109. *Take an inventory at the beginning and end* of the cocktail party. Make sure at the start that none of the seals are cracked (especially if you are paying for a premium brand). And do not allow empties to be used as water bottles as these could be charged by the bartenders as used bottles. No empties at all at the beginning should be the rule. Count again at the end. Add the new bottles brought in. Have the bartender sign the ending inventory sheet.
110. *Instead of eight-ounce glasses* use six- or four-ounce glasses. And cut down on the quantity of liquor proportionately.
111. Save on wages by *cutting down to only half as many bartenders* after the first half hour.
112. When paying by the bottle, notify bartenders to *open only one bottle of an item at a time* as some hotels charge for every bottle with a cracked seal. And be sure to determine in advance who owns the leftover cracked seal bottles. Close the bars progressively and transfer the unopened bottles to the remaining open bars.
113. If the price per bottle with mixer seems exorbitant you may be able to purchase the liquor yourself on the outside and *pay a corkage fee only*.
114. See the "Beverage Checklist" and "Beverage Cost Estimate Checklist" in Chapter 22 for additional ways to control beverage costs. You may save hundreds to thousands of dollars.

Meals

115. When budgeting for meals, *obtain the "total price;"* this means including tax and gratuities.
116. If there is a standard gratuity percentage, negotiate to *pay the gratuity on the amount before tax* is added.
117. *Make meal estimates 10% lower* than expected attendance for voluntary functions. However, be sure to notify the hotel what you are doing. They can usually happily add more servings if notified the morning before the luncheon, but would be reluctant to cut down on the number of guaranteed servings.

118. Watch the scheduled starting time when a banquet room is paid for. *Start promptly as you may be liable for an overtime charge.* Check in advance with the hotel on this point.
119. Judiciously *studying the menu selection* provides savings. Ask the hotel for suggestions of dishes not on the published menus.
120. Serve items on the restaurant or coffee shop menu rather than special luncheon or banquet menus.
121. Tell the hotel you want *six ounces of beef* per serving instead of eight ounces.
122. *Specify the size of the steak;* reduce the size from ten ounces to eight.
123. At the buffet *instruct the meat carver not to work too fast.*
124. *Cut out an appetizer, soup, or dessert. Serve tea cookies* instead of an expensive dessert. Limit the number of courses.
125. *Order fruit cups* instead of expensive shrimp appetizers.
126. *Watch out for luncheon and dinner buffets.* They are more expensive than sit-down dinners.
127. *Shy away from hot breakfasts;* serve continental breakfasts instead. Include cold cereals and bowls of fruit.
128. If you are holding a breakfast buffet and charging guests on a per item basis, *ckeck the coffee shop menu in advance* to determine that the prices are in line.
129. An association *eliminated a "Farewell Breakfast"* as it was found that most conventioneers were leaving the previous night.
130. *If there is a free afternoon, eliminate the luncheon.* Guests can then save this time for their own use and save money by going to the coffee shop.
131. *Leftovers* from a buffet or hors d'oeuvres table can be taken to the hospitality suite.
132. Instruct the waiters to *pour three ounces of wine* per glass; thus, one bottle will serve ten people. Pay on a per-bottle basis. Have the guests pay for a second round should they wish more.
133. If you are paying for more than one round of wine, *serve a white wine at dinner first* as it is less expensive, and serve after the guests are seated and have had some water. Then follow with the more expensive red wine.
134. While the meal is being served *take a guest count* along wtih a member of the hotel staff.
135. Most meeting planners agree that *buffets cost more* than meals served at the table.
136. *Always sell tickets in advance for meal functions*—never at the door. This eliminates the tendency to overestimate the attendance guarantee.
137. *Watch out for those hidden costs.* Ask about all the items you may take for granted as being free. For instance, these items are known to have

been charged: Meeting rooms, tables and chairs, tablecloths, overtime, pencils, pads, easels, gratuity charges, baggage room charges, ashtrays, staff headquarter rooms, corkage fee, air conditioning, etc.

138. *If there is a board of directors luncheon,* ask the hotel to pay for it or provide a special menu at no extra charge.
139. *Ask the hotel to provide skirts at no charge* for head tables.
140. *Check what the hotel is serving to other groups* at the same date; by ordering the same meal costs may be reduced by as much as 10%.
141. *Establish a ticket system for buffets* as most hotels use a plate count rather than a head count. When guests use a fresh plate for a second helping, that means another billing.
142. Rather than serve dessert, set up a special self-serve table as a number of people do not eat desserts.

Entertainment

143. *Ask the hotel for suggestions on planned entertainment.* The cost is generally less than offering a "free" evening on the town to the group.
144. Contact *professional entertainers who are currently appearing at the hotel* for their rates for off-hours.
145. *Check Government Military Units* for marching bands or drill teams.
146. Check the Chamber of Commerce or Convention Bureau for the *availability of a local queen* (Citrus Queen, Rose Bowl Queen, etc.).
147. Ask these same sources if *police bands* are available. Boston and New York have police and fire bagpipe troupes.
148. *Check universities and high schools for marching bands.*
149. *Your hotel may have props left over* from previous meetings. Perhaps even costumes which can be rented. The hotel may have a standard set of props for theme parties.
150. Need actors for skits? *Try university drama departments* or *acting schools.*
151. Plan all rehearsals involving paid help *on straight time*—not overtime.
152. Check the *local sightseeing tour offerings.* Packages can be worked out which include *dinner at a location other than the hotel* and *entertainment at one or more night spots.* Try for the *"first show only"* which is generally less costly and which brings the group back not only fully feted but also in time for a good night's sleep.
153. If required by the union to hire a minimum number of musicians for a room and the minimum is extra large such as 12, *request two six-piece bands,* thus furnishing continuous music.
154. *Bring a tape recorder for music* before the banquet and before and after conference sessions. Check union rules if a band is being hired for the dinner dance.

Flowers

155. You have probably never thought of it, but flowers purchased from a florist are purposely furnished in the bud stage so that the recipient can watch them unfold and come to full bloom over a period of days. So, if the flowers are for a one-time use, check with the florist to see *if fully-opened blooms may be purchased at a lesser price*. Another tip is to have the hotel store the flowers in a cool spot *for use at your other food and social events*. And when you are checking out the hotel, ask if you may use an *out-of-hotel florist*.
156. Think about having *flowers only for the hors d'oeuvre tables* and none for the dinner tables.
157. Or eliminate flowers altogether at the cocktail party and, instead, *use cheese displays for decoration*.

Speakers

158. Transportation and lodging costs can be reduced by *checking for local speakers*.
159. *Use speakers who will be in town at the same time for another engagement.* Check with speakers bureaus, talent agencies, university bureaus, and lecture halls for this possibility. Check with the convention bureau or chamber of commerce for names of associations which will be in town, then check their speakers. You may be able to share the speaker's travel and hotel expenses.
160. Ask if the speaker wishes to take his or her spouse and family along, and make it a combined work/vacation trip *in exchange for a lesser fee*.
161. *Check your own company or association for free speakers.*
162. Rather than a highly-paid professional speaker, think about *inviting a customer, dealer, or distributor* to speak on a subject such as "What a salesman can do for me." Or consider having salesmen give talks on how a difficult or large sale was made.
163. When dealing with agents for speakers *insist that the contract be signed by the speaker*. And contact the speaker by phone or mail to confirm the rate. This is good insurance against rip-offs which have occurred when the contract is signed by the talent agency only. An agent may charge as much as double the fee and sign a contract with the speaker for only half the amount.
164. If the meeting is held in another country, check for *government agency speakers*. They may be available at little or no charge.
165. *Speaker rehearsals and all types of rehearsals involving union members* should be planned for straight time.
166. *Take the speaker along on your discounted group or charter flight.*

167. Specify that the speaker is to be *reimbursed at the tourist fare rate.* Quite often the difference between tourist and first class fare is pocketed by the speaker.
168. *Set a total price for the speaker.* This eliminates the surprise of a spouse or an assistant being brought along for an indeterminate number of days. If the contract states "plus expenses," specify exactly what expenses will be reimbursed.
169. *Try telephoning speakers direct* as this often results in a lower fee.
170. If your organization is large, the prestige of speaking to your group may be such *that a speaker can be obtained at no charge*—especially if it serves as a platform for the speaker's beliefs and if press coverage can be arranged.

Income Boosting Ideas

171. Boost income by *charging a late fee to tardy registrants.*
172. *Sell mailing lists* of attendees.
173. If suppliers have hospitality suites, check into the feasibility of a *surcharge on these suites.*
174. *Sell space in the printed program* for advertisements from suppliers. These can be ads or messages of success for the meeting.
175. *Check if any of your suppliers will sponsor the reception,* coffee breaks, or a luncheon in exchange for a credit line in the program and credit on a table setting place card, or a sign on an easel.
176. If you have the nerve, *charge for the convention program* if it's an association meeting. Attendees will then use the program they picked up at registration, rather than picking up another program at the meeting. It's been done. It cuts down on printing costs.
177. *Invite students to certain events* at a special price.
178. Obtain revenue by *permitting suppliers to set up exhibits* in an exhibition hall.
179. *Sell exhibit space in hospitality suites.*
180. Boost attendance (and income) by providing for *reduced fees for more than one member from a firm.*

Hotel Finances and Auditing

181. Prior to the meeting obtain a clear agreement with the hotel as to *what items are to be charged to the Master Account.* Find out *when the posting occurs,* and the format of these charges. You should furnish a *list of individuals who are authorized to sign bills* charged to the Master Account.
182. Also *provide a list of persons whose bills are to be charged to the Master Account.*

183. *Take a daily random sampling of your guests' charges* to make sure they are being charged at the agreed upon rate.
184. If other associations or companies are holding meetings during your convention, *ask the hotel to assign a specific account number for your group.*
185. Reach an understanding with the hotel *on what guests may or may not charge.* And by the same token, provide more liberal charge privileges for the convention staff and company officials.
186. Have an understanding with the hotel that your organization *is not underwriting individuals' checks.* That is, if this is the way you prefer the situation to be handled.
187. *Sign the tabs daily.* If something is irregular, you will be able to head off a recurrence. Also check all charges to the Master Account.
188. *Audit daily during the meeting.* To prevent extra charges as a last-minute surprise, audit the hotel charges daily by individual and room number. Also check for other expenses charged to your organization by the hotel.
189. The meeting coordinator should *stay on a day after the meeting to go over the bills* before they get to the computer.
190. On the final bill from the hotel make sure that all charges for *sundry items are backed up with signatures.*
191. *Check your attendee roster against the hotel billing* to ensure that only authorized guests have been billed to your organization, that no-shows have not been charged for, and that credit for early checkouts has been given.
192. *Hire a local CPA* by the hour to audit the hotel bill every night.
193. During your negotiations specify that an *itemized* bill is to be presented. You can then go over every item after the conference, checking for errors.
194. In advance of the meeting secure an understanding that the hotel will compute gratuities on the bill *before* the tax is added.

Gratuities

195. Obtain a list of personnel from the hotel who should be tipped. *But don't tip too far up the organization chart. Ask the hotel how much the tips should be*; it may be less than you would normally spend.
196. If your hotel contract calls for gratuities being part of the bill be sure to let your guests know of this fact.
197. Even when gratuities are picked up by the company or association, there are awkward moments when the bellhop delivers the luggage and stands around. To alleviate this situation, and to eliminate double tipping, *mail "Tip slips" in advance to guests.* These are handed out to

bellhops, pool attendants, etc. The slips state that your organization is picking up the gratuity and that the slips have no cash value. Be sure to notify the chief bellhop and pool attendant of this procedure.

Miscellaneous

198. Contact the convention bureau or the chamber of commerce to determine if *registration help is available at no charge.*
199. *Door prizes and welcome gifts* can be donated by suppliers.
200. *Suppliers can be approached for sponsorship of sightseeing tours.*
201. *Shops in the hotel and department stores* can be solicited for door prizes.
202. If there is a matter of choice on dates, *check for fairs, festivals, or religious holidays being held at the site* (both in the U.S. or a foreign country). You'll gain the advantage of pageantry at no charge.
203. Set aside a percentage of the budget *as a reserve* for unexpected costs and inflation.
204. *Budget Control Form.* For a work sheet on estimating and controlling the budget, see the "Budget Planning Checklist," in Chapter 22.
205. *Plan ahead.* Stress to all concerned the need to make plans well in advance so as to avoid the last-minute materials overtime production changes and extra transportation charges. *This avoids overtime charges to you.*
206. *Save money on the telephone credit calls* made by salesmen during the conference by installing phones in the lobby of the meeting site. Usually, the only charge by the telephone company is for the installation. The salesmen dial direct to their customers and sales offices, which is cheaper than credit calls. Your secretaries watch the phones to see that authorized persons use the phones and a central switch at the hotel's main switchboard cuts off the phones during the sessions.
207. *Use students to help out* at registration and to serve as messengers, waiters, busboys, etc. They can be either high school or college students. Services of schools can be utilized for designing programs, printing, decorating, etc.
208. *Having a large amount of photocopying done* at your meeting? Go outside the hotel; it's much cheaper.
209. *Cost cutting ideas for the staff:* Don't serve catered breakfasts or lunch; the coffee shop is cheaper. And place them on a per diem basis for the meals. Buy a coffee maker. Look into the savings of bringing typewriter tables instead of renting desks. Make sure discount room rates apply to staff personnel before and after the meeting.
210. Ask for a number of *complimentary parking spaces at the hotel.*

211. Rather than using air freight, apportion the convention materials among your staff for *taking along as excess baggage.*
212. *If hotel mikes are used in the same room the next day,* don't pay rental for the second day.
213. Spell out in your contract that morning session rooms are to be available for your prop set-up and for rehearsals *the evening before.*
214. *Try to have the hotel limousine* pick up VIPs and speakers.

Chapter 5

Conference Site Selection Tips

Contents

1. Questions to Be Answered Before Determining the Site Area
2. Types of Convention Sites—Advantages of Each
3. Site Selection Assistance
4. Airline Assistance
5. Hold a "Live-In" Inspection
6. Sites That Are Really Different
7. Other Unusual Sites

1. **QUESTIONS TO BE ANSWERED BEFORE DETERMINING THE SITE AREA:**
    Size of group.
    Will participants pay own transportation and hotel?
    Time permitted away from work.
    Location of most of the participants.
    Should meeting be held near headquarters or a factory?
    Is this a reward type of meeting or strictly business?
    What is the level of the group, i.e., mostly VIPs?
    Will wives attend? Children?
    May vacations be taken before or after the convention?
    Should the meeting tie in with an industry convention?

2. **TYPES OF CONVENTION SITES—ADVANTAGES OF EACH.**

    (a) **Large Metropolitan Hotels**—Good for large groups who wish to take advantage of the downtown entertainment. These hotels usually have staffs of specialized personnel.

    (b) **Highway and Suburban Hotels**—Best suited for small groups who tend to get overlooked in large hotels. Generally free convenient parking right outside the room for auto travelers.

    (c) **Airport Hotels**—Especially popular with those in a hurry. Meeting facilities often as good as at large hotels. Disadvantages are that varied evening entertainment is not nearby and that services are generally limited.

    (d) **Resort Hotels and Motels**—The best bet for those who wish to relax amid luxurious resort recreational facilities. Often, meeting facilities are comparable to the large metropolitan hotels. During the off-season, convention group rates are usually surprisingly modest.

3. **SITE SELECTION ASSISTANCE.**

   Convention Bureaus are established in most cities and resort areas. Write to them in care of the chamber of commerce. Some of the bureaus provide convention planning kits.

   Meeting Site Service. *Sales Meetings* Magazine, 1212 Chestnut St., Philadelphia, Pa. 19017, will suggest meeting sites at no charge.

   And each year *Sales Meetings* Magazine publishes an "International Convention Facilities Issue." It gives hotel addresses, convention facilities, number of sleeping and convention rooms, rates, etc.

   Office Meeting Facilities Guide. Provides information on hotels and meeting facilities worldwide. Gives rates, meeting room dimensions and capacities, audio-visual equipment available, special meeting and convention services, and maps of major convention cities, transportation, recreation, etc. Ten dollars for two semiannual issues. From the publishers of *Meetings & Conventions* Magazine. P.O. Box 606, Neptune, N.J. 07753.

4. **AIRLINE ASSISTANCE.**

   The convention sales departments of many major airlines offer assistance in the selection of sites. They will furnish data on hotels, facilities, and ground transportation, and will handle the bookings into the hotels. Air transportation costs to several sites will be computed for you. A great many airlines furnish convention kit checklists to aid in the planning; some even offer professional meeting consultant services.

5. **HOLD A "LIVE-IN" INSPECTION.**

   Stay at the conference site for a few days to get a first-hand view. If possible, take some of the key meeting planning specialists on this trip. Use the opportunity to question the hotel service men, chefs, room manager, and registration manager; check the props, room size, audio-visual facilities, recreation facilities, and exhibit space. This will uncover potential trouble spots and provide time to overcome the problem.

6. **SITES THAT ARE REALLY DIFFERENT.**

   (a) **Ships.**
   More and more companies are discovering the pleasure of conventions on board ships. Shipboard meetings make excellent rewards for salesmen, distributors, and dealers. Convention cruises are offered not only across the oceans, but also along the coasts, the Caribbean, the Great Lakes, the St. Lawrence, and the Mississippi. And one-day charters are possible in many

locations. Thinking need not be confined to large vessels. A flotilla of small craft can be used and the group meetings can be held at a point on shore.

Windjammer cruises for small groups of 20 to 40 people make for memorable meetings. These are available on the East Coast and the Caribbean.

(b) Cruise Agencies:

Windjammer Cruises
P.O. Box 120
Miami, Fla. 33139
(For the Caribbean)

Mystic Whaler
90 Maple Ave.
Hartford, Conn. 06114
(A windjammer)

Travel Center
580 Plandome Rd.
Manhasset, N.Y. 10030
(They also prepare promotional pieces.)

Princess Cruises
3435 Wilshire Blvd.
Los Angeles, Calif. 90010
(Cruises along West Coast and Caribbean.)

Wakefield Fortune, Inc.
52 Vanderbilt Ave.
New York, N.Y.
(Specializes in yacht charters worldwide.)

Matson Lines
100 Mission St.
San Francisco, Calif. 94104
(For Hawaiian trips)

World Yacht Enterprises, Ltd.
14 W. 55th St.
New York, N.Y. 10019
(Yachts for 10 to 200 people worldwide are listed.)

Royal Caribbean Cruise Line, Inc.
853 Biscayne Blvd.
Miami, Fla. 33132

(c) Meeting in a Tent.

Air-conditioned or heated tents complete with black linen for showing movies, floors, and chandeliers can be rented to handle 100 to 1,000 people. There is a special excitement in the atmosphere created by a brightly striped tent.

(d) Planetarium.

The Hayden Planetarium in New York City is rentable for a modest sum. Good for tying in with a special theme.

7. OTHER UNUSUAL SITES.

Let your imagination run wild. Theatres, museums, ballrooms, opera houses, historic buildings, and public buildings can often be rented at rates which are surprisingly low. Two of the world's largest liners, the *Queen Elizabeth* at Hollywood, Florida, and the *Queen Mary* at Long Beach,

California, have been turned into combined hotel and convention center facilities. Or be different by playing host at a guest ranch. And for the hardy there are Playboy Club Hotels at Lake Geneva, Wis.; Jamaica; Great Gorge, N.J., and Puerto Rico. Write Playboy Hotel Division, 919 N. Michigan Ave., Chicago, Ill. 60611.

(a) West Point.
Located right on the grounds of the Military Academy and with a magnificent view of the Hudson is the Hotel Thayer, West Point, N.Y. 10996.

(b) National Parks.
For a starter think of Yosemite National Park which has the deluxe Ahwanee Hotel. Others are Grand Teton National Park's Jackson Lake Lodge, Jackson, Wyo. 83103; Yellowstone's Mammoth Motor Inn, Yellowstone National Park, Wyo. There is also Rocky Mountain National Park, P.O. Box 1080, Estes Park, Colo.

(c) Ski Areas in the Summer.
Try Sun Valley, Idaho; Aspen Meadows, P.O. Box 220, Aspen, Colo. 81611, has excellent convention facilities. Also Snowmass, P.O. Box 5566, West Village, Aspen, Colo. 81611.

(d) Hawaii.
A popular spot. Many companies hold the convention on the ship and fly back. Others fly both ways. Contact Hawaiian Visitors Bureau, 2270 Kalakaua Ave., Honolulu, Hawaii. Offices are also in New York, San Francisco, and Los Angeles.

(e) Mexico.
Write the Mexican National Tourist Council, Mexico House, 677 Fifth Ave., New York, N.Y. 10022, for a copy of "Convention Planning Guide to Mexico."

(f) Canada.
Write to Chief, Convention Promotions, Canadian Government Travel Bureau, 150 Kent, Ottawa 4, Ontario, Canada. Or the Tourist and Convention Bureau of cities such as Ottawa, Ontario, Quebec City, Quebec, Montreal, Quebec. Or how about Chateau Lake Lodge, P.O. Box 1250, Lake Louise, in British Columbia?

(g) Bahamas.
Ministry of Tourism, 1701 First National Bank Bldg., Miami, Fla. 33131, offers a wealth of choice locations.

(h) And More.

There's the Conference Center located in historic Williamsburg, Virginia. Or does the preference run to night life such as Las Vegas? Contact Las Vegas Authority, Convention Center, Las Vegas, Nev. 89109. Tours of *NASA* on Florida's space coast are offered and hotels are nearby. And there is the ever-popular Disneyland. Write to Anaheim Convention Bureau, 800 W. Katella Ave., Anaheim, Calif. 92802. And for splendid desert settings try: Valley of the Sun Convention Bureau, 802 N. Second St., Phoenix, Ariz. 85004.

SITE SELECTION CHECKLIST. See Chapter 22.

Chapter 6

How to Create Interest, Enthusiasm, and Results

Contents

1. Techniques for Conducting Meetings That Are Different
2. Games and Other Ideas for the Group Sessions
3. Special Speaker Sources
4. Thirteen Effective Workshop Session Ideas
5. Dealer or Distributor Programs
6. How to Get the Meeting Off to a Good Start
7. Ways to Involve the Audience
8. Ways to Promote Esprit de Corps
9. Eleven Ways to Get Involvement by Using Questions and Quizzes
10. Sales Training Film Sources

1. TECHNIQUES FOR CONDUCTING MEETINGS THAT ARE DIFFERENT.

(a) Change the Traditional Meeting Pattern.
- If meetings have previously been called by the same name, give the meeting a theme name.
- Change the traditional site; move it to a town where a new plant or store has opened.
- Consider holding one of the breakfasts or lunches at a different location away from the meeting facilities, but tying it in with an inspection trip of a facility near the new eating place.

(b) Give Meeting Rooms Names of Persons You Wish to Honor. Print this room name in the program and on a large poster card at the entrance to the room.

(c) "Learn at Lunch" Session. A leader is appointed for each table. All discuss the same subject, or different topics are assigned at the various tables with attendees selecting the subject of their choice. Make large table tent signs listing the topic. Make extra signs in case some topics are more popular than anticipated.

(d) Conduct an Interview. The company speaker is interviewed on the stage by a reporter who asks questions which bring out the main features of a product, a sales policy, etc.

(e) Giant Screen Television for Simultaneous Meetings in Several Cities. General Electric has a system called "Command Performance Network" which enables a speaker to communicate face-to-face simultaneously with audiences in 5, 18, 25 or more locations. They handle the entire job from planning to production. They maintain giant screen television viewing facilities in Hilton and Sheraton hotels in cities across the country. Write to

How to Create Interest, Enthusiasm, and Results

Command Performance Network, General Electric Company, Electronics Park, Building 2, Syracuse, N.Y. 13201.

(f) Portable Conference Telephone. The Bell Telephone Company has for rent at about $25 a month a Portable Conference Telephone where a spokesman (who is in another city) can talk to the meeting over the portable telephone's speaker or the meeting site's public address system. The entire group can talk to the speaker through two remote microphones—although it may be expedient for the chairperson to relay written questions from the audience. This unit can also be used by a regional sales manager who wants his team to discuss strategy with the boss at the home office, or a trainer or product manager from headquarters who talks with a sales group at a distant point. The number of participants for these regional type of meetings should not be over 12. The set weighs 19 pounds and plugs into any standard telephone jack. Contact your telephone company.

(g) Package the Convention on Film for Nonattendees and as a Sales Training Tool. A film production company can be hired to shoot the entire meeting. This film is then edited down to its highlights for showing to local groups, as a report on happenings, to stimulate next year's attendance, and for sales training purposes. If a trade show is held in conjunction with the conference and if exhibitors' products are used in the film, perhaps some sort of cooperative funding could be worked out.

(h) Video Tape Sales Presentation. Make a video tape of a sales presentation, using your own men as actors. Then play the tape at the meeting and follow this with small group discussions. Video tape is also excellent for bringing shots of the factory or a dealer showroom to the meeting. Video taped programs are easier and cheaper to make than film. Contact: Sony Corp. of America, Industrial Division, 516 W. Florence Ave., Inglewood, Calif. 90301.

(i) Tele-Lecture, Telewriting Service. By using a Tele-Lecture, specialists, experts, or absent members from other parts of the company can address your meeting by telephone, thus eliminating prohibitive travel expenses or conflicting schedules. Your absent company president can send his greetings via this method. Several audiences apart (even overseas), may participate in a panel discussion. Project pictures of the speakers on the screen during the conversation. A conversation between the M.C. and the distant speaker can be held. Roving microphones permit the audience to talk directly to the long-distance speaker and to ask questions. With Telewriting, figures, charts, diagrams, and other hand graphics can be instantly transmitted by telephone. By means of an overhead projector, the image can be projected on a screen for easy reading by large groups. Call the communications consultant of your telephone company.

(j) Arrange Hotel Stage Platforms to Get Close to the Audience by assembling standard hotel platforms in various patterns to fit the meeting requirements. For instance, a walkway can extend out into the audience. Platforms can be stacked so that each part of the stage is at a different height. Place a number of platforms by themselves in various parts of the room; the speaker strolls to each one during the course of the lecture. The audience seating can also be different than the usual; consider placing the audience on different levels. Or place the stage in the center; the audience is seated in boxing ring fashion or in a circle around the stage.

(k) Man's or Woman's Recorded Voice for Introduction. Place the person's voice on a tape recorder. The speaker holds a dialogue with him or her. Provide short pauses on the tape for the speaker or have an assistant control the start and stop of the recorder. Or provide a control for the speaker. Use at the beginning of the speech, also at the end.

(l) Informal Discussion. Get a group of experts together on the stage. Have them hold an informal discussion on the subject instead of using a speaker.

(m) Telephone Customers from Meeting. Amplify the conversation. Notify the customer in advance so he or she can be thinking about the answer. Tell the customer about the general subject, but not specific questions as he or she may read prepared answers.

(n) Open House. If the conference is held near one of your plants, consider taking a trip through the facility.

(o) "Unanswered Questions" Session. Mail a letter to the participants before the meeting listing the subjects of the various sessions. State that if they have questions concerning other subjects to please write them down (on provided cards) and bring them to the conference. And during the meeting provide cards for those who forgot to bring their cards, or for additional questions. The cards are unsigned. A panel of executives is formed and these "unanswered questions" are directed to the individual responsible for that area.

(p) "Signs of the Zodiac" Theme. Print badges with individual signs of the zodiac. Match the badge with the individual's birth date. Use these zodiac signs as a means of assigning discussion groups, for selecting individuals to answer questions, in making assignments, in forming luncheon table groups, etc. Make appropriate comments on the printed program such as "The following signs are being matched for compatibility, for friendship, etc. in assigning discussion groups." Tie in the zodiac theme throughout the program, such as making astrological forecasts for the various parts of the program.

(q) **Offstage Voice Utilized.** For instance, an offstage voice can be a dealer registering complaints about a policy, about a salesman's method of presentation, etc. The speaker answers the dealer's or customer's questions.

(r) **Change of Pace.** Two or three speakers give talks on the same subject. Each discusses a different aspect of the subject. Keep each talk short.

(s) **Speeches Via Closed-Circuit TV.** This method can be utilized at large gatherings where the speaker is unable to attend, or when a number of meetings are held simultaneously in different cities.

(t) **How to Obtain Additional Mileage from Your Speakers.** Place a notice in the convention program that the speakers will be holding shirt-sleeve sessions where additional in-depth questions may be asked. If possible, pick an informal location such as a patio, cabana, poolside, etc.

2. GAMES AND OTHER IDEAS FOR THE GROUP SESSIONS.

(a) **Hold a Demonstration Contest.** Break up the meeting into small groups of about six each. One man in each group is elected to enter the demonstration contest. The other members of the group coach him. Hand out a list of points to be covered in the demonstration. The competing demonstrations are then given. Offer prizes for the best demonstration.

(b) **Problem Solving.** Consider devoting the entire conference to solving a problem and implementing its solution. Make sure that those responsible for authorizing the solution are in attendance. Follow the standard method of problem solving; i.e., (a) define the problem, (b) get the facts, (c) list alternative solutions, (d) select the most fitting solution, and (e) determine the action (what, who, how, when, where).

(c) **Brain Picking.** Form the attendees into discussion groups. All the groups work to develop their best answers to a common problem. If the meeting is large, assign several different problems to various groups. One person in each group is assigned the title of reporter. His job is to report the group's solutions when everyone joins again in the main meeting.

(d) **Computer Marketing Games.** Various sales and marketing games are available for playing on a computer. Use your own computer or telephone the answers to a central computer. Contact IBM or the business course section of a university for such games.

(e) Send a New Selling Procedure to Attendees in Advance of the Meeting. Ask them to try out the procedure and be prepared to evaluate the merits of the new plan and how it can be improved.

(f) Brainstorming. This is creative thinking on a group basis. Assign a non-complex sales problem such as "What are new uses for the product?" "What are new ways of prospecting?" Groups should be small—from 12 to 20 persons. Tell the members to let their imaginations run wild. No negative thoughts are allowed. No evaluations are permitted. Encourage the men to add to or improve already given ideas. Since many hands may be raised at the same time, give priority to suggestions which are "idea improvements" by having the person snap his fingers. Ideas will come fast and furious, so instruct the chairman to appoint two recorders. If desired, appoint a different problem to each group. At the conclusion, all the groups gather to hear summary reports.

(g) Use of Place Cards. Where there are large discussion groups it is advisable to use place cards. Place cards are good for the ego and help the moderator in fielding questions. Lettering on the cards should always be able to be seen from a distance. A height of 1½" should be the minimum. These can be tent type cards, or cards tacked or stapled to blocks of wood. If there are a number of companies represented, it is advisable to include the company name.

(h) Request Some of the Attendees to Come to the Meeting Prepared to Sell a Specified Competitive Product. Groups then explore ways to sell against the competitive product. A reporter from each group then presents a summary at a meeting of all the groups.

3. SPECIAL SPEAKER SOURCES.

(a) Use Customers as Speakers. Invite customers to talk on subjects such as "What I want a salesman to do for me," or "The type of salesmen who receive my business." Also the customer can give information on the sales forecast or technical outlook of his industry.

(b) Special Speaker to Get Audience in Early. Placing a big name speaker first on the program will help bring those convention delegates in early. It is not necessary to save the best speaker for the last.

How to Create Interest, Enthusiasm, and Results 61

(c) **Hire a Woman Speaker.** Check the speaker agencies and large corporations, including airlines. There are excellent speakers available, such as successful models, saleswomen, women executives, and actresses. Surprise the audience by listing the speaker with her first initial only, "J. Smith, noted sales trainer."

(d) **Public Officials as Speakers.** This source of speakers is often overlooked. Use them as speakers on a special subject or as a "welcome to our city" speaker. Most will not charge a fee. Consider asking the mayor or other top man to say a few words of welcome. Once a small meeting was planned for only 70 salesmen for an electronics manufacturer at an Arizona resort. An invitation to the governor to say "Welcome" was extended and was graciously accepted.

(e) **Hire a Psychologist as a Speaker**—especially one who works with salesmen. You will be pleasantly surprised at the interest shown.

(f) **Federal Government Speakers.** There is no charge for Federal government speakers. Speakers are available on a variety of subjects.

(g) **Convention Bureau.** This is an excellent source to contact for local speakers. Often the speakers do not charge—particularly if from a company such as utilities, brokerage houses, banks, etc.

(h) **Check Local Corporate Branches or Local Association Chapters.** They may know of speakers whom they have used and recommend highly.

(i) **Universities.** There may be professors whose specific expertise may be of interest to your delegates.

(j) **Authors of Books and Articles.** There may be authors of current books which are of interest to your group. Authors can be contacted through their publishers. However, check their speaking ability carefully. The author's speaking style may not be the same as his lively writing style.

(k) **Dartnell Corporation.** This company issues a list of well-known speakers especially for sales conventions. The address is 4660 Ravenswood Ave., Chicago, Ill. 60640.

(l) **Sales Meeting Magazine** publishes a list of speakers. It's published annually in the "Guide to Speakers" section of their "International Convention Facilities Issue." Look up a copy at your library or write to them at 1212 Chestnut St., Philadelphia, Pa. 19107.

(m) Speaker Travel Cost Tips. By using local speakers the added expense of travel costs is eliminated. If the meeting is to be held on the East Coast, money can be saved by selecting speakers from the East. If engaging a professional speaker from an agency, check to see if his travel cost can be shared with an organization using his services in the same general area at the same time.

(n) Use a Professional Speaker's Bureau. Top speakers for business meetings and seminar leaders are available through:

National Speaker's Bureau
222 Wisconsin Ave.
Lake Forrest, Ill. 60045

National Lecture Bureau
104 S. Michigan Ave.
Chicago, Ill. 60603

International Speakers Network
1540 Weatherstone Lane
Elgin, Ill. 60120

International Speakers Bureau
P.O. Box 3799, Merchandise Mart
Chicago, Ill. 60654

(o) A "Speaker's Directory" is published by Sales & Executives International, 630 Third Ave., New York, N.Y. 10017.

(p) Sports Speakers may be booked through Burns Celebrity Service, 1 IBM Plaza, Chicago, Ill. 60611.

(q) Chambers of Commerce often have a list of local speakers. Also inquire of the local convention bureau for such a list.

(r) Sales and Marketing Executives Clubs are a source. Also clubs and associations for speakers relating to their specific interest area.

4. THIRTEEN EFFECTIVE WORKSHOP SESSION IDEAS.

Discussion sessions are a particularly effective way of securing audience participation. These sessions offer attendees the chance to let management know of their problems and provide a forum for airing opinions. Solutions arrived at through such group participation offer more likelihood of wholehearted acceptance. Another advantage of discussion sessions is the chance to exchange ideas with peers based on practical experience. This exposure to varied views often leads to better selling methods.

(a) Workshops.
The most useful and lasting learning takes place in an atmosphere in which the learner is doing something, and workshops provide such a vehicle.
Generally, the workshop begins with a lecture. (It is sometimes followed

How to Create Interest, Enthusiasm, and Results 63

by a discussion by the entire audience.) The audience is then broken into small groups which are assigned a problem to solve, or different segments of the problem may be assigned to various groups. The groups then reconvene and a reporter from each group gives its findings.

(b) **Workshop Subjects.**
A sampling of suggested workshop subjects is as follows:
What Do You Know About Your Competition?
How Should Our Promotional Dollars Be Used to Best Advantage?
Correspondence and Paper Work—How to Best Handle
Territory Analysis
Territory Coverage
How to Sell Dealer Promotions
How to Improve Communications Between Field and Factory
How to Make the Distributor Program More Effective
How to Obtain a Larger Share of the _____ Market
Effective Prospecting and Missionary Selling
Improving Sales Training
What Services the Home Office Should Provide to You
How to Obtain More Business by Telephone
How to Provide the Best Utilization of Time
The Best Type of Sales Contests
What Should Be the Content of the Sales Manual?
How to Handle Customer Complaints
How to Improve Report Forms
How to Prepare for the Sales Call
Time Management
How to Combat Price Cutting
How to Make Use of Market Information
How to Take Accounts Away from Competition
Strategy in Selecting Prospects
Product Application Problems
How to Obtain More Business Through Jobbers
Selective Selling (of most profitable lines, most profitable customers, dealers or distributors)
How to Win Customers Away from Competition
Selling Strategy for a Certain Line or Class of Customer
What Type of Competitive Knowledge to Obtain
Improving Forecasts
Daily and Weekly Sales Planning
How to Classify Customers for More Productive Calls
How to Keep Adequate Customer Records

> How to Best Analyze Sales Records
> How to Motivate Distributor Salesmen
> How to Multiply Your Effectiveness Through Distributor Salesmen
> What Services and Benefits We Are Selling
> Seeing the Right Man

(c) Varied Subject Workshops.

At conventions where the interests of the delegates are varied, workshops on different subjects may be held simultaneously. The attendees attend the workshops of their choice.

(d) Workshop Source Material.

A series of 24 four-page brochures are offered by the Business Press Syndicate, Sales Training Division. These brochures provide a good source for workshop material. Some of the titles are "How to Get Appointments," "How Well Do You Know Your Competition?" "We're Satisfied—Why Change?" "What's In It for Me?" "New Business from Your Old Accounts," etc. If desired, these can be paraphrased to fit your selling situations. A method to cover a number of these subjects at a conference is to assign different segments to different workshop groups. The address is 391 Grand Ave., Englewood, N.J. 07631.

(e) Buzz Sessions.

These are used when the group is too large or when time is short. The buzz session can be set up with a chairman and recorder similar to a workshop. The difference is that each group is given only six minutes. It can be used to develop subjects for a panel of experts, or each group may have the assignment of recommending problems for discussion. After the questions are listed before the entire group and voted upon, the buzz groups are assigned the various problems for six-minute solutions.

The buzz session plan can be adopted to audiences in fixed seats by requesting each row to break into pairs for the purpose of making suggestions. Only a sampling of the audience need be polled for their suggestions. It will soon be noted that the ideas suggested begin to form a pattern. The balance of the group can then be called upon to make additional suggestions.

(f) "Listen In on Purchasing" Tape Recording.

This is a tape recording containing realistic interviews between salesmen and purchasing agents. The recording contains four cases, two of which make excellent subjects for workshop discussion. They are: "Back-Door Selling—Whose Fault?" in which a salesman is forced to bypass the purchasing department, and "Back-Up for the Buyer" in which the purchasing manager, buyer and salesman are concerned with cost reduction. "Listen In on

Purchasing" is available both in tape and long-playing record form with accompanying discussion manual from American Management Association, 135 West 50th St., New York, N.Y. 10020.

(g) **Competition for Best Answers.**
A company which has a relatively small number of salesmen broke up its attendees into teams of two men each. These teams were given a common sales problem and competed with each other for the best solutions.

(h) **Salesmen Run Own Show.**
One organization held a series of workshop sessions composed of just salesmen. The object was for the field men to evaluate, criticize, and suggest improved techniques both for themselves and for headquarters. A list of 12 suggested subjects was given to the men with instructions to choose the five most important. They were also given the choice of suggesting alternate topics. A summary of each group's chief recommendation was given in an afternoon session which management attended.

(i) **Sales Manual Written by Salesmen.**
Ideas born in workshops can be given long life by incorporating them in a sales manual. An organization did this by first listing all the duties of a salesman and grouping these under 15 classifications. These became the subjects for workshop groups.

The entire meeting was devoted to the sales manual. Salesmen were appointed as discussion leaders and were given an outline of questions for the discussion. All the groups discussed the same subject for 30 minutes. That was followed by a ten-minute report by each discussion leader. The makeup of the tables was changed for each subject. The reports were tape recorded and from them a sales manual was produced.

(j) **Depth Analysis of a Sale.**
The conference can be devoted to the steps in making a sale—either encompassing all sales in general, or a particular product, or a new product. The depth analysis may cover such subjects as market analysis, investigation of the customer, preparing the presentation, bidding, forecasting sales volume, etc.

(k) **Case Histories.**
Prior to the conference write case histories on hypothetical typical sales situations. Sprinkle with dialogue between customer and prospect if required. The workshop group's job is to offer a critique on how the sale should have been handled. Source material may be in your company's "Lost Order" file.

(l) Make Your Own Tapes of Case Histories to Be Discussed.
Write a case history built around your own custom-selling situation and place it on audio tape or video tape for use at a workshop session.

(m) Feedback.
To ensure that the benefits of participation continue, arrange for feedback so that attendees feel their participation has been meaningful. Ways of accomplishing this can be through a report on solutions to complaints, progress reports on the program instituted as a result of the meeting, or by a written summary of the pertinent meetings.

5. DEALER OR DISTRIBUTOR PROGRAMS.

(a) Idea Showcase. If the meeting is for dealers or distributors, consider requesting that they bring to the convention examples of ideas that worked. Require that the material (photos, diagrams, bulletins, ads, documents) be mountable and fit on standard 2' × 3' cardboard. Give prizes for the best ideas.

(b) Putting Together a Distributor Program. Make it a program where distributors who have been unusually successful in solving a particular problem or who are very successful running a certain aspect of their business, share their experience with fellow distributors. Typical areas of problem solving could be sales, warehousing, accounting, inventory management, new customer prospecting, etc. To assist the speaker, a photographer or a movie cameraman could go to the distributorship to take pictures. When the pictures are shown they will not only provide added interest, but serve as props for the speaker.

6. HOW TO GET THE MEETING OFF TO A GOOD START.

(a) "We Understand Your Problem" Beginning. If there is a big problem in the field, indicate right at the beginning that management is aware of this and that something is being done about it as will be explained as the meeting progresses. A way to dramatize this is to lower the lights and flash a photo on the screen (such as one or two salesmen talking; this can be a negative print to make the person unrecognizable. Or flash on the screen a big "problem" or question mark). A voice or voices backstage narrates the salesman's complaint or complaints. Then the head speaker tells the men they are right and something is being done about it, as they will learn during the meeting.

(b) Breaking the Ice. When there are relative strangers in the small meeting group, give each individual a match and dim the lights. Ask each person to describe his territory, his company or product, or his problem. He speaks until the match burns out.

(c) **Use a tape recorder to play music** for ten or fifteen minutes before the program starts, or you may call on a member who is an accomplished pianist.

(Also see "Meeting Opening Ideas" in Chapter 10.)

7. WAYS TO INVOLVE THE AUDIENCE.

(a) **Role Playing Between Field Sales and Home Office.** If there have been problems in communication between field sales and staff, consider appointing several persons to reproduce a typical problem situation and the attempts to achieve communication. Then, to create empathy, at a signal from the moderator, have the players switch roles.

(b) **Customer Skit.** Salesmen act out a sales call. The person taking the part of the customer asks questions which bring out the product's features and benefits.

(c) **Debate.** Hold a debate on a subject such as "The best way to make a sales presentation on _____ product," etc. Appoint salesmen to the two teams several months ahead of time so they can be marshaling their facts. Let the audience vote on the winners.

(d) **Case Histories.** Instead of a speaker telling the audience how it is done, have several of the salesmen relate histories of how they made successful sales.

(e) **Let the Audience Demonstrate.** If the presentation calls for a demonstration of the product, ask members of the audience to do the demonstrating, with the speaker giving directions.

(f) **Secret Word Game.** This is a take-off on the television program. Use this when salesmen discuss the merits of a product or program on the stage or in discussion groups. Here is how it works: Announce that a five or ten dollar bill will be given to the first person who mentions the secret word. The word can be a product feature or a sales benefit. If the game is played on a stage, place the word on a large placard or blackboard so that the audience, but not the participants, can see the word.

(g) **Role Playing.** As in real life, role playing is the spontaneous acting out of a selling situation. Build the role-playing demonstration around a genuine problem. Select a buyer and a seller from the audience, give them the situation and the problem, and let the action develop naturally. Then the members of the audience discuss the enactment.

(h) There's Money to Be Had. Give a playing card to each person as he enters the meeting room. Tell him to hold on to the card; it is worth money.

At intervals during the meeting interrupt the meeting by ringing a gong or a bell, or shooting a gun. The M.C. announces that there is money to be had by selling the company's line or by learning about the product. And he is going to prove it. He brings out a deck of cards and has someone draw a card. The attendee with the matching card is asked a question. If the answer is correct, he wins the money. If the answer is not known, another card is drawn or the amount is added to a later question. The amount of money given out at each interruption can be increased as the meeting progresses.

If more than 52 are attending, either mark a second deck and do so accordingly for the M.C.; or use a second deck with a different design.

(i) Inquiring Reporter. This is a variation of the role-playing technique. It is effective in telling a company story, in dramatizing the development of a product, in introducing a selling concept, a new division of the company, etc. Set the stage with comfortable chairs to represent a hotel suite. Explain to the audience that an inquiring reporter will be interviewing the company men on this development for a future story. On the stage have actual officials of the company such as the chief engineer, marketing director, comptroller, etc. The reporter asks leading questions from an outline, and the men answer informally and spontaneously. The officials are allowed to reinforce each others' points and to comment to each other.

(j) Workbook Retains Information. Prepare a booklet or loose-leaf binder into which the salesmen write the main points to be retained. Have the speaker stop at each of his few key points and ask the audience to write it down. This spotlights the main points, gives the audience something to do, and is more likely to be remembered. The page headings should, of course, parallel the program. The notebook provides an excellent take-home piece for profitable use.

(k) "Key Question" Jackpot Prize. Develop key questions which represent the heart of the meeting. These can relate to a tour of the factory before the conference, or to the subjects presented and discussed at the meeting. Group the questions to correspond to the four quarters of the conference. Also give a numbered card to each member of the audience. Each man receives a different number. At intervals when attention lags, conduct the drawing of two of the questions. Also draw an attendee number. If the attendee answers correctly, he wins a prize. If an incorrect answer is given, another name is drawn to encourage the collection of the information, print the questions on the program.

(l) Name Written on a Dollar Bill. Everyone is asked to write their name on a dollar bill and drop it into a box or bowl. They are then told that at the end of the session there will be a drawing and the man whose name is drawn wins the pot. However, that man must answer a question from the session or be required to summarize the session. This device helps to ensure attention and taking of notes.

(m) A Champagne Pledge. If a specific accomplishment is to be achieved as a result of the meeting (such as meeting a certain dollar sales goal, landing new accounts, etc.), serve champagne at the meeting's end. Then, as an added bit of drama, one by one or in groups, the attendees smash their glasses into a fake fireplace.

(n) Include a "Question Card" in the Welcome Kit which is given to each person as he arrives at the convention. Ask the conferee to write down any question he might have about the company's plans or about the product. State that the cards will be collected at the opening meeting. The speaker collects the cards as the meeting begins and reads the questions out loud. If it is a large group, announce that only a sampling will be read. As the questions are read, indicate which ones are already being covered at the meeting and which will be passed on to speakers who will try to include the answer in their particular session. Asking for questions indicates to the group that their needs are going to be considered.

(o) "Idea Money." Print up fake money leaving room on the front or back for the writing of an idea. Attendees are told that during the convention they are to contact fellow attendees and write down an idea from the fellow delegate on the bill. Attendees may obtain as many copies of the money as they wish. Prizes are given to those obtaining the greatest number of ideas.

(p) Wheel-of-Fortune Game. Give each person a numbered card and spin a wheel of fortune. The individual with the number which has been spun has to answer a question. If answered correctly he receives a prize. If there are more audience members than numbers on the wheel, the cards can be in several colors. The leader states that the spin is for the green cards this time. Make your own wheel or obtain one from a carnival supply rental company (see the yellow pages of your phone book).

(q) Stump the Experts. Appoint a panel of experts from the audience. Also apppoint an umpire group of three to five persons. The audience asks questions of the panel members who earn or lose points according to the correctness of their answers. The umpire group decides if the answer is correct. A wheel of fortune can be used to determine who in the audience will ask a question. Rotate the panel of experts frequently to give many attendees an opportunity to participate.

For additional information in involving the audience see Chapter 8.

8. WAYS TO PROMOTE ESPRIT DE CORPS.

(a) **Promote Esprit de Corps Among Sales Groups** by encouraging each district to show up on opening morning with distinctive wearing apparel. One group can appear with an imprinted T-shirt. Another group with a different imprinted T-shirt. Others can appear with plastic straw hats, or bandannas, bright old-time arm garters, cowboy hats, derbys, imprinted gold polyester shirts, Gay 90s jackets, Kentucky Colonel ties, distinctive vests, green top hats, etc. At a convention which this writer attended, the British contingent strode in with top hats and canes.

(b) **This Company Will Reproduce an Individual's Own Photo or Drawings on T-Shirts.** It is The Balloon Man, 17301 W. 7 Mile Road, Detroit, Mich., 48235. Other T-shirt manufacturers are: Right-On Graphics, Inc., 2550 West Century Blvd., Suite 427, Los Angeles, Calif. 90045; Sherry Mfg. Co., Inc., 1411 Broadway, New York, N.Y. 10018; Chaseline Division, 4900 Corona Ave., Los Angeles, Ca. 90058; and K-Line Studio, 1226 Ambassador Blvd., St. Louis, Mo. 63132—approximately $1.50 to $2.25 imprinted.

(c) **Some Novelty Hat Manufacturers** are Jacobson Hat Co., Preston & Ridge Row, Scranton, Pa. 18510; Makley's, 441 S. Plymouth Court, Chicago, Ill. 60505. For firemen's hats, oriental hats, racing helmets, western hats, construction hard hats, baseball helmets, or a Colonial tricorn hat it is Lewtan Industries Corp., 30 High St., Hartford, Conn. 06101. They also have color imprinted vests and sleeve garters.

(d) **For Additional Vests** contact Makley's, 441 S. Plymouth Ct., Chicago, Ill. 60605, or Helli Company, 700 North Kilpatrick, Lincolnwood, Ill. 60646. The Helli Company also has garters, ties, bonnets, jackets, and bandannas.

(e) **For the Very Bold** there are bald head wigs, devil masks, and Frankenstein masks from Frank Stein Novelty Co., 1969 So. Los Angeles St., Los Angeles, Calif. 90011. They also carry a line of novelty hats. Obtain fake mustaches of various styles from Jack-Bilt Corp., 906 Central St., Kansas City, Mo. 64105. For the eye-patch look write to Hewig & Marvic, 861 Manhattan Ave., Brooklyn, N.Y. 11222.

(f) **"We Try Harder" Buttons.** One of your sales districts could show up sporting these buttons. Try your local Avis car rental agency for a supply.

9. ELEVEN WAYS TO GET INVOLVEMENT BY USING QUESTIONS AND QUIZZES.

(a) **To Ensure More Attention** conduct a short written quiz before a discussion group begins or before a presentation is made. Ask a dozen questions

How to Create Interest, Enthusiasm, and Results 71

about the main points which the salesman is to remember. The salesman fills in what he thinks are the correct answers. You can be sure that the audience will pay more attention as they listen to the presentation and compare it mentally with their answers. You may choose to conduct this as a longer written inventory test covering items from the entire sales conference.

(b) **Speech Questionnaire.** At the end of a talk hand out a questionnaire. Ask the audience to fill out the first question only. The question is then discussed. Then the audience is requested to answer the second question and this is discussed, etc.

(c) **"Try For More" Quiz.** Place a sign on the platform indicating categories of questions. The contestant chooses the category in which he wishes to compete. First an easy question is given, then each question becomes progressively more difficult The prizes (of money or goods) also increase in value. The contestant has the privilege of quitting at any time and taking his winnings. But any time the contestant fails, the entire amount won up to that point goes into the jackpot.

(d) **Quiz Down.** Remember the old-fashioned spelling bee? Hold one using questions about your product at the end of a particular product presentation, or at the end of the meeting. Pit teams against each other. If a question is not answered by one team, toss it to the other. If the quiz is among individuals, allow two misses before stepping down.

(e) **Customer Voices Asking Questions.** Prerecord on tape the voices of customers asking questions about your product or service. The tape is stopped and the speaker answers the questions as they are asked. Perhaps you will want to have a voice identifying the type of customer before he or she speaks. Arrange to start and stop the tape recorder from the speaker's platform, or cue your assistant.

(f) **Quiz on Agreement/Disagreement.** A good way to obtain participation, to bring out attitudes, and to provide animated discussion is to give an Agree/Disagree Quiz. It works like this: The speaker voices a question and gives an answer; and then asks for a show of hands on whether they agree or disagree. The speaker then gives his opinion of the correct answer. The members of the audience who disagree then state why they disagree and comments are invited from the audience.

(g) **Panel of Interrogators.** Appoint a panel of three or four salesmen to interrogate the speaker on behalf of the audience.

(h) **Examination for Fun and Profit.** Announce at the opening meeting that there will be an examination at the end of the conference. For quick grading, the answers should be true or false, multiple choice, or require only one word or figure. Make the prizes worthwhile, such as a hundred dollar bill and corresponding second and third prizes. You may announce that, in addition, all persons making a score of 80% or better will have their names placed in a hat for a drawing for prizes.

(i) Question Box. Stimulate questions by placing a question box in a conspicuous place. It remains in this spot throughout the meeting. Give the questions to various qualified panel groups for answering at the end of the meeting.

(j) Have Speakers Ask Questions. The speaker asks the audience "What questions do you think the customers will have about the product?" If the speaker doesn't know the answer, he can ask the audience for the answer. Consider asking, "What questions do you think distributors will have?", or "What questions do you have?" If preferred, have the audience write questions on cards during the speech and pass them up to the speaker for answering.

(k) To Encourage Answers from the Audience an assistant passes out a numbered ticket to each person who provides an answer. The matching numbered stub is placed in a container on the stage. This is done throughout the conference. A drawing is then made at the closing session or banquet. A roll of numbered tickets with matching numbers on the stub are usually obtainable from a stationary store.

10. SALES TRAINING FILM SOURCES.

American Management Association
135 West 50th St.
New York, N.Y. 10020

Mass Media
2116 N. Charles St.
Baltimore, Md. 21218

The Dartnell Corporation
4660 Ravenswood Ave.
Chicago, Ill. 60640

Association/Sterling Films
600 Grand Ave.
Ridgefield, N.J. 07657

The Jam Handy Organization
2821 E. Grand Blvd.
Detroit, Mich. 48211

Cally Curtis Company
1111 N. Las Palmas Ave.
Hollywood, Calif. 90038

BNA Communications
9401 Decoverly Hall Rd.
Rockville, Md. 20850

Vantage Communications
Box 545
Nyack, N.Y. 10960

How to Create Interest, Enthusiasm, and Results

Universal Education & Visual Arts
221 Park Avenue South
New York, N.Y. 10003

McGraw-Hill Book Company
Text-Film Department
330 W. 42nd St.
New York, N.Y. 10036

Roundtable Films, Inc.
113 N. San Vicente Blvd.
Beverly Hills, Calif. 90211

Ex-IBM Corporation
7034 Dart Brook Dr.
Dallas, Tex. 75240

Penton Publishing Company
201 East 42nd St.
New York, N.Y. 10017

Modern Media Services
2323 New Hyde Park Rd.
New Hyde Park, N.Y. 11040

Roa's Films
1696 N. Astor St.
Milwaukee, Wisc. 63202

Ramic Productions
58 West 58th St.
New York, N.Y. 10019

Roy Walters & Associates, Inc.
60 Glenn Ave.
Glen Rock, N.J. 07452

Meeting Room Prop Checklist. See Chapter 22.

Chapter 7

How to Make the Most Effective Use of Panels

Contents

1. Types of Panels
2. Panel Sizes
3. Moderator's Duties
4. Planning for the Panel Session
5. Controlling the Panel
6. Ideas for Panels That Are Different
7. Panel Showmanship

What is a Panel? It is a method of developing interaction between a group of experts and the audience. The experts give their views on a subject. A neutral moderator guides the panel. In most cases, this presentation of views is achieved by means of questions and answers by the moderator. Often this type of program includes questions from the audience.

1. TYPES OF PANELS.

(a) **Symposium.** This is a panel where each panelist gives a statement on the segment of the topic assigned to him. Questions are then entertained from the floor.

(b) **Self-Questioning.** The questions come from fellow panel members or from the moderator. Occasionally, the moderator may ask if there are any questions from the floor.

(c) **Classic.** The subject is announced and questions from the audience are immediately answered. No statement of position is made by the panel members.

(d) **Reverse.** The panelists ask the questions and the audience replies.

(e) **Interview.** Used when there are diverse interests represented in the audience. Each panel member represents a different segment of audience interest. When a panel member presents his views, the other members ask questions for their segment of the audience.

(f) **Interrogation.** A group is selected from the audience to ask questions of the panelists for the audience. The interrogators are usually limited to two or three persons. A moderator is also present.

(g) **Debate.** The panelists take sides on an issue.

2. PANEL SIZES.

The ideal size seems to be a panel consisting of three members. A group composed of two to four members is practical, but a group of more than four becomes unworkable.

The problem with a large panel is that it is difficult to control. If each panelist gives a short speech, the total time for speeches becomes too long and there is little time for discussion. There will be too many responses to a question, as all want to participate. This also results in repetition.

3. MODERATOR'S DUTIES.

The moderator's (or chairman, as he is sometimes titled) chief duty is to constantly guide the group so that it stays on the assigned topic. He will ask questions himself to accomplish this guidance. He will also ask questions to clarify a point for audience comprehension. He will encourage the quiet panelist to participate, and will restrain the talkative. When he senses the discussion is getting argumentative or even acrimonious, he uses diplomacy, tact, and humor to clear the air. The moderator will keep track of time so that not too much time is spent on one subject to the detriment of other subjects. Make sure that the moderator is given detailed instructions.

4. PLANNING FOR THE PANEL SESSION.

The panelists should endeavor to determine what is on the minds of the audience. This can be done by holding planning meetings where the panelists and company or association staff members meet. The collective thinking of this diverse group presents a better insight into the audience's interests. At this planning meeting, review the subject to be discussed.

Another effective method is to send a questionnaire to the attendees. For instance, if the subject is a product, ask the attendees their problems with that product, both mechanical and marketing-wise. This method gives the panelists time to research the questions.

Here is another method that you can utilize. Provide question cards at a morning meeting for a panel meeting which is to be held later in the day.

The card-question method enables the panelists to discard questions which are irrelevant or redundant. Another advantage is that the questions can be sorted into logical sequence, and the moderator or panelists can add questions which they feel are required.

5. CONTROLLING THE PANEL.

Basically, controlling boils down to the moderator guiding the discussion so that all panelists participate, and providing guidance in covering the subject adequately.

(a) **How to Control the Time Devoted to Opening Statements.** Make it a requirement that each panelist limit his statement to not more than two sentences or not more than one or two minutes.

(b) Specify to Each Panel Member the Portion of the Topic He is to Cover. This will prevent overlapping. Also, be careful not to assign too large a segment to a panelist. It is better to cover fewer topics thoroughly than a wide range thinly.

6. IDEAS FOR PANELS THAT ARE DIFFERENT.

(a) Set Up a Panel Composed of Top Salesmen. They discuss a subject or subjects such as territory planning, how to prospect, how to sell a certain class of customer, or how to sell a specific product line. Questions may be asked by the audience.

(b) Have a Panel of Salesmen Follow a Speech. Their job is to relay the points made in the speech in terms of their own problems.

(c) Have a Panel of Experts Follow a Presentation of a New Product. They answer questions from the audience. The panel might be composed of the sales manager, product manager, quality control manager, distributor manager, engineering manager, etc.

(d) Have the Audience Set Priorities for Subjects. The moderator asks the audience to indicate by a show of hands its interest in each of the subtopics. He uses this information to confine the discussions to these subjects, thus giving the feeling of audience participation.

7. PANEL SHOWMANSHIP.

(a) Use a "Devil's Advocate" in place of the moderator. This title enables him to be a bit more direct in prodding the panelists for straight answers. It also provides opportunity for informality and humor. Cards from the audience can be handed to him. Garb the devil in appropriate costume—red cape, mask, horns, fork. Check a costume shop for rental of such a garment.

(b) If the Panelists Are Composed of Members of Company Management, rather than have a stage with chairs and a table, draw the curtain and have the panelists sit on the stage apron, thus providing informality.

(c) Provide a Microphone for Each Panel Member, thus eliminating the delays of passing one mike around.

(d) Massive Questioning Technique. The moderator asks a number of related questions at one time. The questions are arranged to enable the panel member to develop his subject logically. There may be only one or two such sets of questions per panelist.

Chapter 8

39 Tested Ideas to Secure Participation

Contents

1. Introduction
2. Tell the Attendees at the Beginning That You Want Their Participation
3. Put on a Skit
4. Sales Situation (Case Study)
5. Group Selling
6. "Carry-the-Ball" Group Selling
7. Start a Blackboard List of Selling Ideas
8. Ask Attendees to Bring Problem Situations with Them from the Field
9. Provide Outlines for Note Taking
10. Sales Planning Forms
11. Hold a "Question-and-Answer" Session
12. Role Playing
13. Problem Solving
14. Hold a Demonstration Contest
15. Gripe Sessions
16. Pit One Side of Audience Against the Other
17. Converting "Features" to "Benefits"
18. Panel of Interpreters
19. Phrases to Use to Encourage Participation
20. Individual Clinics with Experts
21. Repeat the Question

22. Boasting Session
23. Evaluating New or Proposed Programs and Policies
24. Panelists
25. Hold Sales Promotion "Needs" Session
26. "Do-It-Yourself" Customer Presentation
27. "Competition" Sessions
28. Business Simulation and Sales Strategy Games
29. Films Accompanied by a Discussion Leader's Guide
30. Hold Group Contests
31. "How I Made My Best Sale" or "Why Did I Lose an Important Sale?"
32. Representatives Seminar with Management Absent
33. Give Assignments
34. Participative Assistance on Scoring
35. Listening Teams
36. Action Plans
37. Reward Listening Skills
38. Four Test-Yourself Games
39. Other "Participation" Ideas

1. **INTRODUCTION.** At meetings consisting of nothing but speeches, the audience generally will be sitting politely but not listening for a good part of the time; they will be thinking about their own good ideas on the subject and how they are powerless to make a contribution. But a conference with periods for participation makes for enthusiasm and for increased attention. And by affording the attendee an opportunity to take part and exhibit his knowledge, more thought will be given to the subject. There will also be a greater retention of ideas and a more likely acceptance of the decisions made.

2. **TELL THE ATTENDEES AT THE BEGINNING THAT YOU WANT THEIR PARTICIPATION.** Surprisingly, many persons don't realize that their participation is wanted. Explain that everybody benefits when they give their ideas.

3. **PUT ON A SKIT.** Have two attendees come up front and take part in the simulated situation. Then ask members of the audience to give their comments on what went wrong or how the presentation or situation could have been improved. Note: The skit goes much smoother if the two attendees are given the script to rehearse together before the meeting.

4. **SALES SITUATION (CASE STUDY).** Narrate or pass out typewritten sheets spelling out a given sales situation with, perhaps, action having been taken up to a certain point. Then ask the group how they would complete the sale or solve the problem.

5. **GROUP SELLING.** Divide the men into groups with each headed by a knowledgeable salesman or staff member who takes the role of the buyer. The entire group tries to sell the "buyer." The advantage is that all participate and no single person has been singled out as the salesman. This method also serves to encourage constructive cross-talking.

6. **"CARRY-THE-BALL" GROUP SELLING.** If it is felt that a number of the group members may be noncommittal in joining the selling, rather than having volunteers sell to the conference leader, call on each member in turn to take part. First one person takes part, then another is called on to continue the sale, and then another and another.

7. **START A BLACKBOARD LIST OF SELLING IDEAS.** Assign a topic and then call for suggestions from the audience on how to best handle the situation. Typical topics could be: How to arrange a meeting by telephone, or overcoming an objection to price or to delivery. Inform the audience that copies of the lists which have been developed will be mailed to them. If advisable, have the attendees take notes. Cover a number of topics.

8. **ASK ATTENDEES TO BRING PROBLEM SITUATIONS WITH THEM FROM THE FIELD.** Take a vote on which situations will be discussed by the group.

9. **PROVIDE OUTLINES FOR NOTE TAKING.** Outlines of the key presentations are placed in loose-leaf notebooks. Ample space is left after each main point for jotting down notes.

    In addition, the audience can be asked to write down questions for discussion after the speech, or the questions can be submitted to a panel of experts later in the program.

10. **SALES PLANNING FORMS.** Here the company provides a form (on subjects such as planning a sales call, planning the work week, introducing a new product, etc.) and the salesman fills in data as applied to his own territory or account.

11. **HOLD A "QUESTION-AND-ANSWER" SESSION.** There are a number of variations. One is to have the leader ask questions phrased to be of benefit to the group, such as "How would you use this feature to sell a prospect?"

    Individuals can be singled out to answer questions, or there can be volunteers.

    Questions can be printed and passed out to the audience. Members of the group are then called upon to give their opinions as to the proper answer.

    Another method is to pass out blank cards and have the men write questions for which they seek answers. All cards are returned, whether blank or not, thus no one is embarrassed. Ask the group to supply the answers. Have some cards of your own in reserve in case there is a scarcity of questions.

Request for questions can be made in advance by mail. Generally, the questions are confined to one or two subjects. Request each person to prepare a number of questions on each of the subjects. The discussion group at the meeting then provides its opinion as to how the question should be answered.

12. **ROLE PLAYING.** As in real life, role playing is the spontaneous acting out of a selling situation. For example, select a buyer and a seller from the audience, give them the situation and the problem, and let the action develop naturally. Then the members of the audience discuss the enactment.

13. **PROBLEM SOLVING.** Consider devoting the entire conference to solving a problem that is common to most attendees, and implementing its solution. The meeting sessions work on the elements of the problem. Make sure that those responsible for authorizing the solution are in attendance. Follow the standard method of problem solving, i.e., (a) Define the problem, (b) get the facts, (c) list the alternative solutions, (d) select the most fitting solution, (e) determine the action (what, who, how, when, where), (f) assign responsibility.

14. **HOLD A DEMONSTRATION CONTEST.** Break the meeting into small groups of about six each. One man in each group is elected to enter the demonstration contest. The other members of the group coach him. Hand out a list of points to be covered in the demonstration. The competing demonstrations are then given to the entire group. A vote can be taken for the best presentation.

15. **GRIPE SESSIONS.** If handled carefully, such a session can be used as a morale builder by letting the men get gripes off their chests. It is a good method of finding out if there are problems which the group has in common. The other members of the group are asked to help provide the answer. The person may find that co-workers do not consider his gripe important. It is important that action be taken on the complaints.

16. **PIT ONE SIDE OF AUDIENCE AGAINST THE OTHER.** This is especially suitable for smaller meetings. First ask one side and then the other for answers to questions such as: "What are the most profitable sources for prospects for this product?", etc.

17. **CONVERTING "FEATURES" TO "BENEFITS."** List the product features on a board. Then ask the men to translate these features into customer benefits.

18. **PANEL OF INTERPRETERS.** A panel of attendees discusses the points made in a film or speech and translates these in terms of the company's product.

19. **PHRASES TO USE TO ENCOURAGE PARTICIPATION.** Use leading questions—no questions which just elicit a "yes" or "no." For instance, ask after a film is shown or after a skit "Now, why did Jim lose the sale?", or "You have seen the new model with the three-inch reinforced cylinder. How do you translate this into a benefit for the customer?", or "What would you have said to the customer when . . ." Don't use a phrase such as "Any comments?" A good way to open a participation session is to point out that "Everybody knows more than anybody, and that is the reason the session is being held—to obtain the benefit of those ideas." And never ridicule—instead, always show appreciation for a contribution.

20. **INDIVIDUAL CLINICS WITH EXPERTS.** Set aside time for individuals to consult with experts concerning their individual questions and problems. These can be two two-hour periods. The experts can be knowledgeable persons from the industry, or meeting speakers, panelists, and company members from areas such as engineering, sales, credit, production, etc. Set up tables within a room or in several rooms. No appointments are necessary. Guides at the door direct the individual to the proper table. Waiting individuals, if the expert agrees to it, can be directed to the expert's table to listen in on the questions and answers. During question and answer periods on the main program, the speakers can refer the question to a private clinic session.

21. **REPEAT THE QUESTION.** If a question is asked from the floor, be sure to have the leader repeat the question as the individuals sitting in the rows behind the person asking the question are often unable to hear.

22. **BOASTING SESSION.** Various salesmen are called to the platform and given a chance to tell how they accomplish a certain task. It often helps to provide a brief outline which all the salesmen who speak can follow.

23. **EVALUATING NEW OR PROPOSED PROGRAMS AND POLICIES.** Suppose a new policy is being considered. Before the policy is presented, divide the audience into groups and assign to each an analysis of specific customer reactions. For example, it may be a policy concerning pricing—how it affects distributor inventories, salesmen, collections, etc. Each group leader then makes a report based on his group's conclu-

sions. Other topics may concern a proposed advertising program, a choice of priorities in the manufacture of new product lines, a new promotional program, etc.

24. **PANELISTS.** (See Chapter 7 "Panels" on how to use this method of securing audience participation.)

25. **HOLD SALES PROMOTION "NEEDS" SESSION.** Send a letter in advance of the meeting stating that a session will be held during which the needs of participants for sales promotion and back-up material will be explored. Request that the attendees think about their requirements in this area and bring competitive material if possible.

26. **"DO-IT-YOURSELF" CUSTOMER PRESENTATION.** Create an 8½" × 11" booklet with subject headings only. The salesman fills in the blank pages as the meeting progresses. The salesman uses his own words. If desired, this notebook can be the subject of a session where teams put together a presentation. Some or all of the finished presentations can be given before the group. Prizes can be awarded for the best presentation. State that the best presentations will be reproduced and mailed to the attendees.

27. **"COMPETITION" SESSIONS.** This subject is sure to hold a salesman's interest. Here the competitor's strong and weak points are compared to your own product or policy, and appropriate answers and customer presentation strategies are developed. These sessions can be developed around competition to your newly unveiled products. Bring in competitive products for the group's evaluation. Mail copies of the developed competitive profile after the meeting.

28. **BUSINESS SIMULATION AND SALES STRATEGY GAMES.** These games are built around true-to-life situations. Teams are in competition with other groups. Specific games are devoted to a particular problem such as "penetration of a difficult market." The players are required to make a series of step-by-step decisions during which skills and knowledge are acquired as they exchange ideas from their actual experiences.

The games are a means of providing quick involvement. They can last from 90 minutes to a half day and are easy to administer by company executives. For details write to the following organizations:

CMA Meeting Aids
584 Weadley Rd.
Stafford, Pa. 19087

International Business Machines
Armonk, N.Y. 10504

American Management Assn.
135 W. 50th St.
New York, N.Y. 10020

University of Oregon
School of Business Administration
Eugene, Oregon 97403

Games Research, Inc.
48 Wareham St.
Boston, Mass 02118

Star Salesman Services
Star Builders Division
Sales Management Magazine
633 Third Ave.
New York, N.Y. 10017.

Didactic Systems, Inc.
P.O. Box 457
Cranford, N.J. 07016

29. **FILMS ACCOMPANIED BY A DISCUSSION LEADER'S GUIDE** are offered by this film distributor. Titles are "The Hidden Side of Selling" and "The Engineering of Agreement." Length is about 30 minutes. Rental for a week is approximately $40 for black and white and $60 for color. From Roundtable Films, Inc., 321 S. Beverly Dr., Beverly Hills, Calif. 90211.

30. **HOLD GROUP CONTESTS.** Hold contests among the discussion group teams to develop greater enthusiasm. Prizes can be awarded to the best team for each session, or points can be awarded for each session with the winners being the group with the largest number of points earned during the entire meeting. Examples of awarding of points could be the best or greatest number of suggestions for promoting a new product, for invading a new market, for a plan for obtaining the greatest number of new customers of a certain category within 90 days, for ideas on obtaining competitive information, for combating competition, etc. In some areas points could be awarded for answering quizzes on product features, on pricing policies, or on a promotional program. Give a number of prizes—first, second, third—to give more chances for winning.

31. **"HOW I MADE MY BEST SALE" OR "WHY DID I LOSE AN IMPORTANT SALE?"** Basic selling techniques can be imparted by having individual salesmen give short talks on one of the above subjects. The audience then participates in a question and answer period. Either the speaker or the audience members ask the questions and provide the answers. The speaking assignments can be given out before the meeting, or the speakers can be chosen at random.

32. **REPRESENTATIVE'S SEMINAR WITH MANAGEMENT ABSENT.** Two things are certain: (1) representatives are usually too busy to answer letters requesting positive or negative comments to a company's proposed sales plan, proposed new product, or promotion, and (2) if representatives or salesmen are brought together in group sessions with

management attending, an artificial atmosphere is created with the men trying to impress their immediate superiors.

The solution is to hold seminar sessions with management absent. It works like this: Sales management presents the problem, proposed plans, or promotions in a main meeting. The representatives are then divided into groups. If desired, the groups can be separated into those with mutual interests, such as those who sell to a certain class of distributors, those who handle only over-the-counter distributors, those who call only on OEM's, on retailers, etc. Divide into manageable groups of eight to twelve persons. Headquarters' management and regional managers are not present—only local company field sales managers. Each group is assigned a topic on which to give their positive and negative comments, answers to specific questions, and selling suggestions.

A meeting of management personnel should be called for the same period of time to assure that there is no eavesdropping and that they, too, are working (nothing is more morale shattering then to see executives prepare for a round of golf while their men are in session).

When everyone meets again, the group leaders present the views of their team. (It is important to stress to the attendees that their views will be given careful consideration in making adjustments to the proposed plans and promotions.) These reports can be followed by a question and answer session with the flow both from the audience and management.

33. **GIVE ASSIGNMENTS.** It may seem like an imposition, but most individuals appreciate the chance to help out. Through this involvement they take a more active interest in the meeting. Assignments can consist of:

    Writing down points on the blackboard, passing out quiz papers, checking the speaker's time, acting as reporter for a work group, running the projector, recording attendance, introducing speakers, appointment to a panel of questioners, etc.

34. **PARTICIPATIVE ASSISTANCE ON SCORING.** After a quiz, let the men exchange papers and do the grading themselves.

35. **LISTENING TEAMS.** This is a means of achieving purposeful listening. Divide the meeting group into teams, each of which is charged with listening to a certain aspect of a plan being presented. They listen from such points of view as a distributor, a distributor's salesman, a customer, a new member of an association, etc. Each group then presents a summary.

36. **ACTION PLANS.** At the end of the meeting each attendee is requested to write out the action he will take to implement the programs presented. Be sure to have the time frame indicated for the implementation.

37. **REWARD LISTENING SKILLS.** Each person drops his business card in a box at the beginning of the session. Explain that several cards will be drawn at the end of the session and the owner asked to summarize the main points of that session. Prizes are awarded for the best summaries.

38. **FOUR TEST-YOURSELF GAMES.** They are: "The Star Salesman" which rates 82 attributes of outstanding salesmanship; "Time and Territorial Management;" "Eight Keys to Motivation" on how to get the most from your men; and "Before the Call" which covers how to prepare for the sales call. Obtainable from Sales Builders Division, Sales Management Magazine, 633 Third Ave., New York, N.Y. 10017.

39. **OTHER "PARTICIPATION" IDEAS.** Ask questions about the product, policy, or catalog. Award dollar or five dollar bills or silver dollars for correct answers.

    Have a member of the audience assist the speaker in making a demonstration.

    Use the "Magic Word" TV show idea. Announce the magic word at the beginning of the meeting. When a speaker utters the word the first member of the audience who shouts gets a money reward.

    Hold a "Brainstorming" session. Everyone has to contribute at least one idea.

    At the end of the convention the attendees fill in a questionnaire designed to bring out their thinking on what subjects should be discussed at the next meeting.

    Encourage the audience throughout the meeting to place their suggestions in a suggestion box. Read the suggestions by category at the end of the meeting or during several designated times at the sessions.

    Pass a hat around and have the men put questions in it. Then call upon knowledgeable members of the audience to answer the question. Ask if there are any other suggested answers to the question.

    Note: For additional ideas on participation see "Ways to Involve the Audience" in Chapter 6.

Chapter 9

Creative Techniques to Promote the Conference

Contents

1. Planning the Mailings
2. Advance Registration Promotion
3. Assistance from Convention Bureaus, Hotels, and Chambers of Commerce
4. Local Flavor Mailing Ideas
5. Promotion of Foreign Locations
6. Production Aids and Ideas
7. Attention-Getting Mailing Ideas
8. Sources for Stick-Ons, Pop-Ups, 3-D, Fragrances, Invisible Ink, and Theme Mailing Pieces
9. Transportation Giveaways for the Mailing
10. Promotional and Travel Assistance from Airlines
11. How to Publicize the Meeting

1. PLANNING THE MAILINGS.

Promotion of the meeting should begin with the meeting promoter reviewing the "Objectives" of the meeting. Then he should place himself in the attendee's shoes and ask what the attendee will receive from the meeting to compensate for his time and money spent. When the copy for the mailing is written, it should convey to the attendee the key topics to be discussed in terms of the attendee's needs.

Then the promoter is ready to begin planning his series of promotional mailings with attention-getting gimmicks. Keep the mailing content short. It is better to make several short mailings than one bulky mailing, which may not get read.

To get the attendees involved, consider asking them to review a plan and be ready to give their views, to study material on a new product, or to check with retail customers or dealers for opinions on certain proposed products, promotion, or plans.

Announcement Schedule. Most conference planners for an association meeting mail their initial announcement eight to ten weeks before the meeting. Generally, the first announcement lists the dates, the theme, subjects, and some of the speakers. The second mailing, which is from four to seven weeks before the meeting, lists all the subjects and all the speakers. The mailings are in addition to announcements and publicity in trade journals.

2. ADVANCE REGISTRATION PROMOTION.

(a) Advance Registration. Large conventions preregister their guests by mail. It is recommended that convention material (badges, booklets, programs, etc.) not be mailed in advance; the attendees pick up this material at the registration point. There is, of course, a registration booth for those not preregistering.

(b) **Promoting Advance Registration.** Offer "bargain rates" to advance registrants. (In your planning, the "bargain rate" is actually your regular rate; attendees who wait to register at the conference pay a penalty rate.) Do the same when offering tours at bargain rates.

(c) **Mail Phonograph Records.** For large conventions consider producing a short record and mail to individuals. Point out the program content, the romance of the locale (such as sounds of Mexico, Latin songs), the golf course, fishing, etc. Aura Vision, 51 W. 52nd St., New York, N.Y. produces such custom records.

(d) **Tape Recorded Announcements.** If the convention is composed of chapters, sales offices, etc. from various cities, make a tape giving announcements of the main features of the gathering and attractions of the location. This tape can be routed well in advance to the various cities, or duplicates can be made.

(e) **Notify What to Wear.** By all means, in your invitations tell the guests what to wear. Indicate if the banquet dress is formal or informal. For the meetings indicate if casual sports attire is okay. Indicate if the evenings are cool. Also state, if the accommodations consist of separate bungalows, it would be advisable to bring a raincoat. Indicate if ties and jackets are required, the hotel's rules on abbreviated costumes, if ties are required for dining and the rule on turtlenecks, and if whites are required on the tennis courts. Explain the rules on wearing swimming attire in areas other than the pool, and if a sweater is required for an outdoor barbecue.

(f) **What-to-Wear-Trip Tips.** The women especially will appreciate information on what to wear. A number of the airlines publish brochures giving information on what to take and how to pack. TWA has a booklet titled "Basic Travel Wardrobe." Contact your local ticket office, or TWA Travel Advisor, 605 Third Ave., New York, N.Y. 10016.

(g) **Place Mats at Home.** Wives of salesmen of one company received a mailing at home which gave news of the sales conference which their husbands were attending. In the mailing was a record containing details of a contest in which the prize was a four-day trip to Las Vegas. The mailing included six humorous place mats pushing increased sales. The wives were requested to use the mats once a week as a reminder to their husbands to win the Las Vegas trip.

(h) **Send Lucky Key to Treasure Chest.** It's a good way to draw people to the meeting, or to your suite or booth at a convention. A complete Treasure

Chest kit may be obtained from Hewig & Marvic Co. The kit consists of Treasure Chest, padlock, winning keys, a horn buzzer which sings out when there is a winner, key cards for mailing, and dummy keys. Kits range from $50 to about $75. From Hewig & Marvic, 861 Manhattan Ave., Brooklyn, N.Y. 11222. Also from Electronic Treasure Chest Enterprises, Inc., P.O. Box G.C.7, Tijeras, N.M. 87059.

(i) **Self-Smoking Cigarettes.** These tiny cigarettes are only $1/16''$ in diameter. They give out puffs of smoke and keep on puffing continually. Use them on welcome cards to leave in rooms, or use them in advance mailings. What is done is to print an appropriate cartoon, punch a hole, and insert the cigarette in the hole. For instance, use a drawing of a pistol and insert the cigarette in the barrel of the pistol, or have an illustration of a man smoking a cigarette, or make an Indian smoke signal, etc. Source: Display Features, 1415 Thornberry Road, Wyncote, Pa. Approximately $10 per thousand.

3. ASSISTANCE FROM CONVENTION BUREAUS, HOTELS, AND CHAMBERS OF COMMERCE

(a) Convention and Visitors' Bureaus Assistance. Here is a list of items furnished by one resort city convention bureau: Luggage stickers, lapel badges, literature on what to wear, temperatures, brochure of the area, map of golf courses, an illustrated folder with blanks for a printed program or mailed message, palm tree seeds, ribbons for the host, chairman, speaker, exhibitor, guests, etc., details on a shopping "Treasure Hunt" for the ladies, and the providing of registration cards and registration personnel. Write the convention and visitors' bureau at your meeting location and ask what assistance is offered.

(b) Chambers of Commerce. Holding your convention in an area away from the home office? If so, contact that chamber of commerce for items you can use in mailings. For instance, the Phoenix Chamber of Commerce has a "Sunshine Credit Card." The St. Petersburg, Florida, Chamber of Commerce offers a complete "Convention Planning Kit." Others have brochures containing information on the community's recreation, dining, and sightseeing attractions.

(c) Hotel Literature. Don't overlook the hotel for literature which you can mail. Most hotels have postcards and brochures of their establishment and of the surrounding area. Some hotels have a set of teaser mailings and novelties which you can utilize.

(d) Letter from the Golf Pro. If golf is an event at your meeting, consider sending a letter over the signature of the golf pro at your convention site.

Creative Techniques to Promote the Conference

4. LOCAL FLAVOR MAILING IDEAS.

(a) Postcard from the Mayor. Contact the public relations department of the city of your meeting location. Send suggested copy which would appear on a local postcard over the mayor's signature. Your organization, of course, offers to obtain, pay for, print the message, and mail the cards.

(b) Restaurant Menus. If the city is famous for its food, consider reproducing samples of restaurant menus.

(c) Miniature Bottle of Native Liquors and Wines. Depending on regulations in your state, the receipt of a sample miniature bottle makes an unusually good impression and the accompanying message is not easily forgotten.

(d) Publish a Miniature Newspaper. The front page has headlines and sub-headlines on the meeting content and objectives. Include the theme. List the program, the new products, notes on the speakers, entertainers, the panelists, and descriptions of each session.

(e) Custom City Map. Your members will never feel lost again. This meeting aid features a map of any city in the U.S. on your own custom map, plus custom panels. Stock art is available for the panels, such as "People to Contact," "Expense Record," "Booths to Visit," or you can supply a listing of better restaurants, hotels, and points of interest. A custom cover will also be provided. Price is 35¢ each for 500; 25¢, 1000; 19¢, 2,500. From Crestline Co., Inc., 18 W. 18th St., New York, N.Y. 10011.

(f) Local Flavor Ideas. Send something with the mailing piece which imparts the flavor of the area. This could be samples of salt water taffy, semiprecious mineral samples, a can of pine-scented air freshener, or a box of dates ("It's a date"). Enclose free or discount tickets for events or for special discount purchases. Mailing tubes can carry the sample and your letter, or use mailing bags.

If the meeting is held at a European location, or a trip follows the meeting, the mailings can be a pair of wooden shoes, travel brochures, stamps from the countries to be visited, flags, postcards, luggage tags, or even a foreign newspaper.

(g) Send Pine Tree Seedlings to promote a meeting held in a mountain or forest area. These husky young seedling trees are packaged in attractive poly bags or display boxes and can be shipped individually by the suppliers. Spruce, pine, and many other varieties are available. Guaranteed to grow. Van's Pines, Inc., P.O. Box 737, West Olive, Mich. 49460.

(h) **Orange Trees.** Holding your conference in Florida, California, Texas, or Arizona? If so, send a genuine miniature live orange tree to announce the convention location. Obtainable at $1.25 each; mailed from Norman Cox & Co., 2524 First St., Ft. Myers, Fla. 33901. They also have miniature coffee trees, ming trees, palm trees, lime trees, holly trees, and hibicus, rose, and gardenia plants.

(i) **Personal Messages.** An executive obtained brochures from his convention hotel in Mexico. He wrote a personal message on them, then had them mailed from the hotel. The same can be done with postcards.

(j) **State Tourist Magazines.** A company which held a sales conference in Arizona contacted "Arizona Highways" magazine in Phoenix and arranged to have the magazine distributed gratis at the convention resort. Such state magazines could also be mailed in advance to promote attendance.

(k) **Invitation Ideas.** Dab a spot of glue on your invitation and sprinkle sand on it if the convention is to be held in a desert location, or state that it is a sample of sand from the sand trap, or from the beach. Glue on pine needles, or sample of moss from trees in the deep South, etc. Spray pine scent on the mailing if the meeting is to be held in the mountains.

5. PROMOTION OF FOREIGN LOCATIONS.

(a) **Travel Stickers** can be obtained from travel agencies. Also try American Express. These stickers make colorful additions on invitational envelopes or on bulletins.

(b) **Dummy Tickets.** See travel agencies here, too, for making simulated copies of tickets (air, ship or train) for your mailings.

(c) **Travel Posters** can be mailed to your sales offices. Contact airlines, steamship companies, and travel agencies for assistance. Posters may be purchased from Paradise Products, Inc., P.O. Box 568, El Cerrito, Calif. 94530, and from Stancraft Products, 1621 E. Hennepin, Minneapolis, Minn. 55416.

(d) **Vacation.** Think about tying in your conference with a vacation for the family. The Bahamas, Bermuda, Mexico, Canada, Puerto Rico, and Hawaii convention sites offer this possibility as well as resort areas in the 48 contiguous states. Most hotels and airlines have money-saving plans for the family.

(e) **Sell-Your-Way-to-the-Conference.** Hold a conference at a luxurious

Creative Techniques to Promote the Conference   95

place and restrict attendance only to those who win a "Sell-Your-Way-to-the-Conference" contest.

(f) An Incentive Travel Work Kit is offered by Pan American. This airline also provides one and two-color artwork for your use. Write to Pan American World Airways, Inc., P.O. Box 2212, Boston, Mass. 02107.

(g) Films for Group Showings. 16 mm. films on such countries as England, Scotland, Egypt, France, Germany, Greece, India, Israel, Italy, Hong Kong, Thailand, and the U.S.A. may be borrowed from many of the airlines at no charge. Contact your local airline office.

(h) Foreign Mailings. If your meeting is outside of the country, arrange with the hotel to send some of your mailings from that country. Request that a number of colorful stamps be used. Include a picture postcard in your mailing. Another idea is to include a packet of scenic stamps of that country. Any stamp shop can assist on this.

(i) Overseas Mailings. This company will make mailings for you from various foreign countries. They will mail letters or colorful postcards. They will even make mailings on the stationery of famed continental hotels. Contact: National Events & Holidays, Division of Sales Ammunition, Inc., 600 Madison Ave., New York, N.Y. 10022.

(j) Foreign Banknotes for Promotional Mailings. Whether to promote a meeting at a foreign location or for a meeting with a "money" theme, you will find this company a source of inexpensive foreign banknotes. There are Yugoslavian dinars, Brazilian cruzieros, banknotes from Hong Kong, etc. The company also furnishes foreign coins. Mailers for coins and see-through envelopes for banknotes also may be purchased. Write to Deak & Co., 20 Broadway, New York, N.Y. 10006.

6. PRODUCTION AIDS AND IDEAS.

(a) Create a Convention Character symbolizing the meeting. Place the symbol on all of your prepromotion mailings and perhaps even have a live counterpart at the conference. The character can represent the product being introduced, the meeting theme, or symbolize the area in which the convention is being held.

(b) Flash Bulletins and Flashcards consisting of colorful letter-size bulletins and 5" × 8" postcards in a large number of themes are sold by Carr Speirs, 24 Rope Ferry Road, Waterford, Conn. 06385. The price is inexpensive: $7 per

100 in 200 lots; $34.50 in 1,000 lots. Small quantities are seven cents each. Write for catalog.

Excellent modern art letterheads, jumbo cards, regular-size postcards, and envelopes are available from Idea Art, 740 Broadway, New York, N.Y. 10003. Various letterheads are available from Hewig & Marvic, 861 Manhattan Ave., Brooklyn, N.Y. 11222, and from National Creative Sales, Inc., 436 North Ave., New York, N.Y. 10802. Write for catalogs from all and assemble a set to tie in with your conference theme.

(c) **Personalized Jumbo Telegrams.** Dramatic 17″ × 16″ telegrams guarantee readership of your promotional message. Price includes printing of message, individual's address on the telegram, folding, enclosing and mailing. 300 minimum, 40¢ each; 500, 30¢ each; 1,000, 20¢ each; 5,000, 17 1/2¢ each. From Commercial Letter, Inc., 1335 Delmar Blvd., St. Louis, Mo. 63103.

(d) **Colorful Bulletin Postcards.** These are something new. They are low-cost illustrated postcards for short messages. A number of these titles can be used for invitational follow-up mailings. There are titles such as, "Here Ye, Year Ye," "Reminder," "Here's News," "You Are Invited," "Time Is Running Out," "Make a Note," "Keep This Date Open." 250 for $10; 500, $16.50; 1,000, $22.50; etc. From Idea Art, 740 Broadway, New York, N.Y. 10003.

(e) **Mailing Bags of All Types** may be ordered from Milheiser Bag Co., P.O. Box 117, Richmond, Virginia 23208. Also try stationery stores.

(f) **Full-Color Artwork Free.** If your meeting is a large one, try contacting the hotel or convention bureau for full-color artwork for brochures and for your association magazine covers.

(g) **Stock Photographs** are an advantage in that the user sees exactly what he is going to use before the project goes to art, and the photo reflects professional quality. Use for slides, announcements, and brochures. An excellent source is H. Armstrong Roberts, 4203 Locust St., Philadelphia, Pa. 19104. Thousands of photos are in stock—in black and white, and color transparencies. Price depends upon whether it is for local or national advertising, for editorial media size, and frequency of reuse. A catalog of typical photographs is available.

(h) **Horror, Mystery and Science Fiction Movie Stills**—plus stills from hundreds of modern, old time, and classic movies are easily obtainable. Pin-up photos of popular actresses and cowboys also are available. This company is a gold mine of all types of photos. Specify the type of photo you wish and they will probably have it. To obtain a catalog write: Movie Star News, 212 East 14th St., New York, N.Y. 10003.

(i) **Promotional Production Tips.** If the budget does not permit the use of a second color in printing, use colored paper or use a colored ink. Use different colors for each mailing piece. Personalize some of the mailers by handwriting the attendee's name on the heading: "Dear Bill, etc."

7. ATTENTION-GETTING MAILING IDEAS.

(a) **Firecracker Mailings.** Consists of a red cardboard firecracker tube and fuse cap containing a preprinted firecracker bulletin heading. Choice of three letterhead designs, "Here's an Explosive Offer," "It's Hot!," "Hot Savings for You." These are self mailers. From 30¢ to 50¢ per set, Hewig & Marvic, 861 Manhattan Ave., Brooklyn, N.Y. 11222.

(b) **Burning Impressions.** This is an old-favorite item where a cigarette is touched to a designated area on your custom-printed sheet and your meeting message burns into view like a dynamite fuse. Price is $150 for 1,000 custom-made (one color), plus $64 set-up charge on your first order. "Burning Games" (Horseraces, Baseball, Bowling, Golf; and Brand Name where No. 1 always wins) are also offered. Price is .047 each for 500; .039 for $1,000; .029 for 5,000. Price includes your imprint on the cover. Write for descriptions: Hewig & Marvic, 861 Manhattan Ave., Brooklyn, N.Y. 11222.

(c) **A Summons** makes an attention-getting conference invitation. The subpoena notifies attendees to appear at a "Court of New Ideas." The document requests that they appear and show cause why they believe the sales of certain items could not be improved. Use legal language paragraph headings such as "A Summons . . . To Appear . . . Because . . . You Are Notified . . . Be It Known . . . It is Truly Stated, etc." Contact a lawyer, lawbook, or stationery store for legal forms for additional legal language. The conference can carry out the theme with persons put on the stand and examined for new ideas, etc.

(d) **Historical Documents.** Authentic looking antiqued replicas of world-famous documents make mailings intriguing. Over 300 different reproductions are available on parchment paper. Typical are the Mayflower Compact, First Patent, Deed to Manhattan, treasure maps, Declaration of Independence, Jesse James reward poster, Sam and Bell Star Reward Poster, Purchase of Alaska, Civil War Posters, Bill of Rights, General Washington's Call to Arms, Rules of the Tavern, etc. Tie these in with a conference theme. Write for catalog to: Historical Departments Company, 8 N. Preston, Philadelphia, Pa. 19104.

(e) Tiny Pencils enclosed in your invitation mailing make a novel tie-in. Tell the recipient to use it to write the conference date on his calendar. Write W. W. Faber-Castell Pencil Co., Inc., 41-47 Dickerson St., Newark, N.J. 07103.

(f) Foreign Coins. A series of conference mailings can be made on the theme of "Making More Money." Each mailing can contain one or more foreign coins rubber cemented to the letter (or contained in a transparent paper bag which is stapled to the letter). See your local coin dealer for inexpensive coins from many lands. Or contact Hobby Sales, Inc., P.O. Box 4054, Highland Station, St. Paul, Minn. 55116. Or Deak & Co., 29 Broadway, N.Y., N.Y. 10006.

(g) Small Mailing Bag with "It's in the Bag" Imprint can be obtained from Hewig & Marvic Corp., 861 Manhattan Ave., Brooklyn, N.Y. 11222.

(h) Puzzle: "For the Solution to Your Problems" is the name of the heading of a string-and-shipping-tag type of puzzle that makes a remembered meeting notification mailing. Only 17¢ each imprinted for 500; 13¢ for 1,000. From Hewig & Marvic.

(i) Money Envelopes. You'll remember these envelopes with a die-cut hole to show the picture on the currency. They offer great teaser ideas. Samples may be obtained from Bankers Engraving Company, 50 West 17th St., New York, N.Y. 10011.

(j) Pony Express Messenger. Obtain a picture of a pony express messenger for your mailing. Die cut a slit and insert a message in the pouch in the picture.

(k) Puzzle Mailing. Send your invitation in the form of a puzzle. A source of supply is American Publishing Corp., 125 Walnut St., Watertown, Mass. 02172. This is economical only in large quantities. The company will, however, mount and die cut puzzles from sheets supplied by the purchaser. Also Mitche Inc., 17981 Sky Park Circle, Suite N., Irvine, Calif. 92707; Prager Industries, Inc., 100 Jackson Ave., Edison, N.J. 08817; and Du Bois Importing Co., 1914 Portage Ave., South Bend, Ind. 46616.

(l) Antiqued Banknotes. Send banknote replicas in a series of mailings to promote the conferences. Use messages such as "Colonial money may not have been worth a Continental," "You're probably throwing away this $1,000 every year," "There's more of the real thing where this came from," or "Ideas worth thousands of dollars." Over 40 different notes that actually look and feel genuinely old are available—Confederate bills, Colonial currency, New York money, and $10 and $1,000 Bank of the United States banknotes. Only $24 in lots of 1,000. Some can be imprinted. Imprinting costs is $5.25 per thousand. Imprinted window envelopes also available. Write to: Historical Documents Co., 8 N. Preston St., Philadelphia, Pa. 19104.

(m) **Invitation in a Tin Can** makes a different type of mailing. Place in the mail as is. Place a message on the label such as "Open Today" or "Perishable." Look in your classified telephone directory for concerns that sell home canning equipment. American Publishing Co., 125 Walnut St., Watertown, Mass. 02172 will place your mailing in a can, provide labels, and mail for you.

(n) **Secret Message Bullet** promotional mailing consists of your twenty-word message ($1/2'' \times 4''$) inserted into a silver bullet which is sure to get attention. From Hewig & Marvic at 34 cents each for 100; 500 at 29 cents each.

(o) **Pill Promotion.** This can tie in with a theme of "Prescriptions for Sales Success" or "RX for Your Sales Problems." Obtain capsules from your druggist. These capsules are manufactured in various colors. Use pink for "Tickled Pink" messages, green for "Green with Envy," and blue for "Those Monday Morning Blues."

(p) **Jumping Disc Mailing.** These are the paper-thin bi-metal jumping discs which jump up to five feet. They work on the principle of thermodynamics. With your message on it they cost as little as 5¢ each. Use both in an invitation mailing and as a giveaway. From Edmund Scientific Co., 300 Edscorp Bldg., Barrington, N.J. 08007.

(q) **Pencil Caddies** make a good reminder for your convention. This pyramid-shaped box for holding pencils folds flat for mailing. Furnished imprinted for approximately $100 for 500 one color; $125 for two-color. Write for samples from K & D Specialists, 1217 Durham Rd., Riegelsville, Pa. 18077. Also Berkshire Sales Corp., 219 Ninth St., San Francisco, Calif. 94103.

(r) **How About a Plastic Bookmark** for the low imprinted price of only 9¢ each for 1,000. From Hewig & Marvic, 861 Manhattan Ave., Brooklyn, N.Y. 11222.

(s) **If You Are Looking for Letter Enclosures** for promotion of meetings and for travel mailings this company has hundreds of clever novelties from 75 countries and major U.S. cities. Paradise Products, Inc., P.O. Box 568, El Cerrito, Calif. 94530.

8. SOURCES FOR STICK-ONS, POP-UPS, 3-D, FRAGRANCES, INVISIBLE INK, AND THEME MAILING PIECES.

(a) Pop-Up Mailers. Exceedingly colorful pop-up mailers in a variety of designs are offered by two manufacturers. They have stock pop-ups or will make custom pop-ups. There are boats, men, animals, trucks, buildings, boxes, diamond shapes, hexagons, etc. They operate like greeting cards; when opened, a figure which is on a bulletin head pops up. From Scott Crowell Corp., 11 South St., Garden City, N.Y. 11530 and Jannes Associates, 222 W. Huron St., Chicago, Ill. 60610.

(b) Full-Color Postcards, Catalog Sheets, and Brochures. This company specializes in large-volume gang runs in four color. From 6,500 to 12,500 is the minimum. Prices are low: 8½ × 11 catalog sheets cost $90 per thousand for 12,500; $50 per thousand for 25,000. Postcards cost $28 per thousand for 6,500; $17 per thousand for 25,000. Use for your convention (imprint special message locally) and the remainder for promotional use. Write for price list and samples to Colourpicture Publishers, Inc., 76 Atherton St., Boston, Mass. 02130.

(c) Letter Stick-On's. Hundreds of tiny plastic gadgets are available for affixing to your convention promotion letters. Examples are winking eyes, handshakes, hammers, wishbones, shamrocks, gavels, canes, wrenches, golf clubs, jet planes, picture frames, axes, flowers, 8-balls, padlocks, etc. Also in three dimensions are items such as hats, gloves, shoes, bags, telephones, umbrellas, etc. Prices are around 3¢ to 5¢ each in lots of 100; 2¢ to 4¢ in lots of 250. Obtainable from Hewig & Marvic, 861 Manhattan Ave., New York, N.Y. 11222.

(d) Clever "Animated" 3-D Calling Cards, Rulers, Badges, Coasters and Stick-On's may be obtained from Vari-Vue International. These are useful for promotional mailings and giveaways. They have calling-card-size clever animated turning gears in color, winking eyes, shaking hands, rainbows, and stripes. In stock are area codes, calories chart, calendar card, approved state abbreviations, etc. Also available are 3-D rulers with charts converting just about anything—kilos to pounds, temperature, weight, metric, cubic feet, etc. Imprinted badges and coasters can also be purchased. 650 S. Columbus Ave., Mt. Vernon, N.Y. 10551.

(e) Fragrances on Mailings. Useful for a theme such as "The Sweet Smell of Success," or an incentive travel program, or if your resort is in an exotic place. This company can imprint your mailing pieces with specific fragrances: Orlandi Frank, Inc., 31-02 Northern Blvd., Long Island City, N.Y. 11101.

Creative Techniques to Promote the Conference 101

The following firm provides labels which you can place on your mailing piece. The scent is contained in thousands of tiny bubbles which open to release the fragrance when the label is scratched. Hundreds of stock scents may be obtained—the smell of grass, pines, strawberries, dill pickles, mint, new cars, blue cheese, cold lamb, etc. They are relatively inexpensive—around $38 for 1,000. This includes silk screening. From Smell It Like It Is, Inc., 1501 N. W. 14th St., Miami, Fla. 33125, and "Scratch-'N Sniff" labels from 3M Company, Box 33686, 3M Center, St. Paul, Minn. 55101.

(f) **Complete Promotional Mailings.** If the messages fit in with your theme there are a number of complete illustrating mailing pieces ready for your use. For instance: There is a bulletin heading with the message "This Is Your Golden Opportunity," plus gold nuggets packed in a miniature prospector's pan. Price is 75¢ each for 50; 65¢ for 100; 55¢ for 500. There is a Loaded Dice mailer, a Four-Leaf Clover mailer, mailers with a gavel ("For a Man of Decision"), 3-Card Winner mailer, and a Fortune Cookie mailer. From Hewig & Marvic Corp., 861 Manhattan Ave., Brooklyn, N.Y. 11222.

(g) **Invisible Ink Postcard.** These postcards, manufactured in several designs, make an unusual type of promotion mailing. Your message appears when the card is dipped in water. The process can be repeated when the card dries. From Impact Specialties Company, 395 Munroe Circle South, Des Plaines, Ill. 60016.

(h) **How About a "Ghost Writer" Invitation Mailing?** What you send is a teaser letter stating that an important secret message for the recipient's eyes only is enclosed. It's written in secret ink. A developer is included in the mailing. Around 30¢ per kit. You write the message yourself. From Tolch Products, 114 Glenwood Ave., Minneapolis, Minn. 55403.

(i) **Disappearing Message.** Here's a switch. For your ultra-secret communication print the message on a paper which disappears entirely when placed in water. From Gilbreth Company, 212 E. Courtland St., Philadelphia, Pa. 19120.

9. TRANSPORTATION GIVEAWAYS FOR THE MAILING.

(a) **Magic Window Luggage Tags.** These heavy-duty plastic tags are available with your corporate logo or message on one side and write-in personalization feature on the other. The recipient writes in his name in pen or pencil and presses the clear plastic-pressure-sensitive window over the writing surface for permanent identification. 100 for 39¢ each; 250 for 27¢ each; 500 for 24¢ each. From Namemaker Corp., 52 Broadway, Greenlawn, N.Y. 11740.

(b) Airline Souvenir Tie-In's. Airline Merchandising Corp., 52 Broadway, Greenlawn, N.Y. 11740, has items to promote airline travel to the meeting. They offer "Magic Window" luggage tags, airplane desk models, junior flight captain and stewardess hats, T-shirt, flight valets, flight valet bags, embroidered emblems, ballpoint pens, etc. The company supplies items to airport concessionaires.

(c) "Slipper Socks" for Travelers. These washable, long-lasting cotton stretch knit travel socks fit any man's or woman's foot. Your company name, slogan, or trademark is knitted right into the slippers. 100 pairs, $1.50 per pair; 250 paris, 70¢ per pair. From Hewig & Marvic Corp., 861 Manhattan Ave., Brooklyn, N.Y. 11222.

(d) Identification Handkerchief. Have a local clothing manufacturer or seamstress make the top part of a handkerchief for placing in the suit coat pocket. This top half of a handkerchief is slipped between a folded card which can read something like this: "Tuck this card in your suit coat pocket. It will identify you as a _____ Company traveler headed for _____."

Such a card was produced for Eastern Airlines. The simulated handkerchief consisted of tucks of red, white, and red. It was manufactured by Fordham Weaving Company, 203 E. Fordham Rd., Bronx, New York.

(e) Flight Garment Bags can be sent to the attendees. Sterling Products Co., Inc., 1689 Oakdale Ave., St. Paul, Minn. 55118, has clear bags (which also can be used for storage). Price is in the $1.50 range. A variety of other models are offered in price ranges to about $8. Perhaps you will want to award flight bags as prizes for certain accomplishments.

Top Brands, Inc., 520 West 15th St., Oshkosh, Wis. 54901, offers inexpensive imprinted garment bags in a selection of colors at $105 per 100 for men's 40" and $132 per 100 for ladies' 52". Add $12 for artwork and screen cost. Smaller quantities without imprint are in the $1.75 to $2.25 range.

Other sources of garment bags of various grades are: The Biltmore Luggage Co., 304 N. Smallwood St., Baltimore, Md. 21223. Jiffy Garment Bags & Travel Covers, Corydon, Iowa 50060. Neely Mfg. Co., Inc., Corydon, Iowa 50060. And Kordite Corp., Macedon, N.Y. 14502.

10. PROMOTIONAL AND TRAVEL ASSISTANCE FROM AIRLINES.

Take advantage of the services offered by the various airlines; they can make your job easier. Typical promotional assistances that can be provided are:

Destination posters
Telephone or direct mail reminders to prospective
    attendees to arrange for transportation

Creative Techniques to Promote the Conference

Direct mail pieces
Mailing assistance
Imprinted ticket envelopes
Guide books for the convention location offering
    discount coupons
Currency conversion charts
Identification handkerchiefs
Press releases
City maps and brochures
For purchase at cost: Flight bags, overnight kits,
    pocket secretaries, golf bag covers
Restaurant, entertainment, and sightseeing guides
"Suggestions for the traveler" booklet
Pre- and post-conference tour offerings and
    travel planning kits
Movies to arouse interest and promote the trip

Assistance in the planning area is offered by a number of airlines as follows:

Assistance in site selection and facility information
Convention planning checklists
Transportation cost analysis of moving attendees
    from their various points of origin to the
    meeting site
Comparative costs for traveling to various
    convention sites
Budget breakdowns
Centralized invoicing
On-line ticketing (transfers between same airline),
    and off-line ticketing (between two different
    airlines)
Assistance with ground transportation arrangements
Special checking facilities and baggage identification
Assistance with paperwork for flights to other
    countries when necessary
Provide a local destination contact
Arrange for group ground transfers
Special airport personnel assigned to deal with
    baggage handling, routing, and ground transfers
Post-conference travel accommodations, hotel bookings
Assistance in transporting meeting materials
Updates on anticipated arrival times of attendees
Arrange for most convenient departure times and
    connections

104   Creative Techniques to Promote the Conference

    Ticket and reservation confirmation booth at the
        convention site

(a) Airline Promotional Assistance. Note: Check to determine if any of these particular services are still offered as of your convention date and if additional assistance is available. Keep in mind that the airlines often weigh the company meetings as to the potential for the airline—their participation is based on this analysis. However, many of the following items are available regardless of the size of the meeting.

Free Meeting Pro-File Kit comparing costs for different destinations Mailers, stationery Certain destination maps City and area sketches Posters for some cities Publicity releases Group baggage tags Women's program "Travel Tips," recipe booklets Film/Slide presentations	Manager—Convention Sales DELTA AIR LINES Continental Colony Parkway Atlanta, Ga. 30331
Direct Mail Imprintable Brochures Post Tour Imprintable Folders List of Speakers on Variety of Topics "Tips to Air Travelers" Folder Destination Postcards	UNITED AIR LINES Call local offices
Personalized direct mail "Welcome" Folder	Mgr., Convention & Group Sales NATIONAL CAR RENTAL 5501 Green Valley Dr. Minneapolis, Minn. 55437
Air Line Convention Kit Japanese/English Business Cards Group Transportation Bulletins	Convention Manager JAPAN AIRLINES 655 Fifth Ave. New York, N.Y. 10022
"Package Deals" Information	Vice President Marketing CAPITOL INTERNATIONAL AIRWAYS Metropolitan Airport Nashville, Tenn. 37217

Creative Techniques to Promote the Conference

Incentive Travel Check List Simultaneous Translations World-Wide Communications System	Convention Manager SWISSAIR 608 Fifth Ave. New York, N.Y. 10020
Convention Travel Arrangements Handbook for the Lady Traveler Has a "Learning Center" Location "Where to Buy Company Meeting Facilities" Imprintable Tour Folders Convention/Info System at Large Convention Sites Travel Cost Analysis Direct Marketing Campaign Audio-Visual Checklist Chart Personalized Baggage Tags Imprinted Ticket Envelopes Identification Handkerchiefs	Manager, Convention & Corporate Meeting Sales AMERICAN AIRLINES 633 Third Ave New York, 10017
Meeting Planners Booklet	AMERICAN EXPRESS MEETING PLANNERS 770 Broadway New York, N.Y. 10013
Discount Dollars for sightseeing, sporting events, restaurants, car rentals, etc. Booklets "How to Get More for Your Florida and Hawaii Dollar" Baggage tags Arrange for car rentals Free expense record and guide	NORTHWEST ORIENT Contact local travel agent or call 800-328-7747
Shell folder for mailing Post convention tour information Film presentations Promotional letterheads	WESTERN AIRLINES Manager Meeting & Convention Marketing 6060 Avion Dr. Los Angeles, Calif. 90009
Data on Hotel Facilities What's available of interest to the ladies "Flying Golfers Club" Assistance with golf oriented convention including trophies Transportation Planning cost analysis	EASTERN AIRLINES 10 Rockefeller Plaza New York, N.Y. 10020

Meeting Planners Service for qualified groups free of charge Attendance-building programs Special-Handling baggage tags	CONTINENTAL AIRLINES 7300 World Way West Los Angeles, Calif. 90009
Welcome folders giving name, dates, site, and travel information Bulletins to stimulate meeting interest Travel Reminders mailed Planning Checklist Site Selection Assistance Post Conference Trips	AIR CANADA Place, Ville Marie Montreal 113 Quebec, Canada
Conference Planner's Directory to Speakers, Consultants & Suppliers Conference Planner's Handbook	Manager-Commercial Marketing TRANS WORLD AIRLINES, INC. 605 Third Ave. New York, N.Y. 10016

(b) Promotional Assistance Enroute. Check with the airline to determine if the following could be provided:

    Special check-in desk
    VIP arrival service for top executives
    Special group luggage tags
    Group seating arrangements if not a full-plane group
    Individual baggage handling for groups apart from other passengers
    A red carpet rolled out
    A welcome from the flight crew
    Imprinted menus and cocktail lists
    Welcome banner at the destination
    Souvenir photo of the group for each passenger
    Flight souvenirs
    Giveaways for the kids
    Use of the plane's sound system
    Special flight certificates
    Imprinted headrest covers
    Special dress for the hostess
    Ground transportation coordination
    Flower leis

(c) Check the Availability of Group Plans. For instance, at the time of this writing Allegheny Airlines offered savings up to 33% when ten or more people make reservations at least 48 hours in advance. They take off together, but may return separately. Or 20% off for groups of four to nine, who fly together to and from selected cities.

Creative Techniques to Promote the Conference

(d) **Group Ticket Purchasing Tips.** You may not be aware of this. If tickets are purchased for a group leaving from one point, and the trip is arranged by a travel agent, an extra ticket may be obtained for every certain number of persons. And if your group is large enough in total or if you can make one or two stops to pick up other members of the group at other locations, it may be cheaper to charter a plane or split the plane with several other groups. Savings can be up to a third.

(e) **Triangle and Stopover Fares.** Check the airlines or travel agents for some surprising bargains. For only about $5 extra (at the time of this writing) you could fly from Los Angeles to New York by way of Miami, or stop at Las Vegas on the way from New York to Los Angeles. Here are some other fantastic bargains: If flying from a Western city to Anchorage you could fly from there to Hawaii free. If flying from the East Coast to California on Western Airlines, you could throw in Mexico City or Acapulco free! And for modest fees from $1 to $5 to $25 there are other triangle and stopover flights available. Check with your travel agent for suggestions.

(f) **Types of Air Fares.** As you know, air fares seem to be in a constant state of flux. Here is a sampling of the various types of fares for flights within the U.S. available as of this date.

Class	Conditions
First Class	None
Coach	None
Night Coach	Night flights only.
Advance Purchase	60 days before departure reservations and a deposit required. Pay in full 30 days before flight.
Excursion	Ticket paid 7 days before flight. Limited, 7- to 30-day round trips.
Individual Inclusive Tour	Fly Monday through Thursday. You must spend minimum of $65 hotels, sightseeing, and other ground services. Maximum stay 30 days. Minimum is set by each airline.
One-Stop Inclusive Tour Charter	You must make reservations 7 days in advance with a tour operator or travel agent. Minimum stay is usually 4 days. Ground transportation, hotels, and other services must be included in the charges.

Class	Conditions
Children	Limited to children under 12 years.

11. HOW TO PUBLICIZE THE MEETING.

(a) Contact the Local News Media—newspapers, radio, TV. Keep in mind that the information must be of general interest to the public. Slant your news to bring out information that everyone will want to read—such as an industry sales forecast, company growth, success stories, increase in sales, an important new model, or information by an overseas speaker. Familiarize the media with the program, the speakers, and visiting dignitaries.

(b) Advance Copies of Speeches should be delivered to the papers in time to meet their deadlines.

(c) Arrange Speaker Interviews at the TV or radio station. Have on hand photographs and background material, or arrange for the interview to take place as the speaker steps from the plane.

(d) Local Personalities. The local newspaper where the meeting takes place is generally just as interested in their local people as they are in national celebrities. Tell about local people receiving awards, the local mayor making a speech at the meeting, local meeting sponsors, and local companies or clubs involved.

(e) If a Salesman Is Honored at the Meeting, send a news release on the event to his hometown paper.

(f) Timing of Releases. Send the first release about three weeks prior to the meeting. Announce the meeting, the time, the date, location, and number of people expected. About a week before the meeting send a second release. Name the principal speaker, the subject, and his background. Repeat the name of the convention, date, location.

The day before the meeting the media should have in its hands information on the arrival date, time, and location of the principal speaker and newsworthy quotes. Repeat the theme of the meeting and location and date. Place "For release on _____ (date)" on this news release.

If possible, it is best to bring your story personally to the city editor or his assistant. The best impression is made if your visit is brief. Do this two days before the release date.

(g) Extra Coverage. Stories can be written about an unusual entertainer, (get help from the entertainer's agent). Write a paragraph for the society

Creative Techniques to Promote the Conference   109

editor about an executive staying at a local prominent person's house or about a special party for him.

Set up a Press Room for the larger meetings. Include a typewriter, desk, telephone, writing supplies. Have on hand copies of press releases, biographical data, the program.

(h) **Hints on Preparing the Release.** Always double space. Always use 8½" × 11" paper and always print on only one side.

Start the body of the copy about one-third down from the top of the page. This leaves room for the editor to write his own headline and instructions. Margins on both sides should be fairly wide. If the release is more than one page write "more" at the bottom. The top of the succeeding pages should carry identification of the story in case the pages get separated. The end of the release should have "-30-" (a tradition) or "###" or "-end-".

Some editors prefer headlines; some don't. Be safe and put in a headline. Make it short. State clearly what the news release is all about. The lead sentence is the most important part of the release. This should contain the *news*—what is distinctive about the product being introduced at the meeting, the main point the speaker will make, the price cut, etc. If superlatives are used, back them up with the reasons why the product is the best, or the largest, or the cheapest.

Photographs. Provide captions for the photographs. Paste the captions on the back, or if it is a short caption, paste it on under the photo.

Publicity and Public Relations Checklist. See Chapter 22.

Chapter 10

Tested Ideas to Dramatize the Conference

Contents

1. Meeting Opening Ideas
2. Ideas for Starting and Stopping on Time
3. Meeting Accessories
4. Impressive Award Presentations
5. Meeting Room Decorations
6. Distinctive Dress for Speakers and Exhibit Attendants
7. A Test to Guarantee Attention by the Audience

1. MEETING OPENING IDEAS.

(a) Lively Recorded Music Before the Meeting Begins and During Intermission works great with large audiences. Forget about music for small audiences.

(b) "No Sales Meeting Today." Just as the meeting opens, this is what an assistant writes on a blackboard. The M.C. of the meeting then comes on stage and changes the word "No" to "Know!"

(c) Emphasizing Years of Experience. Where the program is composed of workshops or seeks ideas from the attendees, emphasize the weight of their combined ideas by offering a prize for the nearest guess of the total years of company experience in the room.

(d) Laugh-In Joke Wall for an Opener. Remember the Rowan and Martin show with its backdrop simulating a wall and containing cutouts? Have two men on the stage à la Rowan and Martin, and have others behind the wall to poke their heads out of the cutouts with pertinent one-liners.

(e) Start the Meeting with a Tap Drummer if it fits in with the theme. We're talking about the type who is good, loud, and performs all types of gyrations with his sticks. The sales speaker follows up with a statement such as that the purpose of the meeting is to "Drum Up More Business."

(f) Make New Salesmen Feel at Home as Members of the Group by appointing individuals to make sure they are introduced to the other persons. The newcomers should also be introduced at the first few small roundtable sessions.

Tested Ideas to Dramatize the Conference   113

(g) **Flags on Stage.** Instead of just the American Flag, include flags of the states which are represented. Include flags of appropriate nations also.

(h) **Instead of a Coffee Break** make coffee and cokes available throughout the session, if a roundtable set-up is used. Even put a bowl of fruit and nuts on the table.

(i) **If a Late Reception Is Held the Night Before,** plan on having the first session the next morning start at a later than usual time.

(j) **Indoor Poolside Meeting.** Arrange for the use of a hotel's indoor pool. Set up chairs around the edges of the pool. Obtain a large rubber raft which is to be used by the speaker. Keep the pool meeting a secret and initially announce that the meeting takes place in a regular meeting room of the hotel. After everyone is seated announce that the location has been changed and to follow a staff member. Play appropriate nautical music as the guests file in. There can be treasure chests containing product plans or contest prizes hidden in the water and brought up by divers, there can be mermaids, a take-off on "Jaws," etc.

2. IDEAS FOR STARTING AND STOPPING ON TIME.

(a) **Utilize the Hotel Telephone Operators** for "Good Morning" calls to announce the time of the first session and other events.

(b) **A Breakfast Session.** This is a device some conventions use to increase attendance at the first morning session. Call it the "Early Bird" session.

(c) **Appoint a Sergeant at Arms.** He collects 50 cents from each late person at each session. The group decides how to use the money.

(d) **Use Odd Starting Times on the Printed Program.** Such as 7:50 instead of 7:30. Try it. It's effective. It works.

(e) **When the Group Files in They See an Alarm Clock on the Speaker Lectern.** The clock goes off and the meeting begins. (Watch the clock closely; if it doesn't go off exactly as set, turn the alarm on manually.)

(f) **Hold a Drawing for Those Who Arrive Five or Ten Minutes Early.** (Give out numbered tickets to those prompt early birds as they come in the door.) Announce in the printed program that the prompt persons will be eligible for a drawing.

(g) **Make Use of a P.A. System in the Room** where breakfast is served. Make the announcements light and with a touch of humor.

(h) **Use Horse Races to Induce Starting on Time.** Horse races which are on film may be rented. Before each break, give out betting tickets. Explain that the individual must be present during the showing of the race to win. The film is shown at the beginning of various sessions. Films available from A Nite At the Races, 2320 Ave. U, Brooklyn, 11229 and Cinema Races, 271 Schilling Circle, Hunt Valley, Md. 21030.

(i) **The Simplest Idea of All** is to start each session exactly on time! Your meeting's reputation for promptness will gain notoriety as the convention progresses, and will become a tradition for future years.

(j) **Overtime Problems?** Solve the overtime problem by ringing a bell, blowing a whistle, or setting an alarm clock to ring when the speech runs overtime. Utilize a wristwatch alarm, or obtain a clock used in darkrooms which indicates the number of minutes left.

(k) **Devices for Controlling Speaker's Time.** Here is a controller unit which indicates visually to a speaker when his allotted time is starting, when it is nearly over, and when it is finished. The operation is simple and silent. A green light comes on saying "Talk." There is a flashing yellow "Warning" light, and a "Stop" red light. The chairman has a unit which manually controls the speaker's unit. Price is $115. From C.A. Compton, Inc., P.O. Box 1775, Boulder, Colo. 80302. A "Mini-Timer" is available from Hewig & Marvic. It sets from one minute to 60 minutes. A buzzer sounds when time is up—about the size of a watch. Approximately $5.00.

(l) **To Move People Quickly Out of or to Another Room** hire a small band. Add flags and balloon carriers, or have several girls carrying large signs stating "Follow Me!"

(m) **Offer Key to a Treasure Chest.** Announce in the printed program that all who arrive at the opening session by a stated time or any other specified sessions will receive a key to a Treasure Chest. State that 25 of the keys will be lucky keys which open the chest, and that the chest will be opened and prizes given out at the banquet. Obtain the "Treasure Hunt" kit from Dismar Corp., N.W. Corner "A" & Clearfield Sts., Philadelphia, Pa. 19134. Price is $59.95. They are also available from Jet Advertising, 51 Stanton St., Newark, N.J. 07114. An electronic treasure chest can be purchased from Electronic

Treasure Chest Enterprises, Inc., P.O. Box G.C.7, Tijeros, N.M., or Rotadyne, Inc., 8705 Freeway Dr., Macedonia, Ohio 44056.

3. MEETING ACCESSORIES.

(a) Slip-On Plastic Sleeve-Type Chair-Back Covers are an ideal way to call attention to the meeting theme or to a personalized message. For a quote, send quantity, size, and printing copy to Elias Richter Co., 1901 J. F. Kennedy Blvd., Philadelphia, Pa. 19103.

(b) Glass Ashtrays Imprinted with the Meeting Theme or company trademark make a nice added touch. If you are thinking of imprinted beer mugs or glasses, the following firms can supply these also: Sabine Industries, Inc., McKeesport, Pa. 15134, or Hewig & Marvic, 861 Manhattan Ave., Brooklyn, N.Y. 11222.

(c) Personalization. Keep in mind that items may be personalized by writing the name on a piece of gold foil. Obtainable from stationery stores or Hastings Co., Inc., 2314 Market St., Philadelphia, Pa.

(d) Sign Your Name with a Pen Which Writes in Gold. This is an electric pen which writes on wood, paper, plastic, and leather. Personalize binders, briefcases, invitations, and belongings. Use it for signatures, too. Around $9.25. Gold foil refill $2. American Science Center, 5700 Northwest Highway, Chicago, Ill. 60646.

(e) Easel Display Binders. Looking for such binders to furnish to your sales force? This one accommodates $8 1/2'' \times 11''$ pages. It is a regular binder, but when opened has a hinge on the 17″ dimension which makes it a desk easel display. These display binders, writing portfolios, regular binders, protective acetate sheets and dividers are available from Dilly Mfg. Co., 215 East 3rd St., Des Moines, Iowa 50309, and American Thermoplastic Co., 622 Second Ave., Pittsburgh, Pa., 15219.

4. IMPRESSIVE AWARD PRESENTATIONS.

(a) Unroll a Red Carpet for Award Winners. Do it right on stage with the sales manager, president, and other company officials doing the unrolling.

(b) Give Top Salesmen the VIP Treatment But Don't Tell Them Why. Register them in the best rooms or a suite. Provide special easy chairs at the meetings, free drinks, special service by a pretty waitress at coffee breaks, $1 cigars, breakfast in bed, a chauffeur, and top quality wines. Have them feted at dinner. Then tell them why at the conference end when the top men are announced.

(c) To Dramatize an Award, set up a stage about six inches high. The company official making the presentation stands to the right of this platform. The recipients enter from the left. A large rear-projection screen is placed at the back of the stage. As the recipient walks across the stage a slide of the award, and a caption of his accomplishment is flashed on the screen. He then continues across the stage and accepts his award. Another idea is to secure a photo of the winner in advance and include his picture on the screen.

(d) A Theatrical Effect for the Awards Presentation can be achieved by dimming the lights and picking out the winner with a spotlight as he walks to the stage. After each award is made the winner steps out of the spotlight and is seated on a platform on the stage. At the end of the individual award presentations the lights come on to reveal all the winners seated on the platform.

(e) "Reserved for the World's Greatest Salesman" Cushion. Also cushions with inscriptions, "World's Greatest Golfer," "Beer Drinker," "Poker Player," etc. And "RYCDBSOYF" (Remember You Can't Do Business Sitting On Your Fanny). Custom imprints available, too. Cushions are made of corduroy with polyfoam filler and are washable. You can purchase them from The Holmen Company, Inc., Box 205, Frisco, Texas 75034.

(f) Top Quality Exclusive Awards Recognition in the form of custom-made medallions may be obtained from The Medallic Art Co. Sculptors create the likeness of the person to be recognized in the form of a large-size medallion. This is mounted on a plaque. These are truly works of art. They also make custom plaques on which the name of the award winner is inscribed. Their address is 325 East 45th St., New York, New York 10017.

(g) Parchment or Sheepskin Diplomas are impressive awards. This company also will laminate your certificates and diplomas on "Cello-Glass" plaques. A typical price is $13 for an $8'' \times 10''$ certificate mounted on a $10^1/_2'' \times 12^1/_2''$ wooden plaque. The finished product is impervious to dirt and moisture. Contact the Long Island Engraving Co., 120-06 22nd Ave., College Point, N.Y. 11356. Individually lettered scrolls and certificates of appreciation are available from them.

(h) Individualize Awards with Prestype. Assuming that you have printed a certificate for presentation to various individuals, you can add the person's name in an Old English type face or any other type face by using "Prestype." You transfer a letter by just gently rubbing it with a ballpoint pen or pencil.

Prestype sheets containing letters of the alphabet in many different sizes and type faces are obtainable from art supply stores and many stationers. A company which designs award plaques and certificates and on which Prestype may be used is The Neff Athletic Lettering Co., Box 212, Greenville, Ohio 45331. Impressive blank certificates may be obtained from Goes Lithographing Co., 42 W. 61st St., Chicago, Ill. 60621.

(i) **Another Awards Idea.** Obtain head and shoulder photos of the winners. Trace the main features directly on the photos. Then make slides of these photos using high-contrast Kodalith film. The negative is used for the slide; it results in a black background with the drawing in white lines. Project this on the screen before making the award.

(j) **Cigar Store Indian, Totem Poles, and Eagles for Unusual Awards.** The Indian is full size. Made of durable lightweight, weather-resistant, rigid rubber composition which is as hard as wood. This supplier has a full line of additional simulated hand-carved items such as ship's figureheads, Indian heads, Uncle Sam busts, ship's sternboard eagles, gaslight era volunteer firemen, keystone cops, baseball players, 4-foot totem poles, carousel horses, Vikings, Jolly Rogers, Polynesians (etc.) figureheads. Indians cost from $132 to $160 and are available from Alfco-N.Y. Division, Artistic Latex Form Co., Inc., 1220 Brook Ave., Brooklyn 10456.

For additional awards ideas see the "Award Presentation Ideas" Section in Chapter 12. Also see "Gag Gifts and Awards" in Chapter 16.

5. MEETING ROOM DECORATIONS.

(a) **String of Flags.** A string of state flags can be stretched across the meeting room. For about $25 a one-hundred foot string of flags can be purchased from Pratt Poster Company, Inc., 3001 E. 30th St., Indianapolis, Ind. 46218.

(b) **Easy Way to Achieve Dramatic Banners, Posters.** Spell out your meeting slogan. Giant fluorescent paper letters (20″, 28″, 44″ high) are obtainable. Also cloth letter banners made to order. Source: Pratt Poster Company, Inc., 3001 East 30th St., Indianapolis, 46218.

(c) **Pennants and Posters.** You can use professional-looking posters to dress up your stage with a minimal investment. These are posters sold to retail stores for their use. There are all types of posters applicable to sales meetings. Here are a few titles: "Crash! Prices Down. Big Savings!," "Sale," "Clean Sweep Sales," "Fabulous Warehouse Sale," "Carnival of Values," "Spring Discount Festival," "Harvest of Fall Values." These are available in both poster and pennant shapes. Holders are available also. Send for a catalog to start those ideas going. Write to Dismar Corp., N.W. Corner "A" & Clearfield Sts., Philadelphia, Pa. 19134. Another supplier is Gordon-Douglas Co., 2318 Belmont Ave., Chicago, Ill. 60618.

(d) Theme on Banner. As a constant reminder, have a large banner made containing the meeting theme. Place this on the background of the stage for the entire meeting.

(e) Organizational Banners. Need a source for a big beautiful multicolor banner of your organization? Write to Crestline Co., Inc., 18 W. 18th St., New York, N.Y. 10011.

(f) Custom Designed Imprinted Drapes for exhibit displays, or for stage backdrops, are available from the Helli Company. Imprinted table cloths for displays are available, too. Your company logo, trademark, or company name is reproduced in an attractive repeat pattern. Drapes and side panels for a 10' booth are $200; for 20' they are $475. Table display cloths are $26.25 for a 45" × 68" size, and $27.50 for 45" × 72". The address for the Helli Company is 7000 N. Kilpatrick, Lincolnwood, Ill. 60646. Another supplier is Hollywood Banners, 539 Oak St., Copiague, N.Y. 11726. This concern also has a lightweight display booth utilizing the logo drapes.

(g) Satin Banners of top quality come from this company: Hollywood Banners, 539 Oak St., Copiague, N.Y. 11726.

6. DISTINCTIVE DRESS FOR SPEAKERS AND EXHIBIT ATTENDANTS.

(a) Distinctive Dress for Speakers. Equip your product speakers with colorful vests of red, gold, or stripes. These vests may be purchased imprinted or plain, or have all the key people wear imprinted four-in-hand neckties for identification. Kentucky Colonel string ties are also available as well as (skimmers) and imprinted old-fashioned arm bands. Order from Helli Co., 7000 N. Kilpatrick, Lincolnwood, Ill. 60646. Various types of hats are available from Jacobson Hat Co., Inc., Prescott Ave. & Ridge Row, Scranton, Pa. 18510.

(b) Blazers. Borrow this idea from exhibitors by using blazers for all of your speakers. They are available in a variety of colors, styles, fabrics, and weights. Sources of supply: Company Blazers Ltd., 149 Fifth Ave., New York, N.Y. 10010; King Louie International, Inc., 311 W. 72nd St., Kansas City, Mo. 64114. They cost approximately $35. Another supplier is Makley's, 441 S. Plymouth Ct., Chicago, Ill. 60605.

(c) Embroidered Company Emblem. Consider placing an embroidered emblem on the blazers, either over the pocket or as a shoulder patch. High

Tested Ideas to Dramatize the Conference

quality Swiss embroidered emblems are obtainable at approximately $1.50 each in 50-100 quantity from A. B. Emblem Corp., Weaverville, N.C. 28787, or Makley's, 441 S. Plymouth Ct., Chicago, Ill. 60605; Penn Emblem, 10909 Dutlon Rd., Philadelphia, Pa. 19154, and Inter-All Corp., 31 W. State St., Granbury, Mass. 01033.

(d) State Emblems. These are colorful woven emblems of all the states. Size $2'' \times 2^{3}/_{4}''$. Both sew-on and stick-on's available. From Lewtan Industries Corp., 30 High St., Hartford, Conn. 06101.

7. A TEST TO GUARANTEE ATTENTION BY THE AUDIENCE.

When these instructions are printed, fold them in half. Instruct the conference attendees not to open the test until the signal is given to commence.

Name_____

THREE MINUTE COMMUNICATIONS TEST

or

Do You Follow the Instructions?

1. Read everything before beginning.
2. Print your first and last name in the upper right hand corner of this page.
3. Draw a circle around the word "page" in sentence #2.
4. To the right of this line multiply 4×23.
5. Draw a small triangle in the upper left corner of this page.
6. Call out your first name loudly.
7. After the word "Instructions" in the title write "YES."
8. Write your last name here.
9. Draw a rectangle around the word "last" in sentence #8.
10. Add 32 and 153 to the right of this line.
11. Underline numbers 8, 9 and 10.
12. Call out your last name loudly.
13. Circle the triangle drawn in the upper left corner.
14. If you believe that you have followed instructions to this point say "YES, YES."
15. Draw a square around numbers 14 and 15 at the beginning of those sentences.
16. Count out loud from 5 to 1 backwards.
17. Circle entire sentence #16.
18. Say out loud "I FOLLOW INSTRUCTIONS!"
19. Now that you have followed instruction #1 which says "Read everything before beginning," do only sentence #2.

Chapter 11

75 Proven Showmanship Techniques for Presentations and Speeches

Contents

1. Peeks at New Products Under Wraps
2. Hot New Product
3. Magical White Puff of Smoke
4. Fireworks Effect for New Product Information
5. Play Bingo to Teach Product Information
6. Unveil with Balloons
7. Product Samples
8. If the Product Is Too Small to Be Seen When Demonstrated
9. Rooms or Tables for Special Information
10. Illustrate "The Proper Mental Attitude"
11. Another Dramatization of Mental Attitude
12. "Make the Law of Averages Work for You"
13. Dramatizing Enthusiasm
14. Drive Home a Point
15. To Emphasize "The Complete Package"
16. Illustrating the Difference
17. Overcoming Objections
18. Message for the Speaker
19. Use Foreign Language Captions
20. Acronyms
21. Traveling Mike
22. Devil's Advocate or Heckler
23. Write in the Main Points
24. Burn the Speech
25. On-the-Spot Drawings
26. Write-Behind Flats
27. Combination Chalkboard
28. Easel Signs Changed by Models
29. Use Balloons
30. Keep Audience Awake Through Participation
31. State That the Entire Sales Presentation Can be Made to a Prospect in Three Minutes
32. Name the Features
33. Throw Coins
34. Build a House
35. Pitchmaker
35A. Models
36. Keep Attention with Jackpot Prizes

121

37. Crashing Through Door
38. Seductive Voice
39. Mind Reading
40. Descending Sign
41. Pop-Up Signs
42. Money Tree or House
43. Dummies
44. Overcoming a Company Sales Problem
45. Distribute a Special Newspaper Edition
46. Theme Language
47. A Champagne Toast for the Entire Audience
48. Magnify the Demonstration on TV
49. Ideas to Regain Attention
50. Write on Screen Using an Overhead Projector
51. Silhouettes on Rear-Projector Screen
52. Animated Pie and Bar Charts
53. Visual Build-Up
54. Pull Out Letters from a Mailbox
55. Moving Graph Line
56. Old-Time Movie Films
57. Use Black Light
58. Place a Three-Dimensional Symbolic Gadget on the Introductory Page of Flip Chart
59. Bar Charts
60. Simulate an Eye-Testing Chart
61. "Herman Holds a Sales Meeting"
62. "Herman's Secret of Sales Success"
63. Dramatic Balloon Stunt
64. Use "Flash" Paper to Unveil a Vital Statistic
65. Sound Effects Records
66. Use Flannel Boards
67. To Avoid Upside Down or Backward Slides
68. Make Your Own Title Slides—No Developing Required
69. Color Slides for Sales Training Presentations
70. Movie Stills
71. Captioned Slides
72. Kodak Slide Projector
73. Visual Indicator for Changing Slides
74. A Projection Pointer
75. Portable Sound Rostrum

1. **PEEKS AT NEW PRODUCTS UNDER WRAPS.** Obtain suspense by placing tarps or wrapping paper around the new products and placing them on the stage. Periodically during the program have someone, such as a janitor, a model, or an executive, lift the wrapping, peek at the product, and make a suspenseful remark. A slide of the wrapped product can also be flashed on the screen when referred to in speeches. The suspense builds up until the final unveiling. Gain added suspense by placing a sign with a huge question mark next to the product.

2. **HOT NEW PRODUCT.** The speaker handles the "hot new product" with asbestos gloves or heat pads, or warms his hands over it. Another idea is to conceal a heat coil and light a piece of paper or firecracker from it.

3. **MAGICAL WHITE PUFF OF SMOKE.** Use this when presenting a new product. Obtain the equipment from a theatrical prop rental firm. It is called a "smoke pot." It consists of a hot plate in a metal box in which theatrical smoke powder has been placed. The puff of smoke may be ignited from a remote switchboard. A fog machine may also be rented if such a special effect is required.

4. **FIREWORKS EFFECT FOR NEW PRODUCT INFORMATION.** Alert one of your company amateur movie photographers well in advance to take movies of fireworks. Obtain tapes or a record of fireworks sound effects and synchronize these with the film. Flash this on the screen before a new product introduction, or before an award is presented. Also, try a film rental company for a fireworks film.

5. **PLAY BINGO TO TEACH PRODUCT INFORMATION.** This is a good way to induce everyone to read the new production literature, price lists, policies, etc. Short-form Bingo cards (5 squares across) and pencils are passed to the audience. Cards are made up containing product features

and a bingo number. These are drawn from a hat. The M.C. calls out the number and the product feature. The player checks his card and places an X in the proper space. The M.C. makes a few short points about each feature or policy point. To add interest, a slide of the product feature could be projected. (The slides are numbered beforehand for quick selection by the projectionist.) A prize is given for the first person getting five X's in any row, or arrange to have about four winners simultaneously.

6. **UNVEIL WITH BALLOONS.** Cover the new product with light cloth (silk, rayon, or tissue). Place a number of helium-filled balloons directly under the covering cloth. Keep the cloth from rising with one or two master threads. At the strategic moment cut the threads and the covering floats into the air. Practice this. Also note that helium in balloons loses its lifting power after about five hours, so fill the balloons a short time before the presentation.

7. **PRODUCT SAMPLES.** When a new product is introduced, if feasible, give one to each person to inspect, or distribute a sample for each row or small group. Request that questions be asked about the product.

8. **IF THE PRODUCT IS TOO SMALL TO BE SEEN WHEN DEMONSTRATED,** or if it is a large product, but details to be seen are small, rent a TV camera and place several receivers about the room.

9. **ROOMS OR TABLES FOR SPECIAL INFORMATION.** Devote a segment of the meeting for individual person-to-person discussions. Set up tables or assign rooms to various authorities, product experts, customer service, administration, etc. Send a questionnaire in advance, setting up appointments.

10. **ILLUSTRATE "THE PROPER MENTAL ATTITUDE"** by placing a small black dot on a large white poster. Ask the audience what they see. Most will respond that they see a black dot. The speaker tells them they should look for the good in everything. "All of you reported that you saw a small blemish, but none said they saw a fine big white poster. It can be used for a needed directional sign; it forms the base for an effective store poster, etc." The same message can be illustrated by filling a glass up to the halfway mark with water. "Half empty" says the pessimist. "Half full" says the optimist.

11. **ANOTHER DRAMATIZATION OF MENTAL ATTITUDE** is to have a long plank about two inches thick and four inches wide brought to the stage. Volunteers are asked to walk the plank. Then the speaker states

Techniques for Presentation and Speeches 125

that the plank will be placed on the roof connecting two buildings which are ten stories high. Ask for volunteers. There will be none. "Fear" is the downfall. When you are confident you may make the sale!

12. "MAKE THE LAW OF AVERAGES WORK FOR YOU." Illustrate the point "The law of averages states that making more calls will result in more sales" by dumping 500 or 1,000 pennies on a table and then have the table removed. At the end of the speech announce that the law of averages is infallible, and that they will see the proof. State that during the speech people have been backstage counting the pennies and they will give the result on the number of heads or tails. "The law of averages will work for you, too!"

13. DRAMATIZING ENTHUSIASM. To illustrate "Bubbling over with enthusiasm" drop a couple of Bromos in a glass of water.

14. DRIVE HOME A POINT. To make the point that all persons cannot work equally well with the same tools, invite several members of the audience to the stage, give them hammers, and ask them to drive large nails into a thick plank. There will be a difference in the finishing time.

15. TO EMPHASIZE "THE COMPLETE PACKAGE." Use a rope, chain, or ribbon on which signs naming each part of the package have been attached. Place this rope and its attached signs in a handsome giftwrapped package which the speaker unwraps and then draws out the signs one by one. The string of signs is hung across the stage.

16. ILLUSTRATING THE DIFFERENCE. Do this by holding up a cheap and then an expensive cigar. Ask which is the expensive one. This exercise illustrates that when products look alike you have to let the customer know what the differences are.

17. OVERCOMING OBJECTIONS. To emphasize that the customer should be allowed to get his objection or complaint off his mind without interruption, use a balloon stunt. Obtain a large balloon. If possible, paint the word "Objection" on the balloon. State that "Just as the balloon deflates, the customer empties himself of his objections through his flow of words. If the prospect is interrupted, however, the objection is inflated again (blow up the balloon)."

18. MESSAGE FOR THE SPEAKER. Use a faked telephone call by having a phone ring by means of a tape recorder. The speaker picks up the phone and the recorder delivers the caller's message through the auditorium sound system. It can be a request for a clarification of a sales

point, a request for a description of typical prospects, a request that the speaker demonstrate what he is talking about, etc.

19. **USE FOREIGN LANGUAGE CAPTIONS.** Begin each speech and each presentation with the theme or objective of the meeting translated into a different foreign language. This can be accomplished by speaking the words, or the words can be placed on slides.

20. **ACRONYMS.** Assign a single word as the theme of your meeting. Then have each speaker construct a sentence wherein the first letter of each word is taken from a letter in the theme. For instance, suppose your theme is "More." An acronym could be "*Make Orders Really Easy*," or "*Military Orders Require Effort*." Each speaker is instructed that the acronym is to tie in with the speech subject.

21. **TRAVELING MIKE.** A traveling mike carried to the audience can be used to ask for questions, opinions, ideas.

22. **DEVIL'S ADVOCATE OR HECKLER.** Plant a heckler in the audience to clarify or make points. Use sparingly.

23. **WRITE IN THE MAIN POINTS.** Flip charts are a good visual aid control device. They help keep the audience concentrated on the message or the concept being sold. For emphasis, leave blanks in the presentation and write in important numbers or words.

24. **BURN THE SPEECH.** Nothing discourages an audience more than to see a speaker pull out a large number of pages of speech notes. Burn the speech at the lecturn. Then speak from short notes or use a flip chart.

25. **ON-THE-SPOT DRAWINGS.** The speaker professionally draws simple sketches of comic expressions on flip charts and perhaps writes the one-word main caption. (The audience can't see that he is drawing over faint tracings.)

26. **WRITE-BEHIND FLATS.** Stretch a very large piece of white paper over a frame. Several pieces of paper can be glued together to achieve the desired size. Place this paper frame about waist high on a cut-out portion of a flat behind which a man is hidden. As the speaker talks, a shadow of a hand using a felt pen writes on back of the backlighted flat. (The writer is following faint tracings.)

Techniques for Presentation and Speeches   127

27. **COMBINATION CHALKBOARD.** You write on this silver-gray board with special bright colored felt-tip markers. The board cleans easily with a dry chalkboard eraser. Use it also as a projection screen, or as a magnetic display board. Write to Marsh Chalkboard Company, Dover, Ohio 44622.

28. **EASEL SIGNS CHANGED BY MODELS.** Place the easel sign announcing the subject on one side of the stage. A model places the new sign on the easel and walks off to the other side of the stage. There can be changes in costumes and, if affordable, changes in models. For a change of pace, a model can give a speaker a good luck kiss.

29. **USE BALLOONS.** Release a balloon filled with helium or natural gas each time a point is made, or paint a word on each balloon which has been filled with ordinary air. Rub the balloon on your wool suit and you can then (through static electricity) make the balloon stick to a wall and spell out a word or message.

30. **KEEP AUDIENCE AWAKE THROUGH PARTICIPATION** by asking for a show of hands, or have a member of the audience help the speaker make a demonstration. Another method is to have the speaker ask questions, or allow the audience to ask questions.

31. **STATE THAT THE ENTIRE SALES PRESENTATION CAN BE MADE TO A PROSPECT IN THREE MINUTES.** Dramatize this point by displaying a large egg timer. Add interest by not beginning the presentation until about 30 seconds have elapsed. Use the first 30 seconds to talk about how little time it takes.

32. **NAME THE FEATURES.** If a set of sales points or features has been presented, turn over your flip charts and offer money to the first person who can name the points in any order.

33. **THROW COINS.** As sales points are made throw out silver dollars to the audience. Toss out money for correct answers, for thoughtful contributions, for interesting comments, or for ideas.

34. **BUILD A HOUSE.** If it is desired to stress "qualities for success in selling," illustrate this by building a house on a table top. The finished house need be only three or four feet long and two or three feet high (lay a blueprint on the table). Tell the audience that "You first need a good

foundation." Next, state that "You should place yourself in the right frame of mind," or "Right frame of reference." Start construction by placing a rectangular frame on the table. Then continue your speech by placing a solid cardboard on the front of the frame, and attach to this cardboard rectangles simulating a door and a number of windows—each representing a particular point. (The other three sides of the house need not be added.) Then add a roof and a chimney to complete the points in your speech.

35. **PITCHMAKER.** Here's a lightweight frame which sets up somewhat like a Tinkertoy. Onto this 12-lb. frame are placed 22" × 22" panels containing key words or pictures of the product. This is great for illustrating features of a speech. The unit can be assembled into any pattern. The frame with 20 panels ships as a 24" × 24" × 3" package. Cost is around $75.00 from Close Productions, 163 San Carlos Blvd., Fort Myers, Fla. 33931.

35A. **MODELS.** Hire models to assist in making the demonstration. Have them wear company insignia or the conference slogan on their attire.

36. **KEEP ATTENTION WITH JACKPOT PRIZES.** Drop all the attendees' names in a box. Toward the end of several of the sessions when attention flags, draw a name from the box. Have that person answer one to three questions concerning the presentation. If he answers correctly, he receives a prize.

37. **CRASHING THROUGH DOOR.** Stretch paper across a wooden frame and paint a door on it. At the dramatic moment someone crashes through the door and delivers the product, or delivers the proper answer.

38. **SEDUCTIVE VOICE.** A girl with a provocative voice announces each segment of the program. Her voice can be taped.

39. **MIND READING.** Have a mindreader, complete with turban and crystal ball, answer questions about the present and future. Have him talk about sales forecasts, what is expected from the men in the future, advertising results, or results of the marketing plan. Plant assistants in the audience to ask sequenced questions.

40. **DESCENDING SIGN.** Hang introductory signs for presentations so that the signs may be let down with a string from a hidden area above the stage, or thread the twine through an eyelet above the stage and let down the string from the wings.

Techniques for Presentation and Speeches   129

41. **POP-UP SIGNS.** Obtain motorized car antennas. Affix to the antennas one or two words you wish to dramatize and have a remote switch raise the antennas mysteriously. For even more drama paint the signs with fluorescent paint and use a black light.

42. **MONEY TREE OR HOUSE.** Make large posters containing the key words of the presentations. These are placed on racks. As the speech progresses, the posters begin to assume the form of a tree or a house.

43. **DUMMIES.** Want to add humor to a mock selling situation? Then obtain department store dummies to represent a customer or group of customers. Seat or stand these manikins and have a salesman try to sell to these mock individuals

44. **OVERCOMING A COMPANY SALES PROBLEM.** The solutions to the problem can be dramatized by holding a trial. Rig up a desk for a judge and build a witness stand. Company executives are brought in to explain the problem and what is being done. They also mention salesmen who are selling in spite of the problem. These salesmen are also brought in as witnesses. Utilize a defense lawyer and a prosecuting attorney. End with a summation by both attorneys and a decision by the judge.

45. **DISTRIBUTE A SPECIAL NEWSPAPER EDITION.** Have the local convention city newspaper print an edition consisting of four pages of dateless copy except for the headline and its subhead. For the heading print an important meeting announcement such as a policy change or announce the introduction of a new product. During the initial meeting several speakers hint that a policy change or a new product is needed. Then at the meeting's end a newsboy enters shouting the news. The speaker confirms the policy change or new product and the papers are distributed.

46. **THEME LANGUAGE.** Instruct the speakers to use language tying in with the theme. If yours is a baseball theme, use phrases such as "Hit a homer," "Make a home run with customers," "Steal a base on competition," "You can score with this feature," "Be a hitter," etc.

47. **A CHAMPAGNE TOAST FOR THE ENTIRE AUDIENCE.** To celebrate a company anniversary, to toast present or future top salespersons, to tie in with a theme, serve champagne as the closing event of a convention. It can be done for large crowds. The secret is champagne or wine with "twist-off caps" and a sufficient number of waitresses. Use trays accommodating bottles and plastic glasses for about 20 persons. Provide one bottle per two or four guests. To divert the audience's

attention while the serving carts are being wheeled in, dim the lights and put on a short presentation or stunt. Spotlight the presentation, thus diverting attention from the carts being wheeled down the aisle.

48. **MAGNIFY THE DEMONSTRATION ON TV.** Where the product is small, TV sets can be placed at various places among the audience and the demonstration with its close-ups televised.

49. **IDEAS TO REGAIN ATTENTION:**
If the room is warm, if the speech is long, if there have been many speeches, there will be times when the audience becomes glassy-eyed. Some of the tricks of the trade to regain attention and to obtain participation are:
Use a demonstration. Show the product.
Get the audience to participate by asking their opinion.
Slam your fist on the lectern.
Ask for a show of hands from those who agree; from those who disagree.
Pour a glass of water slowly.
Walk to the sides of the stage; walk into the audience.
Tell a story.
Make use of visuals such as placing the key words on a placard, or writing them on a blackboard.
Take a ten-second pause and just look at the audience. Explain the reason for the pause was that you wanted the audience to think about the previous point.
Utilize a pause if members of the audience begin talking among themselves.
The pause works better than an admonishment.
Ask a question. Rephrase the answer in your own words. This aids immeasurably in obtaining a sense of participation.
Request questions from the audience, then ask if anyone in the audience can supply the answer. (Be sure to repeat the question for the benefit of those in the back of the room.)
Wherever possible, use the person's name when calling on him.
Always thank the contributor.

50. **WRITE ON THE SCREEN USING AN OVERHEAD PROJECTOR.** By using an overhead projector, the audience can see the speaker's or assistant's hand write the message or figures, or sketch a design.

51. **SILHOUETTES ON REAR-PROJECTION SCREEN.** Using a rear-projection screen, place silhouettes between the screen and the light

Techniques for Presentation and Speeches   131

source. For instance, you want to say something about the salesman who states, "I need another account like I need a hole in the head." As you speak a cardboard silhouette of a head appears. Then a pistol appears and points at the head. You can also blow cigarette smoke behind the screen near the pistol. The head silhouette is then replaced by a head with a hole in it.

52. **ANIMATED PIE AND BAR CHARTS.** An animated effect can be achieved by covering sections of the chart with paper and removing each pie or bar section as the point is emphasized. If slides are used, each slide can progressively build up the pie or bar chart.

53. **VISUAL BUILD-UP.** If charts are used, take the key charts when finished and line them up against the wall, or tack them up for all to see for reemphasis. Point to each as a summation device.

54. **PULL OUT LETTERS FROM A MAILBOX.** Draw a mailbox on a flip chart. Make a slit in the mailbox and glue a large envelope on the back. Actual letters from customers are drawn out from the mailbox, and excerpts are read aloud.

55. **MOVING GRAPH LINE.** Mount your graph on light plywood or heavy cardboard. Drill a hole at the beginning of the graph line and place staples along the graph line at each change in the curve. Thread a white thread from the hole in the back through the staples and attach a colored cord or ribbon to it. Pulling the thread makes the graph line travel.

56. **OLD-TIME MOVIE FILMS.** A great way to provide humorous relief is to announce a film of your company's product uses, then flash on the screen some applicable old-time movies. For added dramatics, record some player piano music. If your product is used in aircraft, a ten-minute 16mm sound film titled "This Mechanical Age," featuring actual newsreel shots of first flights of ancient planes and how they comically flopped, is available. Obtain from Budget Films, 4590 Santa Monica Blvd., Los Angeles, Calif. Also check under "Motion Picture Film Libraries" in your local telephone directory for this Warner Bros. film or for other old-time movies.

57. **USE BLACK LIGHT** to make easel board messages and displays which glow brightly only under this light. The American Science Center has black light sprays for giving plastic, glass, metal, paper, and even fresh flowers an eerie, luminous glow. It is invisible under ordinary light. The

price of a can of this spray is only $3.50. The company has an ultrawave glass filter for insertion into a slide projector gate for making it a black light spot. The price is $2.50. They sell six large pieces of black light chalk in assorted colors for $6. They also sell fluorescent paints, pencils, and tablets for making water glow. Even fluorescent body paint (that should have interesting possibilities!). American Science Center is located at 5700 Northwest Highway, Chicago, Ill. 60646. Black light lamps are supplied by American Science Center, and Ultra-Violet Products, Inc., 5114 Walnut Grove Ave., San Gabriel, Calif. 91778. The latter company also sells ultra-violet invisible printing ink.

58. **PLACE A THREE-DIMENSIONAL SYMBOLIC GADGET ON THE INTRODUCTORY PAGE OF FLIP CHART.** This can be accomplished by utilizing Velcro tape tabs to adhere the gadget to the page. The gadget could be a dollar mark, a giant hundred dollar bill, a firecracker, a "For Sale" sign, a giant footprint, a question mark, a heel and sole with the caption "Another Giant Step for Mankind," etc. If a company's mistakes are being corrected mount a giant eraser.

59. **BAR CHARTS.** Place Velcro (a special pressure sensitive tape) tabs on your colored bars and slap the bars in place on the flip chart.

60. **SIMULATE AN EYE-TESTING CHART.** Instead of the usual letters which appear on the doctor's chart use the title of the talk. Example: "How to Close More Sales." The word "How" will appear at the top in very large letters; then each succeeding word becomes smaller. Place appropriate vision indicators on each side of the flip chart such as 20/100, 20/50, 20/40, 20/20, 20/10.

61. **"HERMAN HOLDS A SALES MEETING."** A delightful, humorous spoof of all the hackneyed sales-meeting situations we've all experienced. Ideal as a meeting "starter" or program "break." From Dartnell Corp., 4660 Ravenswood Ave., Chicago, Ill. 60640.

62. **"HERMAN'S SECRET OF SALES SUCCESS."** The return of Herman . . . by popular demand. Uproarious scenes lay bare the real secrets behind Herman's stellar rise to the top. Great way to "kick off" a sales meeting.
Both films are ten minutes in length; 16 mm; full color. Purchase price is $125 each. Rental is $50 for each film. Available from Dartnell Corp., 4660 Ravenswood Ave., Chicago, Ill. 60640.

63. **DRAMATIC BALLOON STUNT.** Fill a balloon with confetti and smoke, then tie the balloon stem. Attach a string to the balloon and,

Techniques for Presentation and Speeches 133

using tape on the string, tape the balloon over the wording of the title page of the flip chart presentation. Make a few appropriate opening remarks and break the balloon with a cigarette or pin.

64. **USE "FLASH" PAPER TO UNVEIL A VITAL STATISTIC.** Flash paper is available from magic shops and often from gag novelty shops. Crumple this paper in a pouf style and attach it to the flip chart so that it covers a vital statistic. Touch a cigarette to the paper and there will be a blinding flash and the startling statistic is revealed. This is very effective with before-and-after-figures, in which case flash paper would cover both figures and they would be ignited in a one, two fashion.

65. **SOUND EFFECTS RECORDS.** Thomas J. Valentino, Inc. supplies all types of authentic sound effects on long playing records. They also supply mood music, including bear growls and snorts, applause, jet engines, bugle calls, air hammers, auto races, chimes, doorbells, birds, car skids and crashes, an old car starting, running, backfiring and falling apart, cash registers, cymbals, eight bells, horse effects, trains, harbor noises, waterfalls, carnival background, marches, monkey organs, marching band crowds, and hundreds of other sound effects. Also special records featuring marches, calliope music, silent movie music, carousel music, railroad sounds. Thomas J. Valentino, Inc., is at 150 West 46th St., New York, N.Y. 10036. Another supplier is Musifex Inc., 45 West 45th St., New York, N.Y., or check with the larger record shops. If they don't have the particular effect you wish, they may be able to obtain it for you. Also look in the yellow pages under "Sound Effect Records."

66. **USE FLANNEL BOARDS.** These are boards to which paper or light cardboard items can be affixed by lightly pressing the paper to the board. It works as if a magnet were being used. These boards are excellent for building up figures or sales points. Flannel boards will even hold lightweight products. Several sources of supply are: Oravisual Co., Inc., P.O. Box 1150, St. Petersburg, Fla.; Jacronda Manufacturing Co., 5449 Hunter St., Philadelphia, 31 Pa.; and Charles Mayer Studios, Inc., 140 E. Market, Akron, Ohio.

67. **TO AVOID UPSIDE DOWN OR BACKWARD SLIDES** mark the frame of the slides in a distinctive uniform manner. For instance, place a dot in the upper right corner.

68. **MAKE YOUR OWN TITLE SLIDES—NO DEVELOPING REQUIRED.** This is a quick, easy way to add titles to any 35mm slide show. Simply place a stencil material in the typewriter, cut, and mount.

Kit comes complete with 30 stencils, 30 slide mounts, template, and instructions. About 25¢ per slide. Available from American Science Center Inc., 5700 Northwest Highway, Chicago, Ill. 60646.

69. **COLOR SLIDES FOR SALES TRAINING PRESENTATIONS.** Produce your own slide show on the art of selling. These are 15 slides in full color using professional artwork. Slides depict basic steps of selling such as developing leads, explaining the product, determining the buying influences, overcoming objections, asking for the order, closing the sale, etc. Add your own slides of products or whatever to complete the presentation. $14.25 for set of 15 stock slides. Custom slides to match the sales set also available at $27.50 each. Free sample slide available on request. Order from T-AV Mart, P.O. Box 14647, Austin, Tex. 78761.

70. **MOVIE STILLS.** Make slides from old-time movie still photographs. Place captions on the slide or make appropriate remarks such as "Our new factory," "The girls at the office are behind you," etc. For a source try W. H. Everett, Buck Hill Rd., Ridgefield, Conn. 06877. Granger Collection, 1841 Broadway, New York, N.Y. 10018 (specify the type of picture you wish). American Stock Photos, 6842 Sunset Blvd., Hollywood, Calif. 90028. World Wide Photos, Inc., 50 Rockefeller Plaza, New York, N.Y. 10020. Movie Star News, 212 E. 14th St., New York, N.Y. 10003. And try the yellow pages under "Photographs—Stock Shots."

71. **CAPTIONED SLIDES.** Now you can use professional slides for your captions. Several companies produce these. Visual Horizons Company has 240 full color captioned illustrated slides to choose from. Obtainable are captions such as "Total, Completely New, Solutions, Benefits, Competition, Marketing, Target, Price, Win, Pro/Con," etc. Priced at about $3 individually, or the entire 240 lot for about $90. Visual Horizons, 208 Westfall Rd., Rochester, N.Y. 14620. Also available from Successful Meeting Slides, 1422 Chestnut St., Philadelphia, Pa. 19102; and Cinegraph Slides, Inc., 2675 Skypark Dr., Torrance, Calif. 90505; and from the Slide Innovators, 2020 San Carolos Blvd., Fort Meyers Beach, Fla. 33931.

72. **KODAK SLIDE PROJECTOR.** With this unit you narrate the script, record pulses to change slides at desired points, and your professional slide presentation is ready for use. Perfect synchronization is claimed. It's the Kodak Cinema Sound Model 3000. $595. Available from Visual Horizons, 208 Westfall Rd., Rochester, N.Y. 14620, or try your local Kodak supplier.

Techniques for Presentation and Speeches 135

73. **VISUAL INDICATOR FOR CHANGING SLIDES.** With this unit a lecturer does not need to disturb the audience by calling out repeatedly "Next slide, please." It can also be used to signal his assistant to start a movie projector, tape recorder, etc. The speaker presses a button which flashes on a light to the projectionist. Price is about $50. C. A. Compton, Inc., P.O. Box 1775, Boulder, Colo. 80302.

74. **A PROJECTION POINTER** projects an exceptionally brilliant, triangular-shaped arrow of light. Use it for slides, large easels, chalkboards and posters where the speaker wants to emphasize a particular feature or figure. It can be used with a high intensity projector. The room need not be dimmed. Price is $153. Available from C.A. Compton, Inc., P.O. Box 1775, Boulder, Colo. 80302. Also there is one for $8 from American Science Center, 5700 Northwest Highway, Chicago, Ill 60646.

75. **PORTABLE SOUND ROSTRUM.** Use with audiences up to 500. There are four directional speakers for full audience coverage. It operates on eight size "D" flashlight batteries or standard 115 volt outlet. Cost is about $180. Marketing Distributors, Inc., 3570 Warrensville Center Rd., Shaker Heights, Ohio 44122. Also Oravisual Company, Inc., P.O. Box 11150, St. Petersburg, Fla. 33733.

SPEAKER CHECKLIST. See Chapter 22. For additional ideas see the section titled "How Speakers Use Visual Presentations Effectively" in Chapter 13—"How to Plan, Prepare, and Use Visual Presentations Effectively."

Chapter 12

Using Stunts and Gags to Enliven the Conference

Contents

1. **Stunts for Opening the Conference**
2. **Paging**
3. **Offbeat Newspapers for the Meeting**
4. **Coffee Break Ideas**
5. **Money Ideas**
6. **Humorous Slide and Film Suggestions**
7. **Surprise Humorous Speakers**
8. **Magic Tricks**
9. **Specialty Items**
10. **More Stunts and Gags**
11. **Award Presentation Ideas**

INTRODUCTION

The following stunts and gags are presented for your judicious use in backing up the idea being presented. Use these stunts sparingly. Don't create an environment where the entire meeting is remembered only for its stunts and not for the ideas which are to be carried home. Gimmicks, properly used, can turn a dull meeting into a memorable one in which the meat of the meeting is remembered.

1. STUNTS FOR OPENING THE CONFERENCE.

(a) To Promote On-Time Attendance. Hand a numbered ticket to all attendees who arrive on time for the meeting. A drawing is held for door prizes. This procedure can be repeated at another session, such as the first meeting after lunch.

(b) Open the Meeting with a Bang by renting starter pistols which shoot blanks. They are obtainable from sporting goods stores; or rent one from a theatrical prop company. You can obtain large toy cannons from Conestoga Co., Inc., 732 E. Goepp St., Bethlehem, Pa. 18018. They use carbide to produce a loud bang.

(c) Studio Warm-Up. If it's a large audience, at the start of the meeting use traveling mikes to interview people in the audience. Have two interviewers on different sides of the room. Do this for five or ten minutes; it develops a warm audience and makes the time go by while the late comers arrive.

(d) To Move Persons to the Front Seats. One method is to ask all to stand; then request them to step to the front seats.

(e) Years of Experience. If your meeting has work sessions, open the meet-

Using Stunts and Gags to Enliven the Conference 139

ing with a question, "Guess how many years of experience is represented by this group?" Give a prize for the best guess.

(f) Congratulation Telegram Stunt. This is especially for a newly appointed manager. He reads a telegram which he states has just been received and which he wishes to share with the audience. The telegram congratulates him on his new job or promotion and is filled with a multitude of platitudes concerning his character and ability. As the audience begins to get embarrassed by all this praise, he comes to the end of the telegram which is signed "Mother."

(g) Meeting Opening Stunt. Another opening stunt is to tape money of various denominations to the bottoms of seats. The speaker, after requesting the audience to look under their seats, states "This illustrates the point 'You have to get off your seat to make a sale.'"

(h) "Door Prize." Advertise that a door prize is to be given. When the lucky winner comes to the stage, present him with a door. It's corny, but fun. You can also advertise a "bedroom suite" and give pajamas.

(i) At a Breakfast Guests Were Asked to Peek Under Their Saucers for a Sticker that read "As advertised in a certain magazine." There were five saucers with stickers. Five winners received the product which was advertised. This idea can be adapted to a variety of purposes—to put across sales points, to push a certain product, to indicate that "no stone should be left unturned," etc.

(j) "Chest of Gold." Give keys to all who arrive on time. Do this for several of the sessions. These keys are used later to open a chest filled with a choice of prizes, each of which has been wrapped to conceal its content. The following company markets a "Pirates Treasure Chest," a lock, and keys which will and will not unlock the chest. Write: Jet Advertising, 51 Stanton St., Newark, N.J. 07114. Cost is approximately $60. A complete "Lucky Key" Treasure Chest contest kit is sold by Hewig-Marvic, 861 Manhattan Ave., Brooklyn, N.Y. 11222. They offer the same as above, plus the following at 25¢ each: Pirate map, pirate disguise kit, gold candy coins (package of 10), pirate balloons. Also available are pirate guns and daggers at $1 each, key cards for mailing at $17.50 per thousand, and a horn buzzer at $12.50 which sings out every time there is a winner.

(k) Keys to Profits. A variation of the above is to tape the keys to the bottoms of the seats. The opening speaker announces that the conference is intended to provide "Keys to profits." Then the participants are asked to look under their seats for the lucky keys.

(l) Psychological Stunt to Start a Meeting. Place a diamond made of dots on a poster or blackboard. Ask the audience to copy it. Their assignment is to connect all the dots using four straight lines. Pencils are not to be lifted from the paper. At the end of one or two minutes ask for a show of hands of individuals who have solved the puzzle. Find someone with the correct solution and ask that person to draw the connecting lines on the blackboard.

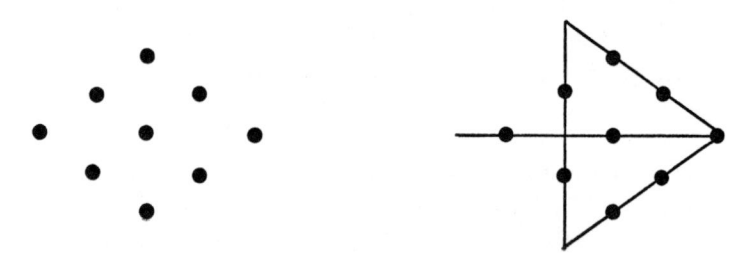

The moral of the story is that tradition, habit, or a wrong frame of reference places us in a rut. We look at old problems using old solutions and don't look for new solutions to these problems.

2. PAGING.

(a) Bellhop Page. Hire a hotel bellhop, or dress up a model, to page each section of your program.

(b) Telegrams. Have a bellboy or waitress deliver gag telegrams to various speakers. The messages can tie in with personages in the news, an incident that has happened to the speaker, etc.

3. OFFBEAT NEWSPAPERS FOR THE MEETING.

(a) Chinese Newspaper. Use this in a mailing announcement, or give to all at a meeting. Contact Chinese newspapers in your local city, or New Kwong Tai Press, 940 Chungking Rd., Los Angeles, Calif. Approximate price is 15¢ per copy, plus $20 for typesetting your headline.

(b) Gag Newspapers. Most of the larger cities and larger resort areas have gag newspapers available. These generally consist of the front page only on which you may have a two-line headline imprinted. Tack a few of the newspapers on a bulletin board each day. Typical headlines could be: "Local Bars Welcome Joe Jones," "Acme Group Hits Boston, 900 Bars Close," "Lover Smith Missing, 67 Girls Commit Suicide," "Jones Refuses Singing Offer at the Met," "Fanny Hill Names Brown in Memoirs," etc.

(c) Old Newspaper. The front page of the New York Times going back to

1851 is available. Pick the date your company was organized, or the date a particular employee joined the company. This will serve as a good start for a speaker when he reads the news headline. Cost is $3 each; send money with order. From Microfilming Corp. of America, 21 Harristown Rd., Glen Rock, N.J. 07452.

4. COFFEE BREAK IDEAS.

(a) Four Coffee Break Ideas.
- Think about having 30-minute coffee breaks if the mix of the attendees is such that much benefit can be gained by a longer socialized coffee break devoted to discussion of the meeting subjects.
- How about coffee break tables on which a small sign has been placed giving the meeting subject. Here persons with like interests can share information on specific topics. Make these large round tables for six to ten persons.
- Place a package of Life Savers, mints, or Chicklets at each person's place in the meeting rooms.
- In addition to the standard coffee and Coke, add fruit, cookies, cheeses, ice cream, or other different items such as fruit punch. Consult the hotel for ideas along this line.

(b) Imaginative Way to Introduce Coffee Breaks. This company offers two different one-and-a-half-minute sound color slide coffee introductions. Sound is provided by an open reel tape or cassette. A printed script is furnished for slide change cues. One module consists of 17 slides using a series of comical live shots of animals. Professional actors on the tape narrate each animal's role, commenting on how great the presentation was, waking up from a nap, learning about the coffee break, etc. On the second module a professional actor does a take-off of the Old Philosopher saying, "How did your stomach feel when you woke up this morning? Did your head feel like an electrical storm was going on when you took your shower? Well, we've got the solution to your problem." The script then leads into the coffee break. The purchase price is $75 dollars each and may be used as many times as you wish. Available on a ten-day review basis from Robert R. Kubick & Associates, Inc., 121 Mt. Horeb Rd., Warren, N.J. 07060.

(c) "An Apple Break." Girls carrying baskets of fruit go down the aisles and hand apples, oranges, etc. to the attendees.

(d) For a Gag, Make Signs saying, "This Coffee Break Sponsored by (competitor name)."

(e) **Music for Breaks.** If the hotel cannot provide music, take along a recorder and play taped music for the coffee breaks and prior to the sessions. For additional information on Coffee Breaks see Chapter 19.

5. MONEY IDEAS.

(a) **Big Money!** These are giant authentic-looking 7" × 17½" bills in denominations of $1, $2, $5, $10, $100, $500, and $1,000. They look almost like the real thing. Printed on two sides, the price is $15 for 100; $55 for 500; $90 for 1,000; $300 for 5,000. You can have them imprinted for a fee, such as $20 for 1,000. This firm also has $100 place mats for the same price and mini-money or mini-money key chains—all great items for sales promotion purposes. Order from Howard Printing Corp., 116 West 32nd St., New York, N.Y. 10001.

(b) **Wooden Nickels.** Have fun with these by tossing the nickels to the audience in response to questions. Obtain from D. Robbins & Co., Inc., 127 W. 17th St., New York, N.Y. 10011. They also have rubber dollars. Another supplier is Falcon Rule Co., Auburn, Maine 04210.

(c) **Your Own Money.** If you are emphasizing profits or commissions, consider printing your own money. Use cartoons or pictures of the president, sales manager, or treasurer. Try slogans such as "Money is like manure—good only when spread around." For the "grand seal" use your company trademark.

(d) **Bowl of Coins.** Obtain a fishbowl with an appropriate size mouth. Fill it with coins and allow persons supplying best or correct answers to retain all the coins they can grab with one hand.

(e) **"A Shower of Money from Heaven"** makes a good stunt when talking about money which can be earned. The money is resting on paper which had been lightly taped to the ceiling or to light fixtures. A strong thread for pulling is attached to the paper.

6. HUMOROUS SLIDE AND FILM SUGGESTIONS

(a) **Humorous Films to Brighten the Meeting.** "Easy on Balance" is a comic montage of athletes caught off balance . . . from a collision between two fielders trying to catch the same ball . . . to a quarterback who is chased back 20 yards, and then miraculously breaks through and runs 35 yards to a first down while his opponents fall all over themselves. The film runs 7½ minutes. Sale price is $180 or $1 per viewer. Also available is a three-minute cartoon

Using Stunts and Gags to Enliven the Conference

film about a boy genius, his invention, and a problem. Rental price is $35. Both can be previewed for $10 each. Use a film as a humorous interlude, prelude to a coffee break, or as an introduction to an R&D speaker. Available from Vantage Communications, Inc., P.O. Box 546, Nyack, N.Y. 10906.

(b) **Old-Time Movie Slides** can be interspersed in the various slide presentations. Speakers can be equipped with suitable explanations such as "our new factory," etc. For photos write to: Movie Star News, 212 E. 14th St., New York, N.Y. 10003, or W. H. Everett, Buck Hill Rd., Ridgefield, Conn. 06877 (203/438-2033); and Granger Collection, 1841 Broadway, New York, N.Y. Make slides of these photos.

(c) **Girl Title Slides.** Make signs on posters of the titles of the various slide presentations. Then take shots of attractive girls from the office holding these signs, or hire models for this purpose.

(d) **Customer Taped Comments.** Before the conference take slides of persons representing typical customers. Ask each an identical question. Place their response on tape, or later have someone dub in voices giving the comments—perhaps preceded with the announcer's description of the person. Run ten to twelve of these typical comments, with each ranging from fifteen seconds to a minute.

(e) **"Kindly Disregard All Previous Presentations"** was the first slide which an ingenious product manager used when he discovered that he was number five on the list of product managers to make a presentation.

(f) **Take Slides or Movies of Your Recreational and Other Events** and show these at the final banquet. This, of course, could be done only at locations where there is fast developing service. For movies use slow motion and fast motion for gags, gag situations on the golf course, simulate men dozing off at a session, men coming out of a small barrel, men running to the golf course, men in slow motion going to a lecture, etc. Polaroid photos can be taken and pasted on the bulletin board.

(g) **Three Humorous Films for Sales Meetings** for after-hours entertainment, or for a hospitality suite. "Plan 15½" portrays Harvey Korman as an evangelistic sales motivator hired to pep up a firm's lagging sales force. "Return from the Road" highlights Korman in a domestic comedy sketch. "Fairwell, George Tugglebolt" parodies the business ritual of a retirement dinner. Rental is $100 each, or purchase for $225 each. May be previewed for $15. Available from Korman-Swanson Productions, Inc., 625 Milwaukee St., Milwaukee, Wis. 53202.

(h) Gag Pictures on Screen Involving Attendees. Use Polaroid's quick-slide process with their camera to take pictures throughout the conference. Look for comic situations at the banquet, the cocktail party, the golf match, the sessions. At the end of the conference or at the banquet show the photos on the screen and ad lib the captions before the slide flashes on the screen. Some examples: Build the slides around the characteristics a successful salesman should have, such as "He is alert"—here, let an attendee in on the gag and show him sleeping during a session. "He is a straight shooter"— golfer behind a tree. "He studies his catalog"—salesman at the bar studying catalog while a girl goes unnoticed. "He should be pleasant"—wearing a frown. "Be careful about drinking"—leaning over water fountain with water dripping off his face. "He should sell all the time"—salesman with leer leaning over a very pretty receptionist. "Salesman should get off by himself and think"— entering men's room. "He is always on time because he eats a light breakfast"—eating big meal. "He looks deeply into every situation"—looking at a girl with low-cut dress. "He works far into the night"—girl on lap. "He is an expert on special applications"—a man in the rough. "He is always on course"—another man in the rough. "He copes with every situation"—another gag golf shot.

Check with your local camera store for information on how to take these Polaroid slide shots. Another idea is to take the shots with an ordinary camera and reproduce these in a post-conference goodwill mailing.

7. SURPRISE HUMOROUS SPEAKERS.

(a) Surprise Speakers. Many "Speakers Bureaus" have surprise humorous speakers available. A Mr. Stuart Cramer masquerades as such diverse characters as a Hindu Swami, Legal Advisor, Dude Ranch Manager, Fertilizer Expert, etc. As a fictitious character he starts his talk in a serious vein and then gradually slips into humorous. He is available through Mr. Meriweather & Co., 2368 Queenston Rd., Cleveland Heights, Ohio.

A master of double talk is "Prof" Harry Stanley. This delightful hoax may be reached at 67-10B 190th Lane, Fresh Meadows, N.Y. 11365.

(b) Information Badges for Speakers. Make a prominent badge for each product speaker or other type of speaker whom your salesmen should consult. Print the message "Ask Me for Information on the XYZ line" on the badge and require the speaker to wear the badge throughout the conference. The badges can be printed on cardboard, and the name of the product inked in.

8. MAGIC TRICKS.

(a) Use Magic Tricks to Illustrate Points. Pull out scarves with messages, illustrate disappearing competition by having an object vanish. See your local magic shop for ideas. "Magicians" are also listed in some telephone books; see them for suggestions, or consider using real magicians. Write: S.S. Adams Co., Neptune, N.J. 07753 for magic tricks.

(b) Puzzles, Magic Tricks, Novelties, Practical Jokes. Write D. Robbins & Company, Inc., 127 W. 17th St., New York, N.Y. 10011. Browsing through their catalog will provide inspiration for a host of ideas.

9. SPECIALTY ITEMS.

(a) Matchbooks. Obtain matchbooks personalized with your meeting slogan or product slogan and company name. Sources: Lion Match Corporation of America, 2 West 45th St., New York, N.Y.; Monogram of California, 500 Hampshire, San Francisco, Calif. Boxes of bantam-size matches are available at $40 per thousand from Glass Industries, 1133 Broadway. New York, N.Y. 10010, or Eliott Sales Corp. 2502 South 12th St., Tacoma, Wash. 98405.

(b) Balloons Imprinted with Meeting Theme. Fill them with helium and decorate the meeting room. These can be used at the banquet later.

(c) Fortune Cookies. Place a message in the cookie promoting a product, theme, etc. Distribute at banquet, in a welcome basket, or during coffee and tea break. A source which will place your message in the cookies: Lotus Fortune Cookie, 436 Pacific Ave., San Francisco, Calif, or contact your local Chinese restaurant for a source of supply.

(d) Blotter Coasters. Use at cocktail parties, banquet, or coffee breaks to illustrate the theme or push a product or idea. Try your local advertising specialty distributor, or Hewig & Marvic, 861 Manhattan Ave., New York, N.Y. 11222.

(e) Baby Photo Contest. Place baby photos of some of the attendees on a bulletin board. Give prizes to those making the most correct identifications.

(f) Special Contest. Announce a special contest to run the duration of the meeting only. Award a gag prize such as a moth-eaten moosehead, as well as a valuable prize.

10. MORE STUNTS AND GAGS.

(a) Cigars for New Product Introduction. A good way to call attention to a new product is to imprint the product name and message "Just Born" on the cigar. For a catalog of imported cigars of every shape and type write: Nat Sherman Co., 1400 Broadway, New York, N.Y. 10018.

(b) Humorous Company Policy Manual. This 24-page manual contains old-time movie stills with captions, such as "Executives," "Coffee Break," "Accounts Receivable," "Employee Selection," etc. Give as a gift to each attendee. Imprinted, the price is about 70¢ each in 150 quantities. Source: Merit Industries, 51 Stanton St., Newark, N.J. 07114.

(c) Illustrating Ad Coverage. Set up a newsstand dealer on the stage and have the dealer shout from the booth how extensive the magazine coverage is. Then bring on a mailman to explain the wide magazine circulation.

(d) Complicated Chart. When the comptroller, sales manager, etc. has a chart of figures, use a very complicated chart as a gag. Then replace it with a simple chart.

(e) The Importance of Observing. Break the ice by having a cook brandishing a large knife chase another down the aisle and across the stage. To impress the importance of observing (or listening), ask questions and have the audience write answers about the incident: color of the hats worn, type of knife, what was said, how many people, etc.

(f) Custard Pie. There was a sales conference where two regional sales managers had previously bet a custard pie in the face for the region with the lowest sales. The climax came when the national sales manager called the two regional sales managers to the stage on a pretext (the winning regional sales manager had been notified beforehand). The loser was requested to look at something at one side and when he turned around he received a pie in the face. This was at the close of the meeting.

11. AWARD PRESENTATION IDEAS

(a) Humorous Award Ideas. Give a deed to one square inch of land in Texas, an island, or other appropriate location. Award a title of nobility, a bit part in a motion picture, a chauffeur and limousine for the duration of the conference, breakfast in bed, special maid service, or any other special service which the hotel can assist you in dreaming up. Free tickets to a show, free shoe shines at the hotel, a two-hour course in bar tending, a hostess complete

Using Stunts and Gags to Enliven the Conference

with golf cart filled with drinks to follow the winner around the golf course, or give a Pet Rock.

(b) **Gifts for VIP's.** Present a giant-size gavel with appropriate inscription. Give the Master of Ceremonies a large ham.

(c) **Certificates of Achievement.** Holding exams, or giving a course at your meeting? If so, consider giving a certificate. Handsome blank engraved certificates are available; you imprint what you wish. Available from Jeffries Banknote Co., 1330 W. Pico, Los Angeles, Calif. 90015, or check your classified telephone directory under "Banknote" companies. Make a ceremony of handing the certificates out by donning a cap and gown. Call your meeting "The College of Product Knowledge."

(d) **Announcing Winners?** Herald each winner with the stroke of a gong. These are available from costume rental shops. Consider scattering the awards throughout the conference at unannounced times. An ornate 8" oriental gong is offered at approximately $20 by Hewig-Marvic, 861 Manhattan Ave., Brooklyn, N.Y. 11222.

(e) **Crowns, Scepters, Tiaras.** Instead of renting such props for crowning the sales leader, here is a source from which they may be purchased. The crowns start at $8 and go up to $71. Other props available are sequin wands, a chain of office, and even halos. Write to Theatrical Accessories, Inc., 1700 Gay Ave. Findlay, Ohio 45840. Also available from Merit Industries, 51 Stanton St., Newark, N.J. 07114; and Frank Stein Novelty Co., 1969 So. Los Angeles St., Los Angeles, Calif. 90011.

(f) **When Announcing an Incentive Program** don't be satisfied with just the announcement of the prizes. Roll out the actual prizes, or show slides of them. If it is an incentive trip, dancers and/or a band can perform, or a short travel film or slides can be shown. TWA will loan at no charge 16mm., 30-minute color sound travel films of various countries. Sets of slides on various countries may also be purchased from them. Contact any of the various airline offices.

For Additional Ideas on Awards, both serious and humorous, see "Impressive Awards Presentations" in Chapter 11 titled "How to Use Showmanship in Presentations and Speeches." Also see "Gag Gifts and Gag Awards" in Chapter 16.

Chapter 13

How to Plan, Prepare, and Use Visual Presentations Effectively

Contents

1. How to Plan Visual Presentations
2. Types of Visual Aids—Advantages and Disadvantages
3. How to Prepare Effective Visuals
4. Cost Estimates of Visuals
5. How to Project Slides and Films to Best Advantage
6. How Speakers Can Use Visual Presentations Effectively
7. Audio-Visual Suppliers

1. HOW TO PLAN VISUAL PRESENTATIONS.

It is assumed that in the preparation of the manuscript, the speaker has (a) determined the size and character of the audience, (b) knows what they can grasp of the subject, (c) has defined what is to be accomplished, (d) has ascertained the time limit, and (e) has learned of the other events on the program.

The speaker should then plan the presentation to bring out a few major points or principles; and not give the audience so much information that it confuses them. This simplicity also provides flexibility in responding to audience reaction and flexibility in making the presentation again to a different audience.

If the manuscript has been written, develop the visualization by underlining the key thoughts and key words. If the manuscript has not yet been written, develop an outline and underline the key words. If you are going to plunge right in without a manuscript or outline, start the planning by listing each major point on a small slip of paper and then place them in the best order.

The same careful planning which goes into the manuscript or outline should go into the planning of the visuals. Plan the visual aids as a support for the presentation; to clarify and strengthen the spoken words. Do not build the speech around the visual aids. Use the visuals only for points which are worth making.

Visual presentations can take the form of (a) a series of colored pictures which tell a story, (b) key words which the speaker amplifies, (c) abstract symbols, (d) charts and diagrams, or (e) a combination of the foregoing.

The best way to plan the visuals is to utilize planning board cards. These are cards about 4″ × 6″ containing an area for sketching the visual, an area for instructions to the production department, and a summary of what will be said as the visual is being shown. Lacking these cards, a supply of 3″ × 5″ cards will accomplish the same purpose.

Furnish the cards in the proper sequence to the production department

Use Visual Presentations Effectively

(artists and photographer) with full information of how the pictures or photographs relate to each other. Be prepared to tell the producing team the budget limitations and the deadline required for rehearsals.

There are a number of do's and don'ts to be observed in making an effective presentation. The following is a distillation of ideas from the experts:

- Convey only one idea per visual. Keep the visuals simple. Remember, you're selling an idea; don't use fancy artwork which overshadows the idea.
- Use an outline drawing, a simple graph, or a single illustrated thought.
- If the audience has to figure out a complex illustration, they won't be listening.
- Don't make the visuals so complete that there is little left for the speaker to say. The visual should be a picture image of what he is conveying orally.
- Confine headlines to not more than two lines.
- A good rule to follow is to confine the entire visual to six or seven words per line, and to not more than six or seven lines per visual.
- The copy on the visuals should be the same words as those which are spoken. Use graphics instead of words whenever possible—a chart, a drawing, a photograph.
- Forget about reproducing detailed data such as a letter. A good test is to measure the width of the proposed line of words or art and divide this by two. Then place the material that many feet from you. If you can read it easily, it will be legible on the screen.
- Another test is to move back a distance to six times that of the width of the original art or lettering to be photographed. If it is readable, it is suitable for photographing and projection.
- If a photo is complex, consider showing a detail on the next slide. The same holds true for a blueprint or other mass of data.
- Convert tabular data to graphs, they can be more easily understood.
- Go over the rough art and edit for simplicity. Eliminate unnecessary grid lines, words, and figures. Abbreviate where possible.
- Plan on showing individual slides no longer than half a minute. Go to a blank slide or a blank colored slide if necessary.
- Plan not to use slides throughout the speech. Arrange to make a straight verbal presentation, then show slides in rapid order to make several points, then back to verbal only. You can even consider mixing in another prop such as a slap board or a flip chart.
- A real attention-getting start can be made by making use of polarized motion on the title slides. The projection unit is the Kodak Motion Adapter which is attached to the front of the slide projector. The adapter contains a polarized disc which rotates in front of the projector lens. The slide contains sections which have a special film, and when the

adapter screen wheel is rotated in front of the slide, an effect of movement is generated.
- Another way to provide an attention-getting start is to take a photo of the speaker, or an attractive girl from the office, holding a placard saying "Kindly disregard all previous presentations."
- A different type of presentation can be made by utilizing two screens with a slide projector for each. Use one slide for the main point to be made such as "The Market," and a slide on the other screen to show segments or figures comprising this market. You may show the product on one screen and flash its features on the other.
- Another variation is the use of "action sequence." This consists of inserting a short motion picture film clip in the middle of a still presentation.
- Consider handling complex subjects by using succeeding slides, each containing the material in the original slide and adding a new element—preferably the new element being the only one in color.
- Build up a long message on slides by projecting the first line only. The second slide contains the first and second line, but the second line is in color. The third slide adds another line, and again only the latest line is in color.
- When using an overhead projector, build up a complex subject by means of transparent overlays. The same method can be applied to the use of the flip charts.
- Another novel overhead projector approach is to plan to show only one section of a transparency at a time. (The remaining portion is covered with opaque paper and removed as the section comes up.)
- If a blackboard is used, look into the possibility of securing one which is two-sided. The front is used to write the points which are being made. As new points are made the old ideas are erased. At the conclusion of the presentation the board is flipped over to reveal the written summary.

2. TYPES OF VISUAL AIDS—ADVANTAGES AND DISADVANTAGES.

(a) Slap Boards, Flannel Boards, Hook n' Loop.

These boards are best suited for fast-moving and dramatic presentations. They are good for putting ideas together, for building up ideas dramatically and for showing relationships. The boards serve as backgrounds upon which drawings, symbols, pictures or words, which have been prepared in advance, are placed. This method adds drama and speed to the presentation.

Some types of boards are made of felt. The material to be slapped on has sandpaper glued on it which, upon slapping, adheres to the board. Another method makes use of small magnets. A leader in popularity now is the Hook n' Loop tape which can be attached to the back of any material (plastic, glass, paper, fabric, rubber, or an actual sample of your product). It is claimed that one square inch of this patented Velcro tape will hold up to ten pounds.

(b) **Opaque Projectors.**

Can be used in a fully lighted room to allow note taking. The speaker thus handles the projector, but has the advantage of being up front and facing the audience. The picture is projected above and behind the speaker. Nowadays, 10″ × 10″ inexpensive transparencies for opaque projectors can be quickly produced right in the office. Production of the visuals can be accomplished by placing a transparency film overlay on virtually any drawn or printed original and then running them through a copying machine. Colorful overlays can be utilized to build up a presentation such as a pie chart. During the projection of the film a pointer can be placed right on the transparency, items can be circled, notes written, and sketches made on the transparency during the presentation.

(c) **Easel Pads.**

Consists of large pads of plain or lined paper on which a speaker writes as he talks. The notes can then be used as a summary. Good for generating discussion. They are simple, inexpensive, and versatile.

A giant easel can be purchased for big meetings or for large or complex charts. It holds pads ruled in light blue 1″ squares which are barely visible from a short distance, and which greatly simplify lettering, drawing, and chart making. The pads are 45″ wide and 34″ high. The easel folds down to $4^{1}/_{2}″ \times 23″ \times 38″$. Two 27″ × 34″ pads can be placed side by side for comparisons. The easel is available at around $125 from Oravisual Company, Inc., P.O. Box 1150, St. Petersburg, Fla.

(d) **Flip Charts.**

An advantage is that the room need not be darkened and the speaker thus maintains visual contact with the audience. The material is prepared beforehand. Not suitable for very sizeable audiences unless the charts are extra large.

(e) **Chalk Boards.**

Good for listing points as the speaker goes along. Useful for developing ideas or to review the material. Fluorescent colored chalk is now available. Rent either blackboards or the newer light colored boards. Disadvantage is that if the board is filled, something must be erased to provide room for the new information.

(f) Recorded Presentations.

These are used where sound alone can serve the purpose such as the recording of a conversation between salesman and customer. The recording can be stopped at appropriate spots and the audience asked how they would handle the subject, then the recording continues. Also they are useful for bringing messages from absent officials. Sound effects can be utilized.

Audio recordings on tape can be made during the meeting for sharing with other groups at a later time. Tapes can be duplicated and used for presenting inspirational talks by professionals. The tapes can be erased and reused, or sections can be spliced in or out.

(g) Slides.

Slides do not take up much room, project to any size, and provide brilliant color. They dominate the room since the room is dark. The slides can be changed to fit individual audiences. Time on the screen can be controlled by the speaker. Slides are relatively inexpensive, quickly produced, and easily portable.

(h) Filmstrips.

Filmstrips are on 35 mm film and will never be out of order. They can be made with or without sound. Silent filmstrips enable the speaker to dwell on any point or to ask or answer questions. Filmstrips are less expensive than movies and relatively easy to produce. Sound can be provided either through disc records or audio cassettes. Write to Project: Filmstrip, 825 S. Barrington Ave., Los Angeles, Calif. 90049 for a do-it-yourself filmstrip kit. Price is $10. It tells you how to write and produce filmstrips and includes production supplies.

(i) Motion Pictures.

Motion pictures are the next best thing to participating in the actual experience. They are generally better than sound filmstrips but much more expensive. Segments may be taken at various times and locations, and edited as required. Cost depends upon the type of sets to be constructed and cost of actors. Camera rental is about $200 per day; projectors about $25 a day; plus the cost of the operators. Professional films can be rented to introduce a subject, or to reinforce the theme of the meeting.

(j) Videotape.

Similar to live TV in that a camera is used to record and special TV sets are used for viewing. The message is placed on a magnetic tape. The tonal quality is equivalent to that of a home TV set. The film can be played back immediately or stored for future use. The image is erasable and the tape can be used again. Unlike motion picture films, a videotape must be shown in the sequence in which it is taken. It cannot be cut for editing. Videotape is useful for training sessions where salesmen can view their presentations. It is excellent for speaker rehearsals, and it can record meetings for viewing at other locations and times.

Costs are approximately $85 per day for recording equipment and $75 to $85 per day for the viewing equipment. An hour of tape (black/white or color) costs about $75. Duplicates are around $50.

(k) Live TV.

Live TV is transmitted by leased telephone wires to TV screens at a number of locations. It has been used for holding multicity sales meetings, new product introductions, etc.

Live TV is effective in that the audience realizes the immediacy—that the words and action are taking place as it happens. It is the next best thing to a personal appearance. Offsetting this is the fact that mistakes cannot be corrected, and the expense of the presentation. The viewers must be present at the correct time, and the audience is limited by the size of the TV screen. However, multiple viewing sets may be placed in the meeting room.

Costs are approximately $1,200 per day for the camera and equipment rental at the broadcasting end, and $12 per day for each receiving set. The telephone line charge averages around $1.35 per hour per mile.

(l) Multimedia.

Multimedia is a combination of still and motion pictures projected simultaneously on odd-shaped screens and accompanied by sound and lighting effects. The speaker can be spotlighted and switches made from live to visual delivery.

Multimedia can be adapted to small or large presentation.

3. HOW TO PREPARE EFFECTIVE VISUALS.

(a) Guidelines for All Types of Visuals.

Keep everything simple. Use few words and few design elements.

Use round numbers or an abbreviated scale; i.e., instead of $386,246 write $386.2.

Do not use vertical-reading words; keep to the horizontal.

Use color judiciously. For example, color the trend lines or bars on a chart and leave all the rest black.

Avoid montages. Use them only to create an impression or as a summary of previous separate points.

Avoid allowing the character on the screen to talk. Get around this by showing the back of the speaker toward the audience and showing the front view of the listener. The listener's expression indicates a conversation is going on.

(b) Flip Charts.

Flip charts do not have to be fancy. Do it yourself by using felt-tipped markers, crayons, grease pencils, and ruled paper pads. Your audience reception may be greater than if you had prepared a professional chart.

Make the lettering visible, the larger the better.

Use one style of lettering throughout.

Don't use many colors. Most professionals use just one color and black.

Don't use dark colored backgrounds. They make the letters difficult to read.

Use only one major thought per sheet.

Place the lettering in the upper two-thirds of the chart pad. This allows for easy reading in the back of the room.

Leave white space on each side of the wording.

Keep the chart simple.

For distances up to 25', don't go under 1" high letters. For 40' use a minimum of 2" letters, and for 50' use a 3" minimum.

Make the letters bold, not thin.

(c) Slides.

Keep the visuals horizontal. When projected, the bottoms of vertical slides generally get lost on the floor—especially in low-ceiling rooms.

Improve legibility of crowded data by condensing the information to rounded figures and to essential information, or break up the data into several slides.

Complex illustrations and blueprints can be simplified by cutting down on the number and wording of captions, simplifying the drawings, and increasing the line widths.

Make the drawings large, bold, and simple. Outline the picture drawings with heavy lines. Use one style for all slides. Sans-serif is best. Helvetica bold is good for headlines and Helvetica regular for body copy. Do not use more than two type sizes for the set of slides.

For drawings, don't use white lines on a black background. It is difficult for the mind to adjust to this form. Draw the black lines on colored stock, not white as a white background produces a glare. A colored film of plastic can be sandwiched between the slide and its mount to produce a colored effect.

When using color, don't use graduated tones.

Do not draw a frame around the art. The frame is provided by the screen and the mask of the slide.

Always use a dark colored background; do not use a white background, as the resulting glare is too much for the audience. Don't use a blue background for black type; the blue washes out.

Use plain or soft textured backgrounds. Fancy backgrounds compete with the message.

Use informal balance in design and in placement of words as a little slippage in precise balance will be magnified many times on the screen.

Use plenty of border space in your artwork to compensate for differences between the framing as seen through the copy camera viewfinder and lens, and the mounting of the transparency.

Simplify the verbiage on the slides.

Lettering guides, ceramic letters, or rub-on transfer letters can be used to produce a professional lettering job.

Colorful, pleasing results for titles can be achieved by using colored crayon or fluorescent colored chalk on black paper.

As a guide to preparing typewritten copy for 35mm slides, draw a rectangle $2^1/_2'' \times 3^1/_2''$. This amount of pica or elite typewritten copy, when projected on a 72 inch wide screen which can be seen at a distance of 45 feet.

The Eastman Kodak Company, Rochester, N.Y. 14650, has several pamphlets: "Effective Slides" #S-22, "Artwork Size Standards for Projected Visuals" #S-12, and "Photo Information Booklet" #AE-83 (75¢) which contain detailed information on the preparation of slides. Also available is a booklet "Slides with a Purpose."

(d) Overhead Transparencies.

Do not make the lettering less than $^1/_4''$. Use a typewriter with bulletin-size type.

Keep the lettering and art within a $7^1/_2'' \times 9''$ area.

Place color on transparencies for greater impact. Utilize color grease pencils, felt pens, color transparent film, or even a colored foil over the entire transparency.

Try using red for the key word, the others in black.

Now available for overhead projectors is a "lightboard" which consists of a pressure-sensitive film placed directly over a cardboard frame. You talk with your pencil. You erase by simply lifting the film from the cardboard and a clean writing surface is automatically formed.

To highlight a special area, or to stress important points on transparencies, superimpose opaque objects for a silhouette effect.

A series of overlays can be built up over a chart, diagram, or drawing.

(e) Type Faces and Hand Lettering.

Keep to one style of type face or one style of hand lettering; variety detracts from the viewer's attention to the message.

If the copy is more than five or six words, use capitals and lower-case letters.

Use sans-serif typefaces such as Helvetica medium or News Gothic bold. Thin lines on serif typefaces generally burn out in the photography and projection.

Provide a maximum contrast of dark letters on a light background, or a dark background with light letters.

Don't use type which is too small. Here's a way to test: If your art is on a 10″ board, you should be able to read the type easily at six feet. If you are using an 8½″ × 11″ board, the minimum height of the letters should be ¼″.

Plan on using at least the height of a capital letter between lines.

White paper which is used for correcting typewritten errors can be used to type white letters on black or dark-colored paper. Set the electric typewriter on "stencil."

Another method is to use regular typewriting on white paper. Photograph the typing and use the negative for the slide. Color can be added by placing transparent watercolor over the negative or using a transparent colored gelatin. Slides consisting of all copy can be produced quickly in one step by using phototypesetting which sets the type to size. Plan on using 8- or 10-point sizes. The machine supplies positive film which then must be reversed.

Type and objects can be combined by first photographing the objects against a black background, then rewinding the film and shooting the matching headline (which is on a reverse) by placing the headline on a lightbox and photographing it.

(f) How to Prepare the Script.

Just as in planning a complete convention program, when producing a script for a slide presentation, keep in mind the objective of the presentation. Every slide should lead toward the objective.

Write the script first or make an outline. Type the script or outline double-spaced on the right half of the paper. On the left half write the caption which should appear on the slide and indicate what type of art should be used.

(g) How to Make Professional Charts in One Easy Lesson.

Write for the Chartpak catalog from Avery Products Co.—Graphics Division. They have a wide variety of graphic tapes in different colors, patterns, widths, and materials. You just press the tapes into position and trim. They also have Chartpak transfer lettering. The address is 2620 So. Susan St., Santa Ana, Calif. 92704.

(h) Your Copy for Slides Is Placed on Stock Art by this company. Send for their "Slide Idea Library" which consists of 220 slide illustrations on a filmstrip. You project the filmstrip to get an idea of what the art looks like.

Use Visual Presentations Effectively

Then you indicate the copy you wish to appear on the slide, and note the numerous color techniques desired as per samples included in the kit. They can even combine four slides on a single slide, which is applicable for showing sequences. Cost for the 220 slide filmstrip is around $5. Also available in a 35mm slide package is a presentation binder for approximately $55. Available from Visual Horizons, 208 Westfall Rd., Rochester, N.Y. 14620.

(i) **Stock Captioned Slides.**

Visual Horizons also offers 240 captioned slides with art. They have six volumes, each of which contains 40 slides. The volumes sell for around $90 each. Send for their illustrated brochure which lists the captions. Individual slides may be purchased at $3 each.

(j) **Old-Time Movie Still Source.**

This source has a set of 100 old-time movie stills of all types. A set of suggested humorous captions to fit the stills comes with it. Price is $39.50 for the set of 100. Available from Studio Archives, P.O. Box 1041, 3950 Laurel Canyon Blvd., Studio City, Calif. 91604.

(k) **Use an Artist's Manikin.** A manikin may be purchased at almost any art store. Generally they are around 15 inches high and can be adjusted to about any position. Have the manikin hold your various captions; or the manikin can hold a prop, or be placed on top of or alongside a product or model of a product.

Note: See Chapter 11 for additional ideas on preparing and presenting slides, and for additional sources of supply of colorful stock captioned art.

4. COST ESTIMATES OF VISUALS.

Slides and Filmstrips (cost per frame):

Average frame containing art and type preparation	$30–$60
Simple paste-up of literature, ad, etc.	$10–$15
Graph or chart (complicated and many words)	$40–$100
Still photograph of the frame (higher costs are for overhead projection)	$10–$20
Frame of speedball lettering	$15–$30
Hand lettering or typeset	$30–$100
Location Photography per photo	$35–$100

Note: Save money by hiring a photographer by the day or half day instead of by the photo.

Filmstrips with Sound   Approximately $700 to $1,000 per minute

Motion Picture with Sound $1,200 to $3,500 per minute
    (Includes script preparation)
Closed Circuit TV $2,500 to $5,000 per location
Studio Recording Time $35 to $80 per hour
    For sound effects, music or
    voice, or mixture of these

5. HOW TO PROJECT SLIDES AND FILMS TO BEST ADVANTAGE.

(a) Fifteen Projection Tips:
  (1) Select a room which has a ceiling high enough to accommodate the screen.
  (2) Make sure in advance that the room can be darkened. If stray light comes in, place the screen in the darkest part of the room.
  (3) Use a large screen. The larger the screen, the greater the emotional impact. A good rule of thumb is to have the screen size not less than six times the distance to the last row of viewers.
  (4) Have the projection screen high enough so that those in the back can see over the heads of those in front. Five feet, and preferably six feet, from the bottom of the screen to the floor should be the minimum.
  (5) For overhead projectors drop the screen from the ceiling so that the operator does not block the view. Tilt the screen so it is at right angles to the projected beam of light to avoid a "keystone" effect.
  (6) Try to seat the audience so that all viewers are no more than ten degrees from the projection axis. If a beaded screen is used, at an angle of 20 degrees the viewer sees an image only half as bright than the viewer seated at ten degrees.
  (7) For easy placement, number the slides in order in the cartridge.
  (8) Make sure all slides are facing in the right direction. Do this by placing a mark in the lower left corner when viewed correctly.
  (9) Check the hotel to see if a union projectionist is required.
  (10) Test the projection equipment beforehand.
  (11) Make sure that the optical system is clean. A dulling film may have settled on the mirror, lamp envelope, lenses, and other glass surfaces.
  (12) Check the bulb. An old darkened bulb will produce less light, and if a lightweight extension cord is used, it may produce a voltage drop which results in less light.
  (13) Be sure to have a spare bulb!
  (14) Place the loudspeaker near the screen (on a chair or table) for a more realistic effect.

Use Visual Presentations Effectively

(15) Make sure that the projector is not turned off when the room lights are turned off!

(b) Types of Screens:

Beaded Screens

They are best for long, narrow rooms. Beaded screens provide a very bright image within a 10 degree range from the projection beam.

Matte Screens

They diffuse light evenly. All viewers see almost equally bright image, regardless of the viewing angle.

Lenticular Screens

They provide an image about three times brighter than a matte screen. Lenticular screens can be seen within a 70 degree angle.

(c) Choosing the Screen Size.

A good rule of thumb to use is that the most distant viewing point should be no more than six times the screen width.

Audience Capacity	Screen Size
25-50 persons	50" width
50-100	60"
150	84"
350	10'
500-1000	14'

6. HOW SPEAKERS CAN USE VISUAL PRESENTATIONS EFFECTIVELY.

(a) Rehearse Well.

The most essential advice is to rehearse the presentation a number of times. Learn the subject well enough to extemporize. By extemporizing, the confidence of the audience will be gained.

(b) Slides And Verbal Filmstrip Presentations.

Arrange for a special extension cord for the remote control of the changing of slide or film scene by the speaker.

Notify the person who provides the projector of the size and type of slide mounting being used (plastic, ready-mounted, glass, metal) to ensure that the right projector and cartridge holder is provided.

(c) Motion Picture and Sound Filmstrips.

Before beginning the showing of a stock film give the title, the purpose of showing it, and how the group can gain from the screening. Alert the audience to watch for certain teaching points. In most cases it is advisable to discuss the film immediately afterward. Ask specific questions such as "What would you have said to the customer when . . ."

(d) Flip Charts.

Place the charts high enough so the men in the back can see. Place the speaker and easel on an 18" platform if required.

Provide adequate lighting for the charts. Try a spotlight.

Keep the charts covered until ready to use. Use a blank page.

Use blank pages for pauses in between the visuals. Flip over all the charts when through.

Read the material on the chart as it appears. This gives time for the audience to read it also. But don't delay after reading, plunge right into the subject.

After reading a chart, refer your attention back to the audience.

As an assist, you can make notes in light pencil on the flip chart. The audience will not be able to see it.

Cover parts of your flip chart or chalkboard beforehand with paste-overs and rip off to reveal the desired points to be made.

(e) Easel Pads.

When writing on an easel pad or chalkboard, keep one side to the audience, not your back. Talk while writing.

As with flip charts, to remember the points to be made, lightly pencil your notes on the pad. The audience will not see them.

You can amaze the audience with your expert art ability by having the sketch drawn ahead of time by the same light pencil technique.

If the information is to be kept visible, tear off the sheets and tape them to the wall.

(f) Slap Boards.

Practice slapping the cards on the board. Have the cards arranged in the proper order.

Restrict the material to be placed on the board to the major point; one word per card is preferred. Instead of words, endeavor to use a symbol, a blown up simple photograph, or a graph line.

And again, don't turn your back to the audience; have one side facing them.

(g) Chalkboards.

Talk while writing and write rapidly.

Use Visual Presentations Effectively

As a rule, write down the points only as they are discussed. Do not list the points in advance.

For variety, use a different colored chalk for each board panel or for the subject of that board.

Tap the board with the chalk to emphasize a point.

If you have to erase a chalkboard, be sure to ask the audience if all have finished with their notes.

And, as mentioned previously, try to obtain a two-sided chalkboard which can be flipped over. Use the back side for the summary which has been written in advance.

(h) Overhead Projectors.

If a listing of figures or points is shown, a help to understanding is to use an opaque sheet on the transparency and reveal a line at a time. Overlays can be used to add information.

Turn on the overhead projector only when you wish to bring attention to the visual message; turn it off when the attention should go to the speaker.

Use a grease pencil to underline or circle a given item as it is being discussed. Cover the transparency with .005 clear acetate for protection. Clean the transparency with a damp cloth for future use. As with an easel pad, you can write on a blank transparency while the audience is being addressed.

To avoid the jerking of hands or the tendency of hands to shake, steady the hand by touching the transparency with a pointer.

(i) Tape Recorder.

Cue the tape with white splicing tape for easy visibility in a darkened room.

For additional information see the section titled "Dramatic Visual Ideas" in Chapter 11.

7. AUDIO-VISUAL SUPPLIERS.

Art Services for Visuals

MM Production Center
320 E. 52nd St.
New York, N.Y. 10022

Vugraphics
1441 Superior Ave., Suite C
Newport Beach, Calif. 92660

Blackboards—Light Background
   Brilliant colored felt-tip pens are used to mark on these boards which have a nonglare white background. They will also accept magnetic numerals and characters. These boards wipe clean with a damp rag. Available from Eberhard Faber, Crestwood, Wilkes Barre, Pa. 18703.

Chart Carrying and Shipping Cases
   Several sizes from $9.95 to $16.00   Oravisual Co., Inc., Box 11151,
                                         St. Petersburg, Fla. 33733.

Charting Materials

Hundreds of varieties of pressure sensitive and dry transfer products. Tapes, symbols, letters. Chartpak, Incorporated, One River Rd., Leeds, Mass. 01053.

Easels

All types are available, including 45″ × 34″ giants, and writing pads to fit. Also available are felt-tip markers and crayons.

Oravisual Co., Inc.
P.O. Box 11151
St. Petersburg, Fla. 33733

Charles Mayer Studios, Inc.
140 E. Market St.
Akron, Ohio 44308

Film Distributors—Free

Association Films
600 Madison Ave.
New York, N.Y. 10022

Modern Talking Picture Service, Inc.
1212 Ave. of Americas
New York, N.Y. 10036

Radiant Films
220 W. 42 St.
New York, N.Y. 10036

Sterling Movies Inc.
375 Park Ave.
New York, N.Y. 10022

Flannel Boards

Folding flannel boards up to 24″ × 48″ are available from Oravisual Co., Inc., Box 11151, St. Petersburg, Fla. 33733.

Hook N' Loop® & Velcro Boards and Supplies

Charles Mayer Studios, Inc.
781 Commins St.
Akron, Ohio 44308

Radiant Manufacturing Company
8230 N. Austin Ave.
Morton Grove, Ill.

Oravisual Company, Inc.
P.O. Box 11151
St. Petersburg, Fla. 33733

Lettering Supplies for Flip Charts

Over 5,300 colorful large, medium, and small lightweight cardboard letters with adhesive for use on charts and signs, including mounting steps, are available. Cost is approximately $30.00

The Holes-Webway Company
St. Cloud, Minn. 56301

Box of 1000 1½″ gummed letters; Oravisual Company Inc.

Dry Transfer Letters for Slide Titles

Arthur Brown & Bro., Inc.
2 W. 46th St.
New York, N.Y. 10036

Prestype, Inc.
Gotham Industrial Park
194 Veteran Blvd.
Carlstadt, N.J. 07072

Use Visual Presentations Effectively

Three-Dimension Letters

Hernard Manufacturing Co.
21 Sawmill River Rd.
Yonkers, N.Y. 10701

Mitten Display Letters
39 West 60th St.
New York, N.Y. 10023

Multi-Media Presentations

Melandrea, Inc. (Spotlight Technique)
17 East 48th St.
New York, N.Y. 10017

Charisma Productions
135-09 Northern Blvd.
Flushing, N.Y.

Overhead Projection Materials Kit

This kit contains all the tools needed to make your own overhead projections. The easy-to-use materials can be applied directly to acetate. There are projectable colors, patterns, printed frames, etc. Cost is approximately $50. Ask for the Chartpak Vim kit at art supplies or drafting supplies stores, or send for literature to:

Chartpak, Inc.
One River Rd.
Leeds, Mass. 01053

Materials for Producing Overhead Transparencies:

Visual Products Division
3M Center
St. Paul, Minn. 55101

Agfa-Gevaert
275 North St.
Teterboro, N.J.

Planning Boards (for A/V)

Aquabee TV Pad #9007, approximately $5.
Michael's Artists & Engineering Supplies, Inc.
7085 Tujunga
North Hollywood, Calif. 91605

Projection Equipment—All Types

Look in *The Audio-Visual Equipment Directory* for listing of over 2000 models of audio-visual equipment. It contains specifications, prices and audio visual manufacturers and dealers. The cost is $8.50. Order from National Audio-Visual Association, Inc., 3150 Spring Street, Fairfax, Va. 22030.

Slide Mounts

Press-O plastic slide mounts are available from Kaiser Products, P.O. Box 3101, Colorado Springs, Colo.

Slide Photography Equipment

The Kodak Visual Maker costs approximately $115 and consists of a Kodak Instamatic, 304 Camera, 8″ × 8″ and 3″ × 3″ copy-stands, and instructions. It makes colored slides from charts, graphs, and three-dimensional objects. No focus or exposure adjustments are required. You can use flash cubes. It can be used as regular camera, too. See your Kodak dealer.

Slides—Custom

Custom slides are produced via mail order at around $13.00 each for slides of charts and graphs, symbols, people, words, backgrounds, or incorporating your printed materials.

The Slide Innovators
2020 San Carlos Blvd.
Fort Myers Beach, Fla. 33931

Cinegraph Slides, Inc.
2675 Skypark Dr.
Torrance, Calif. 90505

Rik Shaw Associates, Ltd.
150 W. 57th St.
New York, N.Y. 10019

Slide—Hot Press Titles

Hot Press Company
2 West 46th St.
New York, N.Y. 10036

Knight Title Service
145 West 45th St.
New York, N.Y. 10036

For additional sources of supply look in the "MEETING SUPPLIES AND SALES PROMOTION BUYER'S GUIDE" under the following headings:

Art Services for Visuals
Blackboards
Chart Carrying Cases/Shipping Cases
Easels
Flannel Boards
Hook N' Loop® & Velcro Boards
   & Supplies
Lettering Supplies—Flip Charts
Letter Supplies—Dry Transfer
   for Slide Titles
Lettering Machines & Devices
Lettering Supplies—Three Dimensional

Planning Boards (for A/V Stories)
Screens
Sound Effects
Projectors—Overhead & Filmstrip
Slide Mounts

Slide—Stock
Stock Shots—Film

Slides—Hot Press Titles
Toning Materials

Chapter 14

How to Enliven the Conference Printed Program

Contents

1. Use Already-Printed Stock Pages
2. Translate the Theme into Foreign Languages
3. Use Cartoons
4. Conference Theme or Company Symbol Drawing
5. Use Art Dealing with the Meeting Theme
6. Acronyms
7. Old-Time Movie Photos
8. Pocket Secretaries Containing Program
9. Specialize in Confucius Sayings
10. Calendar/Planner
11. Speaker Biographies and Photos
12. Place Proverbs and Eipgrams Throughout the Program

The following gives a number of methods by which the printed program can be enlivened.

1. USE ALREADY-PRINTED STOCK PAGES. Use blank pages furnished by the local convention bureau, the chamber of commerce, the hotel or resort, or by the Airlines. Many of these blank programs are in color.

2. TRANSLATE THE THEME INTO FOREIGN LANGUAGES and place the English version last. Example:
Nada sucede mientras no se realice una venta.
Rien n'est fait tant que la venta n'est pas faite.
Nada acontece ate que alguma coisa seja vendida.
De werelde staat stil tot iemand iets verkoopt.
Es geschieht erst dan etwas, wenn verhauft wurde.
Nulla accade fintanto che qualcuno ha venduto qualche costa.
Nothing happens until somebody sells something.

3. USE CARTOONS. Start making a collection of cartoons dealing with your profession. Place these in the printed program and, of course, request permission of the publisher to use them.

4. CONFERENCE THEME OR COMPANY SYMBOL DRAWING. Have cartoons drawn utilizing the conference theme, company symbol, or a mythical participant. Example: If your theme symbol is a tiger, the animal can be depicted as a salesman with a briefcase, wheelbarrowing a load of cash, carrying the product, going into a dealership, signing an order, sitting at the conference table, playing golf, etc. You may prefer to purchase a character type of doll or sets of dolls and photograph them in various positions and with various props. Use captions underneath or draw the words the character is saying similar to the way it is done in the comic strips and insert that drawing into the scene being photographed.

How to Enliven the Conference Printed Program   169

5. USE ART DEALING WITH THE MEETING THEME such as western, gold mining, vacationing, etc. Excellent clipbooks containing hundreds of drawings ready for your use are available from:

Harry Volk, Jr. Art Studios
Pleasantville, N.J. 08232

Redi Art, Inc.
30 East 10th St.
New York, N.Y. 10003

American Marketing Services, Inc.
610 Newbury St.
Boston, Mass.

6. ACRONYMS. If your meeting theme is a single word, construct phrases utilizing each letter in the word. For example, if the theme is "How," use phrases such as:

> House Orders Win
> Help Organize Windfalls
> Hear Our Wonders

7. OLD-TIME MOVIE PHOTOS make great program illustrations. Use humorous captions tying in with your organization. They can be used for invitations, announcements, etc. Several sources are:

Studio Archives	American Stock Photos
P.O. Box 1041	6842 W. Sunset
3950 Laurel Canyon Blvd.	Hollywood, Calif. 90028
Studio City, Calif. 91604	
W. H. Everett	Granger Collection
Buck Hill Rd.	37 W. 39th St.
Ridgefield, Conn.	New York, N.Y. 10018

(He has old-time movie photos with gag captions suitable for sales meetings.)

Old-time movie picture books may be purchased at larger book stores. Your printer can enlarge or reduce the photos. Permission of the book publishers should be obtained.

8. POCKET SECRETARIES CONTAINING PROGRAM. These coat pocket cases are available either in real leather or plastic and usually contain a memo pad. Insert the printed program in with the memo pad. Check your local advertising specialties salesperson, or stationery or department store.

9. **SPECIALIZE IN CONFUCIUS SAYINGS** on each program page, such as:

    Confucius Say: "Don't strive for lighter burdens, but for strong back."

    Confucius Say: "For each man with heroism, ten have ignition trouble."

    Confucius Say: "They fail, and they alone, who have not striven."

    Confucius Say: "Nine tenths of wisdom is being wise in time."

    Confucius Say: "The road to success is always the one under construction."

    Confucius Say: "Facing tomorrow with the method of yesterday brings stagnation."

    Confucius Say: "Men who talk like big wheels are usually spoke-men."

    Confucius Say: "Worry grows lushly in the soil of indecision."

10. **CALENDAR/PLANNER.** If yours is a convention where meeting attendance is optional or there is a choice of meetings to attend, think about producing a calendar/planner. This can be a portion of the printed program or a part of the preconvention packet. Divide the days into hourly blocks and further divide these blocks into quarter hours. The meetings can be listed in these blocks. If there are exhibits, indicate the exhibit hours by shading the blocks. If feasible, provide enough blank space in the blocks for commitment notes.

11. **SPEAKER BIOGRAPHIES AND PHOTOS.** If a long biography is received from the speaker, edit it down to include only the copy relevant to the meeting. If photos are not received from all speakers, place all of the available photos in one group and the biographical copy on another page, thus the missing photos do not become obvious.

12. **PLACE PROVERBS AND EPIGRAMS THROUGHOUT THE PROGRAM.** Consult books of quotations and epigrams at the library. Here are some typical quotations:

The great end of life is not merely knowledge but ACTION.—Huxley

Not what we think we are; but "what we think," we are.

All work and no play makes jack.

Men learn while they teach.—Seneca

A quitter never wins, a winner never quits.

That man is most original who is able to adapt from others.

Great difficulties are the making of great salesmen.

No problem that we face is ever as big as the one we dodge.

Lost time is never found again.

All things come to him who waits, if he works while waiting.

How to Enliven the Conference Printed Program

Knowledge is Power.—Bacon

Try to see yourself as others see you.

The best things are the most difficult.

Nothing was ever achieved without enthusiasm.—Emerson

Everything comes to him who hustles while he waits.

He didn't know it couldn't be done, so he did it.

Truth is always the strongest argument.

To hold interest, ask intelligent questions.

One becomes what he thinks.

You are as old as you think.

The average person rarely uses more than 10% of his potential.—William James

Many a lost sale has been saved by a final try.

It's not what you get, but what you give that counts.

Quality has everything in its favor—including the price.

An ounce of fact is worth a ton of conversation.

Get the customer's viewpoint and you'll get the order.

Big things are not asked of small people.

Never promise more than you can deliver.

No one knows what he can do until he tries.

Objections are requests for more information.

Stop in time to let the buyer sell himself.

A man rarely succeeds at anything unless he has fun doing it.

There's nothing like a little experience to upset a theory.

The reason some people don't recognize opportunity is because it usually comes disguised as hard work.

An expert is someone who is called in at the last moment to share the blame.

Your best advertisement is a tough job well done.

Defeat is but education.

Life is what we make it, always has been, always will be.—Anna Mary Moses

God will not look you over for medals, degrees, or diplomas—but for scars.—Elbert Hubbard

Initiative is doing the right thing without being told.

People can be divided into three groups: those who make things happen, those who watch things happen, and those who wonder what happened.

A smile is the shortest distance between two people.—Victor Borge

Initiative is important, but finishiative is vital.

Man's greatest weakness comes from work not done.

How fast you are going isn't as important as where you are heading.

The road to success is always under construction.

The only thing worse than a quitter is a man who is afraid to begin.

The ladder of life is full of splinters, but they always prick the hardest when we are sliding down.

If you cannot win, make the one ahead of you break the record.

Lack of will power and drive causes more failures than lack of intelligence and ability.

Enthusiasm is knowledge on fire.

Enthusiasm is catching.

Behold the turtle. He makes progress only when he sticks his neck out.

He who whispers down a well
About the things he has to sell
Will not make the shining dollars
Like he who climbs a tree and hollers!

Don't make excuses—make good.—Elbert Hubbard

The rule for every worthwhile man is that no serious job ever shall receive less than his best thought and effort.

Success isn't the result of spontaneous combustion. You must set yourself on fire.

Sears made a fortune with a catalog. Are you using yours?

Dear Lord; I'll row, you steer.

The Chinese ideograph for crisis is two symbols—danger and opportunity.

When a ship misses the harbor, it is seldom the fault of the harbor.

If a man is happy in his work—exerting himself to the full extent of his limitations and capabilities, and enjoying it . . . he is a success.

When the going gets tough, the tough get going.

There is a tide in the affairs of men, which, taken at the flood, leads on to fortune.

No one ever lost an order because quality was too high or service too good.

The impossible is often the untried.

No matter how busy people are, they are never too busy to stop and talk about how busy they are.

If you want a few minutes to yourself, alone and undisturbed—do the dishes.

The only people who listen to both sides of an argument are the neighbors.

Keep smiling. It makes everyone wonder what you've been up to.

The beginnings of all things are small.—Cicero

One percent of the people make things happen . . . nine percent watch things happen and 90 percent ask, "What happened?" and then gripe when they find out.

You are getting old when your back goes out more often than you do.

If at first you don't succeed, you'll get a lot of unsolicited advice.

Changing one thing for the better does more good than proving a dozen things wrong.

Chapter 15

Sales Conference Icebreaker and Welcome Ideas

Contents

1. Advance Registration Promotion
2. "Welcome" Ideas
3. How to Handle the Conference Registration Desk
4. Badge Ideas
5. Hotel Room "Welcome" Ideas
6. Icebreaking Ways to Introduce Guests to Each Other
7. More "Welcome" Ideas
8. "Goodbye" Ideas
9. Briefcases, Folios, Clipboard Sources
10. "Welcome" Gifts
11. Giveaways

1. ADVANCE REGISTRATION PROMOTION.

(a) Advance Registration eliminates the bottleneck at the registration desk and the waits in long lines which make for a poor conference start. Advance registration also enables more accurate advance planning for facilities and the attendant economies of better planning.

Some associations just use the "Beat the Crowd" lure. Others promote advance registration by offering:
1. A registration fee discount (An "Early Bird Bonus").
2. Prizes for preregistrants by means of a drawing at the event.
3. A discounted social function package for preregistrants.
4. Prize drawings for check with order.

(b) Make It Easy to Secure an Attendance Commitment by offering the opportunity on the initial registration form to just say "Yes, I will attend," and a square to be checked which says check enclosed. A later mailing would contain the longer form on hotel requirements, sessions to attend, etc. Schedule the initial mailing four to eight weeks before the event.

(c) Selling the Conference. For meetings where attendance is voluntary don't forget that the prospective attendee may be receiving invitations from a number of different companies or organizations. Also, he is losing productive time away from business and is incurring a large expense. So keep in mind that a selling job must be done. Emphasize the program subjects that deal with solutions to his problems and those that offer opportunities. Play up the caliber of the speakers. Go over the announcement copy with a selling attitude in mind. Include all the necessary information, but keep it short, as you are competing for a busy person's available reading time.

2. "WELCOME" IDEAS.

(a) Luggage Tags. To help expedite the handling of group baggage at the

Sales Conference Icebreaker and Welcome Ideas 175

airport and hotel, send identifying baggage tags and identification badges in advance. These are often available from the hotel, or print the tags yourself. Ask attendees to wear their badges as a means of identification. Imprinted plastic "Economy Tags" for the luggage are available from Glass Industries Co., 1133 Broadway, New York, N.Y. 10010; Hewig & Marvic, 861 Manhattan Ave., Brooklyn, N.Y. 11221; Namemaker Corp., 52 Broadway, Greenlawn, N.Y. 11740; Airways Industries Corp., Airway Park, W. Pittsburgh, Pa. 16160; Art Mold Products, 780 Wellington Ave., Cranston, R.I. 02910.

(b) **Lobby Sign.** Place a "Welcome" placard sign on an easel in the hotel lobby or outside the meeting room entrance.

(c) **Marquee Welcome Banner.** Make a banner and string it across the hotel marquee. Later utilize it in the convention hall.

(d) **Airport Signs.** Be on the lookout for changeable signs at the airport and along the route to the conference site. These are like the signs used to advertise the program at theaters. Employ these for a "Welcome" to your delegates.

(e) **Have Greeters and Hosts on Hand** to extend a warm welcome. "Host" and "Hostess" ribbons are obtainable from trophy shops. These ribbons, as well as "Usher" and "Reception" ribbons, and stock 3″ buttons, are available from Jack-Bilt Corp., 906 Central St., Kansas City, Mo. 64105 and Waldreth Label Corp., 1261 Blue Hill Ave., Boston, Mass. 02126.

(f) **Models or Bunnies.** If you want to make a real hit with the male guests, hire models to serve as hostesses. Bunnies from Playboy clubs are often available in the larger cities. Have someone point out an individual to be greeted effusively with a kiss as a "longtime friend."

(g) **Place the Meeting Theme on the Hotel Marquee** or anywhere else near the entrance.

(h) **Have the Doorman Wear a Large Button with Your Convention Theme.** The bellboys and registration clerks can wear these, too.

(i) **Identify the Convention Staff Members, Who Direct the Operations, with Distinctive Caps or Coats.**

(j) **To Facilitate Quick Registration.** If the attendees travel by chartered bus from the airport to the hotel, obtain a list of arrivals as they enter the bus (perhaps use a quick check-off list) and telephone these names ahead to the hotel for speedy registration.

(k) Provide Adhesive Strips with Room Number for the Luggage. These are blank self-adhesive strips. The strips are placed outside the "Welcome Packet" that is given to each person as he registers. The room number is written on the strip. The delegate then places the strip on his luggage, which has been lined up after it is taken from the bus. Guests can then walk directly to their rooms without waiting for a bellhop; the room key has been included with the "Welcome Packet." The adhesive strips are available from stationery stores.

(l) Giant Balloon Atop Resort. A 12' × 5' balloon may be obtained from William J. Small Agency, Inc., 1318 Beacon St., Brookline, Mass. 02146. Paint the convention theme on it. Also try Edmund Scientific Co., 380 Edscorp. Blvd., Barrington, N.J. 08007, or American Science Center, 5700 Northway Highway, Chicago, Ill. 60640, and Pratt Poster Co., Inc., 3001 East 30th St., Indianapolis, Ind. 46218.

(m) Thirteen by 4-½ Foot Balloon with Two Side Banners and Two Tether Pennants. It will carry your message aloft to altitudes up to 200 feet. Order from Ad-Aloft Division, ILC Dover, P.O. Box 266, Frederica, Del. 19946.

3. HOW TO HANDLE THE CONFERENCE REGISTRATION DESK.

(a) Appoint a Registration Official to ensure that everything goes smoothly. Have a company or organization staff man at the registration desk to answer questions. Identify him or her prominently with a badge with the word "Registration" on it.

(b) Greet Each Person as he registers or enters the meeting room.

(c) Serve Coffee Near the Registration Area or entrance to the meeting room. Call it a "Welcome Corner." Shut off the supply well in advance of the session. It's a place for old friends to meet and a convenient spot to make new friends.

(d) Alphabetize the Badges as they are laid out. If it is a large group, use several tables with a section of the alphabet assigned to each. Consider attaching the badges to thin strips of cardboards to keep badges from getting out of order.

(e) Set Up Separate Desks for convention registration and for ticket sales.

Sales Conference Icebreaker and Welcome Ideas 177

Have a separate desk also for registration for recreation events. Separate desks enable the cashiers to keep more accurate records and facilitates cash balancing.

(f) Round Out the Prices charged for the various functions. This saves considerable time in making change and helps ensure accuracy.

(g) Use a Transparent Window Envelope for the registration materials and have the badge showing in the window. The envelopes are then filed alphabetically.

(h) New Ribbons for Badge Typewriters. The usual convention badge often has the typed name in a dull gray and is hard to read. Be sure to use new well-inked ribbons.

(i) Materials for the Registration Desk.

Member Badges	Cash Box
Ribbons (Host, Committee, etc.)	Scissors
Ballpoint Pens	Some Safety Pins
Pencils	Rubber Bands
Paper Clips	Stapler
Scotch Tape	Heavy Twine
Traveler Sewing Kit	Box for Checks
Guest Badge Holder	Large Manila Envelopes
Jumbo Typewriter	Message Pads
Masking Tape	Band-Aids
Counter Signs as Required	Blank Badges

(j) First Aid for Identification Ribbons. "Host," etc. ribbons which are pinned on can be converted to "Press-On" badges by attaching two-sided masking tape. If two-sided tape is not available, attach one-sided masking tape and give it a twist.

(k) Receipts Timesaver. Combine the receipt and registration into one card. Do this by using a numbered perforated combination registration card and receipt stub. (The receipt numbers appears on both the card and stub.) All the cashier has to do is to fill in the dollar amount and her initials.

(l) Convention Packet. You can be sure that many attendees will have left at home much of the information which has been mailed to them. So repeat the essential items in the convention package that is handed out at registration. The packet includes a welcome message, things to do and see, where to go, where to purchase tickets for meals and other functions, banquet location and time, etc.

(m) Roster of Attendees. In the welcome kit, provide a roster of attendees, giving company name, title, and address. This is easier than exchanging business cards.

(n) Room List. A room list is appreciated by your guests. If your conference is at a resort, enclose a map of the buildings and grounds for ease in locating the rooms.

(o) Hotel Location Map. If delegates are in a number of different hotels, furnish a simple map showing the location of the hotels, event sites, and main points of interest. It is helpful in contacting friends. List the addresses and hotel telephone numbers. Show the bus routes, too.

(p) For Fast Service. Have the persons in your organization who are responsible for hotel arrangements wear special buttons so that hotel personnel may recognize them throughout the duration of the conference, for the providing of special attention.

(q) Message Sign Set. For less than the price of a sign made to order, you can purchase this "Message Master Sign Set." Snap-in plastic letters are placed in a plastic signboard which has five channels. Panel is size 15″ × 27″. Set of two signboards with 100 letters is around $25.00. Available from Crestline Co. Inc., 18 West 18th St., New York, N.Y. 10011.

(r) Hire Airline Hostesses to act as greeters, to man the registration desk, to change signs on the stage, and to act as hostesses at the cocktail parites.

(s) Airline Hostess Source. The agency name is Hospitality Services, Inc. and it has branches located in a number of large cities. Here are two: 246 E. 44th St., New York, N.Y. and 1000 Lake Shore Dr., Chicago, Ill. 60611.

(t) Looking for an Information Booth? This colorful lightweight booth is three feet square and may be quickly converted into an eight-foot table top display. Brilliant colored Veltac fabric and self-adhesive hook tape provide excellent shear strength for hanging product samples. The booth weighs only 85 pounds. They are available from American Display Co., 14918 Minnetonka Blvd., Minnetonka, Minn. 55343.

(u) Walkie-Talkies for locating staff members or receiving messages are a big asset at larger conventions. There are types where you communicate directly, and types where the sender transmits a signal which activates the receiver carried by a selected person—the beeping tone at the receiving end is the signal to call the switchboard operator for his message. All types can be obtained from radio supply storcs.

Registration Checklist. See Chapter 22.

4. BADGE IDEAS.

(a) Badge Hints.
1. Imprinting: Use large typewriter type (a ¼″ bulletin-size typewriter), or use a fiber-tip marking pen.
2. Identify different types of attendees by using different color badge insert stock.
3. For special groups, such as host, guest committee, or press, imprinted ribbons may be purchased from trophy companies. The badge is placed at the top of the ribbon.
Custom Imprinted Copy: Keep it brief. The company logo or organization emblem and the group's name are generally all that is required. Add meeting place and meeting date only if absolutely required.

(b) Leave Plenty of Room for the Individual's Full Name (and city and state, if applicable). Use the first name by which the registrant prefers to be called. For a married woman, use her first name (not Mrs.), followed by her husband's last name, such as Janice Jones.

(c) To Avoid Slighting Anyone, be sure the badges of the on-site registrants and advance registrants are the same style.

(d) Badge Styles. The two most popular badges are a clear acetate with a pin on the back ("Pin back") and "pocket fit." The pocket type enables a program to be placed in it. There are also window buttons consisting of a circular metal or plastic badge with a paper insert, and there are self-adhesive stick-on badges with a mat finish for writing ease.

(e) Ordering. A good practice is to order 10 to 20% extra over the estimated attendance. Be sure to order about 25% extra of the insert cards to take care of writing or typing errors.

(f) Order Early. It takes time to print badge inserts. Allow at least six to ten weeks. This avoids last-minute misunderstandings, and gives time for shipment, lettering, and shipment to the site.

(g) Always Order the Badges and Inserts from the Same Supplier; otherwise they may not match.

(h) Place a Number on Each Badge or use different colored badge paper (or both) to designate to which discussion group or team and subgroup the participant belongs. Session leaders can then tell instantly if the person is in the right group.

(i) State Identification Badges. Colorful state flags are available from postage stamp dealers. These are approximately 1″ square. Paste these on the identification badges. The same type of flags are available for the countries of the world. These can be ordered directly from H. E. Harris & Co., Boston, Mass. 02117. Cost is approximately 25¢ for one set of all the state flags.

(j) "World's Greatest Salesman." Place this caption on the identification badges. For distributors or factory reps attending, use the caption "World's Greatest Distributor," etc. For staff members, use "World's Greatest Backer Upper." For further identification, utilize different colored stock for each classification.

(k) Combination Badge. If there are both men and women attending the function, consider using an all-purpose type of badge. Print your own 2¼″ × 3½″ badge on the "sticky-back" type of stock which has a peel-off backing. Various size sheets are available from printing suppliers. The paper has slits on the backing at various intervals to allow for easy peeling. Print your company logo and any other information on the badge. Obtain both regular and clear plastic pin-on badge holders and the pocket slip-in type. The guests then have a choice of sticking the badge on, pinning it, or slipping it in the coat or shirt pocket.

There is a company which manufactures a badge consisting of a standard pin-on badge mounted on a cardboard pocket slide. The cardboard slide can be removed and the badge pinned on when a pocket is not available. The pocket slide can be printed on both sides with program information. Price for 1,000, including printing, is approximately $175. Ask for the Adco Convention Kit. Available from Directions Unlimited, Inc., P.O. Box 1927, Fairview Heights, Ill. 62208.

Another supplier is Crestline Co., Inc. They have a number of different styles of combination badges and are located at 18 W. 18th St., New York, N.Y. 10018.

(l) Photo Badge and Button-Making Machine makes sales meeting and party introducers, and doubles for the making of I.D. badges and promotional badges. It makes 2⅜″ diameter badges in a minute or two. Badge parts cost about 15¢ each. You can make badges out of photos, magazine cutouts, or drawings. Parts for 25 badges are about $30, with the machine. Extra badge parts to make 100 badges are $13.50. Available from American Science Center, 5700 Northwest Highway, Chicago, Ill. 66646, or Badge-A-Minit, 1820 N. Sterling St., LaSalle, Ill. 61301, or from R.P.M. Associates Ltd., 1820 Sterling St., LaSalle, Ill. 61301.

Sales Conference Icebreaker and Welcome Ideas

(m) Pressure Sensitive Meeting, Party, and Convention Badges. No pins are needed. Just peel off the protective backing and press on. Size 2″ × 3¼″. They can be printed with "Hello! My name is _____," and "Guest." Cost is from 2¢ to 4¢ each. Order from Rueby Process, Inc., 1257 University Ave., Rochester, N.Y. 14607, or Jack-Bilt Corp., 906 Central St., Kansas City, Mo. 64105. Other suppliers are Allen Hollander Co., Inc., 385 Gerard Ave., Bronx, N.Y. 10451, and Crestline Co., Inc. 18 W. 18th St., New York, N.Y. 10018.

(n) Looking for Badge Ribbons with Committee Titles Printed On? There are several companies who manufacture ribbons saying "Host," "Welcome Committee," "Vice President," etc. The regular badge may be placed on one end. Oleet & Co., Inc., 60 Claremont Pl., Mount Vernon, N.Y. 10533 has over 500 different titles in stock! Other sources are: Waldroth Label Corp., 1261 Blue Hill Ave., Boston, Mass. 02126; Jack-Bilt Corp., 906 Central St., Kansas City, Mo. 64105; Rueby Process, Inc., 1257 University Ave., Rochester, N.Y. 14607; Hewig & Marvic, 861 Manhattan Ave., Brooklyn, N.Y. 11222, and Crestline Co., Inc., 18 W. 18th St., New York, N.Y. 10018.

(o) BADGE SUPPLIERS

Seton Name Plate Corp.
592 Boulevard
New Haven, Conn. 06505

C-Line Products, Inc.
1530 E. Birchwood Ave.
Des Plaines, Ill. 60018

Hewig & Marvic
861 Manhattan Ave.
Brooklyn, N.Y. 11222

Jack-Bilt Corp.
906 Central St.
Kansas City, Mo 64105

Oleet & Co., Inc.
60 Claremont Pl.
Mount Vernon, N.Y. 10553

Directions Unlimited, Inc.
Box 1927
Fairview Heights, Ill. 62208

Badges & Labels Corp.
1295 Blue Hill Ave.
Boston, Mass. 02126

Rueby Process, Inc.
127 University Ave.
Rochester, N.Y. 14607

A. Dean Watkins Co.
1209 E. Saginaw
Lansing, Mich. 48903

Elgin School Supply Co.
1007 Solano St.
Sacramento, Calif. 96012

Benply Badges
480 Canal St.
New York, N.Y. 10013

Crestline Co., Inc.
18 W. 18th St.
New York, N.Y. 10018

5. HOTEL ROOM "WELCOME" IDEAS.

(a) Welcome Basket. Place a "Welcome basket" in each room. This can contain small bottles of premixed drinks or wine, cocktail glasses, and assorted cheeses and crackers. Hotels will have suggestions such as adding fruit, etc. Include a "Welcome" card—if possible have the host sign the card.

(b) Drinks on the House. Consider including in each delegate's kit a coupon good for two drinks at the hotel bar. See if the same arrangements can be made with various restaurants or nightclubs for a free drink.

(c) An Unusual Welcome Gimmick. At one convention, a sales manager taped the theme of the meeting on the underside of the toilet lids. Another had helium-filled balloons imprinted with the meeting theme. These were placed in the toilets and the lids then closed.

(d) Handshake Photo. Place in each room a photo of the sales manager extending a handshake. Include a message such as "Glad to see you" or "Welcome to the Conference."

(e) Disposable Pillowcases. Many hotel supply companies stock disposable pillowcases. Imprint these with the word "welcome" and the meeting theme.

(f) Banquet Invitation. Having a banquet? If so, print a special invitation and have the hotel deliver it to the room the day before.

(g) Imprint Invitations on a Balloon. This firm can do it. They have imprinted balloons with restaurant menus and pictures of products—which gives an idea of what can be printed on a balloon. Contact Anderson Rubber Co., P.O. Box 170, Akron, Ohio 44309.

(h) Orchids from Hawaii. Provide corsages for the ladies—either as they check into their rooms, or for the banquet. Small orchids with a plastic lapel pin vial are available from Flowers of Hawaii, 670 S. Lafayette Park Pl., Los Angeles, Calif. 90057. They are inexpensive.

(i) Compressed Sponges. When wet they swell to 16 times the original size. Your message imprinted on various shapes and sizes, such as $100 bills, foot sponges, stop signs, fruit sponges, coin sponges, etc. Available from Sponge Specialties Mfg. Corp., 510 Ocean Ave., East Rockaway, N.Y. 11518.

6. ICEBREAKING WAYS TO INTRODUCE GUESTS TO EACH OTHER.

(a) Place a Letter of the Alphabet on Each Badge. The guests form into groups using the letters to spell the company or association name. Prizes or drinks are given to the first groups formed.

Sales Conference Icebreaker and Welcome Ideas 183

(b) To Get to Know Each Other. Announce that several individuals have been selected as the bearer of gifts. The tenth (or any other number) individual who shakes the mystery person's hand and introduces himself receives a prize. Perhaps sound a gong each time a prize is given. A prize could be chits good at the hotel bar.

(c) Place Signs of the Zodiac on the Badges. The guests select the appropriate badge to match their birthdate. This will be a conversation starter.

7. MORE "WELCOME" IDEAS.

(a) Furnish a Map of the Downtown Area as an aid in locating the chief entertainment spots in relation to the conference location. Check the local chamber of commerce for assistance in finding such a map.

(b) Prepare a Dining Guide to Restaurants. If possible, investigate these yourself, or obtain the opinions of several persons on the merits of a particular restaurant. Ask the restaurant if, in return for their listing, they will offer a free drink or special dessert. Your guests identify themselves to the restaurant by presenting a card.

(c) Convention Publication. Print your own 8½" × 11" newspaper in advance. Make up a simple masthead, set the bold headlines in type, and use typewriter type for the smaller headlines and body copy. The paper can feature stories of the program events of the day, entertainment schedule, personality stories, transportation announcements, product stories, gag headlines, etc. Have the hotel deliver the papers to the rooms.

(d) Local Newspaper with Your Headlines. Get in touch with the local newspaper concerning the possibility of printing copies with a headline pertaining to your convention and including a lead story. The cost is often surprisingly small. This company will provide stock newspapers with your headlines: Headline Printers, P.O. Box 1114, Billings, Mont. 59103.

(e) Identifying Photos of Guests. Take Polaroid photos of all attendees and place them on a bulletin board along with identifying names. You also are giving a bonus, as people love to see themselves.

(f) Slides of Attendees. Take Polaroid slides of the attendees during the conference and show at the final banquet, or use as a means of opening the conference. The slides can be ready for showing within a few minutes. Check your camera store for information.

(g) Speculative Photographer. Many resorts and hotel have photographers on call who will take photographs at no direct cost to your company. They take shots on a speculative basis, post them on a bulletin board, and make them available to the guests at $2 to $3 each.

(h) Bus Entertainment Ideas. If the meeting is at your plant or held at a meeting site away from the hotel, hire a bus for transportation. Use the bus public address system for spot announcements. Serve coffee or cokes en route.

(i) Governmental Welcome Speakers. It's surprising what a store of high-level speakers are available for a short "welcome" to the conference. Write the public relations department of the city and state. You may obtain a mayor or even a governor.

(j) Identification Signs. Don't forget to have ample signs for identifying the meeting rooms. In checking out the hotel, determine the number of "arrow signs" required for directing traffic through the corridors to the meeting rooms.

(k) Daily Instructions Via Cassettes. If the budget permits, provide a tape cassette player for each attendee. When the bellboy shows the attendees to their room, the bellboy switches on the cassette player. It gives instructions about the evening's and the coming day's events, what to wear, the locations, what to bring, and of course, words of welcome. The tapes can be personalized for the occupants of each room. When the convention ends, the attendees take the tapes and player home as a souvenir. Have fun and tape the format in a "Mission Impossible" vein.

8. "GOODBYE" IDEAS.

(a) Goodbye Committee. Have the host say "goodbye and drive safely" at the end of the final banquet. Appoint a committee to help with the checking out. Have prominent company or association officials at the door to say "goodbye."

(b) Post-Convention Booklet. Consider making a souvenir booklet of the convention. It should consist mainly of photographs. Include speakers, workshop session, informal banquet shots, and dance and recreation shots with appropriate captions.

9. BRIEFCASES, FOLIOS, CLIPBOARD SOURCES.

(a) Briefcases. An imprinted plastic briefcase can be utilized as a container for the delegate's convention material. Order these imprinted with your company name and convention slogan. Personalize by writing the attendee's name on the case by means of gold foil obtainable from most stationery stores. For briefcases, see your local advertising specialty salesman, or Glass Industries Co., 1133 Broadway, New York, N.Y. 10010. Other suppliers are American Thermoplastic Company, 622 Second Ave., Pittsburgh, Pa. 15219, Hewig & Marvic, 861 Manhattan Ave., Brooklyn, N.Y. 11222, and S.I. Jacobson Mfg. Co., 1414 So. Wabash Ave., Chicago, Ill. 60605. Cost is approximately $2 to 3 each.

(b) **Folios, Binders, Memo Pads.** A good source is a company especially attuned to convention needs of these items. One company is Crestline Co., Inc., 18 W. 18th St., New York, N.Y. 10018. Another good source is American Thermoplastic Co., 622 Second Ave., Pittsburgh, Pa. 15219, or American Meeting Supply, Lock Box 4037, North Hollywood, Ca. 91607.

(c) **Clipboards.** An appreciated extra is a clipboard for note taking at the meeting and as a gift to take home. Many have an extra pocket and generally include a pad of paper. From Hewig & Marvic, 861 Manhattan Ave., Brooklyn, N.Y. 11222. Other suppliers are Crestline Co., Inc., 18 W. 18th St., New York, N.Y. 10018, Baldwin-Cooke Co., 5714 Dempster St., Morton Grove, Ill. 60053, and American Thermoplastic Co., 622 Second Ave., Pittsburgh, Pa. 15219.

(d) **Pocket Secretaries Containing Program.** These coat-pocket cases are available either in real leather or plastic and usually contain a memo pad. Insert the printed program in with the memo pad. Check your local advertising specialties salesman, or stationery or department store.

(e) **Plastic Shopping Bags and Tote Bags** are welcomed by attendees where exhibits are held in conjunction with the meeting. There are drawstring bags, tote bags, and handle bags in all colors and designs. Available from KCL Corporation, Shelbyville, Ind. 46176; Columbia Plastics Corp., 114 W. 17th St., New York, N.Y. 10011; Nappe-Smith Mfg. Co., Southland Ave., Farmingdale, N.J. 07702; Hewig & Marvic, 861 Manhattan Ave., Brooklyn, N.Y. 11222; and Neely Mfg. Co., Inc., P.O. Box 338, Corydon, Iowa 50060.

(f) **Flight Bags.** Instead of handing guests instructional material in an envelope as they register, consider placing this material in an imprinted flight bag. Great for conventions held at resorts, and they make an excellent take-home souvenir. They are inexpensive, too. Cost is around $3.00 each, plus art. Also available are beach bags and junior flight bags, size 2½" × 4" × 7½". The suppliers offer free preliminary art ideas. Suppliers are Airline

Textile Mfg. Co., 214 S. W. Jackson St., Des Moines, Iowa 50315; Universal Specialty Co., 180 N. Wacker Dr., Chicago, Ill. 60606; and Personident Inc., 164 Pebble Lane, Hewlett, N.Y. 11557.

(g) The Importance of Little Things. Personalization, which costs relatively little, pays great dividends in appreciation. For instance, imprint the individual's name on such items as a binder or meeting notebook, or write in the name in gold foil which is available from stationery stores. One supplier is Hastings & Co., 2314 Market St., Philadelphia, Pa. 19101.

10. "WELCOME" GIFTS.

(a) A Passport Pocket Portfolio makes a nice advance gift for those attending a convention away from the U.S. This pocket portfolio has pockets for passports, airline reservations, tickets, baggage claim checks, money, etc. It is constructed of deep red two-tone leather-grained vinyl. When closed the size is 8¼" × 4¼". Cost is about $1.50 each for 12; $1.32 for 50; $1.15 for 100. Available from Dilly Mfg. Co., 211-215 E. Third St., Des Moines, Iowa 50309.

(b) R.O.N. Kits (from the abbreviation commonly used in the military service and the ariline industry for "remain over night.") These are compact emergency toilet kits. The men's kit contains a Schick razor and injector blades, 1 oz. bottle of hair styling gel, after shave lotion, toothbrush, toothpaste, comb, spot remover, shoe shine packets, and deodorant. The ladies case contains deodorant, hair spray, hand and cleansing cream, toothbrush, toothpaste, emery board, shower cap, and soapflakes. They fit in pocket, attache case, or glove compartment. Cost is about $3.00 each. Available from Airline Textile Mfg. Co., P.O. Box 477, Des Moines, Iowa 50302.

(c) Cameras Make Appreciated "Welcome" Gifts. Cameras are available at prices in the $9.00 range from Imperial Corp., 421 N. Western Ave., Chicago, Ill. 60612, and GAF Corp., 140 W. 51st St., New York, N.Y. 10020. A Magicube camera outfit complete with a role of film is offered at around $6.00 by Jetset Mfg. Co., 9937 W. Jefferson Blvd., Culver City, Calif. 90230.

(d) Sears Roebuck Catalog. Great for the nostalgia theme. Copies are available for the years, 1899, 1900, 1908, 1923. Also available is a 1909-1912 Sears Motorbuggy Catalog. 50-99 copies cost $1.98 each. (Sample copy same price); 100 to 999, 98¢ each; 1,000, 75¢ each. Available from DBI Books, Inc., 540 Frontage Rd., Northfield, Ill. 60093.

(e) Photo Mugs. It takes a bit of detailed effort to obtain photos, but the result is a highly personalized item. It's a "Foto Mug" in which an individual's photo (colored or black-and-white) is sealed onto an insulated plastic dishwasher-safe mug. Use a choice of stock background designs or have a design created for you. Mugs can be individually mailed to the recipient by the manufacturer. Gift certificates are available also. Some suggested uses: As a welcome gift, as personalized trophies, give these out at a coffee break, or as a welcome gift certificate. The recipient mails the certificate and photo to the manufacturer. Available from Foto Mug, c/o Thermo-Serv Company, 2939 Sixth Ave., North Anoka, Minn. 55303.

(f) **Sports Attire for a Welcome Gift.** If the meeting is in a sunny location or includes a golf match, give the attendees a colorful tropical shirt, or golf shirt, and a straw hat or golf hat. Go a step further and include a bottle of their favorite libation. Obtain beverage perferences and clothing sizes from a pre-conference mailing.

(g) **Give Travel-Paks.** This company has a variety of small cases for ladies and men containing all the basic necessities. Prices range from $1.95 to $18.95. The $1.95 kit contains towellettes, cologne, comb, hand and face soap, preelectric shave towelette, razor, shave prep., shoeshine pads, stain remover pads, toothbrush and cover, and toothpaste. Available from Head-to-Toe products, 1697-1725 Elizabeth Ave., Rahway, N.J. 07065.

(h) **Coat of Arms.** Personalize a meeting theme, an incentive program, a mailing, or a welcome gift with an individual's coat of arms on parchment, on a plaque, or on tie tacs. This firm has an appropriate coat of arms for over 500,000 names. Contact the Sanson Institute of Heraldry, 263 Summer St., Boston, Mass. 02210.

11. GIVEAWAYS

(a) **"Money" Theme Welcome Ideas.** These are $1/16''$ cellulose sponges which expand to $5/8''$ when wet. Obtainable in replicas of a penny, nickel, dime, quarter, half-dollar and silver dollar. Bills and bank checks are also available. They can be imprinted with your message. Cost is around 35¢ each. Available from Bass Advertising Specialities, 4317 Lafayette, Bellaire, Tex. 77401. $1,000,000 tie clips, key chains, and cuff links are obtainable through the same source.

(b) **"YCDBSOYC".** For a conference with the slogan "YCDBSOYC"—"You Can't Do Business Sitting On Your Can"—there is a simulated beer can tab with these initials. This brass-plated, silver-oxidized "Tie Clip" is attached to a simulated beverage can top with your imprint. $1.75 ea. for 200, $1.55 ea. for 100. Available from Indiangiver Company, 330 Maple Ave., Westbury, L.I., N.Y. 11590.

(c) **Magnetic Clips** bearing the meeting theme could be considered as a welcome gift. These clips are useful for placing on the dashboard or in the office or home. Cost is approx. 90¢ each. Contact Lewton Industries Corp., 30 High St., Hartford, Conn. 06101.

(d) Shoe Shine Packs. A blend of clear waxes dry quickly to a high gloss without buffing in this "Cinch Pac." They have an imprint area. Cost for 1,000 is $90; 2,000 is $70. Available from Idea Man Inc., 1435 LaCienega Blvd., Los Angeles, Calif. 90035.

(e) Disposable Flashlights for giveaway at resorts or for trip use. They are beautifully styled in contemporary colors. Everything is completely sealed in. Prices include imprinting. Cost is from about $1.50 to $3.00. Order from Safety Premiums, 41 Richmondville Ave., Westport, Conn. 06880.

(f) Four Leaf Clovers make an appreciated welcome gift. Everyone wants to improve their luck. Available in various containers (charms, key rings, etc.) from Daniel's Clover Specialty Co., 4904 Ninth Ave. South, St. Petersburg, Fla., 33707. Key tags cost approximately 30¢ each; letter openers, 35¢; money clips, 30¢.

(g) "You Win, You Lose" Spinner Coins. Sure to be a great favorite with your men are those coins that they can keep for themselves or give to customers. The following company has three stock designs suitable for your imprint: Wendell's, 2424 E. Franklin Ave., P.O. Box 5064, Minneapolis, Minn. 55406. Cost is from $60.00 to $156.00 per 1,000.

(h) Matchbooks. Obtain matchbooks personalized with your meeting slogan or product slogan and company name. Sources: Lion Match Corporation of America, 2 West 45th St., New York, N.Y.; Monogram of California, 500 Hampshire, San Francisco, Calif. Boxes of bantam-size matches are available at $40 to $60 per thousand from Glass Industries, 1133 Broadway, New York, N.Y. 10010, Admatch Corp., 201 E. 42nd St., New York, N.Y. 10017 and Elliott Sales Corp., 2502 South 12th St., Tacoma, Wash. 98405.

(i) Cigarettes with Custom-Made Labels for the Package. Place them on banquet tables, in rooms, etc. They are available in standard soft pack of 20 per package, a hard box of king-size ovals, and filter. Cost is approximately $100 for 250 packages. Contact G.A. Georgopulo Co., 48 Stone St., New York, N.Y.

(j) Survival Kit. This is a small suitcase-shaped cardboard kit, approximately 2″ × 4″ imprinted with your company name. It contains all the obvious necessities to keep your delegates going. Included are such items as Alka-Seltzer, Anacin, Band-Aids, "Do Not Distrub" sign, etc. Order from Hewig & Marvic, 861 Manhattan Ave., Brooklyn, N.Y. 11222.

Sales Conference Icebreaker and Welcome Ideas 189

(k) **Plastic Raincoats, Rainbonnets.** These items fold up into minute packages and thus make a welcome gift for every traveler. Imprinted with your name, they are only 10¢ each in orders of 1,000. Imprinted rain bonnets are 4¢ each in 2,500 lots. Both are useful for customer giveaways. From Plasta-Seal Co., 863 E. 141, Bronx, New York, N.Y. and Advertisers Publishing Co., P.O. Box 602, Ann Arbor, Mich. 48107.

(l) **On-Wheel Tire Gauge and Filler.** This could tie in with the theme or subtheme "Put On The Pressure." It's an inexpensive, well-engineered product which would be welcome by all drivers. It is a tiny gauge that screws on the valve stem and stays on the tire. A twist of the collar delivers an accurate reading without losing air. Adding or removing air is done right through the unit. Proper tire inflation gives improved gas mileage, less risk of blow-out from overheating, and extended tire life. From $1.25 to $1.75 per set of four. From Kalinco, Inc., 1154 Floyd Dr., Lexington, Ky. 40505.

(m) **Anniversary Seals.** If you are having an anniversary and want to dress up presentation binders, welcome gifts, letterheads, envelopes, etc., this source can provide handsome pressure-sensitive labels for you. Available every fifth year from 5th to 50th, plus 75th and 100th. Custom designs also. Size is 1½" diameter. Myron Mfg. Corp., Myron Building, Maywood, N.Y. 07607.

(n) **Imprinted Stickers.** Pressure-sensitive stickers for luggage, folio, briefcases, gift wrappings, etc. in many different shapes, sizes, and colors may be secured from Crestline Co., Inc. 18 West 18th St., New York, N.Y. 10011.

(o) **Americana Giveaways.** As a "Welcome" gift or a favor at the banquet. Most can bear your imprint.
- *Colonial Coins and Currency.* Incentive Sales Co., 15142 Mayberry Circle, Westminster, Calif. 92683. Also available from Historical Documents Co., 8 N. Preston St., Philadelphia, Pa. 19104; and Curtin & Pease, 2725 N. Reynolds Rd., Toledo, Ohio 43615
- *Americana Illustrated Letterholders.* Cost is $1.25 ea. Order from Historic Reproductions, P.O. Box 951, Tauton, Mass. 02780.
- *Bicentennial Map* of U.S. at time of Revolution. Order from Premium Division, Hammond, Inc., Maplewood, N.J. 07040.
- *"Revolutionary Times."* A tabloid size 16-page newspaper with news of the American revolution is available from Incentive Sales Co., 15142 Mayberry Circle, Westminster, Calif. 92683.
- *Historical Documents.* Reproductions of all types such as Declaration of Independence, Colonial recruiting poster, and maps are available from Historical Documents Co., 8 N. Preston St. Philadelphia, Pa. 19104.

Note: For additional information pertaining to making guests welcome, see Chapter 16.

Chapter 16

Do-It-Yourself Ideas for the Reception, Banquet, and Theme Parties

Contents

1. Receptions
2. Cocktail Party Ideas
3. Banquet and Dinner Dance
4. Parties Away from the Hotel
5. Tips on Working with Entertainers
6. After Hours Do-It-Yourself Entertainment Ideas
7. Theme Party Ideas
8. Party and Gag Supplies
9. Patriotic and Americana Favors, Prizes, and Gifts

1. RECEPTIONS.

(a) For a Reception Preceding the Banquet make it no longer than one hour. The reception will, of course, not be as long as a cocktail party. If followed by a full-fledged banquet, you do not wish to serve too much alcohol as it dulls the appetite. If wine is not served at the banquet, consider serving wines only at the reception with dry hors d'oeuvres and cheese. A service bar can be available, but out of sight, for those who do not care for wine.

(b) Comic Waiter. Check talent agencies for a comic waiter, or there may be a budding actor in your organization. I attended a reception where the waiter spilled drinks, bawled people out for dropping ashes and someone for opening a sliding patio door, and objected to people taking too many hors d'oeuvres. He even dropped his tray several times. If you can hire a comic who is proficient in double-talk, he can add even more confusion to the occasion. For a "Reception and Banquet Checklist" see Chapter 22.

2. COCKTAIL PARTY IDEAS.

(a) Cocktail Party Length. If the cocktail party is held before dinner, it should be planned for a duration of one hour or not longer than 1½ hours. Many companies favor leaving the bar open during the dinner. The last-minute rush to the bar is eliminated and generally the bar bill is much lower. To clear out the late hangers-on at cocktail parties, slowly begin to dismantle the bar service 15 minutes before the closing, and dim the lights five minutes before the closing.

(b) Party Host. The host's chief duty is to make sure that the newly-arrived guest is introduced to several people. If the affair is for customers, the guest should be introduced to the representative from his territory and preferably to a V.I.P. also. A second host should be in charge of the bar. All host personnel should wear identification badges.

The Reception, Banquet, and Theme Parties 193

(c) Take Photos of Guests with a Polaroid Camera. Models circulating through the crowd can take these pictures. Better yet, have one or more models with whom the guests can pose. You might want to create a souvenir folder into which the photo is inserted.

(d) Putting Contest at the Cocktail Party. This is always popular. Make the green from Astro Turf or similar material. Try floor covering stores as suppliers. You can insert boards and other objects under the turf to make the green uneven. Each person is given a card entitling him to one or more putts. Those who make the hole-in-one receive the golf ball, a bottle of wine, etc.

(e) If the Cocktail Party is Held Outdoors, Provide for Rain Insurance by making sure there is an alternative location indoors.

(f) To Make a Cocktail Party More Memorable, consider some of these ideas:

   1. Hire a popcorn wagon, a nickelodeon, hand organ, a player piano, a barbershop quartet.
   2. Give out wooden nickels with which to buy drinks, dill pickles, lemonade, jelly beans, popcorn, peanuts.
   3. Hire a fortune teller and/or a handwriting analyst, or a caricaturist.
   4. Set up for an English pub atmosphere with fish and chips, sandwiches, and, of course, several dart boards. For safety, use the suction cup type of darts. There are a host of decorative items available for this theme from Paradise Products, P.O. Box 568, El Cerrito, Calif. 94530. Items such as napkins, English posters, famous street signs, placemats, British flags, bagpipe broaches, rest room signs, Shakespeare posters, coats-of-arms posters, sideburns, and mustaches are available.

(g) Rental Props. Rental companies are an often overlooked source for decorating assistance. Look in the classified telephone directory under "Decorating—Party, Convention." For instance, in the Los Angeles directory one company advertises rental of stages, chairs, tables, bubble machines, columns, and statues. Another rents casino party equipment, animals, and figures. Another offers seasonal decorations for all occasions, and still another advertises entertainment of the 1900's complete with a live show, autos, band organ, popcorn wagon, antique toys, carriages, and an 1800 train.

(h) Make Refreshments Project the Theme. For a circus have popcorn, peanuts, soda pop, hot dogs. If you are using a prospecting theme, think of cookies molded into the shape of a burro, a pick, or a shovel.

(i) Make the Entertainment Fit the Theme. Consider war dances for an Indian theme. Use a magician for another, hula dancers for a Hawaiian theme, or banjo and/or piano player for a honky-tonk theme.

(j) Make Use of Local Customs, Costumes, and Color at the Cocktail Party. For instance, for color and informality the event can take place at poolside. Bring in local vendors such as hot dog, tamale, and soft drink vendors, a popcorn machine on a cart, a native making codfish fritters or corn fritters, meats cooked on a hibachi, or a native cutting coconuts or pineapples for use in drinks. Drink out of coconut halves. You can also have a wood carver, a straw hat maker, jewelry maker, glass blower, etc.

(k) Pose with a Chimp. Scout around talent agencies for the name of an organization that can furnish a chimpanzee. Take shots of the guests posing with the chimp. In New York, contact Carrado Enterprises, 640 West End Ave., New York, N.Y. 10024.

(l) Personal Photo Fun Statuettes. These are humorous photographic cut-outs about 9″ high on which the guest's photo portrait is mounted. Use any Polaroid Land Camera to photograph the subject's head. The face outline is cut with scissors and glued on to the Funny Form statuette. 34 Funny Forms are available: Plump man or woman, bathing beauty, hillbilly, water skier, golfer, fisherman, strong man, gay nineties, male in barrel, honeymooners, wrestler, etc. Price is around 15¢ per Funny Form. Available from A. G. Trumble Co., 3006 Jenkins Arcade, Pittsburgh, Pa. 15222, or Photoform, Inc., 4 West Manila, Pittsburgh, Pa.

3. BANQUET AND DINNER DANCE.

(a) Introducing Couples at Head Table. This can be handled by using an off-stage mike to announce each couple. The couple then walks across the room to the table. A spotlight makes it even more effective.

(b) Dinner Dance Seating. Number the tables. Give a banquet registration card to each registrant. Those who wish to sit together go to the banquet registration desk and turn in their tickets. The registration desk attendant selects a table number from a bowl and assigns that table. Singles take their choice of the empty seats afterward. You may want to make it on a first-come, first-served basis on selecting tables instead of drawing a table number.

(c) Table Host for Convention Banquet. A nice touch to make visitors feel important is to assign a key member of the organization to each table to act as host.

The Reception, Banquet, and Theme Parties

(d) Adapt the Method of Introductions Used by "What's My Line". The first head table member is introduced by an off-stage voice. The member walks to his assigned place. The first individual then introduces the next table member. The second member introduces the third, etc.

(e) Prepare a Small Notice for the Table Informing Guests of the Contents and History of the Local Dish which has been prepared.

(f) Corsages. On the night of the banquet send a corsage to each of the ladies. Orchid corsages for moderate-size groups can be furnished inexpensively from Orchids of Hawaii, Inc. The company guarantees arrival on time and in perfect condition. Address is 305 Seventh Ave., New York, N.Y. 10001.

(g) Imprinted Menu on Balloon. These balloons can be placed at each place setting, or a number of balloons can be attached to sticks, or filled with helium and placed on strings to make an unusual centerpiece. Available from Anderson Rubber Co., P.O. Box 170, Akron, Ohio 44309.

(h) Notify What to Wear. By all means indicate what to wear. Place this information in the invitations, the mailings, and the printed program. State whether dress is formal or informal.

(i) Banquet Music. When the doors are opened music should be playing.

(j) Dancing. Dancing usually starts as soon as the tables have been selected. And a note here, the dance floor should not be immediately in front of the stage. Place two or three rows of tables between the dance floor and stage. This gives the entertainers, when they appear, an audience immediately in front, which establishes audience rapport.

Banquet Checklist. See Chapter 22.
For additional suggestions on the banquet see Chapter 19.

4. PARTIES AWAY FROM THE HOTEL.

(a) Unusual Locations for Parties.
    1. Check for use of historical sites. How about Alcatraz or an old-time opera house? Provide suitable entertainment for these theme places.
    2. Consider an art museum, the hotel swimming pool, the lounge area on top of a hotel, an old estate, an amusement park—and then let the guests wander.
    3. Rent a large airplane for a two-hour combination cocktail party and sky cruise.

4. Use an old-time movie party theme complete with old-time movie posters and movies.

5. Hold the party in a picturesque rehabilitated part of town such as Old Town in Chicago, Underground Atlanta, Ghiradelli Square in San Francisco. On the other hand you could hold the party in a tourist area such as Ports of Call in Los Angeles, or Fisherman's Wharf in San Francisco.

6. Hold a Mexican Fiesta complete with Mariachi band and Mexican liquor and foods. You might even consider a baseball park?

7. Reserve a theatre for the evening and hold the reception in the lobby or on the stage.

(b) Hold the Party (and the Meeting, too) at a Planetarium if the theme fits in—such as "Out of This World," "Out of Sight." Waitresses can wear space helmets.

(c) A Bus Trip with Mystery Destination makes a different way to provide entertainment. Take the bus to a nightclub, a restaurant, a rodeo, an amusement park, or even end up (after 20 minutes of driving) right across the street. Have a bar on the bus. Use the bus P.A. system for the M.C. and for group singing.

(d) Boat Cruise. Consider holding a party on a boat. If you are near a large body of water, check the rental of sightseeing or ferry boats. If you are near a small lake, look into renting several boats—you might have a boat race, or use a boat as transportation to a restaurant across the lake.

(e) Packet Boat Available in New York City. For cocktail parties or for buffet luncheons, consider using this replica of an old-time packet boat. It accommodates 150 guests for cocktail parties and about 70 people for dinners or lunches. Contact World Yacht Enterprises, Ltd., 14 West 55th St., New York, N.Y. 10019.

(f) Train Ride. Check with your local railroad. For a crowd of 200 it's often possible to charter a special train at a modest price. Your invitation can invite the group to travel on the "Company Name Express." Schedule the train to stop at a spot that has a restaurant or nightclub. (You can keep this part as a surprise.) Install a bar on the train, also a small combo. You may be able to fit your event into a regular train schedule, thus saving money. You can charter a bus for the return trip or vice versa.

(g) Train Dinner. In some locations it is possible to arrange to hold a dinner or a cocktail party in a dining car at the railroad station.

(h) A Race Can Be Named After Your Organization if a visit is made by your group to either a horse race or greyhound race.

The Reception, Banquet, and Theme Parties

(i) Get a Local Restaurant to Name a Drink After Your Group. If it's a large group, furnish a special welcome message which can be attached to the menu.

(j) Take Over a Nightclub for a Cocktail Party. Clubs often are more than receptive to a closed party on their usual closed night or slow nights.

(k) Group Theater Parties. This, of course, is most easily accomplished in New York City. However, Chicago, Los Angeles, and many other cities offer plays and musicals at group ticket prices. This event can be tied in with a theater supper at a restaurant other than at the convention site. Participants could be bussed to the restaurant and show. If practical, make it an after-theater supper. These are often less expensive and do away with the time pressure. Another idea is to obtain tickets to a television show. Make a mailing in advance to sign up the attendees for theatre events. The local Convention Bureau can offer suggestions on how to purchase group tickets.

(l) Unconventional Dinner Ideas. How about dinner aboard a ship or a yacht. Sightseeing bus companies offer nightclub tours tied in with a dinner. Consider a riverboat cruise.

(m) Sightseeing Tours. Your recreation time can include an evening sightseeing tour. Most large cities have sightseeing tour companies—Gray Lines is probably the best known. Some tour companies offer a tour where two or three nightclubs are visited; dinner is generally optional. Check with your hotel, chamber of commerce, or the Convention and Tourist Bureau. These agencies are generally a valuable source of tour and entertainment information.

(n) Complimentary Passes. For an entertainment bonus, check the local amusement attractions. Special discount rates or free passes may often be obtained.

5. TIPS ON WORKING WITH ENTERTAINERS.

(a) Tips on Hiring and Working with Entertainers. Have a good M.C. for the event. Be sure to book well in advance. Be sure to get all costs and details in writing. If you are looking for a name entertainer, check with talent agents as to what entertainers will be appearing in or near the convention city. You may thus be able to save on travel expenses. Have a check ready for presentation after the performance; this is customary in the entertainment trade.

If at all possible, make sure that a rehearsal is held, or at least go with the entertainer personally to check the stage, microphone, and props. Go over the schedule with the entertainer as it pertains to the appearance. Make sure, if the entertainer is a speaker, that he or she knows the makeup and purpose of the convention.

Determine well in advance if the entertainer or entertainers require a room with a mirror near the meeting room, in which to freshen up or apply makeup. Rest room facilities may also be required for entertainers.

(b) Engage Entertainers as "Independent Contractors," otherwise your company will be fully liable as an employer in the event of accidents. Obtain a contract which states that the performer is an independent contractor and that the company (or association) is not responsible for control of the performance, for payment of wages, workmen's compensation, taxes, disability benefits, etc. The same applies to models.

6. AFTER HOURS DO-IT-YOURSELF ENTERTAINMENT IDEAS.

(a) Contact the Resort Social Director. Almost all large resort hotels have a hostess or social director who will be only too glad to assist in furnishing ideas or in planning something special. If it's a small hotel, see the manager. Often there is something stored away useful for special entertainment.

(b) Talent Show. Put on an amateur show using your own personnel. Use not only individual acts but skits as well. Consider sending out a questionnaire to your group soliciting talent. To add audience participation, make it a talent contest.

(c) Bingo. Purchase or rent this equipment. Use play money, or use real money and give the house winnings to charity.

(d) Pool Tables. Almost every hotel has ping pong. But have you considered installing several pool tables in rooms adjacent to your hospitality suite? It makes a great adjunct to the nightly poker games. Pool tables can generally be rented for a modest price.

(e) Cinemaraces are authentic motion picture records of official horse races. Guests are given a program with horses' names and performance information for each race. Bets are made for one race and the odds are calculated. The film is shown and the payoffs are made. Then bets for another race are placed. A kit is available complete with play money, programs, mutuel tickets, films, and instructions from Cinemaraces, 271 Schilling Circle, Hunt Valley, Md. 21030. Also available from Armchair Races, Lawrence, Long Island, N.Y. 11559; A Nite At the Races, Inc., 2320 Avenue U, Brooklyn, N.Y. 11229, and Race Nite, Suite 219, 400 Oak St., Cincinnati, Ohio 45219.

The Reception, Banquet, and Theme Parties

(f) **Sports Films, Travel Films.** This outfit furnishes films free from sponsoring companies. Write for catalog on your type of film requirement. Modern Talking Pictures Service, Inc., 1212 Ave. of the Americas, New York, N.Y. 10036.

(g) **Old-Time Movies** can be rented for a song. Write for description of melodramas, also old-time westerns, personalities, and newsreels. Running times are 10, 20, and 30 minutes. Rental is from about $3 to $12 and there is a host of ten-minute silent comedies with Harold Lloyd, Charlie Chaplin, Fatty Arbuckle, Charlie Chase, W.C. Fields, Chester Conklin, etc. Rental is about $4 each. Write for a catalog of these 16mm films from Budget Films, 4590 Santa Monica Blvd., Los Angeles, Calif. 90029. Another supplier is Camera Craft Rentals, 6820 W. Sunset Blvd., Hollywood, Calif., or check the yellow pages under "Motion Picture Film Libraries."

(h) **Dart Boards.** Install these in the hospitality suite. You can have special 12" × 12" boards made for you. On them place a picture of the sales manager, your product, or a competitive product. Order a quantity and send to all of your offices and customers. Available from American Publishing Corp., 144 Moody St., Waltham, Mass. 02154; Cadco, Inc., 310 W. Polk St., Chicago, Ill. 60607; American Premium Co., 125 Walnut St., Watertown, Mass. 02172; and Manton Cork Co., 26 Benson Lane, Merrick, N.Y. 11566.

(i) **Do It Yourself Music.** For the captive group there is group singing, records, a player piano, or a regular piano with hired player.

7. THEME PARTY IDEAS.

(a) **Check the Hotel for Party Themes.** Hotels and resorts often have theme parties in which they specialize. They may thus be a source for the planning of special theme dishes and they may already have appropriate decorations and know of appropriate entertainment sources.

(b) **Party Theme Supplies.** Decorations, napkins, toothpicks, hats, favors etc. for theme parties can generally be obtained from specialized companies in the larger cities. Look under "Party Supplies," "Novelties," and "Carnival Supplies" in the Yellow Pages, or ask for a catalog from Frank Stein Novelty Co., 1969 So. Los Angeles St., Los Angeles, Calif. 90011. Another supplier is Merit Industries, 51-55 Stanton St., Newark, N.J. 07114.

(c) **Costume Ideas.** People need not spend their own money for a costume party. Give them the makings of a costume at the door. It can be a hat, a sash, a bandanna, a veil, a false mustache, an apron, an earring, beads, all types of

Indian headdresses or feathers. Write to Paradise Products, Inc. for a catalog of inexpensive costumes. The address is P.O. Box 568, El Cerrito, Calif. 94530.

(d) Hire One or Several Dance Instructors. They will get the guests to participate.

(e) Source for Decoration Kits for Party Themes. Send for this catalog. It is a gold mine of ideas for thinking up a party theme. The catalog contains just about all items for a theme party. There are decorations, costumes, place mats, drink stirrers, menu covers, napkins, invitations, signs, posters, favors, theme music, records, hats, cocktail picks, and much more. Some of the theme kits are:

Arabian Nights	Hawaiian Luau	Oriental	FROM:
Calypso	Italian	Parisienne	
Circus	Las Vegas	Patriotic	Paradise Products,
Delta Queen	Nautical	Pirate	Inc.
Fiesta	St. Patrick's	Roaring Twenties	Box 568
Western	New Year's	Halloween	El Cerrito, Calif. 94530

(f) Raffle Ticket Source. You don't have to go to the expense of printing raffle tickets. Almost any stationery store will provide you with a roll of numbered "admission tickets." They are inexpensive.

(g) Casino Night. This makes a big hit at any convention. Give each guest a stack of play money. After two or three hours of play, hold an auction of prizes with the guests using their winnings to bid, or the money can be turned in and prizes awarded for the highest amount won. Almost any fair-sized city has a company which rents these games. Look in the classified telephone directory under "carnival supplies," "party goods," "amusement devices." Usually for rent are tickets, play money, poker chips, dice cups, craps, roulette, blackjack, wheel of fortune, and chuck-a-luck. Attendants usually can be hired from the same source, or use your own personnel in shifts. For place mats, invitations, cocktail napkins, menu covers, dice candles, coasters, money bags, etc., write to Merit Industries, 51-55 Stanton St., Newark, N.J. 07114.

(h) Casino Night Party Kit from Harold's Club. A complete party kit of casino games and decorations for about $30. The kit includes 80 humorous signs and posters, three paper craps layouts, three blackjack layouts, six dealer aprons, six visors, six decks of cards, four pairs of dice, 250 cocktail napkins, 3,250 pieces of money, and gaming instructions. Check or money order must accompany order. Order from Harold's Club, P.O. Box 50, Reno, Nev. 89504.

The Reception, Banquet, and Theme Parties

(i) **Fake Money.** For games requiring money, consider printing your own fake money. Use your own design or follow the general layout of a dollar bill. Use cartoons, or actual photos of your treasurer, sales manager, or president. You can use your company trademark as the great seal.

(j) **A Godfather or 1920's Party** complete with gangster and flapper dress and a speak-easy atmosphere. There can be a madam and a player piano. Use checkered tableclothes and candles stuck in wine bottles. Serve pizza. Stage a raid. Again Paradise Products, Inc. comes to the rescue with ostrich plumes, flapper beads, striped vests, street signs, posters, plastic tommy guns, menu covers, invitations, straw skimmers, long cigarette holders, felt flapper hats, name badges, gin bottle candles, sing-a-long song books, bouncer arm-bands, Roaring 20s pennants, crooner megaphones, and speak-easy credit cards.

(k) **Alaskan Gold Rush Party.** Rent a garage or barn, or fix up a hotel room like an old-fashioned saloon. Use red checkered tableclothes and old-time kitchen chairs. By all means have a large keg of beer and peanuts. Bartenders can wear prospector costumes; the waitresses could wear spangles and plumes. The guests can come as sheriffs, prospectors, and bandits. Hang "wanted" posters on the wall. Install a player piano. Serve reindeer (beef) stew and sourdough pancakes.

(l) **Polynesian Beach Party.** This calls for flaming torches, glass floats, fish nets, seashells, fruits. Serve buffet style. Start with Zombies and Mai-Tai cocktails, together with cocoanut chips. For appetizers think of Rumaki, Gee Bo Gai, Fish Fiji. Serve Bongo Bongo soup. For the main course offer Island Chicken, Fufu Oriental, Fish Curry, Chutney Rice, and Island Skewers.

(m) **The Outdoors.** How about a clambake, whether at the beach or miles from the sea. Try an old-fashioned picnic, or a hayride to fit in with your Western theme, or a barbecue with steaks, hot dogs, hamburgers, chicken, or ribs.

(n) **Japanese or Chinese Dinner.** Decorate with parasols, kites, bamboo poles, coolie hats, scrolls, straw mats, lanterns, fans, banners, paper fish, artificial flowers. Waitresses can wear kimonos. Cook the food over a hibachi. To make the party informal, have the guests take off their shoes and sit on the floor.

(o) **Gay Nineties, Micky Finn, or Dixieland Party.** Use the above props plus a Dixieland band. Add pretzels, peanuts, and handlebar mustaches, sleeve garters, bright vests, straw hats, a honky-tonk piano player, a banjo player, and beer steins. Have a sing-a-long with the words projected on the wall. Write to Merit Industries, 51 Stanton St., Newark, N.J. 07114 for a catalog of party decorations.

(p) Hold a Carnival. All the paraphernalia from games to stuffed animals to decorations can be obtained from carnival supply houses. Look under this heading in the yellow pages, or obtain a catalog from Frank Stein Novelty Co., 1969 South Los Angeles St., Los Angeles, Calif. 90011. In the game department they have metal milk bottles, "pitch-a-penny game," dart boards, water pistols, walnut shell games, bingo, dice tables, etc. Run a shooting gallery, guess your weight, ring a bell by hitting a mallet, knock down wooden milk bottles, throw darts and rings, and try the wheel of chance. Have a barker and side show attractions such as a belly dancer or fortune teller.

(q) Sound Effects for Carnival and Circus Parties. Long-playing records of the following may be purchased: authentic carousel music, authentic calliope music, also authentic silent movie music. Available from Thomas J. Valentino, Inc., 150 West 46th St., New York, N.Y. 10036.

(r) For a Circus Theme go all out and rent an elephant, a camel, and monkeys. Provide a photographer for guests to pose with the menagerie.

(s) Patriotic and Americana Party Supply Sources. You can provide colonial tricorne, Uncle Sam skimmer derby, and western hats. Red, white, and blue aprons and vests, embroidered and molded emblems, garters, armbands, etc. are also available. Order from Lewtan Industries, 30 High St., Hartford, Conn. 06101. Place mats, caps, Continental dollars, white wigs, tricornered hats, posters, etc., are available from Paradise Products, Inc., P.O. Box 568, El Cerrito, Calif. 94530.

Additional items can be ordered from Hewig & Marvic, 861 Manhattan Ave., Brooklyn, N.Y. 11222.

Ask your local advertising specialty representatives (yellow pages) for a catalog of the Partyline Company. They have Americana balloons, hats, patriotic leis, Uncle Sam Posters and red, white, and blue plumes. A kit for a party of 50 people costs about $25.

For Americana hats, garters, vests, aprons, jackets, etc., contact Helli Company, 700 N. Kilpatrick, Lincolnwood, Ill. 60646.

Hewig & Marvic can supply favors consisting of colonial coins and currency, historical documents, medallions, jewelry, buckles, mugs, desk sets, napkins, place mats, ash trays, booklets. They also have miniature flags, balloons, bonnets, hats, vests, pens, key chains. Contact them at 861 Manhattan Ave., Brooklyn, N.Y. 11222.

Patriotic balloons, flags, pennants, bunting can be ordered from Bass Advertising Specialties, 4317 Lafayette, Bellaire, Tex. 77401.

(t) Beer-Bust Party. You may obtain authentic German beer steins through this importer. Custom imprinted steins may be obtained for $2.75 from Select Gifts Co., 116 E. 16th St., New York, N.Y. 10003. For "Budweiser Hats" in different styles contact Newark Felt Novelty Company, 50 Jelliff Ave., Newark, N.J. 07108. Paradise Products has a "Bierstube" party decorating kit. Address is Box 568, El Cerrito, Calif. 94530.

(u) A Mexican or Fiesta Party. Decorate with garlands and a 4′ × 50′ backdrop of colorful Mexican and Aztec art from Paradise Products, Inc. This company also has hats for men and women, Spanish combs, hand fans, ladies' aprons, ties, serapes, posters, street signs, strings of peppers, place mats, napkins, place cards, invitations, Spanish postcards, and even Spanish restroom signs.

Use appropriate centerpieces of cactus wood, desert wood or live cactus, or a ceramic Mexican burro.

Serve Mexican foods and have the staff explain the food or make explanatory menus or signs. Give Mexican souvenirs. Hire a Mariachi band or marimba group. Provide Spanish dancers. Play Latin music. Serve Mexican beer and Mexican hard drinks. You can include a Spanish wine, too. Food can be served buffet style.

(v) Nostalgia. Holding a meeting with a "Nostalgia" theme? If so, this company has thousands of items. Here are samples: Old ads, luggage stickers from around the world, apple crate labels, silent movie posters, old railroad and military buttons, beer trays, "Punch" magazines of 1867 and 1868, old sheet music, Gibson girl prints, railroad posters, etc. Order from The Nostalgia Factory, 2019 Peel St., Montreal, Quebec, Canada H3A 1T6. Obtain old-time posters from Bramlee, Inc., 1404 Randall Ave., Levittown, Pa. 19057.

(w) Hawaiian Luau. Hotels and Hawaiian restaurants can help you put on a luau. If you do it yourself, suppliers can furnish decorations of tiki gods, masks, fish nets, glass floats, hurricane lamps, palm trees, and torches. Obtain travel posters from airlines or travel agencies. Order huge bowls of fruit, including entire stalks of bananas. Beach clothes, Bermuda shorts, Hawaiian skirts, muu muus and grass skirts can be the clothing of the day. A local dance studio can give hula lessons at the luau. Give prizes for the best dancers.

(x) Hawaiian Decorations. A jackpot of decoration items at modest cost are available from Orchids of Hawaii, 305 Seventh Ave., New York, N.Y. 10001. They supply fish nets, fishtraps, glass floats, posters, luau mats, totems, palm trees, orchids, reproductions of sea fish, lanterns, palm fronds, grass thatching, tiki masks, and tapa cloth. One of their items is a complete luau kit. Also available are leis (both paper and real), muu muus, aloha shirts, mini swinger skirts, place mats, place cards, and Hawaiian records. Request their catalog which is filled with party tips. An additional source for decorations is Merit Industries, Inc. 51 Stanton St., Newark, N.J. 07114. A great source is

Paradise Products, Inc., P.O. Box 568, El Cerrito, Calif. 94530. Fiesta hats and leis are available from Hewig & Marvic, 861 Manhattan Ave., Brooklyn, N.Y. 11222.

(y) **Luau Party Tips.**

Welcome the guests with a lei. A costumed girl says "Aloha" and greets each guest with a kiss.

Request that guests come in costumes of the islands. Give a prize for the best costumes.

Serve food from low tables and seat the guests on pillows or mats. Regular 3' × 5' unopened meeting tables propped up on boxes will do. Or use plywood slabs. Cover the table with tapa paper, fresh leaves, and orchids.

For large parties arrange for catering from a Polynesian or Chinese restaurant.

Play Hawaiian records. Ask a dance studio to provide an instructor for teaching the basic hula movements. Provide for Hawaiian entertainment if desired.

Soften the lights. Cover with accordion lanterns or use hurricane lamps. If outdoors, use tonga torches.

Serve Luau Drinks. There is Luau Rum Punch, Pink Passion Punch, Planters Delight, Diamond Head Cocktail, Mai Tai-Wicki Wiki, Leilani Sour. Set brimming bowls of fruit about the room. Decorate the mounds of fruit with flowers of spiral leis around them.

Drape a fish net across a ceiling or wall and hang from it cutouts of fish, glass floats, and shells. And fill fish traps with leis for everyone to wear.

Fill the room with potted plants. Dress the windows and doorways with garlands. Place a palm tree or a tiki totem pole in a corner. Use artificial fronds everywhere.

Cover items that detract from the atmosphere with tapa paper, fish netting, palm thatching, travel posters, or luau mats.

For a brilliant array of colors use Hawaiian yard goods for decoration or costumes.

Teach your guests the Hawaiian salute which is "Okole Maluna" pronounced "ok-ko-lay mah-loo-nah." It means "bottoms up."

For an exotic drink freeze fresh Vana orchids (these are small orchids) in the ice cubes.

For appetizers provide hibachis on which the guests heat skewered outrigger balls and pineapple "Alii."

Recipe for Outrigger Balls: Shape softened cream cheese into balls and roll in freshly grated coconut. Serve on colored toothpicks.

Pineapple "Alii" (a-lee-eee): Wrap canned pineapple chunks with bacon; fasten with wooden pick and broil. Serve crisp and hot.

The Reception, Banquet, and Theme Parties

All the decorations including invitations, plates, napkins, and more are available from Paradise Products, P.O. Box 568, El Cerrito, Calif. 94530.

(z) **Other Party Themes.** There are Roman and Italian dinners with candles in the wine bottles, cheeses at the beginning and end, antipasto, Italian bread, and espresso. Also consider a French Dinner, Armenian Dinner, Greek Dinner.

8. PARTY AND GAG SUPPLIES.

(a) **Sports Swizzle Sticks.** There are drink stirrers for all types of sports—golf, tennis, baseball, football, horse racing, skiing, hockey, boating. Ties in with your meeting theme or the recreation. Around $33 per 1,000 imprinted. Available from Bass Advertising Specialties, 4317 Lafayette, Bellaire, Tex. 77401.

(b) **Gag Buttons Add Fun.** Four-inch circular plastic buttons with the following selection of gags are obtainable: Secret Agent; If It's Sin, Count Me In; Double Your Pleasure; Have Car, Will Park; Kiss Me Twice; To Hell With Housework; Have Mate, Will Travel; Official Drinking Team; I Hate Work; I Have A Drinking Problem, I'm Broke; Be Nice To Me, I'm Rich; and To Hell With The Boss may be purchased at about 20¢ each from Centennial Novelty Co., 2684 Lacy St., Los Angeles, Calif. 90031, or N. G. Slaler Corp., 220 W. 19th St., New York, N.Y. 10011.

(c) **Gag Items for the Cocktail Party.** You might want to consider a gag or two to enliven the party. This company has all types of items such as talking teeth, mustaches, shoe squeakers, phony arm cast, spook hands, elbow pillows for sophisticated drinkers, 11" sunglasses, and a super 15" knife and fork set. Available from H. Fishlove and Company, 720 North Franklin St., Chicago, Ill. 60610.

(d) **"Spilled Gags."** This outfit specializes in realistic spills. They have beer, soda (7-Up, etc), coffee, milk, and oil spills. Cost is $6.30 a dozen. Coffee costs $9.75 per dozen and Milk costs $8.10 per dozen. Available from Ooops, P.O. Box 1003, La Mirada, Calif. 90637.

(e) **Yo-Yos and Other Indoor Sports.** Take your pick of these nicknacks, which bear your name. Costs (imprinted) in 1,000 lots are: Yo-Yos, about 25¢ each; spinning tops, 20¢; ball with elastic rubber string, 22¢; paddle ball games, 25¢. Order from Fli-Back Corp., P.O. Box 427, High Point, N.C. 27261. Also available from Hewig & Marvic Co., 861 Manhattan Ave., New York, N.Y. 11222.

(f) More Gag Items. Check a local novelty or joke shop for ideas, or write to D. Robbins and Company. They have goofy teeth, rubber dolls, gay nineties mustaches, skin-head wigs, pop-up ties, four-piece schnozola, a pin-thru nose, giant rubber ears, and specs-fo-young. The address is: 127 West 17th St., New York, N.Y. 10011.

(g) Hats Help Make the Event. There'a a company in Pennsylvania which has a line of hats for every occasion—for the golf course, the beach, meetings, and parties. This partial list will start your imagination: Sturdy beer (Budweiser, Schaeffer), golf, tennis, surfer, gob, tyrolean, and engineer hats Pom-pom styles, zoo hats, safari hats, derbies, pith helmets, and fedoras are also available. In addition, you can order all types of ladies hats, straw hats of all shapes, cowboy, yodeler, admiral, Confederate, Union, Bavarian, and sports hats. Hats for parties include: New Year's, Halloween, St. Patrick's, Carnival, Polynesian, Gay Nineties, Yankee Doodle. Available from: Jacobson Hat Co., Prescott Ave. & Ridge Row, Scranton, Pa. 18510.

(h) Special Hats Add a Festive Atmosphere. For a source of supply for Keystone Cop hats, top hats, skimmer straw hats, derbies, and pith helmets at from $1.00 to $1.50 each, write to Hewig & Marvic, 861 Manhattan Ave., Brooklyn, N.Y. 11222. Additional novelty hat suppliers are:
- Lewtan Industries, 30 High St., Hartford, Conn. 06101
- Paradise Products, Inc., P.O. Box 568, El Cerrito, Calif. 94530.
- Merit Industries, 51-55 Stanton St., Newark, N.J. 07114.

(i) Half-Scale Cars! 1911 Ford flivver, a fire fighter, a "Bitty Bug" and tow truck. They run on 3½ h.p. gas engines. Use them to tool around the resort, deliver beer on the golf course, haul delegates to their cottages, and then give the cars away at a drawing. Around $700 to $900. Write for details to: Unforgettable Cars, Denver Merchandise Mart, Suite 2120, 451 East 58th Ave., Denver, Colo. 80216.

(j) Mini-Kar Raffle Prize or Incentive Award. These are autos averaging five feet long. Powered by a 3½ h.p. heavy-duty engine, they burn up the track with speeds up to 15 miles per hour. There is a fabulous 1911 Ford Flivver, a Flivver Pick-up, a Ford Fire Fighter, a Tow Car, and a Bitty Bug Volkswagen roadster. Prices range from $600 to $750. Available from Mini-Kars, Inc., 410 North Park, Kansas City, Mo. 64120.

(k) A Half-Size Version of the 1910 Mercer which was used both for racing and normal driving would make an unusual door prize. This runabout is a truly classic car. It pulls a 3,500 pound load and has an electric starter and is powered by a 5 h.p. Briggs & Stratton four-cycle gasoline engine. Length is 78″, width 37″. Car is for off-street use only. A four-wheel wagon, which the car pulls, is also available. Price for the runabout is about $3,000; wagon is about $700. Available from The Henry G. Dietz Co., Inc., 14-26 28th Ave., Long Island City, N.Y. 11102.

(l) **1880 "Big Wheel" Bicycle.** A reproduction of the bicycle of the 1880s. 52″ wheel for men, 42″ wheel for ladies. Use as a giveaway, or for riding on the stage. It has wire spokes and hard rubber tires. Cost is approximately $300. Available from Unforgettable Cars, Suite 2220, 451 East 58th Ave., Denver, Colo. 80216. Another supplier is G.E.M. Bicycle Sales & Imports, Inc., 2115 Webster St., Oakland, Calif. 94612.

(m) **Give the World's Greatest Shoeshine.** This shoeshine artist is known from coast to coast. His price for "The World's Greatest Shoeshine" is $5. The address is: World's Greatest Shoeshine, Cleveland Airport, Cleveland, Ohio.

(n) **Gag Gifts from Wretched Mess!** Send for the "Wretched Mess Gift Catalog." It's chockfull of items such as a moose-poker, solid bronze bagel, Polish pencils, genius certificate, brown-bag cards, B.S. remover, belly dancing instructions, book of outhouse photos, hippopotamus repellent, "West Yellowstone Memorial Garbage Dump," "Great Beer Bellies Are Made, Not Born" T-Shirt, and old-time ad posters, etc. Available from Wretched Mess News, P.O. Box C68, West Yellowstone, Mont. 59758.

For Additional Items see "Impressive Award Presentations" in Chapter 11. Also see "Award Presentation Ideas" in Chapter 12.

9. PATRIOTIC AND AMERICANA FAVORS, PRIZES, AND GIFTS

(a) **Genuine Revolutionary War and Civil War Bullets.** These are mounted on 9″ × 12″ plaques with engraved pictures of the Battle of Lexington or Battle of Gettysburg. Cost is $10 each. Available from Pick Point Enterprises, Inc., Mirror Lake, N.H. 03853. These make much appreciated "fighting" awards or gifts.

(b) **Gold Plated Buttons** mounted on flocked background are under glass and framed. There are button collections of Civil War, State Seals, Seals of Thirteen Original Colonies, Railroad, etc., $10 to $20 each. Precision Products & Parts Div., General Time Corp., P.O. Box 338, Davidson, N.C. 28036.

(c) **Plaques of 1776 Coins.** These cost from $3.00 to $4.25. Order from Curtin & Pease, 2725 N. Reynolds Rd., Toledo, Ohio 43615. Four-coin and thirteen-coin framed sets are priced around $4.50 and $8.00 respectively from John P. Anderson Premiums, 2955 Arrow Tr. Riverwoods, Deerfield, Ill. 60015.

(d) Muskets, Pistols, Powder Horns, Cannon. These are authentic replicas and cost from $2 to $200. Available from Gutman Co., Inc., 900 S. Columbus Ave., Mt. Vernon, N.Y. 10550.

(e) Thermo-Serv "Freedom" Collection of insulated mugs, pitchers, coolers. They contain paintings of Paul Revere's ride, Valley Forge, Battle of Lexington, etc. The artwork is very well done. Order from Thermo-Serv Co., Anoka, Minn. 55303.

(f) Colonial Electric Beanpots and Hot Food Trays. Available from Redwood House, 155 River Rd., North Arlington, N.J. 07032.

(g) Paperweights, Mugs, Memo Pad Holders, cigaret boxes, and clocks with dimensional bronze coins created by the numismatic artist Louis Marini make excellent favors or gifts. Request a catalog from World Wide Art Studios, P.O. Box One, Covington, Ky. 38019.

(h) Pewter Spoons. You can obtain a collection of twelve pure pewter spoons depicting great moments in Colonial history. Racks are available also. Cost is about $4 for each spoon. Racks cost $5.50. Available from American Pewter Co., Inc., P.O. Box 1776, Easton, Mass. 02334.

(i) Colonial Pewter Mugs, plates, and serving vessels are reproduced in authentic detail by John Wright, North Front St., P.O. Box 40, Wrightsville, Pa. 17368, and Old Mill Enterprises, Inc., 3125 Nolt Rd., Lancaster, Pa. 17601.

(j) Colonial Banknotes are available from Historical Documents Co., 8 N. Preston St., Philadelphia, Pa. 19104. Colonial Coins can be ordered from Curtin & Pease, 2725 N. Reynolds Rd., Toledo, Ohio 43615.

Chapter 17

How to Program the Ladies' Events

Contents

1. To Invite or Not to Invite the Ladies
2. Staffing for the Ladies' Program
3. Planning the Program
4. Handling the Men's Evening Business Requirements
5. Other Ladies' Program Ideas
6. Ladies' Event Ideas
7. List of Suggested Ladies' Entertainment Events
8. Promoting the Ladies' Program

1. TO INVITE OR NOT TO INVITE THE LADIES.

More and more conventions include the ladies for the following reasons:
- If attendance is voluntary, an invitation to the spouse might tip the balance for the vascillating prospect.
- It provides direct business indoctrination for the wives (they can be invited to several of the sessions), and contact with other wives provides further education.
- Shop talk for the men can be interspersed with social breathers.
- Goodwill is generated by the distaff side being made to feel a part of the business team.

From the woman's point of view, she generally welcomes the change as a fun holiday. Husbands usually prefer to share festive evenings with their wives.

There are also important reasons for *not* bringing the ladies, or at least limiting the invitations to only a few conventions and not as a regular practice.
- Some men are single or cannot bring their wives. These men will generally look for outside entertainment more than usual, and may feel the effects the next day.
- The entire meeting tone is changed when there are wives attending—it is a more festive occasion, when perhaps it should be serious.
- Salesmen or delegates are from many parts of the country. Many would like this opportunity to talk to the fellow at the home office, or to a fellow salesman who has a similar territory; the chances for accomplishing this are small.
- There is a big benefit to salesmen holding informal bull sessions.
- There is less alertness at the sessions. The ladies, if they are invited to the conference, should be entertained, but a diet of staying up to one or two o'clock every night is not conducive to alertness for the attendees or the speakers.

- But if the ladies attend, do it up right. Make them extra welcome. Consider the following suggestions.

2. STAFFING FOR THE LADIES' PROGRAM.

If it is a small conference, it is sufficient to have one of the convention staffers plan and handle the ladies program along with one of the management wives.

Large company or association conventions will require from two to three persons (preferably ladies) full time.

For the large conferences, a chairlady will be required to mastermind the ladies' program. She programs and budgets the events. The chairlady searches out and makes the decisions on which events are to take place. She schedules the timing of the events and makes the arrangements with the hotels and other places of entertainment and recreation, and arranges the transportation.

One of her deputies is the person in charge of *Arrangements*. This "Arranger" (a detail-minded person) handles the mechanical requirements. She handles the decorations, contacts the required vendors, works with the hotel on the menus, obtains music, fills out the name tags, and attends to the corsages, centerpieces, seating requirements, microphone, dais, etc.

The other deputy is in charge of *Publicity and Promotion*. Her assignment is to promote attendance and take care of printing requirements (signs, badges, invitations, programs, tickets). She obtains the door prizes, table souvenirs, prepares the welcome instruction kit, and takes care of the attendant publicity such as bulletin boards.

The chairlady can handle the receiving lines, seating protocol, and introductions, or this can be delegated to her deputies.

If the meeting is held in a city where a wife lives, you have an added bonus in that you have a local person who can deal directly with the hotel and entertainment vendors, and she has a knowledge of the locality.

3. PLANNING THE PROGRAM.

(a) **Plan Far, Far in Advance.** If it is a large meeting, a year is not too far distant.

Plan a program which is so appealing that the wives will want to attend, and the husbands are reassured that their wives have adequate entertainment and will be properly taken care of.

Three useful tips are (a) do not over-program, (b) allow the wives a choice of events, and (c) do not make the events compulsory.

It is better to schedule few events. Planners have found that having too many events tends to draw poor attendance. And if the wives go at all, they don't have a good time.

(b) Send a Questionnaire to the Ladies asking their preferences for ladies' events. Alongside the list of suggested events place check-off squares under these headings: "Like," "Don't Care," and "Strongly Dislike." If you want to grade it finer, add headings "Like Very Much" and "Dislike." Add the business meeting subjects if it is planned to have the ladies attend some sessions.

(c) Don't Fill Every Minute. It's a treat for many just to get away from the kids, so don't start every activity at dawn; they might love to sleep late. Don't require that the ladies participate in each of the special events planned for them. Give them a choice of just lounging beside the pool or doing something on their own with friends.

(d) Do Not Start the Events Too Early. Generally, the events shouldn't begin before 10 a.m. Many women prefer not to get up early—especially if they have been out on the town the night before. You will be a hero if you let it be known that the wives may have the luxury of breakfast in bed.

Have the ladies back by 4 p.m. each day so they can get ready for the evening. If feasible, try to time the events so that the men's meetings, golf, and fishing events break at the same time.

Allow time for leisurely shopping if you are in a big city. If you are at a resort area, leave plenty of time for utilizing the resort recreation facilities. One or two tours will suffice here.

(e) Provide for Easy Mingling to permit chatting on a personal basis. Accomplish this by using private cars if possible. If a bus is used, don't have the entire group march in and out of places to be visited. Instead, while on the bus, explain about the places being visited and then let them wander on their own at each stop and return to the bus at the appointed time.

(f) Program Planning Idea Sources are your hotel, city convention bureaus, chambers of commerce, tour service companies, theater brokers, and the getting together of a group of ladies for the exchange of program ideas. Some hotels and resorts have a social directress who can be contacted for ideas. TWA offers assistance on programs for the ladies. Write to Manager-Convention Sales, 605 Third Ave., New York, N.Y. 10016.

(g) Post-Convention Questionnaire. Ask the spouses to fill out a questionnaire. Not only is valuable information received, but it also is a means of providing participation.

(h) Ladies' Badge Idea. Place the badge on a neckchain. Include a small jewelry item as a part of the neckchain if you wish; it thus becomes a souvenir of the meeting. If it is a "ladies only" convention, the necklace badge can be advertised as given only to advance registrants, others receive only the plain pin-on badges.

(i) After-Dark Activities need not be compulsory events. Other than convention-sponsored events such as a banquet or dance, many couples prefer to meet friends and make plans for the evening as they choose.

4. HANDLING THE MEN'S EVENING BUSINESS REQUIREMENTS.

A solution to the problem caused by the men's requirement for an evening of business conversation exchange is to plan a "For Ladies Only" night. This provides a change of pace for the ladies.

The format can be built around a dinner just for the ladies. Start with a ticket for a cocktail, and during this event have a drawing for door prizes. This is followed by dinner (regular and diet menu). Keep the groups intimate by limiting the table seating to not more than eight. Perhaps during dinner have a strolling accordionist or violinist. Add a festive air with flower centerpieces and souvenirs which can fit in a purse.

After dinner have a short talk by an engaging speaker and, perhaps before that, a demonstration on clothes or makeup. Have a talk on furs, diamonds, perfumes, Steubenware glass, etc.—with one of the items given away.

You can have the ladies transported en masse to a location with dinner and entertainment catering specifically to ladies' tastes. Perhaps a theater party can also be included.

On the date of this evening event, it is suggested that afternoon plans not be made for the ladies. The same holds true for the regular banquet or dance.

5. OTHER LADIES' PROGRAM IDEAS.

(a) Consider Inviting the Ladies to Sit In on some of the business sessions.

(b) Wives at Opening Session. The opening session generally provides an opportunity to invite the ladies for an overview of the entire program.

(c) If Wives Are Invited to Some of the Group Sessions, you'll find the discussions more stimulating if spouses are in different groups.

(d) A Champagne Brunch. There are several features of a champagne brunch which appeal to the ladies—they can eat at whatever time they desire, and they can linger as long as they wish to talk with the other women. So arrange to have plenty of coffee on hand for refills. Another advantage is that women do not prefer three big meals, thus a brunch provides the opportunity to eat as little or as much as desired.

(e) Ladies "Company Orientation" Program. Consider a meeting for the wives to explain the company, its purpose, the problems their husbands face, the opportunities, etc.

(f) Special Breakfast. Consider setting up a special breakfast where the wives are invited with their husbands.

(g) Explore the Idea of Holding a Night Session for the Men to Provide Time During the Day for Couples to Be Together. A work session could be planned for the morning and the afternoon planned for a sightseeing trip, an afternoon at the beach, a couple's golf tournament, etc.

6. LADIES' EVENT IDEAS.

Ladies enjoy events connected with food, clothes or makeup, but the trick is to select and plan affairs which treat these subjects dramatically. Attendance will be increased if the functions planned are things which cannot be seen or done back home.

(a) Introduction Party. Make this a simple event which takes place shortly after arrival. At this time the ladies are introduced to each other. Have a reception line if it is to be a large turnout. Provide badges for all with name and town. Serve punch and cookies. Use this occasion as the time to make announcements concerning entertainment plans. Encourage questions.

(b) Fashion Show Tips. Plan a fashion show only if it features something new or something special such as a collection from a well-known fashion house. Provide the opportunity of purchase at the show's conclusion. The shows are more popular if given before a combined audience of men and women, such as at a luncheon.

(c) "Good Morning" Breakfast for Ladies Only. If there is a ladies business meeting planned for a morning, combine it with a breakfast complete with cheerful decorations or flowers.

(d) Install a Special Ladies Lounge. Have hostesses on hand all day to give information on where to shop, where to eat, and what to do. Have the hostesses make the introductions. Staff the lounge with local wives or hired hostesses. Pipe in music. Serve coffee and cookies all day. Give the lounge a special name in keeping with the meeting theme or locality.

(e) Budget for an Attractively Wrapped "Welcome" Gift for Each Lady.

(f) Set Up a Free Beauty Salon complete with hair stylist for comb-outs. Hire a manicurist and cosmetologist also.

(g) **Breakfast in Bed.** Arrange at least one morning for this special event. Consult with the hotel for any extras—such as a flower from the hotel garden, a special message on the breakfast tray.

(h) **Provide a Corsage** for the dance.

(i) **To Help Defray the Ladies' Program Costs** if it is an association meeting, consider asking exhibitors or allied industries to contribute. For example, a company can sponsor a tour. Door prizes and welcome gifts can be furnished by exhibitors. Prizes or gifts can be furnished by department stores which are to be visited on a shopping tour. Door prizes can be donated by shops in the hotel.

(j) **If in a Gambling Area** (Las Vegas, Tahoe, Puerto Rico, etc.) arrange for an instructional program on how the various games are played. Arrange for a demonstration at an empty gambling table if possible.

(k) **Mementos.** Provide a souvenir of the meeting. This can be a beach bag, native jewelry, towel, a beach hat, native carvings, etc.

7. LIST OF SUGGESTED LADIES' ENTERTAINMENT EVENTS.

(a) **Tours**
  Local Sightseeing
  Garden Tours
  Museum Tour
  Quaint Out-of-the-Way Shopping Tour
  Historical Site, Historical House Tours
  Air Sightseeing Trip
  Botanical Garden Tour
  Department Store and/or Boutique Store Shopping
  Antique Shopping Tour
  Backstage Theatrical Tour
  Ante Bellum Home Tour
  Cultural Center Tour
  Tour of Consulates or Embassies—perhaps with a speaker
     or showing of native products
  Bargain Hunting Expedition (at factory outlet or clearance stores)
  Art Gallery
  Obtain Hotel Assistance or Chamber of Commerce or Convention Bureau Assistance in Tour Planning. They know the area and can recommend tour directors and travel agents for local tours.

(b) **Recreation Events**
   Ladies Golf Tournament
   Fishing Tournament
   Water Ski Lessons
   Card Party
   Tennis

(c) **Plays and Restaurants**
   Exotic Restaurant
   Theater Party Matinee
   Television Show

(d) **Lectures**
   Talk by a Chef
   Lecture on "What Makes a Woman Beautiful"
   Home Decorating (lecture or discussion)
   Astrology Lecture
   Figure Control Lecture
   Personal Financial Planning
   Speaker On a Topical Subject
   Public Affairs Speaker
   "How to Buy" Lecture (for factory outlet tour)
   Why and How to Make Wills and Handling Estates
   Coping with Absent Husbands
   The Generation Gap
   Communication
   The New Morality
   Yoga
   How to Improve Your Memory
   Mental Health
   An Inside Look at the Entertainment Field
   Coffee Session with a Prominent Congressman or Senator
   Contact Airlines for a Hostess or a Speaker
   Consider other speaker experts such as college professors, attorneys, psychologists, businessmen, and businesswomen.
   Obtain speakers through the hotel or speaker's bureau
   And these events need not always be straight lectures—they can be combined with question-and-answer sessions or roundtables.

(e) **Demonstrations—Lessons**
   Use of Cosmetics
   Do-It-Yourself Painting Lesson

How to Program the Ladies' Events

    Gourmet Cooking Demonstration, or Cooking Demonstration of Local Dishes
    Hair Styling Show
    Flower Arrangement Demonstration
    Makeup Demonstration
    Belly Dancing Demonstration and Lessons
    Fashion Show with a Narrator and Door Prizes from Donors
    Backgammon Instruction
    Tour Hint. If you have special tours for the wives, be sure to indicate these are "for ladies only." Sometimes the tours are so inviting that the husbands go on the tour also instead of attending the sessions.

(f) **Information on Speaker Sources** may be obtained from the Chamber of Commerce, universities, associations (such as lawyers, doctors), speaker bureaus, marriage counselors, banks, and foundations. (See the Yellow Pages for each of these categories.)

(g) Leave Plenty of time for a **Question and Answer Period** after a talk is given.

8. PROMOTING THE LADIES' PROGRAM.

The advance publicity and invitation to the wife is generally sent to the husband at his place of business for his decision whether his wife is to attend.

Generally, it is best to send the invitation and a description of the events simultaneously (but in separate envelopes). The description of the program events sells both the wife and the husband on her attendance.

To go along with your mailings, obtain literature from the convention bureau, hotel, sightseeing bureau, etc. Send follow-ups in the form of colored postcards.

Give the ladies an indication of what to wear. State if the events are formal or informal.

Chapter 18

31 Tips for Serving Liquid Refreshment

Contents

1. Provide Cocktail Waitresses
2. That Extra Touch
3. Hors d'Oeuvres
4. Control Expenses by Using Drink Chips
5. Prepour the Drinks
6. Estimating Liquor Consumption
7. Types of Hotel Liquor Service
8. Include a Punch for Nondrinkers
9. Control of Liquor
10. Check Costs for Bartenders
11. Wandering Minstrels
12. Personalized Souvenir Wine Glass
13. "Guide to Professional Hosting"
14. Check the Hotel for Local Beverage Laws
15. Encourage Moving Around
16. Getting Acquainted
17. Beverage Cost Estimate Checklist
18. A Wine Tasting Party Makes a Refreshing Change
19. Physical Arrangements
20. The Average Quantity for a Two-Hour Serving
21. Cheeses
22. A Champagne and Sparkling Wine Party
23. Decorations

24. **Programs**
25. **Wine Tasting Hints for the Guests**
26. **Additional Wine Literature Handouts**
27. **Signs**
28. **Wine Party Themes**
29. **Conduct a Wine Tasting Contest**
30. **Hold a Raffle**
31. **A Wine Expert Adds Prestige**

1. **PROVIDE COCKTAIL WAITRESSES.** Instead of having to wait in line for service at a bar, provide cocktail waitresses who circulate and ask for the guests' drink orders.

2. **THAT EXTRA TOUCH.** Turn your dinner into a festive affair by serving wine with the meal. One or two different wines are sufficient. Be prepared to average two glasses per guest. Have a bottle for every four people. At your cocktail party arrange to have an extra waiter offer drinks and hors d'oeuvres and pick up the glasses.

3. **HORS D'OEUVRES.** This is generally budgeted on a "per person" basis. The hors d'oeuvres can be provided either hot or cold. Also have pretzels, potato chips, and peanuts for those who do not prefer hors d'oeuvres.

4. **CONTROL EXPENSES BY USING DRINK CHIPS.** The chips are handed out at the door. The sponsor thus does not have to worry about the bartender overpouring drinks or the marking of bottles. The hotel is paid on a per chip collected basis.

5. **PREPOUR THE DRINKS.** To prevent a lag in serving prepour some of the drinks.

6. **ESTIMATING LIQUOR CONSUMPTION.** For a predinner cocktail party of 1½ hours figure on an average of 2½ drinks per person. Plan on three drinks if the group is more extroverted. This is an average of one quart of whiskey or gin per seven persons. Liquor consumption at evening parties runs an average of two drinks per person per hour. Western and Southwestern persons generally prefer bourbon; those from the East prefer scotch and rye. Plan on Manhattans and martinis also being called for. Remember to provide a stock of premium beer.

Include soft drinks and tomato juice for the nondrinkers. It is recommended that best brands be purchased and the bottles be displayed prominently on the bar. Many guests may not be able to taste the difference in a mixed drink, but they will be impressed by the labels. Figure on two bottles of soda for each bottle of scotch. For martinis and Manhattans have one bottle of French vermouth on hand for every three bottles of gin or vodka; plan on one bottle of Italian vermouth for every three bottles of whiskey.

7. **TYPES OF HOTEL LIQUOR SERVICE.** (1) *Open Bar:* This is the same as bar service at a public bar except that you have your own private room. The hotel furnishes the bartender, the host pays by the drink. (2) *By the Hour:* The hotel furnishes unlimited drinks and hors d'oeuvres. The charge is based on the number of hours times number of guests. (3) *By the Bottle:* Some bottles include bartender and mix, some do not. It is your responsibility to account for the bottles. (4) *Cash Bar:* Chits are sold to the guests, or the host issues a certain number of free chits to each attendee. It is a good method of controlling the number of drinks before a business session, or to keep out gate crashers. (5) *Corkage:* The term means the host provides his own liquor and the hotel provides the service. Most hotels discourage this.

8. **INCLUDE A PUNCH FOR THE NONDRINKERS.**

9. **CONTROL OF LIQUOR.** Secure an agreement with the hotel that only the original stock of liquor at the bar is to be paid for by you. Your staff members take an inventory before the bar opens. Each bottle is marked with their initials. Additional bottles, if required, are to be initialed also and opened in front of you. Confirm with the hotel that empty bottles are not to be removed. At the end of the function pour the leftover liquor into a common bottle for that particular brand. An ending inventory is then taken. Partials are taken by your staff members.

10. **CHECK COSTS FOR BARTENDERS.** If each bartender pours from $150 to $225 in drinks, there should be no cost for the bartender's services. The ratio generally is one bartender for every 100 individuals. If faster service is desired, a ratio of one bartender and bar for every 75 persons is suggested. Where extra fast service is required, the ratio goes down to one to 50, or use waitresses who obtain drinks from a hidden service bar.

11. **WANDERING MINSTRELS.** If there is musical entertainment, use a strolling group rather than having them sit in a corner. The various parts of the room will thus be enlivened.

31 Tips for Serving Liquid Refreshment 223

12. **PERSONALIZED SOUVENIR WINE GLASS.** You can have these for the meeting, or for the hospitality suite, or open house. Guests share a glass of wine and receive a personalized wine glass. When the guests arrive, the hosts personalize the wine glasses by writing guests' names on the glasses with indelible marking pens. This puts everyone on a first-name basis and enables hosts to remember names. The glass also contains the company logo. Available from Advertising Devices & Specialties, 68-18 138th St., Flushing, N.Y. 11367.

13. **"GUIDE TO PROFESSIONAL HOSTING."** This booklet is offered free by Schenley. The booklet tells what to serve, how to serve, how to be sure you only pay for what is actually served, three ways to estimate your costs for a cocktail party, and how to stop a banquet from eating up your budget. Contact Schenley Affiliated Brands Corp., National Accounts Division, 888 Seventh Ave., New York, N.Y. 10019.

14. **CHECK THE HOTEL FOR LOCAL BEVERAGE LAWS.** There may be days or hours during which liquor may not be served.

15. **ENCOURAGE MOVING AROUND** by not having too many chairs or tables.

16. **GETTING ACQUAINTED.** Use badges. Appoint hosts and hostesses to see that individuals are introduced. Consider assigning persons to key executives and to special guests so that they are introduced to as many persons as possible.

17. **BEVERAGE COST ESTIMATE CHECKLIST.** See Chapter 22.

18. **A WINE TASTING PARTY MAKES A REFRESHING CHANGE** from the usual cocktail party. Such an event is generally less expensive, yet it is looked upon as something special by your guests. Figure the cost as about $8 per person.
    The most common before-dinner event involves tasting an assortment of table wines—reds, whites, rosés and sparkling wines. Serve three or four types of each of these classes. If you wish to be elegant, try champagne tasting.

19. **PHYSICAL ARRANGEMENTS.** Serve each type of wine from a separate table. Place the wine tasting tables around the walls of the room. Place a table containing the wine glasses at the entrance. Each guest is given a glass as he enters. Use the all-purpose type of wine glass which holds at least six ounces. On each of the tasting tables place a pitcher of water and a receptacle. As they move to the different tables the guests

rinse their glasses by holding them **over** the receptacle and pouring water from the pitcher. Arrange to h**ave w**aiters refill the pitchers often.

Arrange to have a pourer behind each table. The pourers should be instructed that not more than one ounce of wine be poured into the glass. If you wish, make it a self-serving affair and make appropriate table signs as to the amount to be poured.

20. **THE AVERAGE QUANTITY FOR A TWO-HOUR SERVING** is two one-ounce tastes of each of the six to eight wines. Estimate 20 bottles of white, 20 bottles of red, and 20 bottles for rosé wine for 125 guests.

21. **CHEESES.** It is customary that small cubes of a bland cheese and cubes of French bread or crackers be served. These are helpful in clearing the palate between wines and are not intended to constitute a meal. For 125 guests figure on about 30 to 35 pounds of cheese. The cheese should be placed in the center of the room.

22. **A CHAMPAGNE AND SPARKLING WINE PARTY** might be considered. On six different tables have an assortment of very dry champagnes ("brut"), medium, and semidry champagnes ("Sec"), pink champagnes or sparkling roses, sweet champagnes ("doux"), and sparkling burgundies.

23. **DECORATIONS.** Purchase clusters of imitation grapes and place these on the tables, also construct trellises and use the grape clusters on them. Wine posters are available at some bookstores, department stores, and gift shops. Also try the gift shops at some of the retail winery sales rooms.

24. **PROGRAMS** can be handed out at the door. The program lists the wines to be tasted and their table locations. If possible, it is helpful to include a brief guide to wine types. Such information is generally available from a winery.

25. **WINE TASTING HINTS FOR THE GUESTS.** Instructions such as the following (courtesy of the Wine Institute), will increase a guests' knowledge and enjoyment of the wine tasting experience:

Notes on Wine Tasting

Wines offer a delightfully wide range of flavor enjoyment. Here are some simple suggestions from professional tasters.

White wines should be tasted before red, where possible. When wines vary in sweetness, taste the "dry" wines before the sweet.

Follow this general pattern, using three senses—sight, smell, and taste:
1. Sight: Hold the glass by the stem; raise it to the light; note color and clarity. (Please retain glass, rinsing between wines.)
2. Smell: Twirl wine in glass. Sniff for aroma and bouquet. (Aroma is grape fragrance; bouquet, the more subtle fragrance that comes later, from fermenting and aging.)
3. Taste: Sip the wine. Hold it in your mouth a moment, slowly rolling it around with the tongue. Note the pleasant tartness or richness, degree of sweetness (if any), body or consistency, distinct flavor. Finally, swallow and enjoy the aftertaste.

Clear your palate with a little bread, cheese, or water between wines.

26. **ADDITIONAL WINE LITERATURE HANDOUTS** are available. Contact wineries for this literature, which is often available at no charge or at a very small charge. The Wine Institute, 717 Market St., San Franciso, Calif. 94103 has booklets on "Introduction to Wines" and on wine cookery. An assortment of colorful wine posters may also be available.

27. **SIGNS.** Place a placard near the entrance requesting that each guest take one glass and retain it throughout the session. Also post several cards throughout the room and at the entrance requesting guests not to smoke. Here is an example:

> Because wine flavors and bouquets are delicate,
> and so that you and the other guests will be
> able to enjoy them to the fullest . . .
> **PLEASE DO NOT SMOKE.**

28. **WINE PARTY THEMES.** Suggested themes can be "Days of Wine and Roses," "Wine, Cheese, and Thou," "In Vino Veritas," or "An Evening with Bacchus." Appropriate decorations for the first theme would include roses. Give the roses away at the conclusion.

29. **CONDUCT A WINE TASTING CONTEST.** Six to eight wines are in the contest. The bottles' labels are masked and are identified by numbers. Guests are given a card containing descriptions of each of the wines. They are asked to place, in a square by each description, the guess of the correct number. Winners can be determined during the wine tasting party or announced at a later time.

30. HOLD A RAFFLE during the wine tasting party. Issue tickets at the door. At intervals during the party hold a drawing for bottles of wine, wine racks, wine recipe books, wine glasses, cheese cutting boards, etc.

31. A WINE EXPERT ADDS PRESTIGE to the event. He can be billed as being available for questions. Contact wineries and wholesalers for experts such as winery representatives.

Chapter 19

How to Plan Meal Functions and Menus

Contents

1. Breakfast
2. Luncheon
3. The Banquet
4. Wines and Drinks
5. Meal Guarantees and Ticket Control
6. Banquet Showmanship Ideas
7. Other Meal Function Ideas
8. Coffee Breaks

1. BREAKFAST.

(a) **To Make the Breakfast Unusual** start with a Bloody Mary—for those who wish one—especially after a celebration the evening before. Better yet, make it a champagne breakfast!

(b) **Dress One of the Waitresses as a Nurse.** Her duty is to dispense aspirin and Bromo Seltzer.

(c) **Breakfast Menu Ideas.** For a treat try fruit in brandy instead of the usual fruit slices, or how about Quiche Lorraine. For a small group think about serving eggs Benedict.

(d) **Provide Local and Out-of-Town Newspapers** for those who wish to catch up on the news.

(e) **If the Hotel Cannot Serve Breakfast a la Carte in the Allocated Time,** here is a suggestion: Provide a separate serving bar for the cereals, juices, and fruit. This bar should be near the entrance. Ask the captain to suggest to the guests that these appetizers be eaten first; this keeps the eggs from growing cold (as would happen if both were served together).

(f) **If Possible, Set Up a Breakfast Next to the Meeting Room.** Late arrivals can thus eat without disturbing the meeting and can listen in on the meeting.

(g) **Vary the Menu of the Buffet Breakfast Each Day.**

(h) **If It Is a Breakfast Meeting,** preset the table with coffee and the appetizers. Then serve the eggs and toast separately.

(i) **For Some Breakfast Meetings It Is Suggested that Continental Breakfasts Be Served** (juices, coffee, tea, milk, and sweet rolls).

How to Plan Meal Functions and Menus

(j) Meal Guarantees. Not everyone shows up for breakfast. Associations generally estimate about 70% will eat breakfast, so make your guarantees accordingly.

2. LUNCHEON.

(a) Remember that Luncheon Buffets Are Expensive. The hotel must prepare much more food than necessary, as it is impossible to accurately guess the tastes of the guests. For a sit-down type of luncheon, if 200 persons are present, only 200 plates are prepared. If the hotel pushes a buffet luncheon, obtain a price comparison between a buffet and a sit-down luncheon.

(b) Check for Meal Duplication. A large hotel may be serving hundreds of functions during a week, so the manager may not be aware of luncheon duplication.

(c) Dining Room Size. Don't pick a room that is too large, as it will appear as though not everyone has shown up. If a small room cannot be obtained, request that room dividers be set up. Conversely, don't obtain a room that is too small; it does not allow space between the tables for seating and movement of the guests and for the service. Figure on two feet of table space per person.

(d) Serve a Glass of Wine at a Luncheon. This is better than having a noontime open bar and adds a festive touch without the letdown from stronger drinks. It's less expensive also.

3. THE BANQUET.

(a) Guard Against Meat Which Has to Be Cut in the Kitchen say some veteran planners. This especially means roast beef. By the time the meat is cut and taken to the table, the last guests being served will be eating cold beef. This caution isn't always true; it depends upon the size of the group, the serving dishes, the number of waiters, and the distance from the kitchen. Sliced turkey also will cool fast. Turkey usually is drier than that served at home, as the hotel cook does not have the time to continually baste the turkey.

(b) Suggestions for Entrees Which Are Cooked Individually:

Lamb chops	Baked stuffed ham	Whole spring chickens
Club steak	Filet mignon and lobster tail	Minute steak
	Top sirloin	

(c) Do Not Always Go by the Standard Menus Shown to You, as the foods listed may be those which make a better profit for the hotel or which are the easiest to prepare. Don't hesitate to ask for additional recommendations or to make suggestions of your own. The food staff is usually delighted in being asked to exhibit their creative talents. Some suggestions are as follows:

Veal Cordon Blue (cheese inside) Filet of Beef Wellington
File of Sole Veronica   Chicken Kiev
Boneless Squab   Braised Swiss Steak Jardinere
Veal Oskar   Entrecote Steak Bordelaise
Roast Tenderloin of Beef with Bernaise Sause

(d) Salads. Caesar salad is the number one choice. Other considerations are green bean salad, romaine with watercress dressing, and spinach salad.

(e) Vegetables. Peas with mushrooms or pearl onions are great; also peas a la Francaise. If the chef recommends gingered carrots, or broccoli hollandaise, or sweet potato souffle, go with his recommendation. Make sure the plates chosen are made colorful by means of the vegetable selected and the use of garnishes.

(f) Desserts. Cherries Jubilee and Baked Alaska have seen their day. Besides, the sauce of Cherries Jubilee tastes bitter. By all means don't go the ice cream roll, cake, pie, or parfait route. Everyone has been subjected to these many times. Ask the chef to recommend something different, such as Coupe Belle Helene (pears and ice cream with chocolate sauce).

4. WINES AND DRINKS.

(a) Wines Add to the Festivity of the Occasion. Wines need not be expensive; a $3 bottle may be as good as a $15 bottle. For insurance, insist on a sample for tasting. Provide for both red and white wines regardless of the entree. You will generally find that wines are less expensive than mixed drinks.

(b) Extra Drinks. The custom generally for those who wish additional drinks or additional wine is to have those drinks signed to the individual's hotel room. Make sure extra waitresses are assigned for this purpose.

(c) Consider Passing Out Cigars After the Dinner. You might want to serve an after-dinner liqueur, or both.

5. MEAL GUARANTEES AND TICKET CONTROL.

(a) Most Hotels Require a Guarantee as to the number of persons served. If your guarantee is 100, the hotel generally will set up and prepare food for four percent above that figure. If 94 persons show up, you are charged for

How to Plan Meal Functions and Menus   231

your 100 guarantee. If 104 are served, the charge is for 104. Be sure to inquire what the cutoff day and hour is for your final guarantee.

(b) For Large Meetings Issue Meal Tickets for Control. Check with the hotel staff on the procedure and timing for collection of tickets. The hotel will give the tickets to you with their bill. Have a few extra tickets on hand for those who may have forgotten their tickets.

(c) Obtain a Written Guarantee on the Meal Charges. Check to make sure there isn't a notation in small print saying "Prices subject to change."

(d) Most Good Planners for Large Banquets Do Not Eat at Their Banquet. They are making sure that the service and banquet functions are going smoothly.

(e) The Table Count. If it is a voluntary group of guests, it is a good idea to make a count at the reception preceding the banquet to make sure there are sufficient tables.

(f) Head Table V.I.P. Service. The only persons who are let in to the banquet room ahead of time, should they desire it, are members of the head table. Do not require the head table guests to hand in their tickets; this is considered poor taste.

(g) Request that Table Service Be Suspended during speeches and during the entertainment. This applies both to food and bar service.

(h) Gratuities. Check the gratuity charge and how it is handled. Are the charges added to the bill or are they optional? Do these include the bartenders, captains, maids? Is there a possibility of an overtime charge?

5. BANQUET SHOWMANSHIP IDEAS.

(a) Add Showmanship by providing a printed menu on which *dishes are named after persons being honored* at the meeting; such as "Peaches Wilson," "Lamb a la Johnson." Another idea is to tie in each dish with a conference meeting product.

(b) If Some of the Dishes Have a Local Flavor, publicize the content and origin of the dish on the menu.

(c) Imprinted Balloons for Banquet. An inexpensive way to add color and excitement to a banquet setting is to provide balloons. Price is approximately

$30 per thousand and includes your meeting slogan imprint. Rent a tank of helium, tie a long string to each balloon and let it float to the ceiling. Hand-operated inflating pumps are also available at about $5. Sources: Maple City Rubber Co., 56 Newton St., Norwalk, Ohio 44857; Pioneer Rubber Co., 429 Tiffin Rd., Willard, Ohio; Anderson Rubber Co., P.O. Box 170, Akron, Ohio 44309.

(d) For Suggestions on Decorations and Favors see the section in Chapter 16, titled "Theme Party Ideas."

(e) Decorate the Tables with Candles. If fire regulations do not permit this, battery-lighted centerpieces can be used.

7. OTHER MEAL FUNCTION IDEAS.

(a) When There Is a Large Function, Set Up a Separate Reception Room for Members of the Head Table.

(b) Prepare a Head Table Seating Plan and give a copy to the M.C.

(c) Outdoor Meal. If at a resort, plan to have at least one of your meals outdoors where your guests can dress informally and colorfully. Hold a barbecue and provide bandannas and western entertainment—perhaps even a rodeo. Other ideas include a Hawaiian Luau, a steak fry, or a fish fry.

(d) Rain Insurance. For the outdoor receptions or meal functions discuss contingency plans with the hotel.

8. COFFEE BREAKS.

(a) Obtain Estimates. Be sure to obtain an estimate of the coffee break costs. Ask for a written statement of the cost per gallon. Do a little arithmetic and you will be shocked to learn that it is costing anywhere from 60¢ to $1.25 per cup. So make a more careful estimate of usage as anywhere from 48 to 50 percent of the coffee that you have paid for is often returned to the kitchen. Also ask for the charges for the pastries and soft drinks.

(b) Coffee Break Location. If possible, plan to serve the coffee in the area away from the meeting room, as the setting up of the service can be a distraction. If the beverage must be served in the room, arrange for the coffee to be wheeled in at the required time on trays which have been preset, or determine if a coffee urn can be obtained which has an alcohol or electric warming unit.

How to Plan Meal Functions and Menus   233

(c) Consider Holding the Coffee Break in the Exhibit Area if it is an association meeting.

For additional information see the section titled "Banquet and Dinner Dance" Chapter 16.

(d) Snacks. Limit the food for the morning break to just donuts and Danish—sandwiches are not necessary. No solid food is required for the afternoon break. However, a fruit adds a welcome touch in the afternoon— such as apples, bananas, grapes, and tangerines.

(e) Ice Cream Cone Break. A pleasant surprise for one of the afternoons is to offer ice cream cones with coffee. At another break offer apple cider, cheese and crackers, hard boiled eggs, or a variety of nuts.

(f) Other Beverages. Don't forget to provide noncaffeinated coffee, tea, juices, and even hot chocolate. Add soft drinks to the afternoon break.

Chapter 20

14 Imaginative Techniques for the Hospitality Suite

Contents

1. Tips on Setting Up and Running the Hospitality Suite
2. Make Sure Your Staff People Are Hosts—Not Barmen or Old Crony Visitors
3. Hospitality Rooms Should Be Away from Hotel Traffic
4. Provide a Private Meeting Room
5. Invitations
6. Executive Hostesses
7. Cabaret Atmosphere
8. Wine Tasting Party
9. Personalized Wine Glasses
10. Advertise an "Evening at the Track"
11. Security and Identification
12. Snacks-On-Your-Own
13. Promoting Attendance at the Hotel
14. A Magician

1. **TIPS ON SETTING UP AND RUNNING THE HOSPITALITY SUITE.** At the average convention, a company hospitality suite generally is a hotel room where drinks and hor d'oeuvres are served. And that's it. One company's hospitality suite is like the next one's. With a little imagination and a very small extra budget, a visit to your suite can turn into a memorable one. Here are some suggestions.

2. **MAKE SURE YOUR STAFF PEOPLE ARE HOSTS—NOT BARMEN OR OLD CRONY VISITORS.** Make sure that the visitors entering the suite are introduced.

3. **HOSPITALITY ROOMS SHOULD BE AWAY FROM HOTEL TRAFFIC.** This will avoid freeloaders.

4. **PROVIDE A PRIVATE MEETING ROOM** adjacent to the hospitality suite for private business conversations.

5. **INVITATIONS.** You will, of course, have mailed out invitations to visit your suite and passed the word to your booth personnel to invite selected visitors to come to your hospitality suite.

6. **EXECUTIVE HOSTESSES.** This company advertises: "Bright, gracious, attractive women who know how to make life easier for the man who makes the plans." Use this company or any similar service as a source for hostesses to make people feel at home, to demonstrate products or services, and to answer questions intelligently. The company's name is Beautiful Women and it has affiliates in 80 major American cities. The address is P.O. Box 2007, 380 Pompano Beach, Fla. 33061.

7. **CABARET ATMOSPHERE.** Obtain small round tables of various sizes. Use white linen tablecloths or red checkered tablecloths. Have candles

at the tables, at the bar, and at the hors d'oeuvre table. Provide gypsy violinists, a piano player, or canned music. Have appropriately dressed barmaids and bartenders.

8. **WINE TASTING PARTY.** A selection of wines, cheeses, crackers, and nuts are the main ingredients. Obtain wine country posters, and provide printed descriptions of the wines. See Chapter 16 for the detailed suggestions for a wine tasting party.

9. **PERSONALIZED WINE GLASSES.** Mail invitations to convention attendees asking them to visit your hospitality suite, where they will share a wine toast and receive a personalized wine glass. When the guests arrive, the hosts personalize their names with an indelible marking pen on a wine glass containing your imprint. The personalization ("Bill," "Jim," etc.) immediately puts guests on a first name basis and enables the hosts to remember names. You can obtain six ounce wine glasses and ten ounce goblets. 144 cost approximately $1.50 each. There is an additional $20 screen charge for each color. Available from Advertising Devices & Specialties, 68-18 138th St., Flushing, N.Y. 11367.

10. **ADVERTISE AN "EVENING AT THE TRACK"** to bring guests to the suite. Give each person who visits the suite an amount of play money to use in playing the horses. Films of horse races are rented for this purpose. At the end of the evening hold an auction for prizes using the play money which has been won. A complete kit for conducting these races may be obtained from: Cinema Races, 271 Schilling Circle, Hunt Valley, Md. 21030 and A Nite At The Races, 2320 Avenue U, Brooklyn, N.Y. 11229.

11. **SECURITY AND IDENTIFICATION.** If your hospitality room or cocktail party is on a floor with a high traffic flow, it is important to guard against gate crashers who can boost costs. Precautions can be in the form of the requirement to show an invitation, name tags, the hiring of a security guard, or a combination of these.

12. **SNACKS-ON-YOUR OWN.** A different touch for the hospitality suite is to let it be known selectively that 11 p.m. snacks will be available in your suite. Serve make-your-own sandwiches, sweet rolls, milk and juice.

13. **PROMOTING ATTENDANCE AT THE HOTEL.** If the suite is open to all, you will want to have a sign in the lobby. If it is a selective affair, invitations can be placed in the guests' hotel mail boxes. Ask the hotel to turn on the red light in the guest's room to signal that a message is

waiting for pickup. If the invitations are not picked up by a certain time, have bellhops make the delivery. Also make sure that adequate directional signs are provided for the corridor.

14. **A MAGICIAN** is a popular entertainer these days. He can utilize the company name and product names as his magic words. Company products can be used as props.

For additional ideas to use at your suite see Chapter 16.

Chapter 21

How to Plan, Promote, and Conduct the Golf Tournament

Contents

1. Planning the Golf Tournament
2. Showmanship Ideas
3. Other Golf Events if Time Allows
4. How to Promote the Tournament
5. Enclosures for Golf Promotional Mailings
6. Golf Evening Entertainment
7. Golf Gags
8. Golf Giveaways
9. Golf Awards
10. Golf Accessory and Giveaway Suppliers

1. PLANNING THE GOLF TOURNAMENT.

(a) Planning Checklist.
- It is assumed that when the meeting site was chosen that reservations for "tournament play" were available.
- Enlist the assistance of the golf pro and the club manager in planning the tournament; this is basic.
- Appoint an individual in your organization to be responsible for the tournament.
- Plan well in advance. Have an alternate day of the week if possible, as the course may be busy.
- Provide a count of number of players.
- Provide the starting times. Request that the times be guaranteed.
- Estimate the costs. Obtain from the club a list of expenses. This may bring up items you may not have thought of, such as locker room attendant, caddies, etc.
- Advise number of rental sets required (indicate number of right and left hand), quantity of rental shoes, approximate number of golf carts.
- Advise who will pay the bills for greens fees, power and hand carts, club rentals for the tournament, and who pays for golf during other days of the meeting. Also find out the number of caddies required, fees, and when available.
- Determine prizes to be awarded.
- Identify V.I.P.'s for special courtesies such as special starting times.
- Advise the club manager if starting times during business meeting hours are to be honored.
- Advise the club manager if nonplayers will be available to assist the pro with tournament scores if required.
- Set the number of refreshment carts required and determine who will drive the carts.

The Golf Tournament

- Determine fee for bucket of balls for driving range.
- Check transportation requirements; the course may be some distance from the meeting site.
- Check clubhouse bar service facilities.
- Check on the lockers. How many are available for men and women, and what is the fee?
- Check on golf club storage facilities.
- Can a golf clinic or exhibition be arranged?
- Obtain a copy of the course rules.
- Determine how the accounting will be handled—which items are to be charged to the master account and which to individual accounts.

(b) Handicapping.

There are several methods of handicapping. Here are some:
a. Ask the player his handicap.
b. Ask the player to provide a golf club card with his handicap.
c. Use the Calloway method.

(c) The Calloway System for Handicapping the Unhandicapped.

Strokes are deducted from the gross score. The greater the gross score, the larger the number of strokes which may be deducted. Examples:

Gross Score	Deduct
One over par to 75	½ worst hole
76 to 80	Worst hole
81 to 85	Worst hole plus ½ of next hole
89 to 90	Two worst holes
91 to 95	Two worst holes plus ½ of next hole
96 to 100	Three worst holes
101 to 105	Three worst holes plus ½ of next hole
106 to 110	Four worst holes
111 to 115	Four worst holes plus ½ of next hole
116 to 120	Five worst holes
121 to 125	Five worst holes plus ½ of next hole
126 to 130	Six worst holes
131 to 135	Six worst holes plus ½ of next hole
136 to 140	Seven worst holes

(d) Pairing.

Pair players according to their skills.

Note: Generally it is best to pair the skill groups according to age or let the members elect to form their own foursomes if they wish. Do this by mail in advance.

(e) Publish the Rules of the Tournament, and other necessary information.

This information should give the rules, the fees, handicap system, system for awarding of prizes, and time of the tournament. Also give credit to the tournament committee members.

(f) Scheduling Large Groups of Players (For a Half Day).

Groups to about 30	All players start from the first tee.
30 to 50	Players start from first tee and tenth tee.
50 to 75	Players start from first tee, tenth tee, and several other available open tees.
75 to 125	Use a "Shotgun Start." Foursomes are placed on each of the tees. All start simultaneously at the firing of a shotgun. All leftover players start from the first hole.
More than 125	Hold a Shotgun Start for half of the group in the morning and half in the afternoon, or consider using two courses. You might consider assigning fivesomes instead of foursomes.

(g) Golf for Couples. Here are several suggested options:
- *Scotch Foursomes.* The partner team plays with only one ball, alternating shots. The partner who may not play well is thus not under competitive pressure.
- Pair the players by handicaps.
- The golfers draw for partners.

(h) Give Prizes for Special Achievements. Here are a few:

Lowest individual score	For selected holes:
Best team	Closest to the pin
Best game	Longest drive
Best individual shots	Longest putt
Fewest total putts	Best chip shot
	Low gross
	Low net
	Individual low scratch

(i) Hold Tournaments for the Nongolfers. These events can be fishing, ping pong, shuffleboard, tennis, bowling, water skiing, etc. The prizes of these other major tournaments should be of the same value as those given for golf. If the swimming area is conducive to it, arrange a snorkel treasure hunt for the swimmers.

(j) Ladies Golf Tournament. Schedule the event while the husbands are in meetings. Consider making it a nine-hole tournament. The wives thus also get to play on the same course. Consider holding a putting contest for those who would rather just putt. Arrange other types of tournaments for the lady nongolfers (canasta, bridge).

Obtain AGS's 4″ × 8″ colorful Official Rules for Golf Tournament and give to each member.

(k) **Rules of Golf.** The tournament chairman should obtain a copy of "The Official Rules of Golf." Available from United States Golf Association, Golf House, 40 E. 38th St., New York, N.Y.

(l) **When It Rains.** *Plan #1:* Schedule the golf tournament for later in the day or the next day. Change the meeting schedule accordingly. If it keeps raining or the meeting time has run out, consider *Plan #2* which is holding a putting contest indoors. Find a room and clear it. Set up a nine-hole course using masking tape for boundaries. Use a glass, placed on its side, as the hole. It may be wise to prepare for this contingency by purchasing indoor putting equipment in advance. Also purchase a roll of indoor artificial turf for some of the holes. Place books, boards, etc. under the turf to make some of the holes interesting. Indoor golf cups may be obtained from C. I. Industries, 3210 N. Pierce St., Milwaukee, Wis. 53212. Obtain turf from a hardware store.

2. SHOWMANSHIP IDEAS.

(a) **Refreshment Carts.** Assign volunteers or, better yet, pretty girls to drive beverage golf carts. Use one cart for each nine holes.

(b) **Golf Flags** can be used to indicate closest to the pin, longest drive, etc. Use the meeting theme insignia or company logo on these golf flags.

(c) **Golf Umbrella.** You may want to purchase a few golf umbrellas for emergencies. A self-opening all-weather Unisel Golf & Fun Umbrella is available for $10. The price is $13 for each imprinted umbrella. Available from Idea Man, 1435 LaCienega Blvd., Los Angeles, Calif. 90035. Another supplier is D. Klein & Sons, Inc., 345 Lodi St., Hackensack, N.J. 07602.

(d) **Fairway Signs.** If a promotion or sales contest is announced at the conference, signs can be placed at various locations on the fairway, at the tee-off location, and on the pin flag. Relate the wording to the contest or the promotion. The signs could be used to point out advantages of a new product. They could also contain a message from the hole sponsor, if several companies are sponsoring the tournament.

(e) **Girl Caddies.** At the 16th hole have girl caddies join the surprised players. This is less strenuous for the girls and fewer caddies are required. This stunt was used in Hawaii with the girls dressed in native costume.

(f) Golf Themes can be easily tied in with the meeting objectives. Thumb through a golf dictionary and you will find ideas for use throughout the meeting program. Here are a few examples: "Drive for show, putt for dough," "Blast out." Competition can be tied in with "Learn from your opponent." "Practice makes perfect!" Problems to be solved can be titled "Sandtraps" or "Bunkers." An idea exchange session can be titled "Learn from the pros." Another session can be titled "How to play out of the rough."

3. OTHER GOLF EVENTS IF TIME ALLOWS.

(a) Driving Contest. Give each contestant five drives with the best three counting. The shots in the fairway are the only ones which count. Place marker flags each 25 yards from 125 to 300 yards. Judges are stationed on the fairway.

(b) Putting Contest. Set up putting contest during free time.

(c) Cross Country Tournament. The starting point should be about a mile from the golf course. The end should be on one of the greens near the clubhouse. Make your own rules such as: the ball must be played from wherever it lies. If unplayable, it may be played from a tee with a penalty of two strokes.

(d) Fewest Putts. The total number of putts for the round is counted. No putts are conceded. Only the shots made from the clipped portion of the green count. If a putter is used to play from off the green, it does not count.

(e) Bingle-Bangle-Bungle. This may be played in addition to the regular game. Three points are earned on each hole. The first player to reach the green (the clipped portion) earns a point. The player whose ball is nearest to the cup after all players land on the green wins a point. And the player who first sinks his putt wins a point. If continuous putting is used, then the earning of the third point is eliminated. Total points won for the course may be counted, or each player wins the difference between his points and the total points of each player with fewer points.

(f) Two-Ball Foursome. There are two players to a team. They use only one ball between them and they alternate the shots. On even tees one partner drives and on odd tees the other partner drives.

(g) Golf Calcutta. This event generally is conducted as follows: Handicaps and other known performance criteria of the individual players or teams are posted. A decision is made in advance and announced that a certain percent

The Golf Tournament 245

of the winnings go to the first, second, and third; and any other place winner desired. An auction is held in which the players or teams go up for bidding. There is only one successful bidder for each player or team; the players may place bids on themselves if they wish. All of the bid money goes in the pot where, after the game, the winnings are shared according to the announced percentage.

4. HOW TO PROMOTE THE TOURNAMENT.

- Mail postcards showing the course along with a message from the pro.
- Set up and promote a golf clinic.
- Obtain photos of the various holes and reproduce and mail.
- Mail score cards in advance. A number of courses have "True Distance Aerial Model" score cards. These cards show aerial views of the holes and give key distances to the obstacles thus enabling the player to study how to play the holes weeks in advance.
- Determine if slides or 16mm motion pictures are available from the meeting site for showing at a preconference meeting.
- Films on the U.S. Opens are available from the United States Golf Association, Golf House, Far Hills, N.J. 07931.
- Send along enclosures from the resort such as ball markers or tees.
- Utilize syndicated art cartoon books for illustrations. See "Clip Art" in Appendix II.
- There are a number of colorful bulletin heads which can be utilized for mailing. Sources are listed under "Bulletin Heads" in Appendix II.
- *Eastern Airlines has a "Flying Golfers Club"* for those who love golf and fly Eastern. Contact any local sales office or their headquarters for promotional items furnished at no charge. Headquarters is 10 Rockefeller Plaza, New York, N.Y. 10020. The extent of promotional assistance depends upon the number of persons in the organization. Assistance includes a tournament Master Score Sheet and an excellent booklet for aiding the golf committee in setting up tournaments titled "Competitive Golf Events." The booklet is published by the National Golf Foundation, 804 Merchandise Mart, Chicago, Ill. 60654.

5. ENCLOSURES FOR GOLF PROMOTIONAL MAILINGS.

(a) "Golf Coach" is the name of a circular slide chart. Give this to each player. Fifteen problems such as "topping," "under trees," and "pitch shot over sand trap to green" are covered. The dial is turned to the answer. The correct stance for the shot is also given. A chart for the correct club for various yardages is pictured. Write to Perry Graf Corp., 2215 Colby Ave., Los Angeles, Calif. 90064.

(b) "Golf Gismo." This consists of an inexpensive small, flat, triangular piece of animated 3-D plastic which is placed under the tee. If you can hold the arrows steady as you address the ball, you are right on the ball. It doubles as an identification tag for your gear. Available from Vari-Vue International, 650 S. Columbus Ave., Mt. Vernon, N.Y. 10551.

(c) "Flip Fact" is the name of a booklet on how to play better golf. Flip the pages and learn how to hit the ball correctly. The booklets may be imprinted. It is available in two colors, and is ⅓" thick, 3" × 4". Available from Hewig & Marvic, 861 Manhattan Ave., New York, N.Y. 11222.

(d) Golf Club Pencils. These are wooden pencils with a driver on the end. They can be imprinted. Available from Hewig & Marvic (above).

6. GOLF EVENING ENTERTAINMENT.

(a) Golf Films make good entertainment. They can be rented at approximately $10 each per showing. Available films include "On the Tee" and "Pitching Wedge." Jack Nicklaus gives tips on how to grip, correct your hook, and line up shots. The films are in color and many of the scenes are in slow motion. Order from United World Films, 221 Park Ave. South, New York, N.Y. 10003; or 542 S. Dearborn St., Chicago, Ill. 60605; Budget Films, 4590 Santa Monica Blvd., Los Angeles, Calif.; United Films, 6420-C, Fair Oaks Blvd., Carmichael, Calif.; or check your Yellow Pages under "Motion Picture Film Distributors." Also contact Modern Talking Pictures, 1212 Ave. of the Americas, New York, N.Y. 10036. They may have free golf films sponsored by a sports manufacturer at the time of your request.

(b) Source for Sports Star Speakers. Contact Burns Sports Celebrity Service, Inc., One IBM Plaza, Chicago, Ill. 60611.

7. GOLF GAGS.

Outfit a number of golfers with the following: golf balls that roll crookedly, balls that leave a trail of smoke, balls that explode, balls that open in the air and release a parachute. Available from D. Robbins & Co., 127 West 17th St., New York, N.Y.

You can obtain a carbide cannon and fire it during the opening and closing shots. Available from Conestoga Co., Inc., 732 E. Goeppe St., Bethlehem, Pa. 18018.

8. GOLF GIVEAWAYS.

(a) Golf, Bowling, Fishing Towels. "Golf is Hell!" is the message on one golf towel. Hamm's beer used a cartoon of their bear hitting a ball. Available with or without chain. Cost is from 71¢ to 85¢ each. Minimum order is 1,200.

Screen set-up charge is about $50 per color. Available from R. A. Briggs & Co., Lake Zurich, Ill. 60047. Another supplier is Crestline Co., Inc., 18 West 18th St., New York, N.Y. 10011.

(b) **Imprinted Golfer's Pocket Saver** keeps all golfer's important pocket items in one handy place—no searching or hunting. Includes pocket for pen or pencil and score card, and four tee holders with four tees and ball marker. The tees and ball marker can be imprinted. Cost is around 33¢ each. Contact S. I. Jacobson Mfg. Co., 1414 So. Wabash Ave., Chicago, Ill. 60605.

(c) **Inexpensive Sports Giveaway Books.** This company has books (averaging 100 pages) on a variety of sports subjects. Size of books is $3¾'' \times 5½''$. The contents tell how to play and give sports records. Available are books on golf, tennis, football, skiing, hockey, bowling, baseball, basketball, fishing, and auto racing. Prices start at 50¢ each for 200. Your logo can be imprinted. Available from Snibbe Publications, Inc., 140 Overbrook Blvd., Bellair Bluffs, Fla. 33540. Slightly more expensive sports books can be ordered from DBI Books, Inc., 540 Frontage Rd., Northfield, Ill. 60093. Also from Crestline Co., Inc., 18 West 18th St., New York, N.Y. 10011.

(d) **Device Which Replaces Divots, Tightens Cleats, Cleans Club Heads,** and has a magnetic cover which holds two wafer-thin ball markers comes in a vinyl case which can be imprinted or silk screened. Cost is around $1 each. Available from Idea Man Inc., 1435 LaCienega Blvd., Los Angeles, Calif. 90035.

9. GOLF AWARDS.

(a) **Awarding of Trophies.** An individual knowledgeable in golf should present the trophies. Better yet, ask the pro to handle the presentations.

(b) **Give Gift Certificates.** Here is an idea which enables winners to choose the prize they really want: give gift certificates redeemable at the golf pro shop. This will solve the problem of size and color preference, and the winner can add money to the certificate to obtain a higher value gift if desired.

(c) **Perpetual Trophy.** If a perpetual trophy is used, also provide smaller trophies which the winners may keep.

(d) **Humorous Sports Award Plaques.** These humorous plaques make unusual awards. They use golf, bowling, and tennis as a theme. They are available in ten varieties for each sport. They feature cheating golfers, four-armed tennis players, and all types of zany sportsmen. The plaque can be personalized. They measure approximately $6'' \times 8''$. Prices range from 10¢ to $4.50. Available from Idea Man Inc., 1435 S. LaCienega Blvd., Los Angeles, Calif. 90035.

(e) Original Golf Awards. Have an artist paint a golf visor to your specifications as an award. Consider doing this with a T-shirt also.

(f) Sports Award Plaques. This company has a series of sports award plaques for tennis, golf, bowling, etc. Contact R. D. Grunert Company, 150 Buckland Ave., Rochester, N.Y. 14518.

(g) Caddy-Cane. This is a unique lightweight balanced golf club carrier. Weight is 21 ounces. It holds ten golf clubs, four golf balls, and six tees. It is made of anodized aluminum and is available in seven different colors. Order from Modern Manufacturing Inc. of Worcester, Brussels St., Worcester, Mass. 01613. List price is about $16, but discounts are available on quantity orders.

(h) This Custom Putter Has Three Weights in the Head, enabling the player to change the weight and distribution. Create the putter that exactly matches "your feel" for that day. Cost is around $25. Available from Yourfeel Products Corp., Premium & Incentive Division, 3300 North Knox Ave., Chicago, Ill.

(i) Crazy Putter. Excellent for a gag prize. It's a stainless steel putter which has a shaft that contains a number of curves. Price is around $30. Available from Chicago Vacuum Casting Corp., 451 Claremont Ave., Chicago, Ill. 60612.

(j) The Better Golf Ball Markers are individually hand cut from real U.S. coins and mounted with a choice of post back or snap back so that the coin can be conveniently stored on a golf glove or bag. Available in a variety of coins such as nickels, dimes, Indian heads, and even Lincoln smoking a pipe. Available from Sterling Creations, P.O. Box 162, San Bruno, Calif. 94066.

(k) Six-Pack Cooler. It holds six beverage cans and keeps them cold for hours. The cans are stacked vertically in this container. They are available with your company logo. Order from Nappe-Smith, Farmingdale, N.J. 07727.

10. GOLF ACCESSORY AND GIVEAWAY SUPPLIERS.

Golf Towels:	Jack Nadel, Inc., 9950 W. Jefferson Blvd., Culver City, Calif. 90230
	Crestline, Inc., 18 W. 18th St., New York, N.Y. 10011
	Golf Ball Advertising Co., P.O. Box 4332, Philadelphia, Pa. 19118.
Golf Bag Covers, Caddy Bags, Shag Bags, Locker Bags:	Airline Textile Mfg. Co., P.O. Box 477, Des Moines, Iowa 50302

The Golf Tournament

Golf Accessories:
 Macademic Sales Corp., 861 Manhattan Ave., Brooklyn, N.Y. 11222
 Ajay Enterprises, 1501 E. Wisconsin St., Delavan, Wis. 53115
 Fred Stoffel Associates, 723 E. California Blvd., Pasadena, Calif. 91106
 Chesal Industries, 3210 N. Pierce St., Milwaukee, Wis. 53212
 JFK Products, Walnut Creek, Calif.

Golf Balls:
 AMF Ben Hogan Co., Premium Sales Dept., 261 Madison Ave., New York, N.Y. 10016
 Plymouth Golf Ball Co., Butler Pike, Plymouth Meeting, Pa., 19462
 Burke-Worthington Div., Victor Golf Co., 8350 N. Lehigh Ave., Morton Grove, Ill. 60053
 Wilson Sporting Goods, 2233 W. St., River Grove, Ill. 60171
 Ram Golf Corp., 1501 Pratt Blvd., Elk Grove Village, Ill. 60007

Golf Caps & Hats:
 Derby Cap Manufacturing Co., 700 W. Main St., Louisville, Ky. 40202
 Golf Ball Advertising Co., P.O. Box 332, Philadelphia, Pa., 19118
 Makley's, 441 S. Plymouth Ct., Chicago, Ill. 60605
 Newark Felt Novelty Co., 50 Jelliff Ave., Newark, N.J. 07108
 Advon Specialties, P.O. Box 552, Hopkins, Minn. 55343
 Lewton Industries Corp., 30 High St., Hartford, Conn. 06101
 Marquardt Advertising Co., P.O. Box 603, Des Monies, Iowa 50303

Golf Visors:
 Roberta's, P.O. Box 630, Shelbyville, Ind. 46176

Golf Clubs & Equipment:
 McDonald & Son Golf Co., 103 S. Island, P.O. Box 214, Batavia, Ill. 60510
 MacGregor/Brunswick, 1-75 Jimson Rd., Cincinnati, Ohio 45215
 ABC Industries, Inc., 827 E. Locust St., Milwaukee, Wis. 53212

AMF Ben Hogan Co., 261 Madison Ave., Morton Grove, Ill. 60053

J. A. Dibow Sporting Goods Corp., 2037 N. Campbell, Chicago, Ill. 60647

Golf Putter & Cup: C. I. Industries, 3210 N. Pierce St., Milwaukee, Wisc. 53212

Golf Shot Computer, Golf Mate, Twirl-A-Dial to correct shanking, topping and slicing: Hewig & Marvic, 861 Manhattan Ave., New York, N.Y. 11222

Golf Tees, Markers, Cleat Wrenches:
Baldwin Cooke Co., 5714 W. Dempster St., Morton Grove, Ill. 60053
C. C. Marketing Services, 70-25 Parsons Blvd., Flushing, N.Y. 11365
Golf Ball Advertising Co., P.O. Box 4332, Philadelphia, Pa. 19118
Art-Mold Products, 780 Wellington Ave., Cranston, R.I. 02910
Cl Industries, 3210 N. Pierce St., Milwaukee, Wis. 53212
Hewig & Marvic, 861 Manhattan Ave., New York, N.Y. 11222

Golf Flags: Valley Forge Flag Co. Inc., One Rockefeller Plaza, New York, N.Y. 10020

Tennis Giftware: For prizes for those tennis athletes write to Beakgaard, Ltd., 1855 Janke, Dr., Northbrook, Ill. 60662

Tennis Hats: Lewtan Industries Corp., 30 High St., Hartford, Conn. 06101

Golf Gags: (Crooked rolling balls, exploding balls, etc.) D. D. Robbins & Co., 127 W. 17th St., New York, N.Y.

Golf Umbrellas:
Golf Ball Advertising Co., P.O. Box 4332, Philadelphia, Pa. 19118
Bass Advertising Specialties, 4317 Lafayette, Bellaire, Tex. 77401

Golfer's Prayer: Carved on simulated wooden plaque. Multi Products, Inc., 824 West 36th St., Chicago, Ill. 60609

Golf Bag Tags: Crestline Co., Inc., 18 W. 18th St., New York, N.Y. 10011

Golf Bag Carry-All: Holds golf bag, clubs, shoes, clothing. Serves as a pilfer-proof shipper. S. I. Jacobson Mfg. Co., 1414 So. Wabash Ave., Chicago, Ill. 60605.

Golf Club Kit: Contains bristle brush, one treated cloth for woods and one for irons, two markers, three tees, golfer's handbook, shoe horn. 50 cost $2.50 each, 250—$2.25. Lewtan Industries Corp., 30 High Street, Hartford, Conn. 60101

Chapter 22

12 Step-by-Step Conference Planning Checklists

Contents

1. Committee Delegation Checklist
2. Budget Planning Checklist
3. Site Selection Checklist
4. Hotel Inspection Checklist
5. Meeting Rooms Prop Checklist
6. Registration Checklist
7. Reception and Banquet Checklist
8. Beverage Checklist
9. Beverage Cost Estimate Checklist
10. Gratuity Checklist
11. Speaker Checklist
12. Publicity and Press Relations Checklist

1. COMMITTEE DELEGATION CHECKLIST.

_____ General Chairman

_____ Steering Committee

_____ Budget & Finance

_____ Transportation

_____ Hotel Reservations

_____ Registration & Welcome Kit (badges, clipboards, programs, announcements)

_____ Hotel Arrangements
  Meals, coffee breaks, seating requirements, gratuities, hotel entertainment, reception, cocktail parties, props.

Program
_____ Product & Sales Presentations
_____ Workshops
_____ Program Requirements Coordinator (details copy & art for slides, flip charts, audio-visual and prop requirements).
_____ Literature & Audio Visual Production
_____ Outside Speakers
_____ Rehearsals
_____ Projectionist, Sound, Lights

Banquet & Entertainment
_____ Hospitality Suite
_____ Banquet Meal and Beverage
_____ Banquet Program
_____ Decorations and Mementos
_____ Outside Entertainers

12 Step-by-Step Conference Planning Checklists 255

	Promotion & Publicity
_____	Printed Program
_____	Invitations, Teaser & Informative Mailings
_____	Publicity
_____	Photographer
_____	Trophies (Sales and Recreation Awards)
_____	Conference Newspaper
_____	Post-Conference Brochure
_____	Signs, Banners, Posters

_____ Golf Tournament

_____ Other Recreation and Tours

_____ Ladies Program

2. BUDGET PLANNING CHECKLIST.

FACILITIES

	Number	@ $	No. Days	$ Total
Guest Rooms	_____			
Single	_____	_____	_____	_____
Double	_____	_____	_____	_____
Suites	_____	_____	_____	_____
Main Meeting Room	_____	_____	_____	_____
Conference Rooms	_____	_____	_____	_____
Hospitality Suite	_____	_____	_____	_____
Ballroom	_____	_____	_____	_____
Administration Room	_____	_____	_____	_____
				$

MEALS & BANQUET

	Persons	@ $	No. Days	$ Total
Breakfast	_____	_____	_____	_____
Lunch	_____	_____	_____	_____
Dinner	_____	_____	_____	_____
Coffee Breaks	_____	_____	_____	_____
Extra for Banquet	_____	_____	_____	_____
Cocktail Party	_____	_____	_____	_____
Hors D'Oeuvres	_____	_____	_____	_____
Decorations				_____
Corsages				_____
Table Wine	_____	_____	_____	_____
Place Cards	_____	_____	_____	_____
Printed Menus	_____	_____	_____	_____
Outside Meals	_____	_____	_____	_____
				$

TRANSPORTATION

	Persons	Average $	$ Total
Plane or Railroad	_____	_____	_____
Car	_____	_____	_____
Transportation from Airport to Hotel	_____	_____	_____
Local Transportation	_____	_____	_____
Car Rentals at Site	_____	_____	_____

PROP RENTAL

$_____ Audio-Visual Rental (projectors, screens, tape recorder)
_____ Other props (blackboards, easels)
_____ Projectionist
_____ Typewriters
_____ Musical Tape   Total Props $_____
_____

HOTEL PERSONNEL CHARGES

$_____ Carpentry
_____ Housemen for setting up auditorium, displays
_____ Sound Engineers
_____ Projectionists
_____ Stage Hands   Total Hotel Personnel $_____

BEVERAGE

$_____ Reception
_____ Cocktail Parties
_____ Dinner
_____ Banquet
_____ Hospitality Suite including snacks
_____ For VIP Suites
_____ Bartenders   Total Beverage $_____
_____ GRATUITIES @ _____%   Total Gratuities $_____

RECREATION

$_____ Golf
_____ Other Recreation
_____ Tours
_____ Prizes   Total Recreation $_____

12 Step-by-Step Conference Planning Checklists   257

OTHER

$____ Welcome Kit (container, writing pads, souvenir, announcements, pens, etc.)
____ Banners & Signs
____ Preconference Inspection Trips
____ Entertainment:
      Cocktail Party $_____
      Dance Orchestra $_____
____ Outside Speakers
____ Printed Program
____ Invitations
____ Teaser Mailings, Attendance Builders
____ Registration Forms, Badges
____ Novelty Items (balloons, hats, etc.)
____ Attendance Prizes
____ Corsages & Flower Decorations
____ Matchbooks, Coasters, Napkins
____ Notices
____ Printed Menus
____ Recognition Trophies & Plaques, Certificates
____ VIP Gifts
____ Daily Newspaper
____ Stenographer
____ Photography
____ Postage, Parcel Post, Express
____ Reserve for Miscellaneous

                              Total Other $_____

MEETING MATERIALS

$____ Flip Charts
____ Slides
____ Printed Literature
____ Displays
____ Cartage & Freight
____ Film Rental

                              Total Meeting Materials $_____

PUBLICITY

$_____ Press Room Rental
_____ Press Party Expense
_____ Typewriters
_____ Telephones
_____ Press Releases
_____ _____
_____ _____ Total Publicity $_____

MISCELLANEOUS

$_____ _____
_____ _____
_____ _____
_____ _____
_____ _____
_____ _____ Total Miscellaneous $_____

GRAND TOTAL ....$_____

3. SITE SELECTION CHECKLIST.

FACILITY NAME: _____

Location _____
Convention Mgr. _____
Phone _____
Checked By _____

Estimated Attendees	
How Many Compulsory	
How Many Voluntary	
Date Main Group Arrives	
Date Main Group Leaves	
Rooms Required:	
Singles	
Doubles	
Suites	
Auditorium Capacity Req'd.	
No. Meeting Rooms Req'd.	
Capacity Each Required	
Exhibit Room Size Req'd.	
Banquet Capacity Req'd.	
Ballroom Required	
Special Food Functions	
_____	

12 Step-by-Step Conference Planning Checklists

Dates Available _____
Number of Guest Rooms _____
Climate _____
Air Conditioned? _____ Guest Rooms _____ Meeting Rooms _____
Room Rate: Singles _____ Doubles _____ Suites _____
American Plan Rate _____ Group Meals Rate _____
Convention Rate _____ Convention Season _____
Gratuity Rate _____
Any Charge for Auditorium? _____
Any Charge for Meeting Rooms? _____
Auditorium Capacity _____ Stage Size _____
Exhibit Space _____
Meeting Rooms Sufficient in Number & Capacity? _____
_____
Liquor Served on Premises? _____
Miles from Airport _____ from Nearest City _____
Transport Service from Airport to Facility _____
Golf Availability _____
Sports Facilities on Site _____
Special Attractions & Services (Tours, On Ocean, Sauna, etc.) _____
_____
Adequate Audio-Visual Facilities on Hand _____
_____

4. HOTEL INSPECTION CHECKLIST.

Inspected By _____   Date _____

HOTEL: _____

Location: _____

Estimated Attendees	
How Many Compulsory	
How Many Voluntary	
Date Main Group Arrives	
Date Main Group Leaves	
Rooms Required:	
Singles	
Doubles	
Suites	
Autitorium Capacity Req'd.	
No. Meeting Rooms Req'd.	
Capacity Each Required	
Exhibit Room Size Req'd.	
Banquet Capacity Req'd.	
Ballroom Required	
Special Food Functions	

Convention Manager _____ Phone _____
Reservation Manager _____
Catering Manager _____
Dates Available _____
Room Rate & Capacity:

	Rate	Capacity
Singles	$_____	_____
Twins	_____	_____
Doubles	_____	_____
Suites	_____	_____

American Plan Charge (with meals) _____
Rates Apply for Pre- or Post-Convention Vacation? _____

Room Inspection:
    Radio _____
    TV _____
    Air Conditioning _____
    Size _____
    Furnishings _____
Check-Out Time _____
Accept Credit Cards? _____ Policy on Checks _____
Policy on Refunds _____
Deposit Required? _____
Advance Reservations Possible? _____
Reservation Cutoff Dates _____
Will Other Guests Be in Hotel? _____
Limo and Bus Transportation. Cost _____ Schedule _____
Entertainment Ticket Service Available _____
Gratuity Policy _____
Any Charge for Meeting Rooms _____
Any Tax _____
Any Other Charges _____
Any Guarantee Policy _____

MAIN MEETING ROOM

    Auditorium Size _____
    Auditorium Ceiling Height _____
    Stage Available _____
    Darkened for Daylight Projection _____
    Air Conditioned _____
    Convenient Storage Room for Props _____
    Type of Chairs _____
    Projection Booth _____
    What are housemen set up rates? _____
    What are rates for stagehands, projectionists, soundmen? _____

SEMINAR ROOMS
    Conveniently Located? _____
    Types of Rooms _____
    _____
    Capacity _____
    Air Conditioned _____
    Closed Circuit TV _____

HOSPITALITY ROOM
    Furnishings, Decor _____
    Bartender Charge _____
    Charge Per Bottle or Per Drink _____
    Charge for Nuts, Potato Chips, etc. _____
    Card Playing Facilities _____
    Does Hotel Have Liquor License _____

MEALS
    Coffee Break Charge _____
    Obtain Sample Menus & Beverage Lists _____
    Average Charge Breakfast _____, Lunch _____,
        Dinner _____. Tip and Tax Included? _____
    For speed, is Buffet Breakfast available? _____
    Does Hotel have special entertainment such as steak fry, luau,
        Bavarian dinner, etc. _____
    Banquet Attendance Guarantee Policy _____
    Room Service Charge _____
    Number of Public Dining Rooms _____
    Obtain Banquet Menus _____
    Hotel Public Dining Room Hours:
        Breakfast _____
        Lunch _____
        Dinner _____

RECEPTION & COCKTAIL PARTY
    Drink Charge _____
    Hors D'Oeuvres Charge _____
    Entertainment Suggestions & Charge _____
    _____

AUDIO/VISUAL
    Screen Available? _____ Size _____
    Blackboards _____
    Easels _____
    Tape Recorders _____ Speed _____
    Slide Projectors: Quantity _____
        Type _____ Slide Size _____

Movie Projector _____ Film Size _____
Spotlight Available _____
Piano _____
Flags & Banners Available _____
Vu-graph _____
Opaque Projector _____

BANQUET

Theme Decorations Available _____

Party Hats, Balloons, etc. Available? _____

Suggested Banquet Entertainment _____

Estimated Additional Costs for Banquet _____

RECREATION

Does Hotel have an Entertainment Director? _____
  Name _____
Types of Recreation on Premises _____

Recreation Available Outside Hotel (fishing, sailing, etc.) _____

Recommended Golf Course _____
  Address _____ Phone _____
  Distance from Hotel _____
Suggested Tours _____

Tour or Bus Company Name _____
  Address _____
Ladies Activities Suggestions _____

OTHER

Any suggestions for a Room Welcome (bottled miniature drinks, cheeses, etc.). _____

Local Memento Suggestions _____

Promotional Aids Available (post cards, brochures, etc.) _____

Any entertainment in public rooms (public dancing, music, movies, etc.)?
_____

12 Step-by-Step Conference Planning Checklists

Photographer:
    Charges _____
    Available on speculative basis? _____
Room Map Available? _____
Baby Sitters _____
Stenographic Service Available? _____
Duplicating Services _____
Car Rentals _____
Hotel Bar hours _____

5. MEETING ROOMS PROP CHECKLIST.

AUDITORIUM

Item	Supplied By Self	Supplied By Hotel
Platforms. Size & Height _____	_____	_____
Stage Risers	_____	_____
Tables & Chairs for Stage	_____	_____
Panel Member Name Plates	_____	_____
Name Plate Holders	_____	_____
Audience Seating Requirements	_____	_____
Speaker Mike	_____	_____
Table Mikes	_____	_____
Traveling Mikes. Quantity _____	_____	_____
Sound Amplifier	_____	_____
Speakers	_____	_____
Lighted Lectern	_____	_____
Gavel & Block	_____	_____
Teleprompter	_____	_____
Movie Screen	_____	_____
Movie Projector. Size _____	_____	_____
Slide Projectors. Size _____	_____	_____
Vu-graph	_____	_____
Opaque Projector	_____	_____
Extra Projection Lamps	_____	_____
Remote Control Slide Changer	_____	_____
Extension Cords	_____	_____
3-Prong Adapters	_____	_____
Projector Table	_____	_____
Overhead Projector	_____	_____
Blackout Curtains	_____	_____
Tape Recorder. Speed _____	_____	_____
Spotlights	_____	_____
Record Player. Size record _____	_____	_____

Record Player Speed _____ _____ _____
Easels _____ _____
Blackboard. Chalk & Eraser _____ _____
Pointer, Hand _____ _____
Pointer, Electric _____ _____
Chart Pad _____ _____
Flannel Board _____ _____
Lobby Sign _____ _____
Room Identification Sign _____ _____
Flags _____ _____
Theme Banners _____ _____
Decorations _____ _____
Flowers or Plants _____ _____
Piano or Organ _____ _____
Projectionist _____ _____
Photographer _____ _____
Ashtrays _____ _____
Drinking Water & Glasses (speaker) _____ _____
Notepads & Pencils _____ _____
Premeeting Music _____ _____
Tables for Displays _____ _____
Blackout Switch _____ _____
Dressing Rooms _____ _____
Storage Room _____ _____
Check Fire Regulations _____ _____
Checkroom _____ _____
Coffee Break _____ _____
Union Requirements _____ _____

SEMINAR ROOMS _____ _____

Chairs _____ _____
Tables _____ _____
Seating Arrangement _____ _____
Easels _____ _____
Chart Pad _____ _____
Grease Pencil or Ink Marker _____ _____
Blackboards _____ _____
Chalk & Eraser _____ _____
Blackout Curtains _____ _____
Slide Projector. Size _____ _____ _____
Extra Projection Lamp _____ _____
Projector Table _____ _____
Extension Cord _____ _____

12 Step-by-Step Conference Planning Checklists

Projector Slide Cartridge _____ _____
Slide Changer Extension Cord _____ _____
Overhead Projector _____ _____
Ashtrays _____ _____
Ice Water & Glasses _____ _____
Pencils & Notepads _____ _____
Pointer _____ _____
Room Identification Sign _____ _____
Directional Signs _____ _____
Coffee Break Arrangements _____ _____
String, rope, tape, thumb tacks for banners & signs _____ _____

6. REGISTRATION CHECKLIST.

Registration Personnel Required:
   Own _____ Hotel _____
Convention Bureau _____

Quantity Required	Item	Supplied By Self	By Hotel
	Printing		
_____	Badges	_____	_____
_____	Badge Holders	_____	_____
_____	Registration Cards	_____	_____
_____	Registration Lists	_____	_____
_____	Tickets	_____	_____
_____	Programs	_____	_____
_____	Meeting Literature	_____	_____
_____	Announcements	_____	_____
	Stationery & Supplies		
_____	Cards & Card Files	_____	_____
_____	Steel Money Box	_____	_____
_____	Numbering Machines	_____	_____
_____	Paper Clips	_____	_____
_____	Pens	_____	_____
_____	Pencils	_____	_____
_____	Rubber Bands	_____	_____
_____	Rubber Stamps	_____	_____
_____	Staplers, Staples, Staple Remover	_____	_____
_____	Typewriters	_____	_____
_____	Typewriter Erasers	_____	_____
_____	Memo Pads	_____	_____

Hotel Furniture

	Work Tables. Size _____.		
	Tables for Guests to Fill Out Forms		
	Chairs		
	Wastebaskets		
	Ashtrays		
	Water Pitchers & Glasses		
	Easels for Signs		
	Bulletin Boards. Size _____.		

Signs

	Welcome Signs		
	Instruction Signs		
	Direction Signs		
	Announcement Signs		

☐ Formalize registration procedure.
☐ Has policy been set on accepting checks?
☐ Policy on refunds.
☐ Any special registration for dignitaries and guests?

7. RECEPTION AND BANQUET CHECKLIST.

Date Held _____ Room _____
Hour _____ Hotel Contact _____

BANQUET
    Will a cocktail precede the banquet?
    Menu selected (fish alternate if Friday)
    Children's plates required
    Dinner wine selected
    Price and tax determined
    Gratuity determined
    Guarantees set. (If a voluntary attendance banquet, guarantee approximately 10% less than estimated attendance.)
    Exact serving time set
    When tables should be cleared
    Decorations selected. (Check the fire laws.)
    Centerpieces?
    Seating style
    Head table seating
    Coat Checking Facilities
    Ticket collection table
    Table for trophy awards, etc.

Music available from house sound system?
Cigars, cigarettes, matches

Props:
Platforms
Lighted lectern and microphone
Water pitcher and glass at lectern
Banners and flags
Spotlights and floods
Tape recorder and operator
Record player and operator
Projection equipment and operator
Easels for signs

Handled by Organization:
Tickets printed and numbered
Ticket collection at door or at tables?
Arrangements for ticket sales to late comers
Menu printed (or printed by hotel?)
Decoration crew designated if handled by organization
Place cards printed or signs for reserved tables
Directional signs
Room entrance easel sign
Number at head table determined
Head table members notified
Corsages furnished by hotel or organization
Corsage delivery to rooms scheduled
Favors selected
Door prizes
Party hats, balloons, banners, streamers
Provide taped or recorded music
Imprinted matches?
Greeters and farewell committee selected
Person assigned to remove organization property

COCKTAIL PARTY OR RECEPTION
Date _____ Location _____

Appetizers selected
Bar facilities
Strolling musicians?
Taped music
Bar operating schedule set
Beverage prices: Per bottle or per drink?
Decorations

ENTERTAINMENT

    Speaker selected and notified
    Entertainers selected
    Fee
    Dressing room required?
    Orchestra

OTHER

    Photographer selected and instructions given
    Master of Ceremonies given instructions

8. BEVERAGE CHECKLIST.

☐ Has a person been appointed to supervise each beverage event?

☐ Does the facility have a license to serve liquor?

☐ What type of bar service will be used:

    ☐ Open Bar. Same as bar service at a public bar except you have your own private room.

    ☐ By the Hour. Hotel furnishes unlimited drinks and hors d'oeuvres. Cost based on number of guests times hours.

    ☐ By the bottle. Check if bartender fee and mix are included.

    ☐ Cash Bar. Use cash or chits.

    ☐ Corkage. You provide the liquor. The hotel provides the service.

☐ Are the room and personnel included in the corkage fee?

☐ Will the hotel serve its brands or your selection?

☐ To speed the service consider using a table instead of a formal bar as people tend to lounge around a bar.

☐ Establish policy with hotel on unused portions. If you pay for opened bottles, the bottle belongs to you. Give to guests or use for private hospitality suites.

☐ Set number of ounces per drink.

☐ Try to buy by the quart or case. It saves money.

☐ Fancy mixed drinks for large gatherings take time. Simple drinks are also more economical. Consider premixing cocktails such as martinis, daiquiris, whiskey sours, manhattans, old fashioneds, etc.

☐ Consider two small bars in different parts of the room to prevent jam-ups.

12 Step-by-Step Conference Planning Checklists

- ☐ Will chits solve problem of recording numbers of drinks, preventing gate crashers, or control number of drinks before a business session?
- ☐ Check the liquor inventory before and after. At $15 per bottle hundreds or thousands of dollars are involved. It's your responsibility.
- ☐ How many bartenders? Plan on one for each 30-40 persons.
- ☐ For additional service plan for an additional waiter or waitress for each 50 persons.
- ☐ Place hors d'oeuvres table so it does not interfere with bar traffic. Plan on one table per 50 persons.
- ☐ Consider having waiters serve hors d'oeuvres in addition to drinks.
- ☐ Is a greeter needed at the door?
- ☐ Set a closing time.

9. BEVERAGE COST ESTIMATE CHECKLIST.

MEASUREMENT CHART

Whiskey & Gin:

@ 1½ oz. per drink:
1 quart = 21 drinks
1 fifth = 17 drinks

Pre-dinner cocktails of 1½ hr:

2½ to 3 drinks per person
Figure 1 quart per 7 persons at the rate of 3 drinks per person.

After dinner:

2 drinks per hour
Figure 1 quart per 10 persons per hour.

Mixers:

Two bottles soda for each bottle of Scotch.
One bottle French vermouth for every three bottles gin.

Cocktails:

One gallon Martinis serves 32 persons (4 oz. glasses)
One gallon Manhattans serves 32 persons (4 oz. glasses)

BUDGET ESTIMATOR

Function: _____ Number Persons _____
Room _____

	Number Bottles	Cost Per Bottle	Total
Whiskey	$_____	$_____	$_____
Scotch	_____	_____	_____
Gin	_____	_____	_____
Vodka	_____	_____	_____
Rum	_____	_____	_____

Premixed Drinks:

_____	_____	_____	_____
_____	_____	_____	_____
_____	_____	_____	_____
_____	_____	_____	_____
Premium Beer	_____	_____	_____
Soda	_____	_____	_____
Ginger Ale	_____	_____	_____
Vermouth	_____	_____	_____
Quinine Water	_____	_____	_____

Soft Drinks:

Coke	_____	_____	_____
_____	_____	_____	_____
_____	_____	_____	_____
_____	_____	_____	_____
Tomato Juice	_____	_____	_____
TOTAL BEVERAGE	$_____	$_____	$_____

HORS D'OEUVRES

Cold $_____
Hot $_____

STAFF

	Number	$ Each	Total
Bartenders	_____	_____	_____
Waiters & Waitresses	_____	_____	_____
Tips	_____	_____	_____
TAX	_____	_____	_____

TOTAL ....$_____

10. GRATUITY CHECKLIST.

The hotel may prefer to establish an overall percentage of your bill for tips which the hotel distributes to its employees. However, you may wish to reward individuals for extra service. In addition, a "thank you" note is also much appreciated.

FOOD & BEVERAGE

- [ ] Maitre d'
- [ ] Head Waiter
- [ ] Banquet Manager
- [ ] Waiters
- [ ] Head Bartender
- [ ] Bartenders
- [ ] Wine Steward
- [ ] Service Bar Manager

SERVICE

- [ ] Superintendent of Service
- [ ] Bell Captain
- [ ] Bell Hops (if attendees notified not to tip)
- [ ] Housekeeper
- [ ] Mails
- [ ] Doorman
- [ ] Parking Attendant
- [ ] Package Room Supervisor

MEETING

- [ ] Houseman
- [ ] Electrician
- [ ] Projectionist
- [ ] Stage Hands
- [ ] Outside Service

11. SPEAKER CHECKLIST.

Invite the speakers well in advance.

THE INVITATION—Include the following:

Reason for inviting
Subject of talk. Type of talk (informative, humorous, inspirational)
Purpose of meeting. Theme
Meeting agenda
Audience composition
   (Type of audience: male, female, mixed)
Audience Size
Site Location

Time limit
Formal or informal attire
Ask for speaker's fee

CONFIRMATION

Confirm fee, expenses, and when payment made.
Confirm date.
Request biographical material and photo.
Ask for speech summary.
Notify if you plan to have a question & answer period.
If talk taped, request permission.
Is speaker's wife coming?
What special equipment is required?
Does he prefer fixed or travelling mike?
Is a spotlight required?
Notify type of room where speech will be given.
Travel instructions.

FOLLOW-UP

Printed or tentative program sent.
Where to go on arrival.
Who will meet him upon arrival.
Notify of publicity arrangements.
Give meeting room location.

PRIOR TO MEETING

Appoint person to introduce speaker.
Appoint question & answer moderator.
Make hotel reservation for speaker.

AT MEETING

Badge or Ticket
Speech equipment set up
Prop Assistant
Introduce speaker to V.I.P.'s and head table.

POST-MEETING

Send "Thank You" letter with copy to his boss.
Send check or gift.
Send publicity clippings.

12. PUBLICITY AND PRESS RELATIONS CHECKLIST.

In Advance

- ☐ Send advance publicity. Release on _____ (date).
- ☐ Send advance major speech releases on _____ (date).
- ☐ Reserve press room, typewriters, telephones.
- ☐ Appoint information center staff.
- ☐ Arrange city editors, radio, and TV contacts.
- ☐ Arrange local convention news bureau contacts.
- ☐ Arrange for photographs for publicity and for organization.
- ☐ Prepare attendance—building publicity program.
  Plan Press Party.
  - ☐ Company Officials   ☐ Food Service
  - ☐ Beverage Service   ☐ Hosts
  - ☐ Registration Staff ☐ Invitations to Press
- ☐ Provide press kit. Product photos, speech, product demonstration. Add meeting photos taken at the conference.

At Conference

- ☐ Send convention photos to newspapers and/or convention news bureau.
- ☐ Send copies of speeches to newspapers and/or convention news bureau.
- ☐ Arrange press conference, radio, and TV interviews for major speakers.
- ☐ Send releases on award winners to home-town newspapers.
- ☐ Provide information and photos to company house organs.

Appendix I

Twentieth Century Jokes and One-Liners for Speakers and Masters of Ceremony

SPEAKER AND M.C. SPECIAL SITUATIONS.

For the M.C.

Introductory remark by toastmaster:
"Gentlemen, you have been giving your attention to a turkey stuffed with sage. Now you will hear from a sage stuffed with turkey."

Clarence Budington Kelland once said, "The obvious duty of a toastmaster is to be so infernally dull that the succeeding speakers will appear brilliant by contrast."

This is Joe Doaks, the First. He's famous. They've named a street after him . . . First Street.

Let's move this right along before the martinis wear off.

Since we have just had the cocktail hour, I am having doubts about my planned words for introducing the speaker—a man who stands alone.

Our next speaker needs no introduction. He didn't show up.

Ideas are contagious to an extent, but I doubt if the people way in the back are close enough to catch anything.

We were going to call this a "shirt sleeve session." But after what happened last year we didn't know if there would be enough shirts.

The gentleman I introduce next is outstanding in his field. Come to think of it "Outstanding in his field" could mean he's either famous or a farmer.

This group represents the finest minds and talents this company has to offer—but before I begin I'd like to pause a moment and say a short prayer for our company.

We have a sobering announcement to make: the bar closes in ten minutes.

When discussing test scores: "We want you to know that the company will pay close attention to those who score A and B. However, we won't be ignoring the people who make a C—one of them might become our president."

I am glad to see so many of you wide awake this morning. You know my wife wakes up early every morning and it really annoys me. But the money she makes on the paper route helps.

Maybe the reason the product is not selling is that it's so great our men hate to part with it.

Our sales manager said the purpose of this meeting was to fire us with enthusiasm.
If I don't get my points across he just might fire me—with enthusiasm.

Response to Introduction

I didn't realize until just now that my obituary had already been prepared.

As the firefly said as he backed into the electric fan, "I'm delighted, no end."

After such a great introduction, I can hardly wait to hear myself speak.

(If bald) Thank you, John for saying in your introduction that I am an expert on _____ (subject). However, there may be something wrong with that assumption. Before they said I was an _____ expert, I was a hair care expert.

Thank you for that great introduction. Some of the facts are extra magnanimous, but speaking as a golfer, I like a good lie.

Thank you for the warm welcome. I feel as welcome as a mini-skirt in a shoe store.

That was a wonderful, warm introduction, Bill. However, if you have a life insurance policy on those jokes, collect on them!

After that handsome introduction I can't quite figure out if I am 12 feet tall or 6 feet under.

Let us say that was an acupuncture introduction—lots of needles.

A man had an accident and his brain was damaged. The surgeon tells the upset wife not to worry, as his hospital is one of the few in the world with a brain bank. "What kind of brain would you like your husband to have?"
    She asked, "What type do you have?" The surgeon told her that they have the brains of company presidents at $50 per ounce, physicists at $75 per ounce, and meeting speakers at $3,000 per ounce.
    "Why," she asked, "do you have to pay $3,000 per ounce for meeting speakers' brains?"
    "Do you realize how many meeting speakers' brains we need to make up an ounce?"

I can see that you don't really believe that introduction. If you did, you would be kneeling, not sitting.

Now I see why they call the previous gentleman a toastmaster. He's the guy who butters you up.

Speech Opening

Friends and nodding acquaintances.

How did I become a speaker? Well, you start off with a mouth full of marbles and you learn how to speak correctly. Then you take one marble out and learn how to speak like that. Then each day you take out one more marble, and when you've lost all your marbles, that's when you become a speaker.

My boss said that opportunity would be knocking, but I think it's my knees shaking.

Before I start my speech, I'd like to say something.

As I understand it, my job is to talk to you. Your job is to listen. If you finish before I do, I hope you'll let me know.

Mark Anthony: "I'm not here to make a speech."
Cleopatra: "Well, I'm not prone to argue."

After I made my last speech I asked a salesman how he would rate that speech. He said, "G.P." I asked what that stood for. He said, "Get Packing!"

I'm not sure if I'm being honored as the first speaker or if they are just making sure that the people who come in late don't miss anything.

I know all of you want to go home early, so let's make this a "meat boycott" meeting. That is, no baloney and no bull.

I gave this speech to my secretary to type. I told her to eliminate anything that sounded dull to her . . . so in conclusion. . . .

I feel like the playwright who asked the critic for his opinion of the play.
    "I found the play most refreshing," answered the critic.
    The author was pleased. "Did you really?"
    "Definitely. I felt just great after I woke up."

I saw an old hillbilly downstairs in the lobby who must have been here on his first visit to the big city. He stopped in front of the small room with the sliding door and watched an elderly lady step in. A light flashed, the door closed and she was gone. A few seconds later the light flashed again and the door opened. A beautiful blonde stepped out.
    "Boy, oh, boy," said the hillbilly, "I wish I had brought my old lady."

Pardon me if I'm nervous. I'm like the patient who was told: "You have bad nerves, you must be drinking nine or ten cups a day."
    "Actually, it's more. I spill more than that."

Some of you may have guessed that I'm a little nervous. Actually, I couldn't be more worried than the guy with sharp toenails in a waterbed.

Last night I suffered a reoccurrence of an ailment that has been very expensive for me. It's Alcoholic Acupuncture. I got stuck for the drinks.

I guess you can tell this is a prepared speech. Just add water.

The speech I gave at a meeting similar to this last month evidently rang a bell. The sales manager rushed up to me after the program and said I was a real ding-a-ling.

Speech Problems

If you are having a speech problem:
   This is the part of my presentation which I call my fish speech. I flounder.

Even if my name were Lipton, I don't believe I could be in more hot water.

When there is a mike problem:
   I'm used to talking loud so I don't need the mike. I have five kids, two TV's, a stereo, and a dog.

When having mike trouble:
   Would someone send for an electrician, please. The mike is on the bum, and what we want is the other way around.

M.C.'s reaction to a beautiful girl, "I second the emotion."

At the end of my last speech a little old lady came up to me and said, "Your speech reminded me of a little dog I have at home." "What kind of dog?" I asked. She explained, "Bull."

When something wrong happens:
   "Don't be concerned. This part is in the program. It's the part we didn't practice."

The Heckler

I see you have put in your two cents worth. It sure isn't overvalued.

A nightclub entertainer who was doing impressions of movie stars was interrupted by a heckler who requested an imitation of Lassie.
   "Of course, I'll do it," said the entertainer, "if you will stand up and play the tree."

For Joke That Bombed

Let's have a moment of silence while I pray for that story.

The way to tell who is the guest of honor at a retirement dinner is to watch all the people. The one who yawns after the boss tells the joke is the one.

When a joke doesn't go over: I think the mike is dead. Or is it me?

My speech saves on heat; it's not so hot.

Speech Closings

And we close with the immortal words of Brigham Young: "I don't care how you brig 'em, just brig 'em young!"

I feel like an Egyptian Mummy: Pressed for time.

The chairman tells me that my time is up. So I will close with the most effective close for a speaker—his mouth.

My final thought. Love thy neighbor—but draw the blinds first.

Talk-Trimmer: To make a long story short, there's nothing like the boss walking in.

Confucius Say: "When speaking—be sincere, be brief, be seated."

ANIMALS.

"I hear you shot your dog. Was he mad?"
"Well, he wasn't very happy about it."

Joe had a dog named Ben. It had pups, so he renamed it Ben Hur.

Do you know how to sculpture an elephant? It's easy. You just take a big block of marble and chip away anything that doesn't look like an elephant.

Mother anteater to baby anteater: "What do you mean you don't like ants!"

Moe: "What is it that says 'Oh boy! Oh boy! Oh boy! Oh boy!!'?"
Joe: "A boy centipede looking at a girl centipede in a miniskirt."

If the father camel has one hump, the mother camel two humps, and the young camel has no humps, what do they name the young camel?
    Answer: "Humphrey!"

Noah, after the flood subsided, opened the doors of the Ark and released the animals. All living things rushed to freedom, except two snakes who lingered in a corner. "Why don't you go forth and multiply?" asked Noah in a stern voice.
    "We can't," moaned one. "We're adders!"

At a dinner at Harpo Marx's home, guests were amazed to find no napkins, but Oscar Levant covered up for his friend. "Due to the high cost of living," he announced, "there are no napkins—but from time to time a wooly dog will pass among you."

Bob has a cat named Sam. He took it to the vet recently. He now calls it "Sam Spade."

What purpose do the Dalmation dogs of fire departments serve?
   To find the fire hydrants.

There was a sign on the door of a small shop saying "Beware of the Dog." But when the customer entered all he saw was a very small dog.
   "Is that the dog to beware of?" he asked incredulously.
   "Right," said the shop owner. "I had to put up the sign because people were always stepping on him."

The salesman stared doubtfully at the rather formidable-looking animal lying on the doorstep. "What breed is your dog?" he asked the little old lady.
   "Don't rightly know," she said. "My husband sent it from Africa."
   "Well," the salesman said, "it's the oddest-looking dog I've ever seen."
   The prim lady nodded her head. "You should have seen it before I cut its mane off."

Aboard ship a magician was entertaining the guests. A parrot was nearby. Everything that was made to disappear, including a rabbit, was greeted by the bird with a raucous "Faker!" Suddenly an explosion destroyed the ship and the parrot landed on a raft occupied only by the magician. After two days of sitting and staring at the man, the parrot finally admitted, "All right, you win! What did you do with the ship?"

It was Easter morning. A rooster was strutting around the barnyard when he came across a basket of gaily colored eggs. He studied the eggs intently and shook his head. After thinking awhile, he made a beeline across the yard and knocked the heck out of the peacock.

Mama Bear to Papa Bear: "This is positively my last year as den mother!"

The farmer just bought a new dog to guard his cantaloupe patch. He calls him "Melancholy."

A farmer vows he increased egg production by putting this sign in the hen house: "An egg a day keeps Colonel Sanders away."

A man offered to sell his dog for $10 and claimed the mutt talked.
   "Please buy me," pleaded the canine. "My owner doesn't feed me, but I'm really a great dog. I was in the last war and won the Silver Star and the Purple Heart."
   The prospective buyer was amazed. "That dog really does talk! Why do you want to sell him for only $10?"
   Replied the owner: "I can't stand a liar."

Joe: "Look at that horse there, scratching his stomach with his hind foot. I wonder what's wrong with him?"
Jim: "Nothing's wrong with him. He's just feeling his oats."

Two kittens were watching a tennis match. One kitten said proudly, "My mother's in that racket."

AUTOS, DRIVING.

In a traffic snarl, one of the inevitable horn tooters began blasting away. A man in a car alongside looked over and politely inquired, "What else did you get for Christmas?"

Halfway down a steep winding hill a man stopped his car to ask an old woman at her gate if the hill was dangerous. "Not here it isn't," she told him. "It's down at the bottom where they all kill themselves."

What would happen if all the cars in the nation were painted red?
   You would have a red carnation.

Mechanic: "Lady, I've found the trouble with your car. You've got a short circuit in the wiring."
Lady: "Well, for goodness sake, lengthen it!"

A careful driver is one who just saw a driver ahead of him get a ticket.

"I'll have to see your license in order to cash your check," the bank teller told the woman at the drive-in window. Without a word the woman drove off, leaving the uncashed check at the window.
   A few minutes later, she pulled up to the window again and asked for her money. The somewhat startled teller repeated that he would have to see her license. "Well, for goodness' sake!" the woman exploded. "If you didn't look at it the first time I pulled away, I'm not going to show it to you again!"

BASEBALL.

Returning to his stadium seat, popcorn in hand, a rather obese baseball fan leaned over and asked a woman seated on the aisle, "Did I step on your feet when I went out?"
   "Well," smiled the woman, ready to accept his apology, "as a matter of fact, you did."
   "Good," exclaimed the portly one, squeezing past her. "This *is* the right row, then."

BOSS.

Said the boss after looking over the contents of the suggestion box: "I wish employees would be more specific. What kind of kite? What lake?"

The pompous, opinionated, and thoroughly disliked office manager announced one morning:
"My wife is pregnant."
After a pause, a slightly audible voice from the rear was heard:
"Whom do you suspect?"

Doctor to a boss being examined: "You don't have ulcers—but you are a carrier."

My sister wrote a glowing report that her son was being promoted and transferred to a Naval air station, where he would be in charge of the Army personnel stationed there. We immediately sent congratulations to our nephew on his new command.
About a week later, we received a letter from him. "I don't know what Mother told you about my new 'command,' " he wrote, "but it was cut in half last week when one of my men went home on furlough."

BUSINESS.

The man went to a loan company and asked how much interest he would have to pay for a six-month loan of $25.
"One dollar and fifty cents," the credit manager told him.
"That's fine," the man said. "I'll take the loan, but I want to leave my new automobile here with you as security until I pay back the $25."
The credit manager protested that such security was not necessary for a small loan, but the man insisted on leaving his car. The next day he mentioned the transaction to a friend.
"They must think you're crazy," the friend said. "Whoever heard of somebody leaving a new automobile with a loan company for six months just for a loan of $25."
"Let them think I'm crazy," the man said. "Tomorrow I'm going to Europe for six months. Where else could I park my car for that length of time for only a dollar and fifty cents?"

A merchant by the name of Chan owned a shop from which his teak carvings kept disappearing. In the mornings he would find a boy's footprints on the floor. He took his problem to the elders of the village and they told him of an ancient legend about a boy who went to live with bears and eventually began to look like a bear, except for his feet. One night the merchant heard a noise in his shop. He rushed in and saw a bear with boy's feet climbing out of the window. He shouted, "Stop, boyfoot bear with teaks of Chan!"

An inventor kept working on a long-range automobile powered by electricity at low cost. One day he walked into his club in New York and said: "I've done it. I went all the way to Mexico City and used electricity instead of gasoline."

When asked how much the trip cost, the inventor answered, "Exactly $4,003. Three dollars for the electricity, and $4,000 for the extension cord."

A Texas counterfeiter had trouble with his machine. Instead of turning out $20 bills, it produced a fine batch of $18 bills. Figuring that his fellow Texans were too smart to be conned, he filled a suitcase with them and headed north to pass them off on Oklahomans. At a hotel in Ada, he asked the man at the desk if he could change an $18 bill.

"Why certainly," the man said cheerily, "how would you like it—two nines or three sixes?"

Definition of a hypocrite: An undertaker trying to look sad at a $7,000 funeral.

One of our star budget watchers protested to his dentist that the $25 estimate was too much for a few minutes time in pulling a tooth.

The dentist replied: "If you wish, I can pull it very, very slowly."

At a script conference when the sponsors began tearing the material to pieces, Fred Allen asked, "Where were you guys when the paper was blank?"

An impressive looking gentleman walked into a fur store with a beautiful blond. They went to the mink coat section where the blonde picked out the finest fur. The man gave his address and references and stated that his references could be checked while the couple was in Atlantic City. The store checked and found that no one would trust him. When the man returned, the manager had to tell him diplomatically of his credit standing. The would-be customer casually brushed this aside saying, "I didn't expect to receive the coat. I just dropped in to thank you for a great weekend."

Two partners were always wheeling and dealing. On a trip the one man called his associate: "I have good and bad news."

"Give me the good news first."

"Instead of $17 million for that company, they want only 14 million."

"That's good! And the bad news?"

"They want $5,000 down."

The man was cleaning out his attic and found a shoe-repair ticket that was ten years old. He took it to the shop and the proprietor started looking for the unclaimed shoes. After about ten minutes the proprietor reappeared and handed the ticket back.

"Did you find the shoes?" asked the customer.

"Yes I did. They will be ready Wednesday."

Overheard: "You conniving, scheming rat-fink, you leave me only one alternative—welcome to the board of directors!"

The inevitable results of improved and enlarged communications between different levels in a hierarchy is a vastly increased area of misunderstanding.

We have met the enemy and he is us.

A man had a store which had just been burglarized. He told a friend who expressed sympathy and asked if he had lost much.
"Quite a bit, but if the burglar had broken in a couple of nights ago it could have been worse."
"Why?" questioned the friend.
"Because the morning of the burglary we marked everything down 40%."

CHILDREN.

Post card from a twelve-year-old camper:
"Dear Mom, Three of the boys in my tent have the dire rear."

Riding home from work, the car pool started to discuss prowlers. One man said he kept a gun handy in case anyone broke into his house. After listening a while, the father of five small youngsters spoke up.
"If a burglar came into our bedroom during the night," he said wearily, "I'd get up and take him to the bathroom."

Two mothers were discussing the problem of getting their children up in the morning.
"I don't have any trouble with Johnny any more," said one. "I just open the door and throw the cat on the bed."
"How does that waken him?" asked the other.
"He sleeps with the dog," she answered.

A doctor received a frantic call from a magazine editor, saying his little boy had swallowed a fountain pen.
"I'll be right over," promised the doctor, "but what are you doing in the meantime?"
"I'm using a pencil," replied the editor.

Father to a young boy scout:
"Well, son, did you do your good deed today?"
"I sure did. Four other scouts and I helped an old lady across the street."
"It took five of you?"
"Yes. She didn't want to go."

Father to teen-age son: "Mind if I use the car myself tonight? I'm taking your mother out and I want to impress her."

"Guess what!" a camper wrote her father. "There is a foot-long catfish under our cabin, two other catfish, and a lot of baby ones. We are feeding them so they will trust us."
"P.S. Could you send me a hook and line?"

The first-graders at an Episcopal Sunday school in San Diego were told to draw their conceptions of the Flight into Egypt. One little girl turned in a picture of an airplane with three people in the back, all with halos, and a fourth up front without one. Preplexed about the fourth person, the teacher asked the little girl who it was.
"Oh," replied the youngster, "that's Pontius, the pilot."

Little Bobby had a forlorn look on his face. "What's wrong, son?" asked his father.
"Just between you and me, Dad," the boy answered, "I can't get along with your wife."

The little boy was making a manful effort to lead a large shaggy dog. "Where are you taking him?" a spectator asked.
"I don't know yet," the youngster replied. "But when he makes up his mind where he wants to go, I'm gonna take him there!"

Proud father to wife as they watch their son lying on the floor studying by light from the TV screen: "Sort of reminds you of Abe Lincoln, doesn't it?"

To Junior: "What do you want to be when you grow up?"
"I'd like a million dollars, a big house, and no bathtubs."
"Why no bathtubs?"
"Because I want to be filthy rich!"

The teen-age daughter finally got off the phone after a half-hour telephone conversation. The father remarked, "What happened? You usually talk two hours"
"Wrong number," replied the daughter.

Five boys decided to skip school one morning because it was such a nice day. When they arrived at school after lunch they explained their car had a flat tire.
"That's okay," smiled the teacher. "However, you missed a test. Just take seats so you are apart from each other."
When they were seated she said: "There is just one question to the test. Which tire was flat?"

"My son's eyesight has just been restored."
"Did he have an operation?"
"No, a haircut."

The small boy in a department store was watching the moving hand rail intently. A guard asked if anything was wrong. "No," replied the kid. "My chewing gum should be back any minute."

My little boy told my wife that he had been playing postman, that he had been putting real letters in the mailboxes on the block. When asked where he got them, he said he found them in his mother's drawer tied up with a ribbon.

The small boy was witnessing a ballet for the first time. After several minutes of engrossed attention, he turned to his mother and in a loud whisper said, "Why don't they just get taller people?"

The crowd of urchins peered wide-eyed as they caught glimpses of the clowns inside the circus tent. A man who had been watching them walked up to the ticket-taker and asked, "Let those boys in and count them as they pass."
    As the last one filed through the gate, the attendant looked at the man and reported, "Sixteen, sir."
    "Shucks," said the man, as he walked away. "Guessed wrong again."

The father noticed that his daughter had a new steady boyfriend and requested that the boy be brought in to see him.
    Several weeks went by and the boy did not meet the father. So he said, "I thought I asked that Bill come in to see me."
    The daughter replied, "I told him. He said he had seen you a number of times but he likes me anyway."

CHRISTMAS.

A man picked the berries from his holly bush, strung them, and made them into vests. He gave them to friends who care for the berry vest.

"Beatnick"—a tired Santa Claus.

This Christmas I received a card with this message:
"A B C D E F G H I J K M N
 O P Q R S T U V W X Y Z"
Puzzled, I called up my friend. He explained: "It's simple. No L."

Two young daughters had been given parts in a Christmas play at school. At dinner that night they got into an argument as to who had the more important role. Judy, aged eleven, was very superior.

"Why, of course, mine's the biggest part," she told five-year-old Lucy. "Anybody'll tell you it's much harder to be a virgin than an angel."

COMPUTERS.

Prospective buyer to electronic-brain salesman: "I think $228,000 is a bit steep. Do you have one with a lower IQ?"

Computer repairman to company executive: "I've found the cause of your slowdown. The big computer is shoving all the work off on the little computer."

COOKING—FOOD.

"I'm not saying she's a bad cook," said the boyfriend, "but I know now why her family prays before every meal."

"My wife worships me!"
   "Really?"
   "Yeah. She places burnt offerings before me every evening."

My wife is always trying to tell me how much the price of food has gone up. She put a plate of food in front of me the other night and said, "It's a hamburger surprise."
   "What is the surprise?" I said.
   "Look for the hamburger."

Waiter: "How did you find your steak?"
Salesman: "I just lifted up one end of the potato and there it was."

"I've got a frog in my throat."
   "Don't complain—I haven't had any meat for weeks!"

Customer: "What are these pennies doing in my soup?"
Waiter: "Well, you said you'd stop eating here if there wasn't any change in the meals."

The father of a young coed majoring in home economics was asking about her courses. "In your cooking class," he inquired, "do they let you eat what you cook?"
   "Let us?" replied the girl. "They make us!"

The two servants were talking over their problems. One said that the lady of the house required her to warm the plates for each of the dinner guests and that it was a lot of work.

"I have the same requirement," said the other, "but it isn't too much work for me. I just warm *her* plate."

The tired businessman returned home from work only to find that his wife hadn't prepared dinner yet.
"Never mind making it now," he retorted. "I'll just go out to a restaurant."
"Please," the wife pleaded, "wait for just five minutes."
"Five minutes?" scoffed the husband. "What can you cook in five minutes?"
"Not a thing," replied his wife, "but it'll only take me that long to get ready to go with you!"

"What shall we eat?"
"Let's eat up the street."
"Let's not, I hate asphalt."

COWBOYS AND INDIANS.

A Hopi Indian had received his call-up instructions and was being questioned by the draft board.
"Do you speak any foreign language?" he was asked.
"Yes," replied the Hopi. "English."

The saloon doors swung open. A cowboy rushed out, took a running jump, and landed in the street.
"What's the matter with you, fella?" asked a bystander. "Did they kick you out, or are you just plain loco?"
"Neither," groaned the bruised cowboy. "But I sure would like to lay my hands on the so-and-so who moved my horse!"

The tribe of Indians struck it rich and decided to send the Chief's daughter to an Eastern finishing school. They figured they also should change the Chief's daughter's name, which was "Happy Tail." They changed it to "Gladys."

Two kids were bragging. One said, "My uncle is the fastest shooting cowboy in West Texas." The other jeered, "Yeah, but my uncle is faster. He shoots even before he gets his gun out of the holster." "What's his name?" "They call him 'Two-toed Pete.' "

The young Indian had just come back to his reservation with a degree in electrical engineering. He told his father, the chief, that he wanted to build a big dam and install a generator.
The chief replied that perhaps his first project shouldn't be so ambitious. "Why don't you build an outhouse with an electric light in it?"

This the young Indian proceeded to do. He was in a flurry of activity as he set up light poles, built the outhouse, and strung the wire.

When he finished, the Chief decided to hold a big celebration and sent invitations for miles around. The cause of the celebration—"This was the first time anyone had wired a head for a reservation!"

Salesman to cute Indian waitress:
"I've got six bits that says I can take you out after work and show you a good time."
Waitress: "I've got a buck that says you can't."

CRIME.

A man telephoned to report that thieves had been at work on his car. "They've stolen the brake pedal, the accelerator, and the dashboard."

The police sergeant said he would investigate. Then the phone rang again.

"Don't bother," said the same voice with a hiccup. "I got into the back seat by mistake."

"Looking for your cashier, are you?" asked the detective. "Is he tall or short?" The bank president groaned, "Both."

"Why are you here again?" asked the warden.
"Because of my belief."
"Your belief?"
"Yes, I believed the burglar alarm was disconnected."

"What are you reading, my man?" asked the prison chaplain.
"Nothing much, Reverend," replied the lifer. "Just the usual escape literature."

Warden of penitentiary on the phone: "You must have the wrong name; there is no one here by that number."

Warden: "I have been warden here for ten years and I think that calls for a celebration. What kind of party would you boys suggest?"
Prisoners: "An open house!"

DOCTORS, OPERATIONS.

The doctor was puzzled by his patient's illness.
"Have you ever had this condition before?" he asked.
"Yes, I have."
"Well, then, you've got it again."

A doctor in our town operates only on midgets—he has very little patients.

Doctor: "Have your eyes ever been checked?"
Lady Patient: "No, they've always been blue."

Ambulance driver: "Give me your name so I can notify your family."
Victim: "My family knows my name."

Patient: "Doctor, I've got amnesia."
Doctor: "How long have you had it?"
Patient: "How long have I had what?"

A meek little man walked into the dentist's office to have a tooth pulled. He was so frightened that the dentist sympathetically offered him a shot of his best bourbon. The little fellow had one shot, then another, and another. After the fourth, the dentist asked solicitously, "Feeling better? A little more courageous?"

"Yeah!" snarled the little man. "Just lay one finger on my teeth and I'll tear your arm off!"

Doctor: "The best thing for you is to quit smoking and drinking and stay away from women."
Patient: "I don't deserve the best, Doc. What's the next best?"

My doctor says I have a persecution complex, but he's just saying that because he hates me.

Colds, of course, eventually go—but usually only blow by blow.

No man is sicker than the man who is sick on his day off.

Our Xerox reproduction machine went on the blink the other day. The repairman discovered someone had dropped a pill in it.

Patient (coming out of anesthetic): "Why are all the blinds down, doctor?"
Doctor: "Well, there's a fire across the alley and I didn't want you to wake up and think the operation was a failure."

Apropos of the season:
   "I'm going to sneeze."
   "At whom?"
   "At-choo!"

A man went to a doctor for a complete physical checkup and when it was over he asked the doctor, "How am I doing?" The doctor looked at the reports and said, "I would appreciate your paying the nurse in cash."

Patient: "What's the trouble, Doc?"
Doctor: "I'm not sure what's wrong with you, but if you were a building you'd be condemned."

"I thought my group insurance plan was fine until I tried to collect—found out I couldn't unless the whole group was sick."

"You should stop taking those sleeping pills," said the doctor. "They will become a habit."
"Nonsense, I've been taking them for ten years and they're not a habit yet."

I just heard about a physician who lost all his money and in desperation he tried to rob a bank. But nobody paid any attention to his hold-up note because they couldn't read his writing.

Doctor: "You should take a hot bath before retiring."
Patient: "But, Doc, I won't be retiring for another 15 years."

In a recent survey, 100 percent of the chain smokers interviewed preferred cigarettes to chains.

A middle-aged woman felt a bit under the weather, so she paid a visit to her doctor. "Well," he asked, "what seems to be the trouble?" "Doctor," she said, lunging into a summary of her symptoms, "I have a general backache, shooting pains in my legs, and bilious attacks." "I see," said the doctor, busily taking notes. "How old are you?" he asked. "I'll be 31 next month," the patient answered coyly. "Hmmm," the doctor mused, adding another note. "Slight loss of memory, too."

"Good morning, Doc, how was my operation?"
"Sorry, fella, but I'm not your doctor. Around here they call me St. Peter."

DRINKING.

"Papa, who is the person who brings you in contact with the spirit world?"
"A bartender, my boy."

The trouble with whiskey is that you take a drink and it makes a new man of you. Then he has to have a drink.

The drunk, sitting at the bar adjacent to a man and his wife, unexpectedly came forth with a resounding burp.
"How dare you belch before my wife!" thundered the irate husband.
The drunk got unsteadily off the barstool and made a sweeping bow. "A thousand pardons, sir," he said, "I didn't know it was madam's turn."

Little Girl: "Mama, Daddy and I stopped on your way home. I had a coke and Daddy had a glass of water with an olive in it."

"Did you get home from the party okay last night?"
"I sure did, except that just as I turned the corner into my street some darn fool stepped on my fingers."

A lion walks up to the bar and says to the bartender. "That blond down there looks good enough to eat. I think I will eat her up." After a while he gets stomach cramps and asks the bartender for an Alka-Seltzer, but in a little while gets still more pains and he says to the bartender, "I wonder what's making me sick?" And the bartender replies, "It must have been that barbiturate."

The tough businessman and meek minister sat side by side in the airliner. The pretty stewardess inquired what they would like. "A double martini!" growled the businessman. The minister was deeply shocked. "Why, I'd rather commit adultery than have such a thing!" he exclaimed indignantly. "Why, so would I," responded the businessman, "but I didn't realize we had a choice."

Small fry to friend, explaining ice bag atop father's head: "Mom says it's a special hat his class wears to show that they've been to their class reunion."

Wife to husband, after several rounds of drinks at a party: "Henry, don't take another cocktail. Your face is already getting blurred."

Noticing a friend tossing off drinks at a bar, the man said to him, "Say, I thought you were allowed only one drink a day—doctor's orders!"
"Sure," said the friend. "I'm following instructions exactly. This drink here, for example, is for August 4, 1985."

In cocktail bar: "Try our miniature highball. Just one and in a miniature troubles are over."

A bouncer threw a noisy roughneck out of the saloon four times in a row, and each time the unwanted drunk staggered back. At last a customer who had watched with interest tapped the bouncer on the shoulder.
"Know why he keeps coming back in?" he asked. The bouncer shook his head.
"You're putting too much backspin on him."

Those bartenders at the cocktail party really know how to pour drinks. With the drink I thought I got a cocktail napkin. Instead, it was a get-well card.

A drunk who had been wandering around Times Square finally went down into the subway at Forty-Second Street. About half an hour later he emerged at Forty-Fourth Street and bumped into a friend who had been looking for him. "Where on earth have you been all this time?" the friend asked.

"Down in some guy's cellar," the drunk said. "And, boy, you should see the set of trains he has!"

A pharmacist found it necessary to leave his drugstore one day. He asked his soda clerk to keep an eye on things until he returned. No sooner had the pharmacist left than in staggered a lushed-up character demanding in a loud voice some medicine to cure his hiccups.

The druggist returned and asked if there had been any customers and the soda clerk replied: "Only one, a drunken guy with a bad case of the hiccups."

"Well," asked the druggist, "did you tell him to come back when I was here?"

"Oh, no," answered the kid soda jerk, "I took care of it myself. I mixed him up a cup of Epsom salts with Citrate of Magnesia, Castor Oil and Mineral Oil; then I gave him some Ex-Lax to nibble on. He took it right then, too."

"Great Scott!" said the druggist, turning pale, "that mixture won't stop the hiccups!"

The soda clerk smiled knowingly and said: "Want to bet? Take a look outside. There he is holding on to that lamppost afraid to hiccup!"

The husband came home intoxicated after a party. As he walked up the front steps of his home, he fell and cut his face. He realized that he must stop the bleeding and clean the cut, so he went to the bathroom very quietly and got to work.

Next morning his wife accused him of coming home drunk, but he denied it. At last she said: "If you were sober last night, how did all that adhesive tape happen to get on the bathroom mirror?"

Did you hear about the drunk who was going to write a drinking song—only he couldn't get past the first two bars.

The drunk stopped a passerby and asked the time. The passerby looked at his watch and told him. "I can't figure it out," muttered the inebriate. "All day long I keep getting different answers."

When he finally got home on payday, he had to admit that he had only $85 left.
"Where's the rest of the money?" his wife demanded.
"Well . . . er . . . I bought something for the house."
"Oh, what was it?" she asked, a bit mollified.
"A round of drinks."

Two men were out on the town and started to go home. The one gave his advice: "When you get in your house undress at the foot of the stairs, fold your clothes neatly, and creep quietly up to your room."

When they met the next day he asked his friend how he made out.

"Terrible. I did exactly as you suggested. But when I reached the top of the stairs I discovered it was the back entrance to the stage of the Roxy Theatre."

A fellow wakes up in his hotel with a first-class hangover and he also finds his wallet is missing. He remembers his friend taking him to a party at a residence and surmises that he left his wallet there. A phone call results in finding out that his friend is now out of town. He remembers the general part of the town, that it was a white house, had a red door, a beautiful hostess, and a gold toilet.

Finally, after miles of cruising he sees what may be the house with the red door. The door is opened by a beautiful blond. He says, "Did you have a party last night?" She replies, "Boy, did we have a party!"

He says, "I think I was here last night and may have left my wallet. I can offer further identification. Do you have a gold toilet?"

She turns her head and yells back into the house. "Henry, I found out what happened to your tuba last night!"

It was the day after the big party. "Tell me," said the unhappy celebrant, "what do you take for a headache?"

Back came the unsympathetic reply: "Liquor—the night before."

Captain of the ship entered into the daily log: "The mate was drunk this afternoon.

A week later, after the mate had been keeping the log for a while, the skipper read the notation: "The captain was sober today."

Two drunks wandered into a railroad trestle one night. "Man! Dig this crazy steep stairway," said one. Replied the other: "Yeah, but also dig these crazy handrails."

EMPLOYEES.

The owner of a big company offered $25 for each money-saving idea submitted by his employees. First prize went to the man who suggested the award be cut to $10.

Boss: "I hear you've been going over my head, Morley."
Morley: "Yes, I have, sir; I've been praying for a raise."

Turned down by the circus owner when he demanded more pay for being shot from a cannon, the Human Cannonball was threatening to quit before the next performance. "Go ahead, quit," said the owner. "I can get a dozen replacements for you at half the salary."

"Maybe you can," said the Cannonball. "But not of my caliber."

The boss asked a job seeker: "I see by your application that you've been fired from every job you had." The applicant said: "Yes, but that proves one thing. I'm no quitter."

ENDEAVOR, SUCCESS.

But this one thing I do, forgetting those things which are behind, and reaching forth unto those things which are before, I press toward the mark.—Philippians 4:13-14.

The courageous man is the man who forces himself, in spite of his fear, to carry on.
—George S. Patton

Some folks are like blisters; they show up when the work is done.

Be kind. Remember everyone you meet is fighting a hard battle.

Occasionally you come across a *concrete mind*—all mixed up and permanently set.

Thought for the day from Moses: "What you know isn't nearly as important as who you know."

Consider the turtle. He makes progress only when his neck is out.

A little learning is a dangerous thing.
—Alexander Pope

Patience is a necessary ingredient of genius.—Disraeli

The best way around is through.
—Robert Frost

No one knows what it is that he can do until he tries.—Publilius Syrus

Wisdom is knowing what to do. Knowledge is knowing how to do it. Success is doing it.

The gem cannot be polished without friction, nor the man perfected without trials.

You never get a second chance to make a good first impression.

If we didn't have problems, we wouldn't have jobs.—Turner Catledge

Some people are cripled by tragedy. Some are crushed. And some are created.

Everytime you sit and watch television you are watching some other guy furthering his career.

No problem is so simple it cannot, through persistent worry, be made complex.

Caution—be sure brain is engaged before putting mouth in gear.

Progress is not created by contented people.

If you think before you speak, the other fellow gets in his joke first.

Some prospects are like wheelbarrows—not much good unless pushed.

He who follows another is always behind.

No problem we face is ever as big at the one we dodge.

Worry grows lushly in the soil of indecision.

In achieving success, backbone is more important than wishbone.

You have not converted a man because you have silenced him.
    —John Morley

We do not meet with success except by reiterated efforts.
    —Francoise De Maintenon

All of the performances of human art, at which we look with praise or wonder, are instances of resistless force of perseverance.
    —Samuel Johnson

The line between failure and success is so fine that we scarcely know when we pass it—so fine that we often are on the line and do not know it.
    —Ralph Waldo Emerson

Personality can open doors, but only character can keep them open.
    —Elmer Leterman

No plan is worth a damn unless somebody makes it work.
    —William Feather

To most people nothing is more troublesome than the effort of thinking.
    —James Bryce

It is more important to know where you are going than to get there quickly. Do not mistake activity for achievement.

Fear fades when facts are faced.

The little blonde coed minced her way into the professor's office the day before final exams and said nervously: "Oh, Professor, I'll do just anything to pass this course!"

"Anything?" asked the professor.

"Oh, yes, just anything. I'll do anything to pass this course!"

The professor sat back, considered for a minute, then asked: "Even study?"

Happiness is not something you get, but something you do.

FISHING & HUNTING.

A recent survey showed the earth's surface is three-quarters water and one-quarter land. Thus it is perfectly clear that the Lord intended men to spend three times as much time fishing as mowing the lawn.

Woman cleaning fish at sink to angler husband: "Why can't you be like the rest of the men? They never catch anything."

The big-game hunter took his wife on a safari. The sportsman bagged a few minor trophies, but the great prize was the head of a huge lion, killed by his wife.

"What did she hit it with?" asked a friend admiringly. "That .303 Magnum rifle you gave her?"

"No," answered the husband dryly, "with the station wagon we rented!"

FOOTBALL.

Football season: The only time of the year when a man can walk down the street with a blonde on one arm and a blanket on the other without encountering raised eyebrows.

A well-known football coach who was addressing a sportswriters' convention began his speech by quoting from a letter he had just received. "You are the greatest football coach in the world," he read. "You are better than Frank Leahy, Knute Rockne, or Bud Wilkinson. And not only are you the greatest coach, you are also the wisest and most handsome." For a moment the sportswriters were stunned at such an exhibition of conceit. Then the coach continued, "Incidentally," he said, "the letter is signed 'Mother.' "

After a flat performance by the offense in an important game, Vince Lombardi showed his displeasure by calling a meeting the following day. He told them that they had forgotten everything that he had drummed into their skulls since opening day in the spring practice and he intended to start back at the beginning. He began by picking up a football. "Now this is a football . . ."

"Just a minute, coach," a player said, "you're going too fast!"

FLYING.

On the plane en route to Honolulu, an elderly gentleman from Chicago taking his first trip asked the woman sitting next to him, "Can you tell me whether the state is pronounced Hawaii or Havaii?"

"Havaii," the lady said.

"Thank you very much," the gentleman said.

"You're wery velcome," the lady answered.

"May I smoke my cigar in here?" the passenger asked the stewardess as he boarded the plane.

"Well, we leave it to your discretion," said the stewardess. "You may smoke if you don't annoy the lady passengers."

"Then I won't smoke. I'd much rather annoy the lady passengers."

In those new jet planes you know you're moving faster than the speed of sound when the stewardess slaps your face before you can get a word out.

The people on the left side of the high-flying plane looked out the window and saw that one engine had stopped. Those on the right side looked out and saw another engine out of commission. Soon a third engine conked out. As you might imagine, panic set in.

The door to the cockpit opened and the pilot appeared, wearing a parachute strapped to his back. "Don't be afraid," he said. "I'm going for help!"

Two elderly ladies boarded a jet and said to the pilot: "Please don't fly faster than sound, we want to talk."

During the takeoff on a training flight, as the observer was tightening a loose hydraulic connection, he suddenly saw that an engine was on fire. Wrench in hand, he turned, touched the pilot calmly on the shoulder with it, and told him, "We're on fire."

He soon had them safely back on the ground, and a short time later the observer was modestly explaining his great presence of mind in a trying situation to an admiring audience. Just then two medics passed, carrying the pilot on a stretcher. Startled, the observer called, "What's the matter with him?"

"Broken shoulder," came the laconic answer.

Airline stewardess: "Use the chewing gum I've handed out; it's to keep your ears from popping at high altitude."

Passenger (after plane lands): "Okay—now how do I get the gum out of my ears?"

The stewardess on a jet flight was saying good-bye to the passengers at the end of the flight, when her eyes suddenly glazed with horror, and she grabbed the arm of one old gentleman whose pants had fallen around his shoes. "Mr. King," she said severely, "it was your safety belt I told you to unfasten."

The private plane approaching an airport called to the tower: "Beechcraft to tower, Beechcraft to tower, can you hear me?" The tower replied, "Tower to Beechcraft, yes, we can hear you. But why are you shouting?"

"Because I haven't got a radio."

Did you hear about the Kamikaze pilot who returned safely after 50 missions?

GIRLS.

Did you hear about the sole survivor of a shipwreck who was finally washed ashore on a South Sea Island? After he dragged himself up on the sand, he looked up and saw tropical foliage of ferns and palms from which emerged a beautiful native girl carrying a frosted martini to him. He drank it and got some of his strength back. She smiled invitingly and said, "Isn't there anything else I can do for you?" She disappeared into the jungle and reappeared with a full-course dinner. After he had eaten, he was getting more of his strength back and feeling like his old vigorous self.

The beautiful South Sea Island girl swayed gently to the soft sea breeze and demurely inquired, "Surely there must be something else I can do for you. Would you like to play around?"

"Good God," he cried, "don't tell me you have a golf course here, too."

The two men watch a girl they know going down the street.
"She's certainly a nicely-reared girl," said one.
"She is," agreed the other, "and she's not bad in front either."

Men do make passes at girls who wear glasses. It depends on their frames.

A young lady with a touch of hay fever took with her to a dinner party two handkerchiefs, one of which she stuck in her bosom. At dinner she began rummaging to right and left in her bosom for the fresh handkerchief. Engrossed in her search, she suddenly realized that conversation had ceased and that all the people were watching her, fascinated. In confusion she murmured, "I know I had two when I came."

At a restaurant an elderly gentleman had made several sly but futile attempts to flirt with the pretty young waitress who was serving him. Finally he grew a little bolder.

"My dear," he purred. "where have you been all my life?"

"Well," chirruped the girl matter-of-factly, "for the first forty years anyway, I probably wasn't born."

"I hear you broke up with Maggie."
    "Yes. She kept using four letter words."
    "What kind of words?"
    "Words like don't, stop, won't."

The sweet young thing is asked to dance by a man in a Navy uniform.
Girl: "And what do you do in the service?"
Man: "I'm a naval surgeon."
Girl: "My, don't they specialize these days!"

A doctor in San Francisco for a medical convention was talking with a spectacular blonde in the lobby of the St. Francis when his wife suddenly emerged from the elevator. Eyeing the departing figure, the wife snapped, "How do you happen to know her?"
"Oh, just professionally," the doctor replied.
The angry wife raised a sarcastic eyebrow. "Yours, or hers?" she meowed.

The girl had been courted for many months by shy Jonathan. She tried flimsy negligees and potent drinks, but he still remained shy. Then one night he told her of a strange dream.
"I dreamed I was chasing you through the woods and you were dressed almost like Eve."
"What happened?" she asked breathlessly. "Did you catch me?"
"Yes, I did. And I crushed you in my arms and began to kiss you."
"And then what?"
"I'm a gentleman," declared Jonathan. "I woke myself up, of course."

You can tell a lot about a girl by looking into her eyes. If she has small pupils, she's a kindergarten teacher.

"Did you hear about the girl with the gleam in her eye?"
"No. What about her?"
"Someone bumped her while she was brushing her teeth."

"What do you give a man who has everything?" the pretty young thing asked her mother.
"Encouragement, dear," she replied.

Wolf to pretty girl at a party. "You look like the outdoor type—let's go out on the patio."

Two girl Fridays arrived in their office one morning. The blonde was wearing a brand new mink coat. "How do I look?" she asked her friend.
Said the friend, "Guilty."

"What do you give a girl who has everything?"
"Penicillin."

He: "Please, darling, whisper those three little words that will make me walk on air."
She: "Go hang yourself."

Man to girl at bar: What does it take to make you dizzy?
Girl: Five dollars—and the name is Daisy, not Dizzy.

GOLF.

Golfer comes home tired. "What's wrong," says the wife. "You're usually enthused and peppy."
"I played golf with Harry today. Harry dropped dead on the 12th hole. From then on, it was hit the ball, drag Harry. Hit the ball, drag Harry."

"I'd move heaven and earth to be able to break 100," the golfer said sadly.
"Try heaven," the caddy said, "you've moved enough earth already."

Sweet old lady to golfer vainly looking for his ball: "Would it be cheating if I told you where it was?"

Two Spanish detectives were standing over the body of Juan Gonzales. "How was he shot?" inquired the first. "I think eet was a golf gun," said the other. "What ees a golf gun?" "I don't know, but eet sure make a hole in Juan."

Golfer to another in the locker room: "Is that a woman's girdle that you're wearing?"
"Yes,"
"How long have you been wearing it?" "Ever since my wife found it in my car."

Golfer: What am I doing wrong?
Pro: You stand too close to the ball after you hit it.

Comedian Joe E. Lewis claims he shoots golf in the low 70's. "If it gets any colder," he says, "I quit."

A visitor at the golf club paid his green fees, found a partner, and teed up. His first wild swing missed the ball completely. "By George!" he exclaimed happily, "It's a good thing I found this out right away! Why, this course is about two inches lower than the one I usually play on!"

Wife: "Why don't you play golf with George any more?"
Husband: "Would you play with a fellow who cheats?"
Wife: "Of course not!"
Husband: "Neither will George."

The golfer teed his ball, looked at the young caddy, and said: "Here's to one long drive and one putt."
He swung erratically, and the ball bounced a few feet.
Diplomatically alert, the caddy handed him the putter and said: "Now for one heckuva putt."

Caddie: "I've got good news and bad news for you, sir. First the good news: you got a hole-in-one on the 6th hole! Now the bad news: we're playing the fifth!"

"I'm sorry," said the dentist over the phone, "but I can't give you an appointment this afternoon. I have 18 cavities to fill."
And he picked up his golf bag and walked out.

Woman golfer to men in foursome ahead: "Do you mind if we play through? My friend is having labor pains."

Two Hollywood producers who had never played golf decided to try the game. At the clubhouse of a famous Palm Springs course they were informed they couldn't play on the particular afternoon they had picked for their initial experience with the game.
"Why not?" they demanded indignantly.
"Because" the pro explained, "there are no caddies."
Then one said, "So who cares? For one afternoon we can take a Buick."

Which reminds us of the golfer who said, "I missed a hole-in-one yesterday by only four strokes!"

A preacher invites a golf pro to play a round of golf with him. At the end of the match the pro tells him that there is a $50 charge. The preacher protests, but finally gives in and tells the pro to come over to the church and he will pay him. He adds, "By the way, bring your father and mother along and I will marry them for you."

Over in Africa some of the native tribes have the custom of beating the ground with clubs and uttering spine-chilling cries. Anthropologists call this a form of primitive self-expression. Over here in America, we call it golf.

Golf is no longer a rich man's game. There are millions of poor players.

One of the quickest ways to meet new people is to pick up the wrong ball on the golf course.

The golfer had just sliced into the rough of the 17th tee and was about to chip out when he noticed a funeral procession going by on the highway. He removed his cap and stood still until the procession had passed. Later, at the clubhouse, a fellow golfer greeted him:
"Say, that was a nice gesture you made today."
"What do you mean?"
"I mean it was nice of you to take off your cap and stand respectfully when the funeral passed," his friend explained.
"Oh, yes," the golfer reflected. "We would have been married 26 years next month."

There's one James Bond fan who even plays golf like his hero. After every hole it's "Oh! Oh! Seven!"

The golfer goes to a spiritualist to ask if there are any golf courses in heaven. She looks into her crystal ball and announces that she has good and bad news for him. The golfer says, "Give me the good news first."

"There are many golf courses in heaven. They are all kept in beautiful green condition, the golf equipment is tops, and the clubhouse with its 19th hole is the best there is."

"And what is the bad news?" the golfer asks.

"You are teeing off next Saturday morning at 9:30."

HUSBAND.

First lady: "My husband was named 'Man of the Year.' "
Second lady: "Well, that shows you what kind of year it's been.

"Is your husband all right after his accident?"
"No, he's not all right; but he's back like he used to be."

A meek little man stepped on the drugstore scale and dropped in his coin. Out came a card reading, "Weight 135."

Nodding in satisfaction, he turned the card over to see his fortune and read, "How are you going to account to your wife for the penny?"

Art Linkletter once asked a Midwestern woman how she got her husband up in the morning. "I put dog biscuits under his pillow," she replied. "Then in the morning I send our boxer in to nose them out. It works every time."

Girls, don't worry if your husband flirts.

My dog chases cars—but if he caught one, he wouldn't know what to do with it.

Entirely too many women get excited over nothing—and then marry him.

When a husband came home unexpectedly, he found a man hiding in the shower and ripped back the curtain. "Stop that!" his wife commanded. "How dare you interfere with his voting!"

MILITARY.

The commanding officer at an Army base in the South was the son of a well-known senator—a fact that he never let anyone forget. He was bawling out a lanky mountaineer one day, and in the course of his tirade asked, "Do you know who my father is?"

The mountain lad looked him straight in the eye. "Why, no, suh," he replied. "Don't you?"

The not-too-popular Admiral reports to the sick bay. He is requested to roll over on his stomach and raise his rear for temperature taking. Then the people leave.
    A friend comes in for a visit and asks the Admiral what he is doing.
    "Can't you see, I'm having my temperature taken."
    "With a daisy?"

Two World War II vets talking: One says: "You know that saltpeter they gave us during the war?"
    "Yes."
    "Well, I think it's finally beginning to work."

A Navy recruit lost his rifle on the firing range. When told that he'd have to pay for it, he protested: "Suppose I was driving a Navy jeep and somebody stole it. Would I have to pay for that, too?" He was informed that he would have to pay for all government property he lost.
    "Now," the recruit said, "I know why the captain always goes down with his ship."

An officer in medieval England made preparations to go to war. He locked his beautiful wife in armor and gave the key to his best friend with these words, "If I don't return in six months, use the key. To you, my good friend, I place it in your trust." About five miles from home he saw a cloud of dust approaching. His trusted friend galloped up and said, "You gave me the wrong key."

MISCELLANEOUS.

A musician worked all week on an arrangement and then his wife didn't go out of town after all.

A man was bitten by a dog and, after several weeks, became violently ill. Upon examining him, the doctor explained, "You've been bitten by a rabid dog and are dying of hydrophobia. The end will come very soon. There's nothing I can do for you."
    The stricken man asked for pencil and paper, then spent several hours thinking and writing. Finally, the doctor broke the silence: "You certainly are making a lenthy will.
    "I'm not making my will," replied the patient. "I'm making a list of the people I'm going to bite!"

"How do you like bathing beauties?"
    "Can't tell, I never bathed any."

"Attention ship-in-bottle makers: I offer my services gratis. I will accept full bottles of wine or other spirits and return them ready for insertion of ship. Prompt, conscientious work guaranteed."

"You look like Helen Brown."
"I look even worse in blue."

The oil tycoon who had come up from roughneck looked out the window of his mansion and said, "Honey, tell the gardener to put some manure on the lawn, it looks shabby." His educated daughter asked her mother why she didn't teach him to say "fertilizer" instead of that horrid "manure."

The mother said, "Oh, no, it took me 20 years to teach him to say 'manure.'"

Q. Do you know how to tell a happy motorcyclist?
A. By the bugs in his teeth!

The man who boasts that he runs things around his house is probably referring to the lawn mower, the dishwasher, the vacuum cleaner, and errands.

First octogenarian: "I can't remember when I went out with girls."
Second octogenarian: "I can, but I can't remember why."

Whistler came home and found his mother scrubbing the kitchen floor on her hands and knees. "Why, mother!" he exclaimed, "Have you gone off your rocker?"

Message inside Chinese Fortune cookie:
"Please disregard message in previous cookie."

Lady Customer: "Do you have alligator shoes?"
Clerk: "Certainly, madam. What size shoe does your alligator wear?"

Mrs. Paul Revere: "I don't care who you say is coming. It's my night to use the horse!"

The man who can smile when things go wrong has thought of someone he can blame it on.

Exasperated dragon: "Mother warned me there'd be knights like this!"

The manager of a theater noticed a man sprawled across three seats and assumed he was a bum trying to keep warm and get some sleep.
"Sit up, or pay for the other two seats!" he demanded.
The only response was a low moan. "Get up or I'll call the police!" the manager persisted.
The manager carried out his threat and an officer arrived.

"Identify yourself, sir," he ordered. "Who are you and where do you come from?"

Groaning loudly, the man got to his feet. Slowly and painfully he managed to answer: "I'm Joe Smith—and I came from the balcony."

During an air raid in London during World War II, a street patrol warden ran up to the opening of a public shelter and called down, "Are there any expectant mothers in there?"

"Don't think so," a feminine voice called back, "We've only been down here a few minutes."

Three motorcyclists in black leather jackets came roaring up to the little roadside diner. Inside, they spotted a truck driver. They pushed his plate of food to the floor and poured his coffee over his head. The truck driver did nothing; he just paid his bill and walked out.

"He's a pretty poor fighter," said the cyclists to the proprietor. "He's a pretty poor driver, too," replied the proprietor. "He just ran over three motorcycles."

"I won't say that it's a matter of life or death. It's much more important than that!"

I forecast that our competitors are going to have a very good year because I hear you can profit from your mistakes.

A six-year-old showed an amazing talent for painting, but each of his canvases was only half filled. A psychiatrist was called in to question the little genius. He asked oblique questions but got nowhere. So he came right out and asked, "Why do you leave the top half of your painting blank?"

"Because, I can't reach that high."

The little old lady entered the department store. Instantly a band began to play, an orchid was pinned on her dress, a $100 bill was put in her hand. She found herself being photographed from all sides and a TV camera beamed down on her.

"You're the one-millionth customer," the master of ceremonies told her, smiling broadly. "And now can you tell us what you came here for today?"

"Yes," said the little old lady. "I'm on my way to the complaint department."

I keep asking for a raise and my boss keeps pointing to the sign on his desk which reads: "The Buck Stops Here."

I tell you it's hot outside. It's so hot that when I stepped outside a few minutes ago I saw a couple of trees fighting. That's right, they were fighting over a dog!

Tell a man that there are two million species of flowers and he will believe you. But if you tell him a door has just been painted, he will touch it to make sure.

A tramp knocked at the door. The lady answered and said: "Has anyone ever responded by offering you work when you knocked?"

"Just once. Other than that, I've met nothing but kindness."

When announcing the results of a vote—
  The cards read 16% undecided for the issue.
  However, 84% will vote for it when hell freezes over.

Thomas Edison had been working on his light bulb invention for years. Finally, at three o'clock in the morning he succeeded. He ran out of the barn, across to the house, and upstairs to his wife and shouted "Look!"

  Mrs. Edison woke up, took a look and said: "For heavan's sakes, Tom, turn out the light and come to bed."

The married couple was reading at home. All of a sudden the wife jumped up and socked him. He got up off the floor and asked what was that for.

  "For being such a lousy lover!"

  They kept on reading. In a few minutes he grabbed his wife and gave her a good spanking.

  "Why are you spanking me?"

  "It's for knowing the difference!"

If a man is bald in front, he is a thinker.
If a man is bald in back, he is a lover.
If a man is bald all over, he just thinks he's a lover.

There was once a chief in Africa who made war on other tribes. He won all his battles and collected many thrones. He stored the thrones in the attic of his hut. One day the ceiling came crashing down and killed the chief. Moral of the story: "People in grass houses shouldn't stow thrones."

Motel clerk: "I can give you a room if you don't mind sharing it with a red-headed school teacher."
Guest: "Well, if that's the way it's gotta be, I'll go along. But I'm a married man."
Clerk: "So is he."

With his hands tied behind him and his back to the wall, a rebel faced a firing squad. An officer approached him. "Do you want a blindfold?"
  Prisoner: "No."
  Officer: "Cigarette?"
  Prisoner: "No."
  Officer: "Drink?"
  Prisoner: "No."

Officer: "Clergy?"
Prisoner: "No."
Officer: "Then get ready to die. Have you anything to say?"
Prisoner: "To hell with the dictator."
Officer: "What's the matter with you—are you looking for trouble?"

The angry little man bounced into the postmaster's office and declared: "I've been pestered by threatening letters and I want something done about it!"

"That's a federal offense," agreed the postmaster. "Have you any idea who is sending these letters?"

"It's those pesty income tax people!"

The fellow across the street has been married for 25 years and has never stopped being romantic. Of course, his wife will break his neck if she ever finds out about it.

Do you know what a Zebra is?
That's 24 sizes larger than an "A" bra.

Q. What do you get when you mix IBM with LSD?
A. A business trip.

Be alert!
The world needs more lerts.

A sweltering Texan staggers out of his Cadillac and collapses in his living room. "Why didn't you roll down the car window, silly?" asked his wife. "What," he says, "and let everyone know I don't have an air-conditioned car?"

Anatomy is something everyone has, but it looks better on a girl.

Sign in the front yard of a house: Anyone Is Welcome to Use Our Lawnmower Provided They Don't Remove It from Our Yard!

Two buckets met each other on the street. One bucket said, "You're a little pale."

"Yes," the other said, "I'm not a well bucket."

Q. Name two ancient sports.
A. Anthony and Cleopatra.

A few years ago a friend was in trouble and I helped him out. "I won't forget you," he vowed. And he didn't. He's in trouble again and just called me.

A sedate lady called to testify in a lewd-and-lascivious trial asked permission to *write* what the defendant had said to her.

When her note was given to the jurors to read, one pretty panelist found the man next to her asleep, pinched him and passed the note on. He read it, smiled at her, nodded and stuck it in his pocket.

NOTICE: Due to the shortage of trained trumpeters, the end of the world has been postponed three months.

"Were either you or your husband married before?"
"Before what?"

A Broadway playboy was in the barbershop: His manicurist was very beautiful. He suggested dinner and a show that evening. "I don't think I ought to," said the girl demurely. "I'm married."

"Ask your husband," suggested the playboy. "I'm sure he wouldn't mind."

"Ask him yourself," said the girl. "He's shaving you."

Bartender: How was the trip across the desert?
Prospector: O.K., but I came across a chap out there who was stumbling along like he had a sun stroke. He'd stagger a few steps and then fall flat on his face. Then he'd push himself up to his knees and crawl a few feet farther and fall on his face again.
Bartender: Where is the poor fellow now?
Prospector: Still out there, far as I know.
Bartender: Didn't you give him a lift?
Prospector: I would have but he was going the other way.

An all-night poker party was being held in a hotel room. As the party progressed, so did the sounds of revelry. Finally, at 3 a.m., a weary guest in an adjoining room started to pound on the wall.

"Well," shouted one of the merrymakers indignantly, "this is a hell of a time to be hanging pictures!"

The man ran frantically down the side of the pier—finally he leaped across a strip of water and landed with a resounding crash on the deck of the ferry.

"I made it!" he shouted with great self-satisfaction as he picked himself up.

"Good show, sir," said the deckhand. "But what was your hurry? We'll be docked in a minute."

The district attorney had spent two hours trying to shake the testimony of a witness. Resorting to sarcasm, he said, "They call you 'Colonel.' In what regiment are you a Colonel?"

"Well," drawled the witness, "It's like this. The 'Colonel' in front of my name is like the 'Honorable' in front of yours. It doesn't mean a thing."

"What would you do with Red China?"
"I would use a purple tablecloth."

"Ringleader"—The first person ever to take a bath.

Mr. Jones sat moodily over his drink and his friend said, "You look pretty down in the mouth, Mr. Jones. What's the matter?"

Mr. Jones said, "My psychiatrist says I'm in love with my umbrella and that's the source of my troubles."

"In love with your umbrella!"

"Yes, isn't that ridiculous? Okay, I like and respect my umbrella and enjoy its company, but *love?*"

Question: Why did the chicken cross the highway?
Answer: To lay it on the line.

Bragging may not bring happiness, but no man having caught a large fish goes home through the alley.

The hungry tramp knocked on the housewife's door.
  "Would you like some of yesterday's soup?" she inquired.
  "Sure would," he answered.
  "Then come back tomorrow," she said.

Three men were trying to sleep in a double bed. One said: "It's too crowded here, I'm getting out." He took his pillow and stretched out on the floor. Then one of the others called from the bed: "You can get back in now; there's plenty of room."

An Australian made himself a new boomerang, and then went crazy trying to throw the old one away.

You may not be aware of this fact, but science tells us that one out of every four people is mentally ill. So if three of your friends are okay, you have a problem.

On a visit to Richmond, Virginia, an English professor decided to see the Edgar Allan Poe home, now restored as a museum. He hailed a taxi and told the driver to take him to the Poe house. After a long drive, the cab pulled up before a weather-beaten structure on the outskirts of town—the Country Home for the Indigent.

The scene takes place at a posh resort. Mr. Smith is sitting at his table, staring at the frail, white-haired old man with baggy eyes at the next table. Each night Smith has seen this frail old man living it up in the company of one or two beautiful young things. Each day and night he is drinking and dancing with a different girl who dreamily gazes into his eyes.

Mr. Smith one night could not restrain himself any longer. He goes over to the other man's table and says, "I want to tell you how absolutely amazing it is the way you live it up day and night at your age. I hope I am not too personal, but how old are you?"

The frail white-haired man shrugged, "Twenty-seven," he said.

The doorbell rings at an apartment and a neighbor stands there trembling with rage. "If you don't stop playing on those blankety-blank drums, I'll go out of my mind."

"I'm sorry," said the drummer, "I think you are too late. I stopped playing 15 minutes ago."

Too often a word to the wise is just enough to start an argument.

To forget the world's troubles, wear a pair of tight shoes.

The safe and sure way to destroy an enemy is to make him a friend.

A smile can add a great deal to one's face value.

Not advertising is like winking at a pretty girl in the dark. You may know what's going on, but nobody else does.

A lady approached a ticket window in the railroad station in Chicago and requested, "I'd like a ticket for New York, please."

"Certainly, madam," replied the ticket agent. "Do you wish to go by Buffalo?"

"Heavens, no!" exclaimed the lady in horror. "I want to go by train."

MONEY, PRICES.

There was a man who years ago was very rich, but now is broke.

A reporter interviewed him and asked where his money went.

"Some of it went for women, some of it for whiskey. The rest I spent foolishly."

The Scotsman became apprehensive when the sea became rough. He asked the Captain what he should do in case he became seasick.

"Do you have a coin?"
The thrifty Scotsman dug into his purse and produced a coin.
Said the Captain, "Hold it between your teeth until we sight land."

You want to experience weightlessness like an astronaut?
That's easy; just get a shopping bag and fill it with $5 worth of groceries.

My wife and I ate in the hotel coffee shop this morning. When she looked at the menu she said, "What will you have—bacon or eggs?
I said, "You mean bacon and eggs."
She said, "Look at the prices!"

The passenger was in an argument with the conductor over the train fare. The passenger got so disagreeable that the conductor picked up the man's suitcase and threw it out just as they were crossing a river.
The passenger screamed, "First you try to rob me, and now you're trying to drown my boy!"

'Twas in a restaurant they met,
Romeo and Juliet.
He had no cash to pay the debt,
So Romeo'd what Juliet.

"Eggs are 60¢ a dozen. Cracked ones are 30¢ a dozen."
"Crack me a dozen."

The peddler who sold shoelaces was stationed outside an office building. Each day an executive passed and gave him a dime without taking a shoelace. One day, the peddler, after receiving the dime, said, "I don't like to complain, but laces have gone up to 20¢ now."

This hotel really charges for everything. There's an odometer on the toilet tissue holder.

"Why are you so glum?"
"Remember two weeks ago? That worthless stock I had went up and I made $15,000 and last week a distant uncle died and left me $25,000."
"Yes, I remember. But why are you so depressed now?"
"Because this week, nothing!"

The collection agency began its letter saying, "We are surprised that we have not received anything from you."
Back came the answer, "I don't know why you are surprised. I didn't send anything."

A young husband realized that it was time to start saving money. He decided not to use the streetcar any more. One evening he ran behind the streetcar, came home gasping, and said to his wife, "Dear, I saved 20¢ by running behind the streetcar."

"You're a fool!" said the wife. "You could have saved $2.25 by running home behind a cab!"

Statistics show that the best time to buy anything is about 40 years ago.

"What would you do if you found a million dollars?"
"Well, if it was a poor person who lost it, I would return it."

Everybody says it's hard to meet expenses . . . I meet them everywhere.

There was a successful businessman with his expensive Cadillac at the college class reunion. He confided to a former classmate that he was lousy at math and had flunked accounting.

"How did you became such a success then?" asked the classmate.

"I found an item which I bought for $1 and sold for $4, and I seem to be doing pretty well on the three percent profit."

POLITICIANS.

A Presidential candidate was campaigning in the West and was giving a speech at an Indian reservation. "If I am elected, my friends, my party will love you as our neighbors."

"Buzzonga! Buzzonga!" cheered the Indians. ". . . and we will eliminate war, poverty and disease!" he continued. "Buzzonga! Buzzonga!" thundered the Indians, the excited squaws holding their papooses in the air to better see the speaker. "We will teach all citizens to have tolerance and understanding . . ." continued the candidate. "Buzzonga! Buzzonga!" roared the tribe in tribute to the white man's ending his speech.

Later, while talking to the Chief, the politician noticed an odd breed of horses grazing in a nearby field. Explaining his interest, he asked if he could walk among them and look them over. "Sure, you can," replied the Chief, "but be careful that you don't step in the Buzzonga!"

The reporters were getting frustrated because the politician they were interviewing was deftly refusing to be pinned down on any issue. Finally one reporter said, "We're having trouble getting straight answers from you. Why don't you answer just this one question. What is your favorite color?"

"Plaid," replied the politician.

The Democratic mayor had an interesting and effective technique for winning votes. He gave taxi drivers, waiters, and barbers no tips at all, then advised them. "Be sure to vote Republican!"

A man of mediocre intellect who had become a prominent politician once amazed Parliament with a brillant speech. As he sat down amid thunderous applause, a single voice in the Opposition cried out: "Author! Author!"

PREACHERS.

Two priests were on a walk and came upon a rabbit who was stretched out and gasping its last breath. The first priest said, "Oh, look at that poor little rabbit." The second priest pulled a bottle out of his pocket and sprinkled the animal. Immediately, the rabbit got up and scampered away. The first priest said, "It's a miracle! It's a miracle!" "Oh, no, it wasn't," said the second priest. "It was my hare restorer."

The following admonition was addressed by a Quaker to a man who was pouring forth a volley of unparliamentary language against him:
"Have a care, friend, thou mayest run thy face against my fist."

The father came home and found his daughter crying her heart out. "What's the matter," he said.
"I'm in love with Sam, but we can't get married because we're Catholic and he's Jewish."
"Why don't you convert him? Describe to him the beauty of the churches, the great rituals, the music, the stained glass."
Several weeks later he finds his daughter again crying her heart out. "What's the matter," he exclaimed.
"Now Sam wants to become a priest!"

"What must you do to obtain forgiveness for your sin?" asked the Sunday school teacher.
A hand promptly went up: "Sin."

The car the nuns were driving ran out of gas. A passing motorist told them they could siphon gas from his tank, but they didn't have anything to put it in.
The nuns has been on a nursing assignment, so they put the gas in a bedpan. As they were putting the gas into their gas tank, a passing truck driver slowed down and said to his assistant, "That's what I call real faith."

PRODUCT.

The president of an auto manufacturing company received a telephone call. "Was it your company which announced that you had put together a car in seven minutes?"
"You are right," said the proud executive. "Why did you call?"
"Well," replied the caller, "I'm the one who got that car."

A Japanese company decided to build a new car. They engineered and built it within two weeks.
They didn't have a name for it so they decided to contact the Germans who had a reputation for coming up with good descriptive names.
Back came the answer, "Datsun."

The development of a new product is a three-step process: first, an American firm announces an invention; second, the Russians claim they made the same discovery 20 years ago; third, the Japanese start exporting it.

After the employee attended a new product meeting which went into great detail, he was asked if he had a better understanding. "Yes, I'm now confused on a much higher plane!"

SALESMEN.

The wife received a phone call from her husband saying he was going fishing for the weekend. He asked her to be sure to pack his gold silk pajamas as he likes to relax in these after a shave and shower when he comes in from fishing.
When he got back home he related several anecdotes about his fishing experiences and then asked his wife why she didn't pack his gold silk pajamas.
"I did. I put them in your fishing tackle box."

The sales manager was checking the references of an applicant for a sales job. "Was he a steady worker?"
"Steady," said the former employer, "he was almost motionless."

You can tell that Bill is a great salesman. He is the type of guy who can sell cracked eggs at 15¢ extra because he called them "pre-broken."

A salesman, after driving all day, stopped at a small town. He asked the gas station attendant, "Is there any night life here?"
"Not now," said the attendant. "She moved to Kansas City."

A clothing salesman was requested to take an especially loud suit and sell it to a blind man. He came back with the suit and was scratched up and his own suit torn.
The sales manager asked if he got into a fight with the customer.
"No, I didn't. But I sure got in one heck of a fight with his seeing eye dog!"

The sales manager told the advertising copywriter that he wanted to hire a product information expert, an engineer, a trouble shooter, a merchandising expert, a top-notch marketing man, a public relations expert. The copywriter asked if he should advertise for all six in one ad, or run six separate ads.
"I'm not looking for six men," replied the sales manager. "I'm looking for a professional salesman."

"Now here is where you are going to see a miracle," said the vacuum cleaner salesman as he dumped a pile of dust and dirt on the floor.
"It will be a miracle all right, there ain't no electricity here!"

A salesman in Ann Arbor dialed a number which was answered by a small boy.
"Is your father home?" he asked.

"No."
"Is your mother there?"
"No."
"Is there anyone else there?" he asked.
"Just my sister."
"Will you let me talk to her?"
After several minutes, the boy returned and said, "I can't lift her out of the play pen."

He who works with his hands is a laborer;
He who works with his hands and head is a craftsman;
He who works with his hands, head, and heart is an artist;
He who works with his hands, head, heart, and feet is a salesman.

A shoe manufacturer decided to open the Congo market and dispatched two salesmen to the undeveloped territory. One man cabled back: "Prospects here are nil. Nobody wears shoes." The other man cabled: "Market potential is terrific! Everybody here is barefooted!"

"I got two orders today," declared the new salesman.
"Splendid," said the boss. "What were they?"
"Get out and stay out!"

Since I started in sales I'm my own boss.
How's that?
I'm not taking orders from anybody.

Customer: "I'm thinking of placing a $10,000 order with your company. How much will you take off for cash?"
Salesgirl: "Everything but my earrings."

A salesman, trying to figure out how to make his way out of the Kaiser Steel plant in Fontana, asked a secretary, "How do I get outside?"
She replied, "Dial 9."

Bos: "What's this big item here?"
Salesman: "That's my hotel bill."
Boss: "Don't buy any more hotels."

The husband came home and asked his wife, "Did the man come today who guaranteed to get rid of our crabgrass?"
"Yes, we are going to get a swimming pool."

Three salesmen were holding a conversation. The food salesman said, "I hate to see a woman dine alone." The liquor salesman said, "If there's anything I hate, it's to see a woman drink alone."
And the mattress salesman said not a word!

There is a company which uses an ink blot test to hire salesmen. They show the applicant an ink blot. The applicant who tries to sell the company a new pen gets the job.

We have a top notch sales force. But the trouble is that we don't sell notches.

Bill says he is a really good salesman. He reports he doesn't need leads from us. People tell him where to go.

Competitive salesman confiding to one of our men: "I won't go into all the details; in fact, I've already told you more about it than I heard myself."

Wife: "What's all the excitement about—why are you throwing things out of drawers? What have you lost?"
Salesman: "I got an order today, and I've mislaid the address of my firm."

Nearing the close of the day, an executive admitted an insurance salesman and said, "You can flatter yourself, for I have refused to see five salesmen today."
    The man replied, "Yes, I know—I was the five."

Salesman: "I've been trying all week to see you. May I have an appointment."
Businessman: "Make a date with my secretary."
Salesman: "I did, and we had a grand time, but I still want to see you."

Definition of a good salesman. One who can make his wife sympathize with the girl who lost her compact in his car.

A meddling old lady accused one of our star salesmen of having reverted to drink because with her own eyes she had seen his company car parked outside a tavern.
    The accused made no verbal defense, but the following evening he placed that same company car in front of her house and left it all night.

The sales manager was talking confidentially to his secretary about Sam. "It's a wonder he can sell anything. Just watch, I asked him to bring me a package of cigarettes on his way back from lunch. I'll bet he won't remember to come back from lunch, never mind remembering the cigarettes."
    Just then the door flew open and in burst Sam. Happily he shouted, "Guess what, while at lunch I met Mr. Smith who hasn't bought anything in seven years. We got to talking and by the time we finished lunch, he gave me this $400,000 order!"
    "See," said the sales manager to his secretary, "he forgot the cigarettes."

SALES MANAGER.

The newly appointed vice president of sales was conducting his first press conference. A reported asked: "When you select your staff, will you consult with the powerful interests that control you?"

"Young man," said the vice president, "let's keep my wife out of this discussion."

The sales manager, trying to instill a little pep into his sales force, said:
"Gentlemen, every morning as soon as I wake up, regardless of the hour, I touch the toes of my shoes 25 times."
From the rear of the room, a voice asked, "Is that before or after you put them on?"

The sales manager really hated any phone operator who answered with the phone number instead of the company name, and the secretary who asked "Who's calling?"
He really got even when an operator answered "241-6002." And when he asked for Mr. Smith, she asked, "Who's calling?" With sweet revenge he answered, "264-9006."

Two salesmen were verbally raking their sales manager over the coals.
"To me," said one, "he's a pain in the neck!"
"That's funny," said the other, "I have a much lower opinion of him."

Sales Manager.: I think we ought to drop the XYZ line.
Boss: Why?
Sales Manager: Because we set a sales target of 100,000 and sold 13.
Boss: This is no time to get superstitious.

The sales manager asked the new salesman what the $28.56 item was on his trip expense account, labeled "ESP." "What is this extra-sensory perception expense?"
"Oh, it doesn't mean that. It stands for 'error some place.'"

Americans, as I've discovered in my medical practice, seem unable to relax. A business executive came to my office for a routine checkup. He showed visible signs of overwork. I warned him to slow down, take up a hobby—perhaps painting—to relax. He readily agreed, and left the office.
The next day he phoned and announced enthusiastically, "Doc, this painting is wonderful! I've finished a dozen already."

The kid asked his mother why his daddy brought home a briefcase crammed full of papers each night.
The mother explained that he had so much work that he couldn't finish it, so he brought it home.
The son replied, "Well, why don't they put him in a slower group?"

SECRETARY.

The boss is in the hospital on account of his knee. His wife found a red-haired secretary on it.

Overheard in an elevator: "She's such a slow typist, every time the little bell rings on her typewriter, she thinks it's time for a coffee break."

"Do you have a Saxhauer in your Company?"
"Hell, no, we don't even have a coffee break!"

Said the newly hired secretary to her boss: "Do you want double spacing on the carbons too, sir?"

The beautiful secretary returned from her vacation. The boss asked, "What's new?"
"I have good news and I have bad news."
"Give me the good news first."
"You're not sterile."

Boss: "Do you file your nails?"
Secretary: "No, I just throw them away after I break them."

SEX.

The Most Virtuous Lady in the World died and found herself in hell. She phoned St. Peter, who asked her to be patient because heaven was overcrowded. Two weeks later she phoned St. Peter again. They were teaching her to drink and smoke.
Patience, St. Peter urged; a room in heaven would be available for her shortly.
The next week the Most Virtuous Lady phoned again: "Hello, Pete? Forget it . . ."

As he approached the haberdashery counter of a large department store, a well-dressed gentleman was greeted by a shapely clerk.
"Good afternoon," she murmured softly. "And what is your desire?"
"My desire," he said, after giving her a long, appreciative look, "is to sweep you into my arms, rush out of this store and make mad, passionate love to you. But what I need is a pair of socks."

A pretty young nurse was selling poppies when a potential buyer, a young man, told her that he would give her a $5 bill for a poppy provided she would promise to nurse him if at any time he went to the hospital. She agreed.
"By the way," the young man asked, "where is your hospital?"
"I am at the maternity hospital," meekly replied the pretty young nurse, putting the money into the box.

The nine-year-old boy came home from a new school to which he had been transferred and asked his father, "What's sex?" The father was prepared and spent ten minutes explaining the subject fully. After the father finished, the boy looked at him questioningly, showed him an enrollment card and said, "Yes, but how am I going to get all that in this little square?"

There was a man who was advised by his physician to run ten miles a day to improve his love life. After two weeks he phoned his doctor as instructed. "Has it helped your sex life?" asked the doctor.

"I don't know," replied the patient. "I'm 140 miles from home."

The rural businessman received a questionnaire from the State. One of the questions was: "How many employees do you have broken down by sex?"

He wrote in his answer: "I think we have more of a problem with liquor."

A man was appointed a judge at a beauty contest. He went up to a man in the group and said, "Are you the head judge?"

"Yes, I am."

"That's good," said the first man, "then I'll take the legs!"

There was a Sultan who had a harem. He kept the harem five miles from his palace. He would send a servant to get one of his wives whenever he wanted one.

The Sultan lived to the ripe old age of 98. His servant lived to 32. All of this goes to show you that it's not women that kill you, but the running after them.

I know of two maiden sisters who had a cat named Tom. They never let him out except when he was on a leash.

The younger sister got married. A few days after the honeymoon the older sister received a letter from her newly married sister. Eagerly awaiting the details of the honeymoon, she tore the envelope open. Inside was only one sentence, "Let Tom out!"

I heard that Libras are sexy and fun-loving. So I found a girl who was a Libra and married her. And it's true. When I make love to her, she laughs.

The lady had just had her tenth child. It was a boy. The hospital nurse asked her, "Was it what you really wanted?"

"All I really wanted was just a good night kiss!"

Definition of an operator: A male telephone operator alone with 50 girl operators.

Diary of a girl on her first trip to Europe:
Mon.:   I felt honored that the Captain seated me at his table.
Tues.: The Captain invited me to the bridge.
Wed.:   The Captain made some advances to me.
Thurs.: The Captain invited me to his cabin.
Fri.:   The Captain said that if I didn't, he would sink the ship.
Sat.:   Tonight I saved the lives of 475 passengers.

TAXES.

Man to tax examiner: "But I've always deducted my liquor bill as a medical expense. My friends and I drink to each other's health."

Man filling out his income tax papers: "Who says you can't be wounded by a blank!"

Internal Revenue Agent: "Tell me, Father, did that fellow Richards really donate $5,000 to your church?"
Father: "Not yet, but he will . . . he will."

TOURISTS.

The tourist was visibly impressed. "You say you have 365 days of sunshine in your part of Arizona?" he asked.
"Indeed, I do, sir," replied the Arizonan. "And that figure is a very conservative estimate.

"I got up at dawn to see the sunrise," boasted a tourist.
"Well," commented his friend, "you couldn't have picked a better time."

Guide in bus: "We are now passing the largest distillery in the state!"
Voice from the rear: "Why?"

"That is Black Mountain?"
"Yes, sir—highest mountain about Lake George."
"Any story or legend connected with that mountain?"
"Lots of 'em. Two lovers once went up that mountain and never came back again."
"Indeed! Why, what became of them?"
"Went down the other side."

WIFE.

Spendthrift wife to husband, upon opening his anniversary present to her: "Oh, darling, a mink coat. Is it genuine mink?"
Husband: "Well, if it's not, I'm out $25."

An insanely jealous woman compelled her husband to undergo a rigid inspection after every night out with the boys. If she discovered a single hair on his clothes, there would be a terrible row. One night, having found nothing, not even a single hair, she burst into tears and cried: "Even baldheaded women, now!"

Druggist: "Did that mud pack I suggested improve your wife's appearance?"
Husband: "Only for a few days. Then it wore off."

A chap at breakfast early one morning was glancing through the used car want-ads and could hardly believe his eyes when he saw one that read: "Cadillac convertible, used 2 weeks. Perfect condition. $100."

He hurried to the address listed. A woman answered the doorbell and took him to the garage. Sure enough, there it was—shiny, white, handsome and expensive!

As he handed over the money, he asked how it was possible she could sell the car for so little.

"Well," said the woman gently, "my husband bought it just before he passed away last month. In his will he requested that it be sold and the money given to his secretary."

The husband was fed up with domestic life. One evening he said to his wife, "Look, your mother's been living with us for 18 years. Why doesn't she go back to Kokomo?"

"My mother?" repeated the wife, "I thought she was your mother!"

"My mother-in-law is a dear and I can't wait for the season to open."

I asked my wife what she wanted for her birthday. She said she wanted something which was hard to break—like a $500 bill.

The wife was complaining that her husband didn't appreciate her and that wives ought to get together and strike.

Husband: "Go ahead. I've got a honey of a strikebreaker in mind."

"You've got to stop running around with women. If you don't, you won't last another week!"

"I'm okay. There's nothing wrong with me," said the patient. "Why can't I run around with women?"

"One of them is my wife."

The housewife had her hands in dough, and she was annoyed to find that the knock at the door was that of a tramp.

"Please lady," he whined, "could you help a poor man out of his troubles?"

"Gladly," snapped the woman, "would you rather be shot, poisoned, or hit with an axe?"

The wife was admonishing her husband for going back for "seconds" too many times at the party.

"Doesn't it embarrass you, going back for more food so many times?"

"No, darling," he replied, "I tell them it's for you."

Man to friend: "Nobody can cook like Mabel. But they came pretty close to it when I was in the Army."

"I can't marry Henry, mother, he's an atheist and doesn't believe there's a hell."

"Marry him, Susie, and between us we'll convince him he's wrong."

"I suppose you'd call this horrible thing modern art," a woman customer said to the owner of an art gallery.

"No, madam," he replied. "You're looking in the mirror."

When the woman motorist was called upon to stop, she asked indignantly, "What do you want with me?"

"You were traveling at 40 miles an hour," answered the officer.

"Forty miles an hour? Why, I haven't been out an hour," said the woman.

Two women were discussing the impending marriage of one of their daughters. The other woman said, "Well, if you dislike this Henry so much, why are you consenting to the marriage?"

"I guess the thing is," rasped the first woman, "I'm sort of looking forward to being his mother-in-law for awhile."

"Tell me, Mr. Zimmer," said the marriage counselor, after several sessions, "did you wake up grouchy this morning?"

"No," said Zimmer, "I let her sleep."

Mrs. Smith: "Why did you get rid of your waterbed?"
Mrs. Jones: "Harold and I were drifting apart."

At one of our meetings a fellow flinched every time an auto horn sounded on the street. He jumped so often that he disturbed the other salesmen. So we stopped the meeting and asked him for an explanation.

He said, "A few days ago my wife ran away with our chauffeur. Every time I hear a horn, I'm afraid it's that chauffeur bringing her back!"

There was the husband who was so happy that his wife hired a detective to find out why.

Mr. Jones flew into the closet just ahead of his pursuing wife and locked the door.

"Come out of there, you worm," she said as she banged on the door.

"I will not," shouted Jones from the closet.

"Do as I say," thundered Mrs. Jones.

"I won't," yelled her husband. "I'll show you who's master of this house."

"So you deceived your husband," said the friend. "No, he deceived me. He said he was going out of town and he didn't."

Defense lawyer, to woman on trial for her life:
"Now tell the jury why you shot your husband with a bow and arrow."
"I didn't want to wake the children."

The little bride was lecturing her husband. "Listen," she said sternly, "I want you to do as I say. When my mother comes to visit us I want you to take her out somewhere!"

The groom blinked mildly. "It's no use doing that," he answered. "The last time she was here I took her out, but she found her way back."

Appendix 2

Meeting Supplies and Sales Promotion Buyer's Guide

A

ACUPUNCTURE CHART
   Edmund Scientific Co.
ADDRESS BOOKS
   Robinson Reminders
   Stationers Specialty Corp.
AD REPRINT FRAMES
   Sutton Designs, Inc.
ADVERTISING SPECIALTIES
   Autopoint Co.
   Arthur Blank & Co., Inc.
   Hagerstown Leather Goods Co.
   Baldwin Cooks Co.
   Hewig & Marvic
   Idea Man
   Impact Specialties Co.
   Lewtan Industries Corp.
   Macademic Sales Corp.
   Paper Mate Co.
   Pilgrim Plastic Products Co.
   Rueby Process, Inc.
   Fred Stoffel & Associates
AIRLINE SOUVENIR PRODUCTS
   Airline Merchandising Corp.
AIRPLANES—Paper
   Carlisle Co.
   Dennis Hommel Associates
AIRPLANES—Toy
   Sportswood Specialty Co.
   Tester Corp.
ALBUMS—Photo & Scrapbook
   Peerless Plastics
   Holmes-Webway Co.
ALMANACS
   Bantam Books, Inc.
   Dell Publishing Co., Inc.
   Hammond, Inc.

Buyer's Guide

ANIMATED CALENDARS, RULERS, etc.
  Visual Penagraphics, Inc.
  Visual Graphics Co.
APPLIQUES (see "Embroidered appliques")
APPOINTMENT BOOKS
  Brandmark Sales
  Keith Clark, Inc.
  Dymo Products Co.
  General Diaries Corp.
  Ready Reference Publishing Co.
APRONS
  Artistic Apron House, Inc.
  Helen of Troy
  R. A. Briggs Co.
  Fruit of the Loom, Inc.
  Helli Company
  Hewig & Marvic
  The Holemen Company
  Lewtan Industries Corp.
  P&M Apron & Novelties, Mfg. Co.
ART (see "Clip Art," also "Transparencies")
ASHTRAYS
  Adams Mfg. Co.
  Anchor Hocking Glass Corp.
  Color Craft Co.
  Contemporary Ceramics
  Crestline Co., Inc.
  Federal Glass
  Hewig & Marvic
  Jeanette Glass Co.
  Macademic Sales Corp.
  Savine Industries, Inc.
ASHTRAYS—Ceramics
  World Wide Art Studios
ATLASES (also see "Maps")
  Hammond, Inc.
  The George F. Cram Co., Inc.
  G & C Merriam Co.
  Rand McNally Co.
ATTACHE CASES
  American Tourister Luggage
  American Meeting Supply
  Ernest Hazel Jr., Inc.
  Day-Timers
  Leather Specialty Co.
  United States Luggage
AUTO-½ & ⅓ Scale, Antique
  The Henry G. Dietz Co., Inc.
  Mini-Kars, Inc.
  Unforgettable Cars, Inc.
AUTO ACCESSORIES
  Amity Leather Products
  Aladdin Industries, Inc.
AUTO PAD HOLDERS
  Bridgeport Leather Specialty Co.
AWARDS (also see "Plaques, Trophies")
  Creative Rewards
  Rueby Process, Inc.
  Arlen Awards
  Creative Awards by Lane
  Seth Thomas
  Bruce Fox, Inc.
  Philadelphia House

B

BADGE HOLDERS
  American/Durein Co.
  Directions Unlimited, Inc.
  Elgin School Supply Co., Inc.
  Oleet & Co., Inc.
  Seton Name Plate Corp.
  American Meeting Supply
BADGE MAKING MACHINE
  American Science Center
  Badge-A-Minit
  Edmund Scientific
  R.P.M. Associates, Ltd.
BADGES (also see "Buttons—Badges")
BADGES
  Adcraft Manufacturing Co.
  Badges & Labels Corp.
  Benply Badges
  Hewig & Marvic
  J.J. Mfg. Co., Inc.
  Philadelphia Badge Co.

BADGES—Adhesive
  Jack-Bilt Corp.
BADGES—Celluloid
  Oleet & Co., Inc.
BADGES—Clear Holders
  Macademic Sales Corp.
  Green Duck
BADGES—Clear Plastic
  C-Line Products, Inc.
  Crestline Co., Inc.
  Jack-Bilt Corp.
  Oleet & Co., Inc.
  Seton Name Plate Corp.
BADGES—Combination
  Crestline Co., Inc.
BADGES—Combination Men &
Ladies & Printed Program
  Directors Unlimited, Inc.
BADGES—Medallion Type
  Green Duck
BADGES—Metal
  Oleet & Co., Inc.
  Directors Unlimited, Inc.
BADGES—Plastic, Adhesive
  Jack-Bilt Corp.
BADGES—Pressure Sensitive
(Stick On)
  Badges & Labels Corp.
  Crestline Co., Inc.
  Jack-Bilt Corp.
  Oleet & Co., Inc.
  Rueby Process, Inc.
  A. Dean Watkins Co.
  Allen Hollander Co., Inc.
BADGES—Ribbon (see "Ribbons")
BAGS—Beach
  Airline Textile Mfg. Co.
  Pipcraft Mfg. Co.
  Aladdin Industries, Inc.
  NASCO, Inc.
BAGS—Flight
  Aladdin Industries, Inc.
  Airline Textile Mfg. Co.
  Natco Products Corp.
  Northwest Airlines
  Personident, Inc.
  United Air Lines

  Universal Specialty Co.
BAGS—Insulated
  Hamilton-Scotch Corp.
  Holiday Line, Inc.
BAGS—Litter
  Airline Textile Mfg. Co.
  Aladdin Industries, Inc.
  Marquart Advertising Co.
  Rueby Process, Inc.
  U.S. Pencil & Stationery Co.
BAGS—Plastic
  KCL Corporation
BAGS—Shopping
  Columbia Plastics Corp.
  Nappe-Smith Mfg. Co.
  Hewig & Marvic
BAGS—Tote (also see "Beach Bags")
  Cardinal China Co.
  Chase Bag Co.
  Miller Belt's Ltd. (Denim)
  Nappe-Smith Mfg. Co.
  Neely Mfg. Co., Inc.
  Sibs Associates, Inc.
BAGS—Travel
  Neely Mfg. Co., Inc.
BALLOONS (also see "Inflatables")
  Anderson Rubber Co.
  Automatic Balloon Systems, Inc.
BALLOONS—4' Diameter
  Dismar Corp.
  Maple City Rubber Co.
  Mark Promotions
  Macademic Sales Corp.
  Oak Rubber Co.
BALLOONS—Giant
  Pratt Poster Co.
BALLOONS—Giant 12' × 5'
  William J. Small Agency, Inc.
BALLOONS—8' Weather & 3'
  American Science Center
BALLOON INFLATER
  Auto. Helium Balloon Sys. Inc.
BALLS
  AMF Voit, Inc.
BALLS—Miniature Football, Basketball, etc.
  Hewig & Marvic

Buyer's Guide

BANDANNAS
  Helli Company
BANK NOTES (also see "Money" and "Coins")
  Deak & Co., Inc.
BANKS
  Advertisers Publishing Co.
  Anchor Hocking Corp.
  Bathrico, Inc.
  Cycor, Inc.
  Macademic Sales Corp.
  Mitché, Inc.
  Marquart Advertising Co.
  Paragon Plastics, Inc.
  Vernon Co.
BANNERS (also see "Flags, Banners")
  Pratt Poster Company, Inc.
BANNERS
  Pratt Poster Company, Inc.
BANNERS—Custom Satin
  Hollywood Banners
BANNERS—Individual letters
  Dismar Corp.
BANNERS—Organizational
  Crestline Co., Inc.
BAR ACCESSORIES
  Advertising Gifts, Inc.
  Aladdin Industries
  Better Living Laboratories, Inc.
  Ekco Housewares Co.
  R. A. Briggs & Co.
BAROMETERS & HYGROMETERS
  Advertising Gifts, Inc.
  Seth Thomas Div. General Time
  Taylor Inst., Consumer Div.
  Welby Clock Div., Elgin Natl.
BATH MATS
  Aldon Rug Mills, Inc.
  Superior Products
BEACH BAGS—(see "Bags")
BEACH TOWELS (see "Towels")
BEANPOT—Bicentennial
  Redwood House
BEARDS & MUSTACHES
  Paradise Products, Inc.
BEER HATS
  Jacobson Hat Co.

BEER STEINS—Custom
  Select Gifts Co.
BELTS
  Buxton, Inc.
  Hickock Mfg. Co.
BEVERAGE SETS
  Anchor Hocking Glass
  Federal Glass
BICENTENNIAL GIVEAWAYS
  Hammond, Inc.
BICENTENNIAL ITEMS
  The New Spirit of '76 Foundation
BICENTENNIAL PARTY ITEMS
  Hewig & Marvic
  Rueby Process, Inc.
BICYCLES—Hi Wheelers
  G.E.M. Bicycle Sales & Imports
  Unforgettable Cars
BILLFOLDS
  Boyes Mfg. Co., Inc.
BINDERS
  Crestline Co., Inc.
  Day-Timers
  Dilly Mfg. Co.
  Inter-City Mfg. Co.
  S.I. Jacobson Mfg. Co.
BINDERS—Presentation
  C-Line Products, Inc.
BINDERS & FOLDERS
Presentation
  American Thermoplastic Co.
  Myron Manufacturing Corp.
BINGO (see "Games")
BLACKBOARDS
  American Visual Aids
  Maggie Magnetic, Inc.
  Marsh Chalkboard Co.
  Multi Products Industries
  Oravisual Company, Inc.
BLACKBOARDS—Chalkboard
  Marsh Chalkboard Company
BLACKBOARDS—Light Background
  Eberhard Faber
BLACK LIGHT and Accessories
  American Science Center
BLAZERS
  Holloway Sportswear, Inc.

BLAZERS *(cont.)*
   King Louie International Inc.
   Makley's
BLOUSES
   Medalist Industries, Inc.
   The Van Heusen Co.
BOATS
   Snark Products, Inc.
   General Foam Plastics
BONNETS
   Hewig & Marvic
BOOKENDS
   Nettle Creek Industries
   John Wright/York Metal Crafters
BOOKS
   Time-Life Books
BOOKS, BOOKLETS
   Better Homes & Gardens Books
   Hammond, Inc.
   Historic Reproductions
BOOK MARKS
   Advertisers Publishing Co.
   Hewig & Marvic
   Incentive Specialities, Inc.
   J.M. Lesser Co., Inc.
BOOKS—Sports
   Crestline Co., Inc.
   Snibbe Publications, Inc.
BOOTHS (see "Displays")
BOTAS
   Algoma Net Co.
   Gutman Cutlery Co., Inc.
BOTTLE & JAR OPENERS
   Ekco Housewares Co.
   Kroftware Corp.
BRANDING IRONS
   M & D
BRIEFCASES
   Amity Leather Products
   American Meeting Supply
   American Thermoplastic Co.
   Aycock Enterprises, Inc.
   Baldwin Cooke Co.
   Crestline Co., Inc.
   Elco Mfg. Co., Inc.
   Olympic Luggage Co.
   Peerless Plastics
   U.S. Luggage & Leather Prods.
   Glass Industries Co.
   Ernest Hazei, Jr., Inc.
   Shaw-Barlon, Inc.
   Hewig & Marvic
   Jacobson Mfg. Co.
   Macademic Sales Corp.
   Olympic Luggage Co.
   Rueby Process, Inc.
   Shaw-Barton, Inc.
BUCKLES
   Avedon Mfg. Corp.
   Hickock Mfg. Co.
   His Lordship Products Co.
BUCKLES—Custom
   Lee Company
   Lewis Buckle Co., Inc.
   Liberty Dee & Mould Corp.
   Metalart Buckle Co.
   Premium Mills, Inc.
   Ruebro Mfg. Co., Inc.
BULLETIN BOARDS
   American Visual Aids
   Ghent Enterprises, Inc.
   Multi Products Industries
   J. L. Weiner Co.
BULLETIN HEADS
   Carr Speirs
   Day-Timers
   Hewig & Marvic
BULLETIN HEADS (illustrated)
   The Drawing Board
   Idea Art
   National Creative Sales
BULLETS—Revolutionary & Civil War
   Pick Point Enterprises, Inc.
BUMPER STICKERS
   Oleet & Co., Inc.
   Hewig & Marvic
   Random Specialties Co.
   Jack-Bilt Corp.
BUMPER STRIPS
   Oleet & Co., Inc.
BURNING GAMES
   Hewig & Marvic
   Macademic Sales Corp.

Buyer's Guide

BUSINESS CARD CASES (see "Calling Cards")
BUTTONS (Badge)
  Adcraft Manufacturing Co.
  Creative House Promotions
  Dymo Products Co.
  Hewig & Marvic
  Macademic Sales Corp.
BUTTONS—Celluloid
  N.G. Slater Corp.
BUTTONS—Label
  Lar Lu Manufacturing
  Metal, Photo, Identification Co.
BUTTONS—Civil & Revolutionary War, State Seals, etc.
  Precision Products & Parts Div.
BUTTONS—Gag
  Centennial Novelty Co.
  N.G. Slater Corp.
BUTTONS—Metal Badge
  Crestline Co., Inc.

C

CALCULATORS & COMPUTERS
  Canon U.S.A., Inc.
  Casio, Inc.
  Litronix
  Norvus Consumer Products
CALENDARS
  Acorn Co.
  Advertising Publishing Co.
  Rand McNally & Co.
  Redi-Record Products Co.
  The Vernon Co.
CALENDARS, CARD
  Adcraft Mfg. Co.
  Brown & Bigelow
CALENDARS—3D
  Visual Graphics, Inc.
CALENDAR—Desk
  Macademic Sales Corp.
CALENDAR PAPERWEIGHT
  Baldwin Cooke Co.
CALENDAR TOWELS
  Stevens Linen Division

CALENDARS—Card & Wall
  Shaw-Barton, Inc.
  Vernon Company
CALENDARS—Watch Plastic Overlay
  Crystal Date Watch Calendar Co.
  The Vernon Co.
CALENDARS—Wristband
  Marquart Adv. Co.
CALLING CARD CASES
  Advertising Publishing Co.
  Advertising Leather Specialty Co.
  Winston Mfg. Co.
  Frederick H. Beach, Inc.
  Forbes Products Corp.
CALLING CARD FILE
  Baldwin Cooke Co.
CAMERAS—Promotional
  Argus, Inc.
  GAF Corp.
  Imperial Camera Corp.
  Jetset Manufacturing Co.
CANDLES
  Nasco Inc., Premium Div.
  Ronson Corp.
CANES
  Advertisers Publishing Co.
  Helli Company
CANNONS—Miniature, Noise
  Conestoga Co., Inc.
  Gutman Cutlery Co.
CANS—Message in a Can
  American Publishing Co.
CAPS (see also "Hats")
CAPS
  Derby Cap Mfg. Co.
  K-Studio
CAPS—Baseball
  Swingster Wearables
  ABC Sportswear
CAPS (also see "Golf Caps")
CAPS & HATS
  Chase Bag Co., Chaseline Div.
CAPS—Sports
  Marquart Advertising Co.
CARDS, PLAYING
  Advertising Leather Specialty Co.
  Baumgarten's Exclusive Imports

CARDS, PLAYING *(cont.)*
  Promotional Products Co.
CARD TRICKS
  Morgan Press, Inc.
  Stancraft Products
CARICATURE PORTRAITS
  Barbary Denny Caricatures
CARNIVAL GAMES
  Frank Stein Novelty Co.
CARRY-ALLS
  Baldwin Cooke Co.
CARRYING CASES—for Charts
  Oravisual Company, Inc.
CARS (see "Auto")
CARS—Antique
  First-A-Long Enterprise, Inc.
CAR TRUNK LITERATURE ORGANIZER
  Tiffin Metal Products
  Fidelity Products
  Trav-L-File Co.
  Robert James Co.
CARTON CUTTERS
  Pacific Handy Cutter, Inc.
CARTOONS (see "Illustrations")
CASINO PARTY KIT
  Harold's Club
CASSETTES
  Pickwick Int'l Inc.
  RCA Records
  Rival Mfg. Co.
CASSETTE DUPLICATION
  DAK Industries
CERTIFICATE BLANKS
  Goes Lithographing Co.
  Jeffries Banknote Co.
CERTIFICATES, CITATIONS—Lettered
  Ames & Rollinson, Inc.
CHAIRS—Folding
  Telescope Folding Furniture Co.
CHARTING MATERIALS
  Chartpak, Inc.
CHRISTMAS DECORATIONS
  Airline Textile Mfg. Co.
  General Foam Plastics Corp.
  J.M. Lesser Co., Inc.

  Norma Lites, Inc.
  Orchids of Hawaii
  Paper Novelty Mfg. Co.
CHRISTMAS IN-STORE DECORATING KITS
  Kurt S. Adler, Inc.
CIGAR STORE INDIAN
  Alfco-N.Y. Div.
CIGARS—Imprinted
  Nat Sherman Co.
CIGARETTES—Custom Labeled
  G. A. Georgopulo Co.
CLIP ART
  Clip Art Services
  Dynamic Graphics, Inc.
  Hart Publishing Co.
  Idea Art
  Redi Art
  Valdes Associates, Inc.
  Harry Volk Art Studio
  Volk Corporation
CLIP DISPENSER—Magnetic
  Leeco Mfg. Corp.
CLIPBOARD FOLDERS
  Crestline Inc.
CLIPBOARD KITS
  American Thermoplastic Co.
CLIPBOARDS
  Alcron, Inc.
  Amerline
  Baldwin Cooke Co.
  Crestline Co., Inc.
  Ernest Hazel, Jr., Inc.
  Hewig & Marvic
  Myron Manufacturing Corp.
CLIPS, UTILITY
  Advertisers Publishing Co.
  Green Duck Co.
  Promotional Products Co.
CLOCKS/TRAVEL ALARMS
  Bradley Time Div., Elgin
COASTERS
  Advertisers Publishing Co.
  American Polystyrene Corp.
  Hewig & Marvic
  Federal Glass

Buyer's Guide

Macademic Sales Corp.
Mitché, Inc.
Rueby Process, Inc.
COASTERS—Ceramic
  World Wide Art Studios
COASTERS—Cork
  Manton Cork Corp.
COASTERS—Metalized Cardboard
  Smith Pacific
COAT OF ARMS
  Sanson Institute of Heraldry
COAT OF ARMS—Embroidered
  Aycock Enterprises
COFFEE BREAK FILM
  Robert R. Hubrick & Assoc., Inc.
COFFEE MUGS (see "Mugs")
COIN BANKS (see "Bank")
COIN PLAQUES
  Curtin & Pease
  John P. Anderson Premiums
  Precision Products & Parts Div.
COIN PURSES
  Boyes Mfg. Co., Inc.
COIN REPLICAS (large)
  Pico International Corp.
COINS
  Creative House Promotions
  Hewig & Marvic
  Royal Anthenia Galleries (Ancient)
COINS—Anniversary
  Wendell's
COINS—Colonial
  John P. Anderson Premiums
COINS/COMMEMORATIVE &
CUSTOM
  Greenland Premium & Fulfillment Center
  Mount Everest Mint
COINS—Custom
  The Osborne Coinage Co.
  Hewig & Marvic
  Leyse Aluminum Co.
COINS—Foreign
  Deak & Co., Inc.
  Hobby Sales, Inc.
COINS—Historical
  Curtin & Pease

COINS—Miniature
  Museum Coins
COINS—Spinner
  Wendell's
COINS—Stretch
  Sasco, Inc.
COLOGNE—In Pen
  Copy & Graphics, Inc.
COLOGNE PACKETS
  Sales Catalysts, Inc.
COLOR PRINTING (small runs)
  Koodet Color Corp.
COLOR PRINTS
  Spectra Color Lab, Inc.
COMBS
  Gillette Appliance Div.
  B.B.B. Plastic Products
  Beacon Plastics Corp
  Ben S. Loeb
  Van Schaack Premium Corp.
COMIC BOOKS
  Benjamin Co., Inc.
  Dell Publishing, Co.
  M.B. Rosen & Son Co.
COMPANY POLICY MANUAL
(HUMOROUS)
  Merit Industries
COMPASS
  The Sherril Corp.
COMPASS—Auto
  Hull Manufacturing Co.
COMPASSES
  Taylor Instrument Co.
  Gutman Cutlery Co.
CONTEST HANDLING SERVICES
  D.L. Blair Corp.
  Promotions for Industry, Inc.
CONTEST INCENTIVE SERVICES
(see "Incentive Plans")
COSMETICS
  P 3 Enterprises
  Songrand Corp.
  Vis-Zon-De Cosmetics
CREDIT CARD WALLET
  Day-Timers
CRESTS—Monogrammed
  Seaton Name Plate Corp.

CROWNS, SCEPTERS, TIARAS
  Frank Stein Novelty Co.
  Merit Industries
  Theatrical Accessories, Inc.
CUFF LINKS
  The Easton Company
  Art Carved Incentive Sales Div.
  Green Duck Co.
  Hickock Mfg. Co.
  Wilnor Products
  Martguild, Inc.
CUSHION—"World's Greatest Salesman"
  The Holmen Company, Inc.
CUTTERS—Box
  Pacific Handy Cutter, Inc.

D

DART BOARDS
  Synergistics Research Corp.
  American Premium Corp.
  American Publishing Corp.
DART BOARDS—Cloth
  Cadaco, Inc.
DART BOARDS—Custom
  Manton Cook Co.
DATE BOOKS, DIARIES
  Myron Manufacturing Corp.
DAY-TIMERS
  Day-Timers Co.
DECALS
  Crestline Co., Inc.
  Imprint Art Products
  Jack-Bilt Corp.
DESK ACCESSORIES
  3M Company
  Better Ideas
  Custom Caddy
  Dymo Products Co.
  Ernest Hazel Jr., Inc.
  Park Sherman
  Arthur Salm, Inc.
  Shaw-Barton, Inc.
DIAMONDS (genuine & simulated)
  Art Carved/JR Wood Inc.
  Eternalight
  Waltham Watch Co.
DIARIES
  Distinctive Diaries Ltd.
  Forbes Products Corp.
  Ready Reference Publishing Co.
DIARIES, BUSINESS
  Day-Timers
DICE—Imprinted
  Crisloid Plastics, Inc.
DICE, LOADED, REGULAR
  Macademic Sales Corp.
DIPLOMAS—Parchment, Sheepskin
  The Long Island Engraving Co.
DIRECTOR'S CHAIR—Imprinted
  Domestic Industries
  The Telescope Fldg. Furn. Co.
DISAPPEARING MESSAGE
  Gilbreath Company
DISPLAYS
  The Brewster Corp.
  Dimensional Displays & Design
DISPLAYS—"Grand Opening," "Sale"
  Gordon-Douglas Co.
DISPLAYS—Lightweight Portable
  Arlington Aluminum Co.
  The Blue Thumb Co.
  Display Sales, Inc.
  Display Workshop, Inc.
  Downing Displays, Inc.
  Exposystems
  GP Enterprises
  Charles Mayer Studios, Inc.
  Merry Products
  Oravisual Co., Inc.
  Package Exhibit Programs
  Port-A-Splay
DISPLAYS—Lightweight Self-contained
  Arlington Aluminum Co.
  Display Producers, Inc.
  Display Sales, Inc.
  Merchandise Displays, Inc.
  Package Exhibits Programs, Inc.
DISPLAYS—Plexiglass Dome
  Ray Products, Inc.

Buyer's Guide

DISPLAYS—Self Pack
  Display Sales, Inc.
  Downing Displays, Inc.
  Package Exhibit Programs, Inc.
  Visual Communications
DISPLAYS—Table Top
  American Display Co.
  Arlington Aluminum Co.
  Autofold Displays
  Berm Studios, Inc.
  Display Sales, Inc.
  G.P. Enterprises
  Wm. Hayett, Inc.
  Merchandise Displays, Inc.
DIVIDERS (INDEX)—Custom
  American Thermoplastic Co.
DOLLAR BILLS—Personalized
  Thurston Moore & Associates of Denver
DRAPES—Custom Imprinted
  Hilli Company
  Hollywood Banners
DRINKWARE, Plastic Imprinted
  Macademic Sales Corp.

E

EASELS
  Arlington Aluminum Co.
  Charles Mayer Studios, Inc.
EASEL BINDERS (see "Binders—Presentation")
EASEL CARDS
  Dismar Corp.
EASELS, PORTABLE
  Oravisual Company, Inc.
EMBEDIMENTS—Lucite
  Creative Dimensional Products
  Distinctive Embediments, Inc.
  Hewig & Marvic
EMBLEMATIC JEWELRY
  Green Duck
EMBLEMS/EMBROIDERED
  A-B Emblem Co.
  Apache-Totem Badge & Emblem
  Marley's
  Penn Emblem
EMBLEMS—Embroidered State
  Lewtan Industries Corp.
EMBLEMS—Iron On
  Joy Insignia, Inc.
EMBLEMS, JEWELRY
  J.J. Mfg. Co., Inc.
  Mitché, Inc.
EMBLEMS—Metal
  His Lordship Products Co.
  J.J. Mfg. Co., Inc.
  Mount Everest Mint
EMBLEMS—Molded
  Adcraft Mfg. Co.
  Award Incentives, Inc.
  Hewig & Marvic
EMBLEMS—Molded—Custom & Stock
  Lewtan Industries Corp.
EMBLEMS—Sportswear
  Lar Lu Manufacturing
EMBLEM/STICK ON, SEW ON
  Rueby Process, Inc.
  Idea Man
EMBROIDERED APPLIQUES
  S&A Appliques, Inc.
  Inter-All Corp.
EMERY BOARDS
  H.C. Cook Co.
  Macademic Sales Corp.
  Finger Tip Specialties, Inc.
EMOTION METER—Electronic
  Edmund Scientific Co.
EXECUTIVE FLY SHOOTER
  Stancraft Products
EXHIBIT BOOTHS (see "Displays")
EXHIBIT BOOTHS—Lightweight
  Hollywood Banners
EXHIBIT BOOTHS, Portable
  Hollywood Banner
EYEGLASS TISSUE
  Macademic Sales Corp.

F

FILMS—Coffee Break
  Robert R. Kubrick & Assoc.

FILMS/FREE
Association Films
Modern Talking Pictures
Radiant Films
Sterling Movies, Inc.
FILMS—Humorous
Vantage Communication, Inc.
FILMS—Sales Training
American Management Assoc.
Association/Sterling Films
BNA Communications, Inc.
Cally Curtis Co.
The Dartnell Corp.
Ex-IBM Corp.
The Jam Handy Organization
Mass Media
Modern Media Services
Penton Publishing Co.
Ramic Productions
Roa's Films
Roundtable Films, Inc.
McGraw-Hill Book Co.
Universal Education & Visual Arts
Vantage Communications
Roy W. Walters & Associates, Inc.
FILMS—Travel & Sports
Modern Talking Pictures
FILMSTRIP PRODUCTION KIT
Project: Filmstrip
FILMSTRIPS—Custom
Custom Slides, Inc.
FILMSTRIPS—Photography
Custom Slides 'N Prints
FIRECRACKER MAILINGS
Hewig & Marvic
FIRST AID KITS
Advertising Publishing Co.
Brandmark Sales
Eagle Novelty, Inc.
Forest City Products, Inc.
Hewig & Marvic
Premium Sales Division,
  Johnson & Johnson
Macademic Sales Corp.
FISHING EQUIPMENT
Tony Acceta & Son
Al's Goldfish Lure Co.
Longfellow Sales Corp.
South Bend Tackle Co., Inc.
FLAGS
Anderson Associates
Atlast Flag Corp of America
Fabriko, Inc.
Gordon-Douglas Company
Merit Industries
Paradise Products, Inc.
Velva-Sheen Mfg. Co.
FLAGS (AMERICAN)
Marquart Advertising Company
FLAGS, BANNERS, PENNANTS
American Cap & Pennant Co.
Eagle Regalia Co.
FLAGS—Desk Size
American House of Flags
FLAGS—Golf
Valley Forge Flag Co., Inc.
FLAGS—Miniature Paper
H.E. Harris & Co.
FLAGS, PENNANTS, BUNTING
Bass Advertising Specialties
Greene Specialties
National Forge Flag Co., Inc.
FLAGS—State
Pratt Poster Co., Inc.
FLAGS—State Pennant, String of
Pratt Poster Company, Inc.
FLANNEL BOARDS
Jacrenda Manufacturing Co.
Charles Mayer Studios, Inc.
Oravisual Company, Inc.
FLASHLIGHTS
Adva-lite
Advertisers Publishing Co.
Garrity Industries
Incentive Aids Co.
Market Pro., Inc.
Ray-O-Vac, Div., ESB Inc.
Union Carbide Corp.
FLASHLIGHTS—Disposable
Churchill Marketing Corp.
Safety Premiums

Buyer's Guide   337

FLIGHT BAGS (see "Bags-Flight")
FLIP CHART PADS, PAPER
   Charles Mayer Studios, Inc.
   Oravisual Company, Inc.
FLOOR STANDS, Poster Frames
   Arlington Aluminum Co.
   Merry Products
FLOWERS, ARTIFICIAL
   Laride Corp.
FLOWER SEEDS
   W. Atlee Burpee Co.
FLY SWATTER—Executive
   Stancraft Products
FOLIOS—Imprinted
   Crestline Co. Inc.
FORTUNE COOKIES
   Lotus Fortune Cookie Co.
   Hewig & Marvic
FOUR-LEAF CLOVERS
   C.C. Marketing Service
   Daniel's Clover Specialty Co.
FRAMES—Ad Reprint
   Sutton Designs, Inc.
FRISBEES
   Wham-O Mfg. Co.
FUNNY FORMS
   Photoform, Inc.
   A.G. Trumble Co.

G

GAG GIFTS
   Wretched Mess Co.
GAG, JOKE NOVELTIES
   American Novelty Co.
   Haines House of Cards
   H. Fishlove & Co.
   Ooops
   D. Robbins & Co., Inc.
GAMBLING SUPPLIES (see also "Casino Kit")
   Paradise Products, Inc.
GAMES
   3M Company
   Aladdin Industries, Inc.
   American Premium Corp.
   Atlantic Playing Card & Match Co.
   Bar-Zim Mfg. Co.
   Bingo King
   Holes-Webway Co.
   Seymour Company
   Stancraft Products
GAMES—Simulation
   Science Research Associates
GARMENT BAGS
   The Baltimore Luggage Co.
   Bogene, Inc.
   Jiffy Garment Bags & Travel Covers
   Kordite Corp.
   Neely Mfg. Co., Inc.
   Sterling Products (Flight Bags)
GARMENT BAGS—Imprinted
   Top Brands, Inc.
GARTERS
   Helli Company
   Ris-Gay Division
GARTERS—Sleeve
   The Lewtan Company
   Frank Stein Novelty Co.
GEM STONES
   Ramona Mining & Mfg. Co.
GHOST WRITER KIT
   Tolch Products
GIVEAWAYS
   Idea Man
   Macademic Sales Corp
   Rueby Process, Inc.
GLASSES—Custom
   Anchor Hocking Corp.
   Brockway Glass Co.
GLASSES—Plastic
   Glasses Galore, Inc.
   Rueby Process, Inc.
GLASSWARE
   American Historical Replica Co.
   Anchor Hocking Corp.
   Federal Glass
   Rickes Crisa Corp
   Corning Glass Works
   Federal Glass Co.

GLASSWARE—Monogrammed
  Museum Coins, Glassware Div.
GLOBES (also see "Maps")
  George F. Cram Co.
  Hewig & Marvic
  Replogle Globes, Inc.
  Rand McNally & Co.
GOLD BARS (replica)
  Museum Coins
GOLD FOIL (Packets)
  Hastings & Co., Inc.
GOLD INGOTS—Custom
  Great Western Trading Co.
  Green Duck
GOLD NUGGETS
  Carson's
  Ferguson Gold Mining Co.
  Macademic Sales Corp.
GOLD PANNING KITS
  Ferguson Gold Mining Co.
  Marshall Manufacturing Co.
GOLD SIGNATURE PEN (writes in Gold)
  American Science Center
GOLF ACCESSORY PRIZES
  Chesal Industries
  J.F.K. Products
  Fred Stoffel & Associates
GOLF BALLS
  AMF Ben Hogan Co.
  Burke-Worthington Div.
  Golf Ball Advertising Co.
  Plymouth Golf Ball Co.
  Ram Golf Corp.
  Fred Stoffel & Associates
  Victor Golf Equipment Group
  Wilson Sporting Goods
GOLF BALLS—Imported
  Burke-Worthington Div.
GOLD BALL MARKERS
  Dick Watson
GOLF CAPS
  Advon Specialties
  Derby Cap Manufacturing Co.
  Golf Ball Advertising Co.
GOLF CASE TRAVEL GAG
  S.I. Jacobson Mfg. Co.

GOLF COACH (Slide Chart)
  Perry Graf Corp.
GOLF EQUIPMENT
  ABC Industries, Inc.
  AMF Ben Hogan Co.
  J.A. Dubow Sporting Goods Co.
  Dunlop Sporting Goods
  McDonald & Son Gold Co.
  MacGregor/Brunswick
  A.G. Spaulding & Bros., Inc.
GOLF FLAGS (see "Flags-Golf")
GOLF GAG NOVELTIES
  D. Robbins & Company, Inc.
GOLF GIZMO
  Vari-Vue International
GOLF GLOVES
  Ajay Enterprises
GOLF HATS (ses "Hats-Golf")
GOLF INSTRUCTION FILMS
  Budget Films
  United World Films
GOLF ITEM GIVEAWAY
  Idea Man
GOLF KIT
  Lewtan Industries Corp.
GOLF POLO SHIRTS—Imprinted
  Ebert Sportswear
GOLF PUTTER
  C.I. Industries
GOLF SHIRTS, SWEATERS
  Golf Ball Advertising Co.
GOLF SHOT COMPUTER
  Hewig & Marvic
GOLF TEES
  Amerline Corp.
  C.C. Marketing Service
  CI Industries
  Marquart Advertising Co.
GOLF TEES, DIVOT FIXERS, MARKERS
  Baldwin Cooke Co.
  Cosom Corp.
  Golf Ball Advertising Co.
  Art-Mold Products
GOLF TOWELS
  Golf Ball Advertising Co.
  Jack Nadel, Inc.

GOLF UMBRELLAS
Golf Ball Advertising Co.
Idea Man
GREETING CARDS
Berkey Film Processing
Nasco Inc. Premium Div.
Shaw-Barton, Inc.
GUNS—REPLICAS (see also "Cannons")
Gutman Cutlery Co., Inc.
Replica Models

H

HANDKERCHIEF—Traveler Identification
Arrow Co.
Artistic Monogram Co.
HANGERS
Baumgarten's Exclusive Imports
Carlisle Mfg. Co.
HATS
Derby Cap Mfg. Co.
Jacobson Hat Co.
Makley's
Miller Belts, Ltd.
John B. Stetson Co.
HATS—Chef
The Holemen Company, Inc.
HATS—Comic
Lewtan Industries
HATS—Golf
Derby Cap Mfg. Co.
Makley's
Frank Stein Novelty Co.
HATS—Novelty
Helli Company
Jacobson Hat Co., Inc.
Lar Lu Mfg.
Lewtan Industries Corp.
Newark Felt Novelty
Frank Stein Novelty Co.
HATS—Party
Hewig & Marvic
Paradise Products, Inc.
Merit Industries, Inc.
Rueby Process, Inc.
Idea Man
HAT—Skimmers
Jacobson Hat Co.
HATS—Sports
Derby Cap Mfg. Co.
HATS—Straw Cowboy
Advertisers Publishing Co.
HISTORICAL DOCUMENTS
Creative Ideas for Industry
HISTORICAL MONEY
(also see "Coins," "Antiqued Banknotes")
Historical Documents Co.
HORSE RACE GAMES
A Nite At The Races, Inc.
Armchair Races
Race Nite
The Races, Inc.
Cinemaraces

I

ICE BUCKETS
Flambeau Products Corp.
Thermo-Serv
ICE SCRAPERS
SV Tool Company
Hycor Inc.
Mc Donough Inc.
S/V Tool Co.
ILLUSTRATIONS (also see "Clip Art")
Redi-Art, Inc.
Valdes Associates, Inc.
Dynamic Graphics, Inc.
Harry Volk Art Studio
Volk Corporation
INCENTIVE PLANS
American Heritage Industries
Creative House Promotions, Inc.
Incentive Co. of America
Key to Sales Co.
King Korn Incentive Co.
Key Incentives, Inc.
E.F. MacDonald Co.
Motivation, Inc.

INCENTIVE PLANS *(cont.)*
   Performance Incentives Corp.
   Sperry Hutchinson Co.
INCENTIVE TRAVEL
SOUVENIR MAILERS
   Paradise Products Inc.
INFLATABLES
   Alvimar Mfg. Co.
   General Fabrics Corp.
   Vision Wrap Industries, Inc.
INGOTS (see "Gold Ingots")
INVISIBLE INK POSTCARD
   Impact Specialties Company
IRON-ONS
   Holoubek Studios

J

JACKETS (also see "Blazers")
JACKETS—Athletic
   ABC Sportswear
   Swingster Wearables
JACKETS—Personalized
   Holloway Sportswear, Inc.
JACKETS—Promotional
   Ebert Sportswear
   Helli Company
   Horizon Sportswear, Inc.
   Makley's
   Varsity House/Chév Craft
JEWELRY
   Art Carved Div., J.R. Wood & Sons
   Avedon Mfg. Corp.
   Award Incentives Corp.
   Benrus Watch Co., Inc.
   Coro, Inc.
   Curtin & Pease
   Imperial Jade Mining, Inc.
JEWELRY—Costume
   Coro, Inc.
   J.J. Mfg. Co., Inc.
JEWELRY—Custom Design
   Avedon Mfg. Corp.
   The Easton Company

JEWELRY—Emblematic
   Green Duck
JEWELRY—Gems
   Coro, Inc.
   Designcraft Jewel Industries
JEWELRY—Symbolic
   Creative Rewards
JEWELRY CASES
   Coro Inc.
   Matson Mfg.
JOKES (see "Gags")
JUMPING DISC
   Edmund Scientific Co.

K

KEY CASES
   Amity Leather Prod. Co.
   Columbia Plastics, Inc.
   Ernest Hazel Jr., Inc.
   Leyse Aluminum Co.
   J. J. Mfg. Co., Inc.
   Mark Promotions
   M.E. Moss & Co.
   Shaw-Barton, Inc.
KEY CHAINS
   Accutec, Inc.
KEY CHAINS (Coin replica)
   Curtin & Pease
   Historical Documents Co.
KEY CHAINS (Pull apart)
   Directions Unlimited
KEY CHAINS—Rabbit Foot
   Flair Craft Furs
KEY FOBS
   Macademic Sales Corp.
   Art Mold Products
KEY FOBS—Custom
   His Lordship Products Co.
KEY FOBS (Glow in dark)
   The Ever-Lite Co.
KEY FOBS, KEY CASES
   Art Mold Products
   Boyes Mfg. Co., Inc.

Buyer's Guide

KEY HOLDER—Magnetic
  Rueby Process, Inc.
  Idea Man
KEY MARKERS (Identifies Keys)
  Crystal-Date Watch Calendar Co.
KEY RINGS—Separating for Home and Car
  Baldwin Cooke Co.
KEY TAGS
  Baldwin Cooke Co.
  Marquart Advertising
  Macademic Sales Corp.
  Advertisers Publishing Co.
  B.B.B. Plastic Products
  Hewig & Marvic
  J.J. Mfg. Co., Inc.
  Mark Promotions
  Wendell's
KEYS—Emblematic
  Amity Leather Prod. Co.
  Avedon Mfg. Co.
  J&J Mfg. Co., Inc.
KITES
  Central States Diversified, Inc.
  Go Fly a Kite, Inc.
  Hi-Flier Mfg. Co.
KNIFE—Pocket
  Boker Mfg. Co.
  Baldwin Cooke Co.
  Razosharp
  The H. C. Cook Co.
  Gutman Cutlery Co., Inc.
  Hill Novelties Mfg. Co.
  Kinny Co.
  Robeson Cutlery Co., Inc.
  Imperial Knife Associated Cos.
  Kinney
  W.E. Basset Co.

L

LABEL MARKERS
  Duramatic Co.
  Dymo Products Co.
  Name Maker Corp.
  Hermes Engravers, Inc.
  Seton Name Plate Co.
LABELS—Pressure Sensitive
  Allen Hollander Co., Inc.
  Jack Bilt Corp.
  Dilly Mfg. Co.
LAMINATING KITS
  Lami Film Self-Sealing Plastic
LECTURN, PORTABLE—Sound
  Oravisual Company, Inc.
LECTERNS
  Dimensional Displays & Design
LETTER GADGETS
  Hewig & Marvic
  Macademic Sales Corp.
LETTERHOLDERS—Bicentennial
  Historic Reproductions
LETTER OPENERS
  Advertisers Publishing Co.
  Art-Mold Products Co.
  Baldwin Cooke Co.
  Bayes Mfg. Co., Inc.
  Brown & Bigelow
  Ernest Hazel Jr., Inc.
  Gutman Cutlery Co.,
  Green Duck Co.
  Imperial Jade Mining, Inc.
LETTER OPENERS—Sword
  The Beachcombers
LETTER PASTE-ON GADGETS
  Hewig & Marvic
LETTERING MACHINES & DEVICES
  Keuffel & Esser Co.
  Varigraph
  Varityper
LETTERS—Dry Transfer for Slide Titles
  Arthur Brown & Bro., Inc.
  Prestype, Inc.
  Gotham Industrial Park
LETTERS—for Displays
  Port-A-Splay Co.
LETTERS—for Flip Charts
  The Holes/Webway Co.
  Oravisual Company, Inc.

LETTERS—for Signs
  Scott Plastics Co.
LETTERS—Individual Initials
  Desk Sign Mfg. Co.
LETTERS—Plastic
  Charles Mayer Studios, Inc.
LETTERS—Three Dimensional
  Hernard Mfg. Co.
  Mitten Display Letters
LETTERS—Transfer
  Letraset
Avery Products Graphics Div.
LICENSE PLATES—Custom
  Columbus Manufacturers, Inc.
LIGHTERS
  Advertisers Publishing Co.
  Alfred Dunhill of London, Inc.
  His Lordship Products Co.
  J.A. Meyers & Co.
  Bic Pen Co.
  Creative Rewards
  Garrity Industries
  Gillette Co.
  His Lordship Products Co.
  Miller Advertising Service
  Ronson Corp.
  Scripto, Inc.
  Zippo Mfg. Co.
LITERATURE ORGANIZER, (see
"Car Trunk Literature Organizer")
LITERATURE—Racks
  Arlington Aluminum Co.
  Beemark Plastics
  Dimensional Display & Design
  Exposystems
  Kole Enterprises, Inc.
  Charles Mayer Studios, Inc.
  Oravisual Company, Inc.
  Polygraphics, Inc.
  Sutton Designs, Inc.
LITTER BAGS (see "Bags")
LUCITE EMBEDMENTS
  Arlen Awards
LUGGAGE (also see
"Garment Bags")
LUGGAGE
  Airways Industries, Inc.
  American Tourister Luggage
  Samsonite Corp.
  U.S. Luggage Corp.
LUGGAGE & TAGS
  Airline Merchandising Corp.
  Art Mold Products
  Bayes Mfg. Co., Inc.
  Glass Industries Co.
  Idea Man
  Macademic Sales Corp.
  Namemaker Corp.
  Rueby Process, Inc.
  James Specialty Co.
  Seton Name Plate Co.

M

MAGIC CARD TRICKS
  Stancraft Products
MAGIC TRICKS
  D. Robbins & Co., Inc.
  S.S. Adams Co.
MAGNETIC CLIPS
  Lewtan Industries, Corp.
MAGNETIC KEY HOLDER
  Directions Unlimited
MAGNETS
  Magnaplan Corp.
MAGNIFIERS
  Bausch & Lomb, Inc.
MAILING NOVELTIES (Also see
"Letter Gadgets")
  Paradise Products, Inc.
MANICURE KITS
  Griffon Cutlery Corp.
  Ernest Hazel, Jr., Inc.
  Noymer Mfg. Co.
  Mark Promotions
  J. Wisse & Sons
  World-Wide Gifts
MAPS
  The George F. Cram Co., Inc.
  Follet Publishing Co.
  Hammond, Inc.
  Rand McNally & Co.
  Replogle Globes, Inc.

Buyer's Guide

MAPS—Antique
  American Map Co.
  Historical Documents Co.
MAPS—Bicentennial
  Premium Division
MAPS, CITY—Custom Folders
  Crestline Co., Inc.
MAPS—Historical
  American Map Co.
MARBLES
  Berry Pick Industries, Inc.
  Bitro-Agate Co.
MASKS
  Frank Stein Novelty Co.
MATCHES—Box & Book
  Admatch Corp.
  Elliot Sales Corp.
  Glass Industries
  Lion Match Corp. of America
  Monogram of California
  Universal Match
MATS—Beach
  Flex-Mat Corp.
MATS—Table
  Bright of America, Inc.
  Nasco Inc., Premium Div.
MEASURING TAPES
  Justus Roe & Sons, Inc.
MEDALLIONS—Custom
  Medallic Art Company
MEDALS
  His Lordship Products, Inc.
  The Mount Everest Mint, Inc.
  Medallic Art Company
MEGAPHONES—Mini
  Advertising Counselors
MEMO BOOKS
  Autopoint Co.
  Minute Man Line
  Redi-Record Products Co.
  Robinson Reminders
MEMO NOTE HOLDERS
  Advertising Replicas, Inc.
  Creative Rewards
  Hewig & Marvic
MEMO PADS
  American Premium Corp.
  Crestline Co., Inc.
  Ernest Hazel Jr., Inc.
  Historic Reproductions
MENDING KIT
  Hewig & Marvic
  Idea Man
  Rueby Process, Inc.
MESSAGE SIGN SET
  Crestline Co., Inc.
METRIC CHARTS, RULES
  Baldwin Cooke Co.
  National Dealer's Service, Inc.
METRIC WALLET CARDS (3-D)
  Visual Graphics
MILES PER GALLON TAGS
  Macademic Sales Corp.
MINERALS POLISHED
  Ambidextrous, Inc.
MINTING—Custom
  The Mount Everest Mint, Inc.
MITTS—Cooking (also see "Potholders")
  R. A. Briggs Co.
MODEL T CARS (see "Autos")
MONEY CLIPS
  Advertisers Leather Specialty Co.
  Amity Leather Products
  Frederick H. Beach, Inc.
  Buxton, Inc.
  Creative Rewards
  Hickok Mfg. Co.
  His Lordship Products Co.
  Imperial Jade Mining Co.
  Martguild, Inc.
  Irving Weissler Co.
  Vernon Company
MONEY CLIPS ("$1,000,000")
  Museum Coins
MONEY CLIPS—Actual Coin
  S&S Associates
MONEY CLIP—Coin Replica
  Curtin & Pease
  Historical Documents Co.
MONEY CLIPS—Continental Dollar
  Curtin & Pease
MONEY CLIPS—Custom
  The Easton Company

MONEY—Confederate
 Impact Specialties
MONEY—Play
 Paradise Products, Inc.
MONEY—Playmoney Imprinted
 Texantics Unlimited Products
MONEY ENVELOPES
 Bankers Engraving Co.
MONEY/MAKING MACHINE
 Hewig & Marvic
MONEY PREMIUMS
 Sasco, Inc.
MONEY TREE SPOUTING SEED CARD
 Hewig & Marvic
MOOD MUSIC
 Thomas J. Valentino, Inc.
MOTION PICTURE FILM STOCK SHOT LIBRARIES
 Lem Bailey
 Fotosonic, Inc.
 Sherman Grinberg Film Library
MOUSETRAP PAPER CLIPS
 A.N. Brooks Corp.
MOVIES—Old Time
 Budget Films
 Camera Craft Rentals
MOVIE STILLS—Old Time
 American Stock Photos
 W.H. Everett
 Granger Collection
 Studio Archives
MOVIE STILLS—(Modern & Old Time)
 Movie Star News
MUGS (also see "Cups")
 Arnart Imports, Inc.
 American Heritage Industries
 Contemporary Ceramics
 Benner Glass Co.
 Contemporary Ceramics
 Federal Glass & Div. Feders Paper Board Co., Inc.
 Macademic Sales Corp.
 Mitché, Inc.
 World Art Studios

MUGS—Beer, Imprinted
 Sabine Industries
MUGS, Insulated, Bicentennial
 Thermo-Serv Co.
MUGS—Plastic Imprinted
 Thermo-Serv Co.
MUGS & PLATES—Colonial Pewter
 John Wright
 Old Mill Enterprises, Inc.
MULTIMEDIA CONTROL
 Communications Group
 Columbia Scientific Industries
MUSTACHES & BEARDS
 Merit Industries

N

NAIL CLIPPER
 Hewig & Marvic
NAMEPLATES
 AAA Nameplate Awards, Inc.
 Adcraft Mfg. Co.
 Advertising Plastics Co.
 Distinctive Embediments, Inc.
 Desk Sign Mfg. Co.
 Imperial Awards
 Seton Name Plate Corp.
 Spear Engineering Co.
NAMEPLATES, DESK & DOOR
 Day-Timers
NAMEPLATES—Pressure Sensitive
 Topflight Corp.
NAPKINS
 Hewig & Marvic
 Marquart Advertising Co.
NECKTIES, TIES—Custom Made
 Pick & Smith, Ltd.
NEWSPAPER—Bicentennial
 Incentive Sales Co.
NEWSPAPER—Chinese
 New Kwong Tai Press
NEWSPAPER HEADLINES
 Headline Printers
NEW YORK TIMES—
Front Pages Since 1851
 Microfilming Corp. of America

Buyer's Guide

NOISEMAKERS
  Green Duck Co.
  G. W. Rodin Co.
NOSTALGIA ITEMS
  The Nostalgia Factory
NOTEBOOKS
  Historic Reproductions
NOTE PAD HOLDER KITS
  American Thermoplastic Co.
NOVELTIES
  American Premium Corp.
  Mark Promotions
NOVELTIES—Carnival
  Frank Stein Novelty Co.

O

ORANGE TREES
  Norman Cox & Co.
ORCHIDS
  Flowers of Hawaii
  Orchids of Hawaii, Inc.
  Paradise Products, Inc.
OVERHEAD TRANSPARENCIES
MATERIALS KIT
  Agfa-Gevaert
  Visual Products Division
  Chartpak, Inc.

P

P.A. SYSTEM—Portable
  Argos Products Company
PAPER CLIP HOLDER—Magnetic
  Directions Unlimited
  Baldwin Cooke Co.
PAPER CLIP DISPENSER—Magnetic
  Leeco Manufacturing Corp.
PAPER CLIPS (Giant Imprinted)
  Marquart Advertising Co.
PAPER CLIPS—Large Imprinted
  Isis Products Ltd.
PAPERWEIGHTS
  Cambor Enterprises, Inc.
  Contemporary Ceramics
  Distinctive Embediments, Inc.

Display-Weight
  Kingwood Ceramics
  Lava Simplex International, Inc.
  Loyal Gift Products
  Wendell's
PAPERWEIGHTS—Awards
  Creative Rewards
  Crestline Co., Inc.
PAPERWEIGHTS—Commemorative
  Indiangiver Company
PAPERWEIGHTS—Globe
  Hewig & Marvic
PAPERWEIGHTS—Marble
  Paperweights, Inc.
  Crestline Company, Inc.
PAPERWEIGHTS—Plexiglass,
with World Inside
  Baldwin Cooke Co.
PARACHUTE—Toy
  Edmund Scientific Co.
PARTY DECORATIONS
  Gordon-Douglas Company
  Merit Industries, Inc.
  Paradise Products, Inc.
  Frank Stein Novelty Co.
PARTY DECORATIONS—
"Americana"
  Rueby Process, Inc.
  Hewig & Marvic
PARTY FAVORS
  Mitché, Inc.
  G. W. Rodin Co.
PASS CASES
  Golden Era/Div. Shiman Ind., Inc.
  Adams Mfg. Co.
  Adcraft Mfg. Co.
  Advertising Leather Specialty Co.
  Prince Gardner Co.
PASSPORT CASES
  Frederick H. Beach, Inc.
PASSPORT POCKET PORTFOLIO
  Dilly Mfg. Co.
PATCHES (also see Emblems)
  ABC Industries
  Canyon House
  Emblemcraft Ltd.

PATCHES, EMBROIDERED
  A-B Emblem
PATCHES (trademark)
  Conrac Industries, Inc.
PEARLS
  Coro, Inc.
PEN & PENCIL SETS
  Autopoint Co.
  Brown & Bigelow
  Esterbrook Pen Co.
  Gillette Co., Premium & Incentive Sales
  Mark Promotions
  Norma Pencil Corp.
  Shaw-Barton, Inc.
  W. A. Sheaffer Pen Co.
PENCIL CADDY—Aluminum Tankard
  Crestline Co., Inc.
PENCIL CADDY—Pop Up
  K&D Specialties
  Berkshire Sales Corp.
PENCIL CADDIES—Calendar
  K&D Specialties
PENCIL HOLDERS—Ceramic
  World Wide Art Studios
PENCIL SHARPENERS—Electric
  Panasonic
PENCILS—Mechanical
  Autopoint Co.
  Holes-Webway Co.
  Lindy Pen Co.
  Listo Pencil Corp.
  Ritepoint Corp.
PENCILS—Miniature
  W. W. Faber-Castell Pencil Co.
PENCILS—Wood
  Marquart Advertising Co.
PENLIGHTS
  Accutec, Inc.
  Adva-Lite
  Garrity Industries, Inc.
  Rueby Process, Inc.
  PENNANTS (also see "Flags" and "Banners")
    Chase Bag Co.
    Dismar
    Gordon-Douglas Company
    Jones Decorating Co.
    Mark Promotions
    Pratt Poster Company, Inc.
PENS—Ball Point
  Rueby Process, Inc.
  W. A. Sheaffer Pen Co.
  Shaw-Barton, Inc.
  Hewig & Marvic
  Accutec, Inc.
  All-Rite Pen Co.
  Autopoint Co.
  Esterbrook Pen Co.
  Eversharp Pen Co.
  Garland Industries
PENS—Desk
  Hallmark Cards, Inc., Writing Instrument Div.
  Kraftware Corp.
  W. A. Sheaffer Pen Co.
  Brown & Bigelow
  Parker Pen Co.
PENS—Jumbo 10″
  Berkshire Sales
  BIC Pen Corp.
PENS—Marking
  Bic Pen Corp.
  W. A. Sheaffer Pen Co.
PERFUME SPRAY POCKET DISPENSER
  Copy & Graphics, Inc.
PERFUMES—Colognes
  C. C. Marketing Service
  Parfums Originale
  A. Stein & Co., Inc.
  Van Schaack Premium Corp.
  World Wide Gifts
PERFUMES—Pursepack
  Rueby Process, Inc.
  Idea Man
PEWTER
  Oneida Ltd.
  Wallace Silversmiths
PHONE DIALERS & RINGS
  Macademic Sales Corp.
PHONOGRAPH RECORDS
  Pickwick International, Inc.

Buyer's Guide

    Aura Vision
PHOTO BADGE MAKING MACHINE
    Edmund Scientific Co.
PHOTO BUTTONS
    N. G. Slater Corp.
FOTO MUGS
    Foto Mug
    Thermo-Serv Co.
PHOTO PRISMS
    Creative Rewards
PHOTO—Old-Time Movie
    American Stock Photos
PHOTOS—Old-Time Movie Stills
    W. H. Everett
PHOTOS—Quantities
    Quantity Photo Co.
PHOTOS—Stock
    H. Armstrong Roberts
    Creative Photographic Library
    World Wide Photos, Inc.
PICNIC SETS
    Ever-Ware, Inc.
PICNIC SETS & HAMPERS
    Aladdin Industries
    W. C. Redmon Sons & Co.
    Thermos Div.
    Thermo-Serv Co.
PIPES—Peace
    Gutman Cutlery Co.
PITCHERS
    Aladdin Industries, Inc.
    The Pfaltzgraff Co.
    Thermo-Serv Co.
PITCHMAKER
    Close Productions
PLACE MATS
    American Premium Corp.
    Artistic Monogram
    Bright of America, Inc.
    Brown & Bigelow
    Mitché, Inc.
    Stancraft Products
    Stevens Linen Associates
    Surfset Inc.
    Wirley Ind., Inc.

PLACE MATS—Imprinted
    Hewig & Marvic
PLANNERS—Pocket
    Baldwin Cooke Co.
PLANNING BOARDS (for A/V)
    Michaels Artists & Engineering Supplies, Inc.
PLANTS—Live
    Asgrow Seed Co.
    Norman Cox & Co.
    Jackson & Perkins
PLAQUES
    Adcraft Mfg. Co.
    American Premium Corp.
    Arlen Awards
    Creative Rewards
    Crestline Co., Inc.
    Harris Engraving Co.
    Hewig & Marvic
    Idea Man
    Imperial Awards
    The Neff Athletic Lettering Co.
    Reuby Process, Inc.
    Seton Name Plate Corp.
    World Wide Art Studios
PLAQUES—Do It Yourself
    Creative Products Co.
    The Harnett Co.
PLAQUES—Humorous
Sports Awards
    Creative Rewards
    Idea Man
    Fred Stoffel & Associates
PLAQUES—Laminated
    The Award Company of America
    Perma Plaque Corp.
PLAQUES—Sports Awards
    R. D. Grunert Company
PLAYING CARDS
    Advertising Publishing Co.
    Morgan Press
    Shaw-Barton, Inc.
    Stancraft Products
    Western Publishing Co.
    The United States Playing Card
    U.S. Games Systems, Inc.

PLAYING CARDS—Jumbo
   Stancraft Products
   United States Playing Card Co.
POCKET KNIVES
   Bill-Mar Specialty Co.
   Camillus Cutlery
   Vernon Company
POCKET PROTECTORS
   Acme Leather Goods Co., Inc.
   Forbes Products Corp.
   Hewig & Marvic
   S. I. Jacobson Mfg. Co.
   Professional Products Co., Inc.
   Bayls Mfg. Co.
POINTER—Flashlight
   American Science Center
POINTER—Projection
   C. A. Compton, Inc.
POINTERS—Telescoping
   Perrygraf Division
     Nashua Corp.
POKER CHIPS—Imprinted
   The Osborne Coinage
POP-UPS, 3-D
   Jannes Associates
   Scott Crowell Corp.
   Structural Graphics
PORTFOLIOS
   Macademic Sales Corp.
PORTRAITS—Hand Printed
   Gentry Galleries, Ltd.
POSTER FRAMES (see "Floor Stands")
POSTER FRAMES
   Multiplex Display Fixture Co.
POSTERS—Old-Time
   Gramlee, Inc.
POSTERS—Photo Blow-Ups
   Blue Ribbon Promotions, Inc.
POSTERS—Promotional, Store
   Dismar Corp.
POSTERS—Travel
   Merit Industries
   Paradise Products, Inc.
   Stancraft Products
POTHOLDERS
   Artistic Monogram
   Chaseline, Inc.
   R. A. Briggs & Co.
   Hewig & Marvic
   Macademic Sales Corp.
   Marquart Advertising
PRECIOUS STONES
   Imperial Jade Mining, Inc.
PREMIUM INCENTIVE PROGRAMS
   Top Value Enterprises
   Travelers Premium Company, Inc.
   Bulova Watch Company,
     Incentive Sales Div.
   Performance Incentives Corp.
PREMIUM/PRIZE IDEAS
   Idea Source Guide (Magazine)
   Incentive Marketing (Magazine)
   Potentials in Marketing (Magazine)
   Premium Incentive Business (Magazine)
PRESENTATION ALBUMS
   The Holes-Webway Co.
PRESENTATION BINDERS
   S.I. Jacobson Mfg. Co.
PRESENTATION COVERS
   Day-Timers
PRESSURE GAUGES—Tire
   Lewtan Industries Corp.
PROJECTORS—Film Strip
   DuKane Corp.
   La Belle Industries
PROJECTORS—Overhead
   Buhl Projector Company, Inc.
   Visual Products Division 3M Co.
PROJECTORS—Slide
   Creation, Inc.
   La Belle Industries, Inc.
PROJECTORS—with Cassette Sound
   Creatron, Inc.
PROMOTIONAL KITS (for stores)
   Dismar Corp.
PURSES
   Promotional Mailings
   Hewig & Marvic
   Advertising Leather & Specialty
   Craftsman Billfolds

Buyer's Guide

U.S. Luggage & Leather Prod. Co.
PUZZLES
  S. S. Adams Co.
  American Premium Corp.
  American Publishing Corp.
  Du Bois Importing Co.
  Joslin Photo Puzzle Co.
  Milton Bradley Co.
  Mitché, Inc.
  Rand McNally & Co.
  Whitman Publishing Co.
PUZZLES—Custom
  Prager Industries, Inc.
PUZZLE—Shipping Tag
  Hewig & Marvic

Q

QUARTER—JUMPING
  Edmund Scientific Co.

R

RAFFLE TICKETS
  Frank Stein Novelty Co.
RAILROAD SPIKE SCULPTURES
  Garo Art Metal Co., Inc.
RAILROAD SPIKES (Paperweights)
  Harmon Marketing Corp.
RAIN BONNET
  Advertisers Publishing Co.
  Larido Corp.
  Macademic Sales Corp.
  Rueby Process, Inc.
RAINCOAT—Plastic
  Advertisers Publishing Co.
  Plasta-Seal Co.
RAINWEAR—Ponchos & Bonnets
  Columbia Plastics, Inc.
  Peerless Plastics
  Promotional Products Co.
REAR PROJECTION SCREENS
  Prima Education Products
RECOGNITION PROGRAMS (also see "Incentive Plans" and "Awards")
  Creative Rewards
  Arlen Awards
  Rueby Process, Inc.
RECORD BOOKS (also see "Diaries")
  Distinctive Diaries, Inc.
  Dymo Products Co.
  Minute Man Line
  Prentice Hall, Inc.
  Robinson Reminders
RECORDS—Party Albums
  Merit Industries
RECORDS—Phonograph
  Alphatape Sales Co., Inc.
  Columbia Special Products
  Jubilee Records
RECORDS—Sound Effects
  Thomas J. Valentino, Inc.
RECORDS/TAPES
  Eva-Tone Soundsheets
  Fleetwood Recording Co., Inc.
  Sales Motivators, Inc.
REFLECTOR STICK-ONS
  Safety Premiums
REPLICAS—Product
  Reuby Process, Inc.
  Arlen Awards
RIBBONS—Badge
  3M Co.
  Crestline Co., Inc.
  Hewig & Marvic
  Idea Man
  Jack-Bilt Corp.
  Macademic Sales Corp.
  Oleet & Co., Inc.
  Rueby Process, Inc.
  Frank Stein Novelty Co.
  Waldoroth Label Corp.
RINGS
  Art Carved/J.R. Wood Inc.
  Jayposon Jewelry Mfrs.
  Luxury Incentives
    Frederick Siebel Associates
ROBES—Blankets
  Fairbault Woolen Mill Co.
ROBOTS
  Quasar Industries, Inc.

ROOM TAGS
　Creative Awards by Lane
RUBBER DOLLARS
　Hewig & Marvic
　Impact Specialties
　Macademic Sales Corp.
RULERS
　The Cooper Group
　Falcon Rule Co.
　B.B.B. Plastic Products
　Eagle Rule Mfg. Co.
　Leyse Aluminum Co.
　Macademic Sales Corp.
　Perrin Products
　Rueby Process, Inc.
RULERS (6" 3-D)
　Visual Graphics, Inc.

S

SASH—Advertising
　The Lewton Company
SCENTS
　Smell It Like It Is.
SCENTS—on Labels
　3 M Products
SCENTS—on Printed Products
　Orlandi Frank, Inc.
SCISSORS
　Mc Donough, Inc.
SCRAPERS, INC.
　Hewig & Marvic
　Key Tag Mfg. Co.
SCREENS
　Da-Lite Screen Co., Inc.
SCREWDRIVERS
　Alexander Mfg. Co.
　National Dynamic Classics Ltd.
SCROLLS
　Ames & Rollinson, Inc.
　Goes Lithographing Co.
SEALS—Anniversary (Paper)
　Myron Manufacturing Corp.
SEARS ROEBUCK CATALOG
　DBI Books, Inc.
SECRET MESSAGE (also see "Ghost Writer" also "Invisible Ink")

SECRET MESSAGE—in Bullet
　Hewig & Marvic
SEEDS/BULBS
　Applewood Seed Co.
　Asgrow Mandville Co., Inc.
　W. Atlee Burpee Co.
　Luther Burbank Seed Co.
　Orchids of Hawaii
　Vaughan's Seed Co.
SEWING KITS
　Avant Products
　Advertisers Publishing Co.
　Random Specialties Co.
　Larido Corp.
　Macademic Sales Corp.
　Random Specialties Co.
　Mark Promotions
SHADING ZIP-A-TONE
　Para Tone, Inc.
SHAKERS, SALT & PEPPER
　Anchor Hocking Glass Corp.
　Better Specialties
SHAMROCKS
　Orchids of Hawaii, Inc.
SHARPENING STONE
　Advertising Publishing Co.
SHEET PROTECTORS
　C-Line Products, Inc.
　Day-Timers
SHIRTS
　Artistic Monogram
　Puritan Sportswear Corp.
　Truvalue Shirt Co., Inc.
　Victoria Products, Inc.
SHOE HORNS
　Art-Mold Products Co.
　Custom Metal Products
SHOESHINE PACKETS
　Penman Sales Co.
SHOE SHINE TRAVEL POUCH
　Fred Stoffel & Associates
SHIPPING BAGS—POLY
　Hewig & Marvic
SHOPPING BAGS
　Oleet & Co., Inc.
　Rueby Process, Inc.

Buyer's Guide

SHOWER CAPS
  I. B. Kleinert Rubber Co.
  Seal Sac, Inc.
SIGN LETTERING KITS
  Dewey-Carter Co.
SIGNS
  Nettle Creek Industries
  Vernon Co.
SKIMMER HATS
  The Lewtan Company
SLIDE ART—Do It Yourself
  Frank Holmes Laboratories, Inc.
  Prima Education Products
  Singer Education Div.
SLIDE ART—Stock & Custom
  Cinegraph Slides, Inc.
  Lab Services
  The Slide Innovators
  Visual Horizons
SLIDE CHARTS
  Addressograph Division
  American Slide Chart Corp.
  Graphic Calculator
  Perrygraf Corp.
SLIDE DUPLICATION
  Custom Slides Inc.
SLIDE MOUNTS
  Kaiser Products
SLIDE PROJECTOR—
Cassette Sound
  Visual Horizons
  Singer Education Div.
SLIDE RULES
  Hoffman Products
  Jeppesen & Co.
  Keuffel & Esser Co.
SLIDE TITLES—Make Your Own Kit
  American Science Center
SLIDES—Custom
  Cinegraph
  Cinegraph-2
  Rick Shaw Associates Ltd.
SLIDES—Stock
  Successful Meeting Slides
SLIDES—Title
  Custom Slides, Inc.
  Technamation, Inc.
SLIDES—Visual Signal Accessory
  C. A. Compton, Inc.
SOAP
  Command Creations, Inc.
SOAP—Custom
  Hewitt Soap Co., Inc.
SOCKS—Slipper, Imprinted
  Hewig & Marvic
SOUND EFFECTS (also see "Records")
  Musifex Inc.
SOUND SYSTEM—Portable
  Shure Brothers, Inc.
SOUVENIRS (see "Travel Souvenirs")
SPEAKING TIME CONTROLLER
  C. A. Compton, Inc.
SPINNER COINS
  American Thermoplastic Co.
  Hewig & Marvic
  Glass Industries Co.
  Wendell's
SPONGES (swell to 16 times size)
  Sponge Specialties Mfg. Corp.
SPOONS—Bicentennial Pewter
  American Pewter Co., Inc.
SPORTS BOOKS (see "Books")
STAPLE REMOVERS
  Bates Mfg. Co.
  Swingline, Inc.
STAPLERS
  Arrow Fastner Co.
  Bates Mfg. Co.
  Van Schaack Premium Corp.
STATIONERY
  Bright of America, Inc.
  Elmira Greeting Card Co.
  Mitché Inc.
STEINS
  World Wide Act Studios
STEINS—Imported
  Thermo-Serv Co.
STICKERS—Pressure Sensitive, Imprinted
  Crestline Co., Inc.

STIRRERS—Drink & Picks
   Beacon Products Corp.
   Gay Fad Studios
STIRRERS—Picks
   Imperial Jade Mining Co.
   Stir-It, Inc.
STRAW HATS
   Jack-Bilt Corp.
STRAW HATS—Skimmers
   Oleet & Co., Inc.
STRAWS
   Columbus Plastic Products
STRING BOW TIE
   The Lewton Company
SUIT BAGS—Carry On (Also see "Garment Bags")
   Neely Mfg. Co., Inc.
SUN GLASSES
   American Optical Co.
   Bausch & Lomb Optical Co.
   Bushnell & Co.
SUNGLASSES—Imported One Way
   Design Specs, Inc.
SUNTAN LOTION—Imprinted
   Macademic Sales Corp.
SUN VISORS
   The Lewton Company
SURVIVAL KIT
   Macademic Sales Corp.
SURVIVAL KITS—for Conventions
   Hewig & Marvic
   Aycock Enterprises, Inc.
SUSPENDERS
   A. Stein & Co.
SUSPENDERS—Imprinted
   Lewtan Industries Corp.
SUSPENDERS—Police & Firemen
   Ay-Won Belt Mfg. Corp.
SWEATSHIRTS—Imprinted
   Ebert Sportswear
SWIZZLE STICKS—Sports
   Bass Advertising Specialties
SWORD—Excalibur
   Better Ideas
SWORDS & SWORD PLAQUES
   Gutman Cutlery Co., Inc.

T

TABLE CLOTHS—Plastic & Paper
   Fruit of the Loom, Inc.
   Sorg Products Co.
TABLE-TOP DISPLAYS
(see "Displays")
TAGS—Golf Bag
   Crestline Co., Inc.
TAPE MEASURES
   The Cooper Group,
     Spec. Sales Div.
   Crestline Co., Inc.
   Greenland Premium Center
   Hewig & Marvic
   Lewtan Industries Corp.
   Parisan Novelty Co.
TELEGRAMS—Giant
   Commercial Letter, Inc.
   Mailographic Co., Inc.
TELEPHONE DIALERS
   Art-Mold Products Co.
   Beacon Products Co.
TELEPHONE TIMER
   Baldwin Cooke Co.
TEMPLATES—Custom
   Addressograph Corp.
TENNIS EQUIPMENT & CLOTHES
—(Ball markers, tennis bags, tennis blazers)
   Backgaard, Ltd.,
TENNIS GIFTWARE
   Backgaard, Ltd.,
THEME SUPPLIES—
Parties & Mailings
   Paradise Products, Inc.
THERMOMETER—Desk
   Hull Manufacturing Co.
THERMOMETERS
   Airguide Instrument Co.
   Berkshire Sales Corp.
     (Ruler/Thermometer)
   Hull Manufacturing Co.
   Ohio Thermometer Co.
   Robert Parker Research, Inc.
   Taylor Instrument Co.

Thermoptics, Inc.
John L. Chaney Instru. Co.
THERMOMETERS—Digital
  George Jerome
  Rueby Process, Inc.
THERMOMETERS—Digital Thermal
  Idea Man
THIMBLES
  Brown & Bigelow
Promotional Products Co.
THREADERS
  Green Duck Co.
  Scott Mitchell House, Inc.
  Two Brothers, Inc.
THREE-D BUSINESS CARDS, RULERS, CALENDARS
  Visual Graphics
THREE-D CALLING CARDS, RULERS, BADGES—Animated
  Vari-Vue International
TIE BARS—"$1,000,000"
  Museum Coins
TIE BARS—Clips
  A. T. Cross Co.
  Green Duck Co.
  Hewig & Marvic
  Martguild, Inc.
  J. R. Wood, Inc.
  Wil-Nor Products
TIE BARS—Custom
  The Easton Company
  His Lordship Products Co.
TIE CLIP—Beer Can Tab
  Indiangiver Company
TIES—Custom
  Artistic Monogram
  Sparky of Chicago
  G. S. Harval & Co., Ltd.
  Wm. Chelsea Ltd.
  Pick-Smith Ltd.
  Prince Consort Tie Co.
TIES—Kentucky Colonel
  Helli Company
TIES—Money Design
  Prince Consort
TIES—String

Lewtan Industries
TIME MAGAZINE "Man-of-the-Year" MIRROR
  Vizuall Company, Inc.
TIMERS
  Advertisers Publishing Co.
  Creative Dimensional Products
  Ekco Housewares Co.
  McGraw Edison Time Products
  Shatas-Timecrafters
  Sundials & More
TIRE GAUGE
  Kalinco, Inc.
TIRE GAUGE KEY CHAIN
  Baldwin Cooke Co.
TITLE SLIDES (see "Slides-Title")
TOILETRIES
  Alfred Dunhill of London, Inc.
  Viz-zan-De Cosmetics, Inc.
TOILETRY KITS, MEN & WOMEN
  Macademic Sales Corp.
TONING MATERIALS—for Slides
  Burges Color Corp.
  Para-Tone, Inc.
TOOL KITS
  Greenland Premium Center
  The Cooper Group,
    Spec. Sales Div.
  Bayes Mfg. Co., Inc.
  Brandmark Sales Co.
TOOL SET—Miniature
  Baldwin Cooke Co.
  Gries Reproducer Co.
  Hill Novelties Mfg. Co.
TOP HAT
  The Lewtan Company
TOTE BAGS (see "Bags")
TOTEM POLES
  Alfco-NY Div.
Artistic Latex Form Co., Inc.
TOWELS—Beach
  R. A. Briggs & Co.
  Plectox Products Co.
  Sherry Mfg. Co., Inc.
TOWELS—Calendar
  Stevens Linen Division

TOWELS—Crying
   Paradise Products, Inc.
TOWELS—Golf
(see "Golf Towels")
TOWELS—Guest
   Ames Shower Curtain, Inc.
   Windsor Industries
   World-Wide Gifts
TOWELS—Imprinted
   R. A. Briggs
   Sherry Mfg. Co., Inc.
TOWELS—Sports
   Crestline, Inc.
   R.A. Briggs & Co.
   Crestline Co., Inc.
TOYS—Product Replicas
   Aluminum Specialty Co.
   F&F Mold & Die Works, Inc.
   Multiple Products, Inc.
   American Premium Corp.
   Product People
   Replica Models, Inc.
TRANSLATIONS—Simultaneous
   Round Hill, Inc.
   Hargrove Display
   Accomplished Office Services
TRAVEL INCENTIVE PROMOTION ITEMS (see "Theme Supplies")
TRAVEL KITS
   Airline Textile Mfg. Co.
   Ami Co., Inc.
   Cornwall Corp.
   Elco Mfg. Co., Inc.
   Ernest Hazel Jr., Inc.
   Gerber Products Co.
   Macademic Sales Corp.
   Hewig & Marvic
   M&L Plastic Specialties
   Wright Leather Specialty Co.
   Stebco Products Corp.
TRAVEL PLANS
   Incentive Co. of America
   King Korn Incentive Co.
   E. F. MacDonald Co.
   Northwest Airlines, Inc.
   Performance Incentives Corp.
   Sperry Hutchinson Co.
TRAVEL POSTERS
   Stancraft Products
TRAVEL SOUVENIRS
   Paradise Products
TRAYS
   Advertisers Publishing Co.
   Bennet Products Corp.
   Lith-o-Ware Products, Inc.
TREASURE CHEST
   Ron Henry Associates
   Hewig & Marvic
   Macademic Sales Corp.
   Republic Co.
   Rotadyne, Inc.
TREASURE CHEST—Electronic
   Electronic Treasure Chest Enterprises, Inc.
TREASURE HUNT KIT
   Dismar Corp.
   Jet Advertising
TREE SEEDLINGS
   Van's Pines, Inc.
TRICKS—Money
   Sasco, Inc.
TROPHIES
   Award Incentives, Inc.
   Creative Awards by Lane
   Creative Dimensional Prod. Corp.
   Crestline Co.
   Ownes Trophy Co.
   Arlen Awards
   Imperial Awards
   Kraftware Corp.
   Modern Onyx Mfg. Co.
T-SHIRTS
   Allison Mfg. Co.
   B&R Promotional Products
   Chaseline Div. Chase Bag Co.
   Ebert Sportswear Premium Div.
   K-Studio
   Makley's
   Norwich Mills, Inc.
   Right-On Graphics, Inc.
   VIP Industries

Buyer's Guide

Sherry Mfg. Co., Inc.
T-SHIRTS—Glow in the Dark
   Pro Faces, Inc.
T-SHIRTS—Imprinted
   Velva Sheen Mfg. Co.
T-SHIRTS—Photographs Reproduced
   The Balloon Man
T-SHIRTS—Scented
   Seeko Promotions
TUMBLERS—Plastic
   Thermo-Serv Co.
TURNTABLES—Display
   Electro-Motion Corp.

U

UMBRELLAS—Golf
   Bass Advertising Specialties
   F. Hollander & Son, Inc.
UMBRELLAS—Golf (Imprinted)
   Fred Stoffel Associates
UMBRELLAS—Imprinted
   D. Klein & Son, Inc.
UTILITY CASE—Pocket
(Contains bottle opener, nail file, 4 hooks for keys, screwdriver)
   Bray Co.

V

VACUUM BOTTLES
   Aladdin Industries, Inc.
   Hamilton Scotch Corp.
VELCRO BOARDS
   Charles Mayer Studios
   Oravisual Company, Inc.
   Radiant Manufacturing Co.
VESTS—Advertising
   Helli Company
   Lewtan Industries Corp.
   Makley's
VISORS
   Lar Lu Manufacturing
   Sand Manufacturing

W

WALLETS
   Swank, Inc.
   Advertising Leather Specialty Co.
   Amity Leather Products
   Frederick H. Beach, Inc.
   Buxton, Inc.
   Day-Timers
   Ernest Hazel Jr., Inc.
WALLET & BILLFOLDS
   Shaw-Barton, Inc.
WATCH—Photo Disappearing
   H&L Stanley
WHISTLES
   Bruce-Brent Co.
   Spotswood Specialty Co., Inc.
WINDSHIELD SCRAPERS
   S. V. Tool Co., Inc.
WINE BAGS—Spanish Bota
   Algoma Net Co.
   Gutman Cutlery Co., Inc.
WINE GLASSES—Personalized
   Advertising Devices & Specialties
WOODEN NICKELS
   Directions Unlimited, Inc.
   Falcon Rule Co.
   Impact Specialties Co.
   D. Robbins & Co., Inc.
   Wendell's
WRITING PORTFOLIOS
   Dilly Mfg. Co.

XYZ

YARDSTICKS
   The Cooper Group, Spec. Sales Div.
YO-YOs—Lighted
   Kozmic Electric
   Hewig & Marvic
   Fli-Back Corp.
   Union Wadding Co.
XOGRAPHS
   Visual Panographics, Inc.

Directory of Suppliers

AAA Nameplate Awards, Inc.
600 E. 28th St.
Kansas City, Mo. 64109

A-B Emblem
Div. of Conrad Industries
Weaverville, N.C. 28787

ABC Sportswear
1247 N. Lake Ave.
Pasadena, Calif. 91104

Accomplished Office Services
5 Beekman St., Suite 214
New York, N.Y.

Accutec, Inc.
168 Main Ave.
Wallington, N.J. 07057

Acme Leather Goods Co., Inc.
347 Fifth Ave.
New York, N.Y. 10016

S. S. Adams Co.
P. O. Box 369
Neptune, N.J.

Addressograph Division
Addressograph Multigraph Corp.
1239 Central Ave.
Hillside, N.J. 07205

Admatch Corp.
201 E. 42nd St.
New York, N.Y. 10017

Adva-Lite
Airport Station
St. Petersburg, Fla. 33732

Advertising Counselors
P.O. Box 98
Greenville, Ohio 45331

Advertising Devices & Specialties
68-18 138th St.
Flushing, N.Y. 11367

Advertising Gifts, Inc.
36 E. 31st St.
New York, N.Y. 10010

Advertisers Publishing Co.
P. O. Box 602
Ann Arbor, Mich. 48107

Advertising Replicas, Inc.
84 Fifth Ave.
New York, N.Y. 10011

Advon Specialties
P. O. Box 552
Hopkins, Minn. 55343

Agfa-Gevaert
275 North St.
Teterboro, N.J.

Airguide Instrument Co.
2210 Wabansia Ave.
Chicago, Ill. 60647

Directory of Suppliers

Airline Merchandising Corp.
52 Broadway
Greenlawn, N.Y. 11740

Airline Textile Mfg. Co.
P. O. Box 477
Des Moines, Iowa 50302

Airway Industries, Inc.
Airway Park
W. Pittsburgh, Pa. 16160

Ajay Enterprises
1501 E. Wisconsin St.
Delavan, Wis. 53115

Alfco—N.Y. Div.
Artistic Latex Form Co., Inc.
1220 Brook Ave.
Bronx, N.Y. 10456

Algoma Net Co.
2266 N. Prospect Ave.
Milwaukee, Wis. 53202

Allison Mfg. Co.
350 Fifth Ave.
New York, N.Y. 10001

Alvimar Mfg. Co.
51-02 21st St.
Long Island City, N.Y. 11101

American Display Company
14918 Minnetonka Blvd.
Minnetonka, Minn. 55343

American/Durein Co.
5541 San Leandro St.
Okland, Calif. 94621

American House of Flags
Customs House Station, P.O. Box 2888
San Francisco, Calif. 94126

American Management Assn., Inc.
135 West 50th St.
New York, N.Y. 10020

American Map Co.
1926 Broadway
New York, N.Y. 10023

American Marketing Services
610 Newbury St.
Boston, Mass.

American Meeting Supply
Lock Box 4037
North Hollywood, Calif. 91607

American Novelty Co.
1209 Broadway
New York, N.Y. 10001

American Pewter Co., Inc.
P. O. Box 1776
Easton, Mass. 02334

American Premium Corp.
125 Walnut St.
Watertown, Mass. 02172

American Publishing Co.
125 Walnut St.
Watertown, Mass. 02172

American Publishing Corp.
144 Moody St.
Waltham, Mass. 02154

American Science Center
5700 Northwest Highway
Chicago, Ill. 66646

American Slide Chart Corp.
201 N. Gables Blvd.
Wheaton, Ill. 60187

American Stock Photos
6842 Sunset Blvd.
Hollywood, Calif. 90028

American Thermoplastic Co.
622 Second Ave.
Pittsburgh, Pa. 15219

American Visual Aids
80 39th St.
Brooklyn, N.Y. 11232

Ames & Rollinson, Inc.
215 Park Ave. South
New York, N.Y. 10003

Amity Leather Products
P. O. Box 339
West Bend, Wis. 53095

Ambidextrous, Inc.
8 West 19th St.
New York, N.Y. 10011

Anderson Associates
Div. of L & C Mfg. Co., Inc.
8673 S. Vincennes Ave.
Chicago, Ill. 60620

John P. Anderson Premiums
2955 Arrowwood Dr.
Riverwoods
Deerfield, Ill. 60015

Anderson Rubber Co.
P. O. Box 170
Akron, Ohio 44309

Apache-Totem Badge & Emblem, Ltd.
70 W. 40th St.
New York, N.Y. 10018

Argus, Inc.
2080 Lunt Ave.
Elk Grove, Ill. 60003

Argos Products Company
600 S. Sycamore St.
Genoa, Ill. 60135

Arlen Awards
68 Brook Ave.
North Plainfield, N.J. 07061

Arlington Aluminum Co.
19303 W. Davison
Detroit, Mich. 48223

Armchair Races
Lawrence,
Long Island, N.Y. 11559

Arnart Imports, Inc.
212 Fifth Ave.
New York, N.Y. 10010

Art Carved/J. R. Wood, Inc.
216 E. 45th St.
New York, N.Y. 10017

Art Mold Products
780 Wellington Ave.
Cranston, R.I. 02910

Associations Films
600 Madison Ave.
New York, N.Y. 10022

Association/Sterling Films
600 Grand Ave.
Ridgefield, N.J. 07657

Atlas Flag Corp. of America
1311 E. Jackson St.
Eldorado, Ill. 62930

W. Atlee Burpee Co.
9375 Burpee Bldg.
Philadelphia, Pa. 19132

Directory of Suppliers

AuraVision
51 W. 52nd St.
New York, N.Y. 10019

Autofold Displays
2564 Via Tejon
Palos Verdes Estates, Calif. 90274

Automatic Helium Baloon Syst.
450 S. Beverly Dr.
Beverly Hills, Calif. 90212

Avant Products
P. O. Box H 3085
New Bedford, Mass. 02741

Aycock Enterprises
60 E. 42nd St.
New York, N.Y. 10017

Avery Products-Graphics Division
2620 S. Susan St.
Santa Ana, Calif. 92704

Ay-Won Belt Mfg. Corp.
41 E. 11th St.
New York, N.Y. 10003

The Award Company of America
1700 26th Ave.
Tuscaloosa, Ala. 35401

B & R Promotional Products
292 Fifth Ave.
New York, N.Y. 10001

Badge-A-Minit
R.P.M. Associates, Ltd.
1820 N. Sterling St.
La Salle, Ill. 61301

Badges & Labels Corp.
1295 Blue Hill Ave.
Boston, Mass. 02126

Baekgaard, Ltd.
1855 Janke Dr.
Northbrook, Ill. 60662

Baldwin Cooke Co.
5714 Dempster St.
Morton Grove, Ill. 60053

Lem Bailey
7934 Santa Monica Blvd.
Hollywood, Calif. 90046

The Balloon Man
17301 W. 7 Mile Rd.
Detroit, Mich. 48235

The Baltimore Luggage Co.
304 N. Smallwood St.
Baltimore, Md. 21223

Bankers Engraving Co.
50 W. 17th St.
New York, N.Y. 10011

Bantam Books, Inc.
Premium Marketing Div.
666 Fifth Ave.
New York, N.Y. 10019

Barbary Denny Caricatures
8071 Ainsworth
La Palma, Calif. 90623

Bar-Zim Mfg. Co.
930 Newark Ave.
Jersey City, N.J. 07306

Bass Advertising Specialties
4317 Lafayette
Bellaire, Tex. 77401

W. E. Bassett Co.
259 Roosevelt Dr.
Derby, Conn. 06418

Bathrico, Inc.
4615 W. Roosevelt Rd.
Chicago, Ill. 60650

Bayls Mfg. Co.
22 W. 21st St.
New York, N.Y. 10010

Frederick H. Beach, Inc.
36 E. 31st St.
New York, N.Y. 10016

Beemak Plastics
7424 Santa Monica Blvd.
Los Angeles, Calif. 90046

Benjamin Co., Inc.
485 Madison Ave.
New York, N.Y. 10022

The Beachcombers
P. O. Box 250
Fort Myers, Fla. 33902

Benply Badges
480 Canal St.
New York, N.Y. 10013

Berkshire Sales Corp.
219 Ninth St.
San Francisco, Calif. 94103

Berm Studios, Inc.
404 Industrial Park Dr.
Yeadon, Pa. 19050

Better Ideas
2250 Arbor Blvd.
Dayton, Ohio 45439

Bil-Mar Specialty Co.
1739 E. Parkhaven Dr.
Cleveland, Ohio 44131

BNA Communications, Inc.
9401 Decoverly Hall Rd.
Rockville, Md. 20850

Bradley Time Div.
Elgin National Industries, Inc.
1115 Broadway
New York, N.Y. 10010

Bramlee, Inc.
1404 Randall Ave.
Levittown, Pa. 19057

Brandmark Sales Co.
5778 N. Lincoln Ave.
P. O. Box 59320
Chicago, Ill. 60659

Bray Co.
510 N. Compton Ave.
St. Louis, Mo. 63103

The Brewster Corp.
Old Saybrook, Conn. 06475

Bright of America, Inc.
300 Greenbriar Rd.
Summersville, W. Va. 26651

R. A. Briggs & Co.
155 S. Old Rand Rd.
Lake Zurich, Ill. 60047

A. N. Brooks Corp.
P. O. Box 3550
Merchandise Mart
Chicago, Ill. 60654

Arthur Brown & Bro., Inc.
2 W. 46th St.
New York, N.Y. 10036

D. L. Blair Corp.
460 Park Ave.
New York, N.Y. 10022

Arthur Blank & Co., Inc.
119 Braintree St.
Boston, Mass. 02134

Directory of Suppliers

Blue Ribbon Promotions, Inc.
350 Fifth Ave.
New York, N.Y.

The Blue Thumb Company
5247 San Fernando Rd. West
Los Angeles, Calif. 90034

Budget Films
4590 Santa Monica Blvd.
Los Angeles, Calif.

Buhl Projector Co., Inc.
1776 New Highway
Farmingdale, N.Y. 11735

Bulova Watch Co.
Incentive Sales Div.
630 Fifth Ave.
New York, N.Y. 10020

Burges Color Corp.
84 Fifth Ave.
New York, N.Y. 10011

Burke-Worthington
8350 N. Lehigh Ave.
Morton Grove, Ill. 60053

Buxton, Inc.
P. O. Box 1650
Springfield, Mass. 01101

C. C. Marketing Service
P. O. Box 116
Flushing, N.Y. 11365

Cadaco, Inc.
310 W. Polk St.
Chicago, Ill. 60607

Cally Curtis Co.
1111 N. Las Palmas Ave.
Hollywood, Calif. 90038

Cambor Enterprises, Inc.
64 Hillside Ave.
Verona, N.J. 07044

Camera Craft Rentals
6820 W. Sunset
Hollywood, Calif.

Camillus Cutlery
Camillus, N.Y. 13031

Canyon House
466 Lexington Ave.
New York, N.Y. 10017

Cardinal China Co.
P. O. Box D
Carteret, N.J. 07008

Carlisle Co.
P. O. 463
San Carlos, Calif. 94070

Carr Speirs
24 Rope Ferry Rd.
Waterford, Conn. 06385

Carson's
P. O. Box 848
Montrose, Colo. 81401

Centennial Novelty Co.
2684 Lacy St.
Los Angeles, Calif. 90031

Central State Diversified, Inc.
5221 Natural Bridge
St. Louis, Mo. 63115

John L. Chaney Instrument Co.
Lake Geneva, Wisc. 53147

Chartpak, Inc.
One River Rd.
Leeds, Ma. 01053

Chase Bag Co.
4900 Corona Ave.
Los Angeles, Calif. 90058

Chaseline Division
Chase Bag Co.
4900 Corona Ave.
Los Angeles, Calif. 90058

Chaseline, Inc.
Chase Bag Co.
P. O. Box 60
Reidsville, N.C. 27320

Wm. Chelsea Ltd.
P. O. Box 159
Scarsdale, N.Y. 10583

Chesal Industries
3210 N. Pierce St.
Milwaukee, Wis. 53212

Churchill Marketing Corp.
25 Third St.
Stamford, Conn. 06905

C. I. Industries
3210 N. Pierce St.
Milwaukee, Wis. 53212

Cinegraph
2 N. Riverside Plaza
Chicago, Ill. 60606

Cinegraph Slides, Inc.
7215 Garden Grove Blvd.
Garden Grove, Calif. 92641

Cinemaraces
271 Schilling Circle
Hunt Valley, Md. 20130

Keith Clark, Inc.
Union & Division St.
Sidney, N.Y. 13838

C-Line Products, Inc.
1530 E. Birchwood Ave.
Des Plaines, Ill. 60018

Clip Art Services
P. O. Box 1142
Pomona, Calif. 91769

Columbus Manufacturers, Inc.
P. O. Box 423
Columbus, Miss. 39701

Commercial Letter, Inc.
1335 Delmar Blvd.
St. Louis, Mo. 63103

Communications Group
Columbia Scientific Industries
3625 Bluestein Blvd.
Austin, Tex. 78762

C. A. Compton, Inc.
P. O. Box 1775
Boulder, Colo. 80302

Conestoga Co., Inc.
732 E. Goepp St.
Bethlehem, Pa. 18018

Conrac Industries, Inc.
Weaverville, N.C. 28787

The H. C. Cook Co.
28 Beaver St.
Ansonia, Conn. 06401

Copy & Graphics, Inc.
271 Madison Ave.
New York, N.Y. 10016

Norman Cox & Co.
2524 First St.
Ft. Myers, Fla. 33901

George F. Cram Co.
P. O. Box 426
Indianapolis, Ind. 46206

Creation, Inc.
32 Cherry Lane
Floral Park, N.Y. 11001

Directory of Suppliers

Creative Awards by Lane
32 W. Randolph St.
Chicago, Ill. 60601

Creative Ideas for Industry
915 W. Montana St.
Chicago, Ill. 60614

Creative Photographic Library
2038 Milan Ave.
South Pasadena, Calif. 91030

Creative Products Co.
P. O. Box 131
Issaquah, Wash. 98027

Creative Rewards
P. O. Box 186
Ashton, R.I. 02864

Creative Rewards
Torrey Rd.
Cumberland, R.I. 02864

Crestline Co., Inc.
18 West 18th St.
New York, N.Y. 10011

Crisloid Plastics, Inc.
Eddy & Porter Sts.
Providence, R.I. 02905

Curtin & Pease Co.
2725 N. Reynolds Rd.
Toledo, Ohio 43615

Custom Caddy
8242 McCormick Blvd.
Skokie, Ill. 60076

Custom Slides, Inc.
2018 Lyndale Ave. South
Minneapolis, Minn. 55405

Dak Industries
10845 Vanowen St.
North Hollywood, Calif. 91605

Da-Lite Screen Co., Inc.
Warsaw, Indiana 46580

Daniel's Clover Specialty Co.
4904 Ninth Ave. South
St. Petersburg, Fla. 33707

The Dartnell Corp.
4660 Ravenswood Ave.
Chicago, Ill. 60640

Day-Timers
Allentown, Pa. 18001

DBI Books, Inc.
540 Frontage Rd.
Northfield, Ill. 60093

Deak & Co., Inc.
29 Broadway
New York, N.Y. 10006

Dell Publishing Co., Inc.
One Dag Hammarskjold Plaza
New York, N.Y. 10017

Derby Cap Mfg. Co.
700 West Main St.
Louisville, Ky. 40202

Design Specs, Inc.
25 S. Dove St.
Alexandria, Va. 22314

Desk Sign Mfg. Co.
223 South 61st St.
Philadelphia, Pa. 19139

Dewey-Carter Co.
228 Wood St.
P. O. Box 822
Doylestown, Pa. 18901

The Henry G. Dietz Co., Inc.
14-26 28th Ave.
Long Island City, N.Y. 11102

Dilly Mfg. Co.
211 E. Third St.
Des Moines, Iowa 50309

Dimensional Displays and Design, Inc.
1222 University Ave.
St. Paul, Minn. 55104

Directions Unlimited, Inc.
P. O. Box 1927
Fairview Heights, Ill. 62208

Dismar
A & Clearfield Sts.
Philadelphia, Pa. 19134

Display Producers, Inc.
P. O. Box 231
Southfield, Mich. 48075

Display Sales, Inc.
5555 Fair Lane
Cincinnati, Ohio 45227

Display Workshop, Inc.
150 Huyshope Ave.
Hartford, Conn. 06114

Display-Weight
10800 S.W. 7th Ave.
Miami, Fla. 33156

Domestic Industries
P. O. Box 6
Blackwood, N.J. 08012

Downing Displays, Inc.
300 Genessee St.
Cincinnati, Ohio 45202

The Drawing Board
P. O. Box 505
Dallas, Tex.

DuBois Importing Co.
1914 Portage Ave.
South Bend, Ind. 46616

DuKane Corporation
2900 Dukane Dr.
St. Charles, Ill. 60174

Dynamic Graphics, Inc.
6707 N. Sheridan Rd.
Peoria, Ill. 61614

Dymo-Products Co.
149 E. 39th St., Suite 120
New York, N.Y. 10016

Eagle Novelty, Inc.
191 Mountain Ave.
Springfield, N.J. 07081

The Easton Company
Attleboro Industrial Park
Attleboro, Mass. 02703

Eberhard Faber
Crestwood
Wilkes Barre, Pa. 18703

Ebert Sportswear
P. O. Box 632
Columbia, S.C. 29202

Edmund Scientific Co.
300 Edscorp Bldg.
Barrington, N.J. 08007

Electronic Treasure Chest
    Enterprises, Inc.
Box G.C.7
Tijeras, N.M. 87059

Electro-Motion Corp.
Sixth St. & Highland Ave.
Verplanck, N.Y. 10596

Elgin School Supply Co. Inc.
1007 Solano St.
Sacramento, Calif. 96021

Elliott Sales Corp.
2502 South 12th St.
Tacoma, Wash. 98405

Directory of Suppliers

Elmira Greeting Card Co.
656 State St.
Elmira, N.Y. 14902

Emblemcraft, Inc.
115 West 23rd St.
New York, N.Y. 10011

Eternalight
1156 Ave. of Americas
New York, N.Y.

Eva-Tone Soundsheets
2051 Waukegan Rd.
Deerfield, Ill. 60015

W. H. Everett
Buck Hill Rd.
Ridgefield, Conn. 06877

The Ever-Lite Co.
150 Express St.
Plainview, L.I., New York 11803

Ex-IBM Corp.
7034 Dart Brook Dr.
Dallas, Tex 75240

Exposystems
5652 Saunders Settlement Rd.
Lockport, N.Y. 14094

W. W. Faber-Castell Pencil Co., Inc.
41-47 Dickerson St.
Newark, N.J. 07103

Falcon Rule Co.
Auburn, Maine 04210

Faribault Woolen Mill Co.
Faribault, Minn. 55021

Ferguson Gold Mining Co.
c/o Michael M. Grayson Consultants
7 Barton Ct.
East Brunswick, N.J. 08816

Fidelity Products Co.
705 Pennsylvania Ave. So.
Minneapolis, Minn. 55426

First-A-Long Enterprises, Inc.
P. O. Box 366
Hagaman, N.Y.

H. Fishlove & Co.
720 N. Franklin St.
Chicago, Ill. 60610

FlairCraft Furs
P. O. Box 874
Rogers, Ark. 72756

Fleetwood Recording Co., Inc.
321 Revere St.
Revere, Mass. 02151

Fli-Back Corp.
P. O. Box 427
High Point, N.C. 27261

Flowers of Hawaii
670 S. Lafayette Park Place
Los Angeles, Calif. 90057

Forbes Products Corp.
1465 Jefferson Rd.
Rochester, N.Y. 14632

Fordham Weaving Co.
203 E. Fordham Rd.
Bronx, N.Y.

Forest City Products, Inc.
722 Bolivar Rd.
Cleveland, Ohio 44115

Foto Mug
c/o Thermo-Serv Co.
2939 Sixth Ave. North
Anoka, Minn. 55303

Fotosonic, Inc.
15 West 46th St.
New York, N.Y. 10036

Bruce Fox, Inc.
1909 McDonald Lane
New Albany, Ind. 47150

G & C Meriam Co.
47 Federal St.
Springfield, Mass. 01101

GAF Corp.
140 W. 51st St.
New York, N.Y. 10020

Garco Art Metal Co., Inc.
Brigs Ave. & Kate St.
Durham, N.C. 27703

Garrity Industries, Inc.
Garland Drive
Stamford, Conn. 06907

G.E.M. Bicycle Sales & Imports
2115 Webster St.
Oakland, Calif. 94612

General Fabrics Corp.
173 Oak St.
Marion, Ohio 43302

General Time Corp.
Precision Products Div.
P.O. Box 338
Davison, N.C. 28036

Gentry Galleries, Ltd.
Hotel Martinique Penthouse
New York, N.Y. 10001

G. A. Georgopulo Co.
48 Stone St.
New York, N.Y.

Ghent Enterprises, Inc.
P. O. Box 8828
Canton, Ohio 44711

Gilbreath Company
212 E. Courtland St.
Philadelphia, Pa. 19120

Gillette Co.
825 26th St.
La Grange, Ill. 60525

Glasses Galore, Inc.
P. O. Box 30185 AMF
Memphis, Tenn. 38130

Glass Industries Co.
1133 Broadway
New York, N.Y. 10010

Goes Lithographing Co.
42 West 61st St.
Chicago, Ill. 60621

Go Fly a Kite, Inc.
1434 Third Ave.
New York, N.Y. 10028

Golf Ball Advertising Co.
P. O. Box 4332
Philadelphia, Pa. 19118

G.P. Enterprises
4630 Campus Dr. Suite 203
Newport Beach, Calif. 92660

Green Duck
255 S. Elm St.
Hernando, Miss. 38632

Green Duck
P. O. Box 30085
Memphis, Tenn. 38130

Gordon-Douglas Company
2318 Belmont Ave.
Chicago, Ill. 60618

Granger Collection
1841 Broadway
New York, N.Y.

Graphic Calculator
234 James
Barrington, Ill 60010

Directory of Suppliers

Great Western Trading Co.
P. O. Drawer 16147
Phoenix, Ariz. 85011

Greene Specialties
1000 Calbrillo Park Dr.
Santa Ana, Calif. 92701

Sherman Grinberg Film Library
630 Ninth Ave.
New York, N.Y. 10036

R. D. Grunert Company
150 Buckland Ave.
Rochester, N.Y. 14618

Gutman Cutlery, Co., Inc.
900 S. Columbus Ave.
Mount Vernon, N.Y. 10550

Haines House of Cards
2465 Williams Ave.
Norwood, Ohio 45212

Hammond, Inc.
515 Valley St.
Maplewood, N.J. 07040

Hargrove Display
2660 Woodley Road, N.W.
Washington, D.C.

Harmon Marketing Corp.
527 Madison Ave., Suite 912
New York, N.Y. 10022

Harold's Club
Party Kit
P. O. Box 50
Reno, Nev. 89504

The Harnett Co.
951 Main St.
Woburn, Mass. 01801

H. E. Harris & Co.
Boston, Mass. 02117

Harris Engraving Co.
801 Hogan St.
Jacksonville, Fla. 32202

Hart Publishing Co., Inc.
15 W. 4th St.
New York, N.Y. 10012

G.S. Harvale & Co., Ltd.
1290 Ave. of the Americas
New York, N.Y. 10019

Hastings & Co., Inc.
2314 Market St.
Philadlephia, Pa. 19122

Wm. Hayett, Inc.
207 W. 25th St.
New York, N.Y. 10001

Headline Printers
11 North 17th St.
P. O. Box 1114
Billings, Mon. 59103

Helli Company
7000 N. Kilpatrick
Lincolnwood, Ill. 60646

Ron Henry Associates
3009 Fifth Ave.
Beaver Falls, Pa. 10510

Hernard Mfg. Co.
21 Sawmill River Rd.
Yonkers, N.Y. 10701

Hewig & Marvic
861 Manhattan Ave.
Brooklyn, N.Y. 11222

Hewitt Soap Co., Inc.
333 Linden Ave.
Dayton, Ohio 45403

Hi-Flier Mfg. Co.
510 E. Wabash Ave.
Decatur, Ill. 62525

His Lordship Products Co.
245 Seventh Ave.
New York, N.Y. 10001

Historical Documents Co.
8 N. Preston St.
Philadelphia, Pa. 19104

Historical Reproductions
P. O. Box 951
Tauton, Mass. 02780

Hobby Sales, Inc.
P. O. Box 4054
Highland Station
St. Cloud, Minn. 56301

The Holes-Webway Co.
Webway Park
St. Cloud, Minn. 65301

Allen Hollander Co., Inc.
385 Gerard Ave.
Bronx, N.Y. 10045

F. Hollander & Son, Inc.
10 W. 33rd St.
New York, N.Y. 10001

The Holmen Company, Inc.
P. O. Box 205
Frisco, Tex. 75034

Holloway Sportswear, Inc.
607 Pike St.
Jackson Center, Ohio 45334

Hollywood Banners
539 Oak St.
Copiague, N.Y. 11726

Frank Holmes Laboratories, Inc.
1947 First St.
San Fernando, Calif. 91340

Holoubek Studios
12420 W. Derby
Butler, Wis. 53007

Dennis Hommel Associates
261 Hamilton Ave., Suite 415
Palo Alto, Calif. 94301

Horizon Sportswear, Inc.
1 Ajax Dr.
Madison Heights, Mich. 48071

Hull Manufacturing Co.
P. O. Box 246
Warren, Ohio 44482

Idea Art
740 N. Broadway
New York, N.Y. 10003

Idea Man
1435 S. La Cienega Blvd.
Los Angeles, Calif. 90035

Idea Source Guide
P. O. Box 66
Fairless Hills, Pa. 19030

Impact Specialties Co.
395 Munroe Circle South
Des Plaines, Ill. 60016

Imperial Awards
10661 W. Pico Blvd.
Los Angeles, Calif. 90064

Imperial Camera Corp.
421 N. Western Ave.
Chicago, Ill 60612

Imperial Jade Mining, Inc.
2118 Blaisdell Avenue
Minneapolis, Minn. 55404

Imprint Art Products
1401 Maple Ave.
Fair Lawn, N.J. 07410

Incentive Marketing
633 Third Ave.
New York, N.Y. 10017

Directory of Suppliers

Indiangiver Company
330 Maple Ave.
Westbury, L.I., N.Y. 11590

Inter-All Corp.
31 West State St.
Granby, Mass. 01033

Inter-City Mfg.
7401 Albama Ave.
St. Louis, Mo. 63111

Isis Products Ltd.
P. O. Box 332
Radio City, N.Y. 10019

Jack-Bilt Corp.
906 Central St.
Kansas City, Mo. 64105

Jacobson Mfg. Co.
1414 S. Wabash Ave.
Chicago, Ill. 60605

Jacobson Hat Co., Inc.
Prescott & Ridge Row
Scranton, Pa. 18510

Jacronda Manufacturing Co.
5449 Hunter St.
Philadelphia, Pa.

The Jam Handy Organization
2821 E. Grand Blvd.
Detroit, Mich. 48211

Jannes Associates
222 W. Huron St.
Chicago, Ill. 60610

Jayposon Jewelry Manufacturers
73 Canal St.
New York, N.Y. 10002

Jeffries Banknote Co.
1330 West Pico Blvd.
Los Angeles, Calif. 90015

George-Jerome
18219 Parthenia St.
Northridge, Calif. 91423

Jet Advertising
51 Stanton St.
Newark, N.J. 07114

Jetset Manufacturing Co.
9937 W. Jefferson Blvd.
Culver City, Calif. 90230

J.F.K. Products
Walnut Creek, Calif.

Jiffy Garment Bats & Travel Covers
Corydon, Iowa 50060

Johnson & Johnson
Premium Sales Division
501 George St.
New Brunswick, N.J.

Jones Decorating Co.
2807 Sunset Blvd.
Los Angeles, Calif. 90026

Joslin Photo Puzzle Co.
302 Bel Air Rd.
Southhampton, Pa. 18966

Joy Insignia, Inc.
P. O. Box 68
Guttenberg, N.J.

Kaiser Products
Box 3101
Colorado Springs, Colo.

Kalinco, Inc.
2434 W. Fletcher
Chicago, Ill. 60618

KCL Corporation
Shelbyville, Ind. 46176

K & D Specialties
P. O. Box 164
Riegelsville, Pa. 18077

Keuffel & Esser Co.
60 E. 42nd St.
New York, N.Y. 10017

King Louie International, Inc.
311 W. 72nd St.
Kansas City, Mo. 64114

Kingswood Ceramics
P. O. Box 30
E. Palestine, Ohio 44413

Kinney Co.
123 Stewart St.
Providence, R.I. 02903

D. Klein & Son, Inc.
345 Lodi St.
Hackensack, N.J. 07602

Kole Enterprises, Inc.
3553 N.W. 50th St.
Miami, Fla. 33152

Kordet Color Corporation
15 Neil Ct.
Oceanside, N.Y. 11572

Kordite Corp.
Macedon, N.Y. 14502

Kozmic Electric
417 N. Third St.
Philadlephia, Pa. 19123

K-Studio
1226 Ambassador Blvd.
St. Louis, Mo. 63132

Robert R. Kubrick & Associates
121 Mt. Horeb Rd.
Warren, N.J. 07060

La Belle Industries, Inc.
501 S. Worthington St.
Oconomowoc, Wis. 53066

Lab Services
2018 Lyndale Ave. South
Minneapolis, Minn.

Larido Corp.
251 Park Ave. South
New York, N.Y.

Lar Lu Manufacturing
1250 E. Sanborn
Winona, Minn. 55987

Lee Company
350 Fifth Ave., Suite 4619
New York, N.Y. 10001

Leeco Mfg. Corp.
12 Holmes St.
Milburn, N.J. 07041

Letraset
2379 Charleston Rd.
Mountain View, Calif. 94040

Lewis Buckle Co., Inc.
541 S. Vermont Ave.
Palatine, Ill. 60667

Lewtan Industries
30 High St.
Hartford, Conn. 06101

Liberty Die and Button Mold Corp.
475 Tenth Ave.
New York, N.Y. 10018

Lion Match Corp. of America
2 West 45th St.
New York, N.Y.

Litronix
19000 Homestead Rd.
Cupertino, Calif. 95014

Directory of Suppliers

The Long Island Engraving Co.
120-06 22nd Ave.
College Point, N.Y. 11356

Lotus Fortune Cookie Co.
436 Pacific Ave.
San Francisco, Calif.

Luxury Incentives
Frederick Siebel Associates
641 Lexington Ave.
New York, N.Y. 10022

McGraw Edison Time Products
P. O. Box 1639
Laurinburg, N.C. 28352

McGraw-Hill Book Company
Text-Film Dept.
330 W. 42nd St.
New York, N.Y.

Macademic Sales Corp.
861 Manhattan Ave.
Brooklyn, N.Y. 11222

Magnaplan Corporation
North Main St., Box 431
Champlain, N.Y. 12919

Mailographic Company, Inc.
315 Hudson St.
New York, N.Y. 10013

Makley's
441 S. Plymouth Court
Chicago, Ill. 60605

Manton Cork Corp.
26 Benson Lane
Merrick, N.Y. 11566

Maple City Rubber Co.
Norwalk, Ohio 44875

Marquart Advertising Co.
P. O. Box 603
Des Moines, Iowa 50303

Marsh Chalkboard Company
Dover, Ohio 44622

Marshall Manufacturing Co.
2375 15th St.
Denver, Colo. 80202

Martguild, Inc.
540 E. Washington St.
Chagrin Falls, Ohio 44022

Mass Media
2116 N. Charles St.
Baltimore, Md. 21218

Charles Mayer Studios, Inc.
140 E. Market St.
Akron, Ohio 44308

MacDonald Signs
1315 W. Business Highway 83
Alamo, Tex. 78516

M & D
1821 West C. St.
North Platte, Neb. 69101

Medallic Art Company
325 East 45th St.
New York, N.Y. 10017

Merchandise Displays, Inc.
44 Webb St.
Dayton, Ohio 45403

Merit Industries
51 Stanton St.
Newark, N.J. 07114

Merry Products
P O. Box 703
Columbus, Neb. 68601

Metalart Buckle Co.
166 Valley St.
Providence, R.I. 02909

Michaels Artists & Engineering
    Supplies, Inc.
7005 Tujunga
North Hollywood, Calif. 91605

Microfilming Corp. of America
21 Harristown Rd.
Glen Rock, N.H. 07452

Miller Belts, Ltd.
10270 St. Rita Lane
Cincinnati, Ohio 45215

Mini-Kars, Inc.
410 North Park
Kansas City, Mo. 64120

Mitché, Inc.
17981 Sky Park Circle, Suite N
Irvine, Calif. 92707

Mitten Display Letters
39 West 60th St.
New York, N.Y. 10023

Modern Media Services
2323 New Hyde Park Rd.
New Hyde Park, N.Y. 11040

Modern Talking Pictures
1212 Ave. of the Americas
New York, N.Y. 10036

Monogram of California
500 Hampshire
San Francisco, Calif.

Thurston Moore & Associates
    of Denver
6840 S. Sheridan Blvd.
Littleton, Colo. 80123

Morgan Press, Inc.
145 Palisade St.
Dobbs Ferry, N.Y. 10522

The Mount Everest Mint, Inc.
141 Terwood Rd.
Willow Grove, Pa. 19090

Movie Star News
212 East 14th St.
New York, N.Y. 10003

Multiplex Display Fixture Co.
1555 Larkin Williams Rd.
Fenton, Mo. 63026

Multi Products Industries
824 W. 36th St.
Chicago, Ill. 60609

Museum Coins
P. O. Box 206
Flushing, N.Y. 11352

Musifex, Inc.
45 W. 45th St.
New York, N.Y.

Myron Manufacturing Corp.
Myron Building
Maywood, N.J. 07607

Name Maker Corp.
30 Irving Place
New York, N.Y. 10003

Jack Nadel, Inc.
9950 W. Jefferson Blvd.
Culver City, Calif. 90230

Namemaker Corp.
52 Broadway
Greenlawn, N.Y. 11740

Nappe-Smith Co.
Southard Ave.
Farmingdale, N.J. 07727

Nasco, Inc.
P. O. Box 576
Springfield, Tenn. 37172

Directory of Suppliers

Natco Products Corp.
West Warwick, R.I.

National Creative Sales
435 North Ave.
New Rochelle, N.Y. 10802

National Dealer's Services, Inc.
33-49 Rockwell Pl.
Brooklyn, N.Y. 11217

National Flat & Display
43 W. 21st St.
New York, N.Y.

Neely Mfg. Co., Inc.
P. O. Box 338
Corydon, Iowa 50060

Newark Felt Novelty
50 Jelliff Ave
Newark, N.J. 07108

The Neff Athletic Lettering Co.
P. O. Box 218
Greenville, Ohio 45331

New Kwong Tai Press
940 Chungking Rd.
Los Angeles, Calif.

The New Spirit of '76 Foundation
World Center Building
918 16th Street, N.W.
Washington, D.C.

A Nite At The Races, Inc.
2320 Avenue U
Brooklyn, N.Y. 11229

Norvus Consumer Products
National Semiconductor
1177 Kern Ave.
Sunnyvale, Calif. 94086

The Nostalgia Factory
2019 Peel St.
Montreal, Quebec, Canada H3A 1T6

NVF Company, Container Div.
P. O. Box 160
Kennett Square, Pa. 19348

Old Mill Enterprises, Inc.
3125 Nolt Rd.
Lancaster, Pa. 17601

Oleet & Co., Inc.
60 Claremont Pl.
Mt. Vernon, N.Y. 10553

Ooops
P. O. Box 1003
La Mirada, Calif. 90637

Oravisual Company, Inc.
P.O. Box 11151
St. Petersburg, Fla. 33733

Orchids of Hawaii, Inc.
305 Seventh Ave.
New York, N.Y. 10001

Orlandi Frank, Inc.
31-02 Northern Blvd.
Long Island City, N.Y. 11101

The Osborne Coinage Co.
2851 Massachusetts Ave.
Cincinnati, Ohio 45225

Owens Trophy Co.
5535 N. Lynch Ave.
Chicago, Ill. 60630

Pacific Handy Cutter, Inc.
2454 N. Chico Ave.
South El Monte, Calif. 91733

Package Exhibits Programs, Inc.
7380 N. Lincoln Ave.
Lincolnwood, Ill. 60646

Paper Novelty Mfg. Co.
166 Henry St.
Stamford, Conn. 06904

Paperweights, Inc.
100 Broadway
Garden City Park, N.Y. 11040

Paradise Products Inc.
P. O. Box 568
El Cerrito, Calif. 94530

Para-Tone, Inc.
512 W. Burlington Ave.
La Grange, Ill. 60525

Park Sherman
465 Eagle Rock Ave.
Roseland, N.J. 07068

Penman Sales Co.
41-02 23rd Rd.
Astoria, N.Y. 11105

Penn Emblem
10909 Dutton Rd.
Philadelphia, Pa. 19151

Penton Publishing Co.
201 East 42nd St.
New York, N.Y. 10017

Performance Incentives Corp.
5199 E. Pacific Coast Highway
Long Beach, Calif. 90804

Perma Plaque Corp.
6515 Sunset Blvd.
Hollywood, Calif. 90038

Perrin Products
Pond St.
Randolph, Mass. 02368

Perry Graf Corporation
2215 Colby Ave.
West Los Angeles, Calif. 90064

Personident, Inc.
164 Pebble Lane
Hewlett, N.Y. 11557

Philadelphia Badge Co.
924 Cherry Street
Philadelphia, Pa. 19107

Philadelphia House
858 Sussex Blvd.
Broomal, Pa. 19008

Photoform, Inc.
4 West Manilla
Pittsburgh 20, Pa.

Pick Point Enterprises, Inc.
P. O. Box Mirror Lake,
N.H. 03853

Pick & Smith Ltd.
230 Birch Hill Rd.
Locust Valley, N.Y. 11560

Pickwick International, Inc.
135 Crossways Park Dr.
Woodbury, N.Y. 11797

Pico International Corp.
1830 S. Hill St.
Los Angeles, Calif. 90015

Pilgrim Plastic Products Co.
278 Babcock St.
Boston, Mass. 02215

Plasta-Seal Co.
863 E. 141st St.
Bronx, New York, N.Y.

Pleetox Products Co.
1919 Delmar
St. Louis, Mo. 63103

Plymouth Golf Ball Co.
Butler Pike
Plymouth Meeting, Pa. 19462

Directory of Suppliers

Polygraphics, Inc.
2037 Wales Rd., N.E.
Massillon, Ohio 44646

Port-A-Splay
14918 Minnetonka Blvd.
Minnetonka, Minn. 55343

Potentials in Marketing
731 Hennepin Ave.
Minneapolis, Minn. 55403

Prager Industries, Inc.
100 Jackson Ave.
Edison, N.J. 08817

Pratt Poster Co., Inc.
3001 E. 30th St.
Indianapolis, Ind. 46218

Precision Products & Parts Div.
P. O. Box 338
Davidson, N.C. 28036

Premium Incentive Business
1501 Broadway
New York, N.Y. 10036

Premium Mills, Inc.
71 Oliver Rd.
Paramus, N.J. 07652

Prestype, Inc.
Gotham Industrial Park
194 Veteran Blvd.
Carlstadt, N.J. 07072

Prima Education Products
Irvington-On-Hudson, N.Y. 10533

Prince Consort Tie Co.
16 S. Eutaw St.
Baltimore, Md. 21201

Pro Faces, Inc.
2001 S. Bannock St.
Denver, Colo. 80223

Professional Products Co., Inc.
347 Fifth Ave.
New York, N.Y. 10016

Project: Filmstrip
825 S. Barrington Ave.
Los Angeles, Calif. 90049

Promotions for Industry, Inc.
6545 Carnegie Ave.
Cleveland, Ohio 44103

Quality Photo Co.
119 W. Hubbard St.
Chicago, Ill. 60610

Quasar Industries, Inc.
380 Main St.
Hackensack, N.J. 07601

Race Nite
400 Oak St., Suite 219
Cincinnati, Ohio 45219

The Races, Inc.
2320 Avenue U
Brooklyn, N.Y. 11229

Radiant Films
220 W. 42nd St.
New York, N.Y. 10036

Radiant Manufacturing Co.
8230 N. Austin Ave.
Morton Grove, Ill.

Ram Golf Corp.
2020 Indian Boundary Dr.
Melrose Park, Ill.

Ramic Productions
58 West 58th St.
New York, N.Y. 10019

Ramona Mining & Mfg. Co.
P. O. Box 847
Ramona, Calif. 92065

Rand McNally & Co.
822 N. Central Park
Skokie, Ill. 60076

Ray Products, Inc.
11565 Federal Dr.
El Monte, Calif.

Razosharp
421 Stockholm St.
Brooklyn, N.Y. 11237

Redi Art
740 Broadway
New York, N.Y. 10003

W. C. Redmon Sons & Co.
Peru, Ind. 46970

Redwood House
155 River Rd.
North Arlington, N.J. 07032

Replica Models
610 Franklin St.
Alexandria, Va. 22314

Replogle Globes, Inc.
1901 Naragansett Ave.
Chicago, Ill. 60639

Rick Shaw Associates Ltd.
250 W. 57th St.
New York, N.Y. 10019

Right-On Graphics, Inc.
2550 W. Century Blvd., Suite 427
Los Angeles, Calif. 90045

Ris-Gay Division
Beltex Div.
P. O. Box 278
Barnhart, Mo. 63012

Roa's Films
1696 North Astor St.
Milwaukee, Wis. 63202

D. Robbins & Co., Inc.
127 West 17th St.
New York, N.Y. 10011

H. Armstrong Roberts
4203 Locust St.
Philadelphia, Pa. 19104

Robert James Co., Inc.
3600 7th Ct. St.
Birmingham, Ala. 35222

Justus Roe & Sons. Inc.
217 River Ave.
Patchogue, N.Y. 11772

M. B. Rosen & Son. Inc.
2801 N. Tryon St.
Charlotte, N.C. 28206

Rotadyne, Inc.
8705 Freeway Dr.
Macedonia, Ohio 44056

Round Hill, Inc.
581 W. Putnam Ave.
Greenwich, Conn.

Roundtable Films, Inc.
113 N. San Vicente Blvd.
Beverly Hills, Calif. 90211

R.P.M. Associates, Ltd.
1820 Sterling St.
La Salle, Ill. 61301

Ruebro Mfg. Co., Inc.
1002 Grand St.
Brooklyn, N.Y. 11211

Rueby Process, Inc.
1257 University Ave.
Rochester, N.Y. 14607

S & A Appliques, Inc.
799 Broadway
New York, N.Y. 10003

Directory of Suppliers

Sabine Industries, Inc.
McKeesport, Pa. 15134

Safety Premiums
41 Richmondville Ave.
Westport, Conn. 06880

Sales Catalysts, Inc.
105 East 29th St.
New York, N.Y. 10016

Sales Motivators, Inc.
8400 Julianne Terr.
Golden Valley, Minn. 55427

Arthur Salm, Inc.
1169 Egan Industrial Blvd.
St. Paul, Minn. 55121

Sand Manufacturing
9107 Chesapeake Dr.
San Diego, Calif. 92123

Sanson Institute of Heraldry
263 Summer St.
Boston, Mass. 02210

Sasco, Inc.
2781 Philmont Ave.
Huntingdon Valley, Pa. 19006

Science Research Associates
259 E. Erie St.
Chicago, Ill. 60611

Scott Crowell Corp.
11 South St.
Garden City, N.Y. 11530

Scott Plastics Co.
P. O. Box 2958
Sarasota, Fla. 33578

Scripto Inc.
P. O. Box 4847
Atlanta, Ga. 30302

Seeko Promotions
P. O. Box 128
Tappan, N.Y. 10983

Select Gifts Co.
116 E. 16th St.
New York, N.Y. 10003

Seth Thomas Div., General Time
135 S. Main St.
Thomaston, Conn. 06787

Seton Name Plate Corp.
592 Blvd.
New Haven, Conn. 06505

Shatas-Timecrafters
Commerce Campus
Middlebury, Conn. 06762

Shaw-Barton, Inc.
545 Walnut St.
Coshocton, Ohio 43812

Nat Sherman Co.
1400 Broadway
New York, N.Y. 10018

The Sherrill Corp.
Mexico, Ind. 46958

Sherry Mfg. Co., Inc.
1411 Broadway
New York, N.Y. 10018

Shure Brothers, Inc.
222 Hartrey Ave.
Evanston, Ill. 60204

Singer Education Div.
3750 Monroe Ave.
Rochester, N.Y. 14603

N. G. Slater Corp.
220 W. 19th St.
New York, N.Y. 10011

Slide Chart Corp.
50 W. Barnard St.
West Chester, Pa. 19380

The Slide Innovators
2020 San Carlos Blvd.
Fort Myers Beach, Fla. 33931

William J. Small Agency, Inc.
1318 Beacon St.
Brookline, Mass. 02146

Smell It Like It Is
1501 N.W. 14th St.
Miami, Fla. 33125

Smith Pacific
5300 W. 104th St.
Los Angeles, Calif. 90045

Snibbe Publications, Inc.
140 Overbrook Blvd.
Belleair Bluffs, Fla. 33540

Spectra Color Lab, Inc.
11037 Penrose St.
Sun Valley, Calif. 91352

Sponge Specialties Mfg. Corp.
510 Ocean Ave.
P. O. Box 96
East Rockaway, N.Y. 11518

S & S Associates
2781 Philmont Ave.
Huntingdon Valley, Pa. 19006

Stancraft Products
1621 E. Hennepin
Minneapolis, Minn. 55414

H & L Stanley
423 Guaranty Bldg.
Cedar Rapids, Iowa 52401

Stebco Products Corp.
3950 S. Morgan
Chicago, Ill. 60609

Sterling Movies, Inc.
375 Park Ave.
New York, N.Y. 10022

Frank Stein Novelty Co.
1969 So. Los Angeles St.
Los Angeles, Calif. 90011

Sterling Products
1689 Oakdale Ave.
St. Paul, Minn. 55118

Stevens Linen Division
P. O. Box 220
Webster, Mass. 01570

Fred Stoffel & Associates
723 E. California Blvd.
Pasadena, Calif. 91106

Structural Graphics
P. O. Box 70
Old Lyme, Conn. 06371

Studio Archives
P. O. Box 1041
3950 Laurel Canyon Blvd.
Studio City, Calif. 91604

Successful Meeting Slides
1422 Chestnut St.
Philadelphia, Pa. 19102

Sundials & More
New Ipswich, N.H. 03071

Surfset Inc.
35 Haddon Ave.
Shrewsbury, N.J. 07701

Sutton Designs, Inc.
P. O. Box 342
Interlake, N.Y. 14847

S. V. Tool Co., Inc.
P. O. Box 466
Newton, Kans. 67114

Directory of Suppliers

Swank, Inc.
6 W. 32nd St.
New York, N.Y. 10001

Swingster Wearables
Div. of Nat Nast Co.
P. O. Box 415
Bonner Springs, Kans. 66012

Synergistics Research Corp.
30 W. 22nd St.
New York, N.Y. 10010

Taylor Instruments
Consumer Division
Arden, N.C. 28704

Technamation, Inc.
30 Sagamore Hill Dr.
Port Washington, N.Y. 11050

The Telescope Folding Furniture Co.
Granville, N.Y. 12832

Texantics Unlimited Products
2120 McKinney Ave.
Houston, Tex. 77003

Theatrical Accessories, Inc.
1700 Gay Ave.
Findlay, Ohio 45840

Thermoptics Inc.
P. O. Box 504
Livermore, Calif. 94550

Thermo-Serv
239 Sixth Ave. North
Anoka, Minn. 55303

3-M Products
P. O. Box 33686
3 M Center
St. Paul, Minn. 55101

Tiffin Metal Products
450 Wall St.
Tiffin, Ohio 44883

Time-Life Books
Time & Life Bldg.
New York, N.Y. 10020

Tolch Products
114 Glenwood Ave.
Minneapolis, Minn. 55403

Top Brands, Inc.
520 West 15th St.
Oshkosh, Wis. 54901

Top Value Enterprises
3435 Wilshire Blvd., Suite 221
Los Angeles, Calif. 90010

Top Value Enterprises
Dayton, Ohio

A. G. Trumble Co.
3006 Jenkins Arcade
Pittsburgh, Pa. 15222

Travelers Premium Company, Inc.
110 Fifth Ave.
New York, N.Y. 10011

Trar-L-File
P. O. Box 16106
Memphis, Tenn. 38116

The United States Playing Card
Beech & Park
Cincinnati, Ohio 45212

United World Films
221 Park Ave. South
New York, N.Y. 10003

U. S. Games Systems, Inc.
468 Park Ave. South
New York, N.Y. 10016

U. S. Luggage Corp.
951 Broadway
Fall River, Maine 02724

U. S. Pencil & Stationery Co.
West Caldwell, N.J. 07006

Union Wadding Co.
125 Goff Ave.
Pawtucket, R.I. 02862

Universal Education & Visual Art
221 Park Ave. South
New York, N.Y. 10003

Universal Match
463 Paul Ave.
St. Louis, Mo. 63135

Universal Specialty Co.
180 N. Wacker Dr.
Chicago, Ill. 60606

Valdes Associates, Inc.
P. O. Box 382
Westbury, L.I., New York 11590

Thomas J. Valentino, Inc.
151 W. 46th St.
New York, N.Y. 10036

Valley Forge Flag Co., Inc.
One Rockefeller Plaza
New York, N.Y. 10010

Van's Pines, Inc.
West Olive, Mich. 49460

Vantage Communications
P. O. Box 546
Nyack, N.Y. 10960

Varigraph
1480 Martin St.
Madison, Wis. 53713

Varityper
720 Frelinghuysen Ave.
Newark, N.J. 07114

Vari-Vue International
650 South Columbus Ave.
Mt. Vernon, N.Y. 10551

Varsity House: Chev Craft
1533 Alum Creek Dr.
Columbus, Ohio 43209

Velva Sheen Mfg. Co.
2860 Virginia Ave.
Fairfax, Cincinnati, Ohio 45227

Vernon Company
604 W. 4th St. North
Newton, Iowa 50208

Victor Golf Equipment Group
8350 N. Lehigh Ave.
Morton Grove, Ill. 60053

VIP Industries
1543 14th St.
Santa Monica, Calif. 90404

Vision Wrap Industries, Inc.
250 S. Hicks Rd.
Palatine, Ill. 60654

Visual Communications
700 Ashland Ave.
Folcroft, Pa. 19032

Visual Graphics
P. O. Box 5646
Arlington, Tex. 76011

Visual Horizons
203 Westfall Rd.
Rochester, N.Y. 14620

Visual Panagraphics, Inc.
P. O. Box 5646
Arlington, Tex. 76011

Directory of Suppliers

Visual Products Division
3M Center
St. Paul, Minn. 55101

Vizuall Company, Inc.
14 E. Sixtieth St.
New York, N.Y. 10022

Harry Volk Art Studio
P. O. Box 4098
Rockford, Ill. 61110

Volk Corporation
P. O. Box 72
Pleasantville, N.J. 08232

Waldoroth Label Corp.
1261 Blue Hill Ave.
Boston, Mass. 02126

Roy W. Walters & Associates, Inc.
60 Glenn Ave.
Glen Rock, N.J. 07452

Index

A

Accessories for Meetings, 115
Acronyms in Printed Program, 169
Acronyms—Use in Speeches, 126
Action Plans, 87
Action Taking Place After Meeting, 15
Ad Coverage, 146
Advance Registration Mailing, 174
Advance Registration Promotion, 90
After Hours Do-It-Yourself Entertainment, 198
Agreement/Disagreement Quiz, 71
Air Fares—Types of, 33, 107
Airline Group Travel Purchasing Tips, 107
Airline Hostess Source, 178
Airline Promotional Assistance, 104
Airline Promotional Assistance Enroute, 106
Airline Souvenir Tie-Ins, 102
Airline "Flying Golfer's Club," 245
Airlines—Site Selection Assistance, 51
Airport Signs, 174
Alarm Clock on Speaker's Lectern, 113
American Plan—Savings, 31
Americana Giveaways, Gifts, 189, 207
Analysis of a Sale, 65
Animated Pie and Bar Charts, 131
Anniversary Seals, 189
Announcement Schedule, 90
Answers Encouraged from Audience, 72
Apple Break, 141
Art and Acting School Talent, 42
Artwork—Free from Hotels, etc., 36
Ashtrays with Meeting Theme, 115
Assignments—Participation, 87
Associations—Speaker Source, 61
Attention Ensuring, 70
Attention Regaining Ideas, 49
Audience Demonstrate, 67
Audio Visual Scripts, 158
Audio Visual Suppliers, 163
AUDIO VISUALS—HOW TO PLAN, PREPARE AND USE, 149
Auditing Hotel, 45
Authors—Speaker Source, 61

Award Presentation Ideas, 115, 116, 147
Awards—Golf, 247
Awards—Humorous Ideas, 147
Awards Individualized with Prestype, 116

B

Baby Photo Contest, 145
Badge Ideas, 179, 180
Badge Making Machines, 180
Badge Styles, 179
Badge Suppliers, 181
Badges—Alphabetize them at Registration, 176
Badges—from Hotels, 34
Badges—Ladies, 212
Badges—Letter of Alphabet on, 182
Badges—New Ribbons for Typewriters, 177
Badges—Ordering of, 179
Badges—Signs of Zodiac on, 183
Badges—Speaker, 144
Badges—Three-D, 100
Balloon Filled With Confetti and Smoke, 132
Balloon—Invitation, 182
Balloon—Menu Imprinted on, 195
Balloons—for Banquet, 231
Balloons Imprinted with Meeting Themes, 145
Balloons—in Speech, 127
Balloons—New Product Introduction, 124
Bands—Government Units, 42
Bands, Marching from High Schools, 42
Bands—Police, 42
Banknotes—Antique, 98
Banknotes—Colonial, 208
Banknotes—Foreign, 95
Banners—Organization, 118
Banners, Posters—Lettered, 117
Banners—Satin, 118
Banquet, 229
Banquet and Dinner Dance, 194
Banquet Checklist, 266
Banquet—How to Plan, 227
Banquet Invitation—Delivery of, 182
Banquet Showmanship Ideas, 231
Bar Charts, 132

Bartenders—Check Costs of, 39
Beauty Salon—Ladies, 215
Beef Serving, 41, 229
Beginning of Meeting Ideas, 66
Bellhop Page, 140
Beverage Checklist, 268
Beverage Cost Estimate Checklist, 269
Beverage Laws—Check Hotel, 223
Beverage Savings, 39
Bicycle—Big Wheel, 207
Binders, 185
Bingo, 198
Bingo to Teach Product Information, 123
Blackboard List—Group Selling, 82
Black Light, 131
Blazers, 118
Boasting Session, 84
Boat Cruise, 196
Book Mark, 99
Bookmatches, 145, 188
Bowl of Coins, 142
Brainpicking, 59
Brainstorming, 60
Breakfast Announcements thru PA System, 113
Breakfast in Bed—Ladies, 215
Breakfast—Ladies Special, 214
Breakfast Program Timing, 15
Breakfast Savings, 41
Breakfast Session, 113
Breakfast Stunt, 139
Breakfast—Unusual, 228
Breaking the Ice, 66
Briefcases, 185
Brunch—Champagne, 213
Budget—Constructing and Organizing, 12
Budget—How to Plan, 19
Budget—Notify Hotel, 20
Budget Planning Checklist, 255
Budget Responsibility, 19
Budget—Rough Draft and Firm, 19, 20
Budget Savings—Door Prizes, 46
BUDGET—WAYS TO STRETCH, 31
Buffets—Cost of, 41
Buffets—Luncheon, 229
Build a House, 127
Bulletin to Attendees on How to Gain Mileage from the Conference, 18
Bulletin Postcards, 96
Bullets—Revolutionary and Civil War, 207
Burn Speech, 126
Burning Impressions Mailing, 97
Bus Entertainment Ideas, 184
Bus Rental Subsidy, 33
Bus Trip with Mysterious Destination, 196
Business Stimulation and Sales Strategy Games, 85
Buzz Sessions, 64
Buttons—Gold Plated Period, 207
Buttons—"We Try Harder," 70
BUYER'S GUIDE—MEETING SUPPLIES AND SALES PROMOTION, 326

C

Cabaret Atmosphere for Hospitality Suite, 236
Calendar Planner, 170
Calcutta—Golf, 244
Camera—Source of Inexpensive, 186
Cannon, 246
Carnival Sound Effects, 202
Cars—Half Scale, Mini, 206, 207
Car Rental Discounts, 33
Cartoons—Imprinted Program, 168
Case Histories, 65, 67
Case Histories—Make Own Tapes, 57
Case Study—Problem Situation from Field, 82
Case Study—Sales Situation, 81
Casino Night, 200
Casino Gambling Instructions, 215
Cassette Instructions Daily, 184
Certificates of Achievement, 147
Chalkboard—Combination, 127
Chalkboards, 153
Chalkboards—Using Effectively, 162
Chamber of Commerce Assistance, 92
Chamber of Commerce—Local Queens, 42
Chamber of Commerce—Speaker Source, 62
Champagne Pledge, 69
Champagne Toast for Audience, 129
Change of Pace, 59
Charging Privileges—Savings, 45
Chart—Complicated, 146
Charts—Preparing, 158
CHECKLISTS, 253
Chest of Gold, 139
Chimp—Pose with, 194
Chinese Newspaper, 140
Chip and Dip Reception, 38
Cigarettes with Custom Labels, 188
Cigars After Dinner, 230
Cigar Store Indian Award, 117
Cigars—New Product, 146
Cinamaraces, 198
Circus Theme Supplies, 202
City Map—Custom, 93
Clinics with Experts, 84
Clipboards, 185
Closed Circuit TV—Speeches, 59
Coasters—Blotter, 145
Coat of Arms, 187
Cocktail—Hotel Sponsored, 39
Cocktail Party Ideas, 192
Cocktail Party at a Night Club, 197
Cocktail Party—Savings, 37
Cocktail Waitresses, 218
Coffee Break Estimates, 232
Coffee Break Ideas, 113, 141, 232
Coffee Break Location, 232
Coffee Break Savings, 37
Coffee Breaks Sponsored by Supplier, 44
Coffee Served Near Registration Area, 176
Coffee Throughout Session, 113

Index

385

Coins—Foreign, 95, 98
Coins—Plaques, 208
Coins—Throw, 127
Colonial Banknotes, 208
Color Postcards, Brochures, 96
Committee Delegation Checklist, 254
Committee Name Badges, 181
Communication Test, 119
"Company Orientation" Program for Wives, 214
Company Policy Manual—Humorous, 146
Company Symbol Drawing on Printed Program, 168
"Competition for Best Answers," 65
"Competition" Session, 85
Competitive Prices—Savings, 34
Competitive Product—Prepare to Sell, 60
"Complete Package" Emphasized, 125
Computer Marketing Games, 59
Confucius Sayings, 170
Contest—Demonstration, 59
Contest—Hold Group, 86
Controlling Speaker's Times, 113
Convention Bureau Promotion Assistance, 92
Convention Bureaus—Speaker Source, 61
Convention Character—Create a, 95
Convention Newspaper, 183
Convention Packet, 177
Corsages, 195, 215
COST SAVINGS, 31
Costume Ideas, 199
Crashing Through Door, 128
Critique—Meeting, 26
Crowns, Scepters, Tiaras, 147
Cushion—"Reserved for Worlds Greatest Salesman," 116
Custard Pie, 146
Customer Skit, 67
Customer Taped Comments, 143
Customer Voices, 71

D

Dance—Dinner, 194
Dance Instructors, 200
Dancing, 195
Dartboards, 199
Dealer Programs, 66
Debate, 67, 146
Debate Panel, 76
Decoration Kits for Theme Parties, 200
Decorations for Meeting Room, 35, 117
Demonstration Contest, 59, 83
Demonstration Magnified on TV, 130
Demonstrations, Lessons—Ladies, 217
Depth Analysis of a Sale, 65
Desserts, 230
Devil's Advocate, 126
Devil's Advocate—Panels, 78
Dining Room Size, 229
Dinner Dance—Seating, 194

Dinner Ideas—Unconventional, 197
Dinner—Train, 196
Diplomas—Sheepskin, Parchment, 116
Directional Signs Reuse, 34
Disappearing Message, 101
Discussion—Informal, 58
Disposable Flashlights, 188
Distributor Programs, 66
Dixieland Party, 201
Dollar Bills—Names Written On, 68
Door Prizes, 139, 215
DRAMATIZING THE PROGRAM, 111
Drapes—Imprinted, 118
Drawing Prizes for Early Birds, 113
Drill Teams—Government, 42
Drink Chips, 221
Drink—Names After Group, 197
"Drive Home a Point," 14
Dummies in Selling Reinactment, 129

E

Easel Display Binders, 115
Easel Pads, 153
Easel Pads—Using Effectively, 162
Embroidered Company Emblem, 118
Entertainers—Hiring, 197
Entertainers—Independent Contractors, 198
Entertainers—Tips on Working with, 197
Entertainment—by Hotel, 42
Entertainment—After Hours, 198
Entertainment—Golf, Evening, 246
ENTERTAINMENT IDEAS—DO-IT-YOURSELF, 191
ENTERTAINMENT—LADIES, 209
Entertainment—Theme, 193
Enthusiasm Dramatized, 125
ENTHUSIASM, INTEREST AND RESULTS—WAYS TO CREATE, 55
Entree Suggestions, 229
Esprit De Corps—Ways to Promote, 70
EVALUATING AND FOLLOWING UP THE MEETING, 25
Evaluation Questionnaire Distribution, 26
Evaluations—Types of, 26
Evening Activities—Couples, 213
Evening at the Track, 237
Evening Meetings—Scheduling, 15
Evening Session, 214
Examination for Fun and Profit, 71
Exhibit Area Coffee Break, 233
Exhibit Set-Up Charges—Savings, 35
Eye-Testing Chart Simulated, 132

F

Fashion Show Tips, 214
"Features to Benefits"—Converting, 83
Features—Name the, 127
Federal Government Speaker, 61

Feedback, 66
FEEDBACK—MEETING, 26
Film—Convention on, 57
Film—Golf, 246
Film Sources—Sales Training, 72
Films Accompanied by Discussion Leader's Guide, 86
Films—Free, 35
Films—Humorous, 142
Films—Projecting, 160
Films—Sports, 199
Films—Travel, 35, 199
Films—Free Foreign Travel, 35, 95
Filmstrips, 153
Filmstrips—Using Effectively, 162
Firecracker Mailings, 97
Fireworks Effects, 123
Flags—Golf, 243
Flags on Stage 113
Flags, String of for Meeting Room, 117
Flannel Boards, 133
Flash Bulletins, Flashkards, 95
Flash Paper to Unveil Statistic, 133
Flats—Write behind, 126
Flight Bags, 185
Flight Seat—Complimentary, 33
Flight Garment Bags, 102
Flip Chart—Write in Main Points, 126
Flip Charts, 153
Flip Chart—Three Dimensional Symbol, 132
Flip Charts—Using Effectively, 162
Flip Charts—Preparing, 156
Flower Savings, 43
Folios, 185
Foreign Language Captions—Speeches, 126
Foreign Promotional Mailing, 94
Fortune Cookies, 145
Four Leaf Clovers, 188
Fragrances on Mailings, 100

G

Gag Buttons, 205
Gag Items for Cocktail Party, 205
Gag Supplies, 205
Gags—Golf, 246
Gag Slides Involving Attendees, 144
GAGS, 137
Gambling Instructions, 215
Game—Secret Word, 67
Game—Stump the Experts, 69
Game—Wheel-of-Fortune, 69
Games, 59, 88
Garment Bags, 102
Gay Nineties Party, 201
"Ghost Writer" Invitation Mailing, 101
Giant Balloon Atop Meeting Site, 176
Gifts—Welcome, 186
Giveaways, 187
Giveaways—Americana, 189
Giveaways—Golf, 246
Godfather Party, 201

Gold Rush Party, 201
Golf—Callaway System, 241
Golf Events—Other, 244
Golf—Handicapping, 241
Golf—Ladies Tournament, 242
Golf—Putting Contest Indoors, 193
Golf Accessory and Giveaway Suppliers, 248
Golf Awards, 247
Golf Evening Entertainment, 246
Golf Gags, 246
Golf Giveaways, 246
Golf Planning Checklist, 240
Golf Pro-Promotional Letter from, 92
Golf Promotion Enclosures, 245
Golf Showmanship Ideas, 243
Golf Tournament—How to Promote, 245
GOLF TOURNAMENT—HOW TO PROMOTE AND CONDUCT, 239
"Good Morning" Wake Up Calls, 113
Good Start—Meetings, 66
Goodbye Ideas, 184
Government Welcome Speakers, 184
Graph Line—Moving, 131
Gratuities, 231
Gratuity Checklist, 271
Gratuity Savings, 45
Greet Each Person, 176
Greeters and Hosts on Hand, 175
Gripe Session, 83
Group Contests, 86
Group Function Rates, 31
Group Plans—Airline, 33, 106
Group Selling, 81
Group Sessions—Wives at, 213
Group Ticket Purchasing Tips, 107
Guarantees—Food Function, 40
Guarantees—Meal, 229
Guide to Professional Hosting, 223
Guns—Muskets, Pistols, Powder Horns, 208

H

Handkerchief—Identification, 102
Handshake Photo—As Welcome in Room, 182
Hats—Novelty, 70, 206
Hawaiian Luau, 203
Head Table Seating Plan, 232
Head Table—Introducing Couples, 194
Head Table—VIP Service, 231
Head Table—"What's My Line" Introduction, 194
"Herman Holds a Sales Meeting" Film, 132
Historical Documents, 189
Historical Documents Mailing, 97
Hors d'Oeuvres, Savings, 37, 221
Horse Race Named After Company, 196
Horse Race to Induce Starting on Time, 114
HOSPITALITY SUITE—HOW TO RUN, 235
Hospitality Suite—Savings, 40
Hospitality Suite Surcharge, 44
Host—Party, 192
Hostesses—for Hospitality Suite, 236
Hot New Product, 123

Index

Hotel Charges, 32
Hotel Daily Audit, 45
Hotel—Notify of Budget, 20
Hotel Inspection Checklist, 259
Hotel Literature Assistance, 92
Hotel Location Map, 178
Hotel Low-Demand Periods, 31
Hotel Promotional Assistance, 92
Hotel Service Evaluation, 27
Hotel—Printed Material Available, 36
House Brands, 39
"How I Made My Best Sale," 86
HOW TO PLAN A SUCCESSFUL PROGRAM, 7
Humorous Slide and Film Suggestions, 142
Humorous Sports Award Plaques, 247

I

ICEBREAKER AND WELCOME IDEAS, 173
Icebreaking, 66
Icebreaking Ways to Introduce Guests, 182
Ice Cream Break, 233
Idea Money, 69
Idea Showcase, 66
"Illustrating and Difference," 125
"Importance of Observing" Stunt, 146
Incentive Program Announcing, 147
Incentive Travel Work Kit, 95
Income Boosting Ideas, 44
Individual Clinics with Experts, 84
Individual Sessions, 15
Informal Discussion, 58
Information Booth, 178
Inquiring Reporter, 68
Insurance, 16
Interrogator Panel, 76
Interview-Conduct, 56
Interview Panel, 76
Interviews—Speaker, 108
Introductions—Head Table, 195
Introduction Party—Ladies, 214
Invisible Ink Postcard, 101
Invitation—Tin Can, 99
Invitation Ideas, 94
Invitations—Hospitality Suite, 236
Invitations on Balloon, 182
Involvement—Ways to Get Audience, 67
Involving Audience—Questions and Quizzes, 70

J

Japanese Dinner, 201
JOKES AND ONE-LINERS, 275
Jumbo Telegrams, 96
Jumping Disc, 99

K

Keep Attention With Prizes, 128
"Key Question" Jackpot Prize, 68
Key to Treasure Chest for Early Birds, 114
"Keys to Profits" Stunt, 139

L

Ladies—Invite or Not Invite, 210
Ladies at Business Sessions, 210
LADIES EVENTS—HOW TO PROGRAM, 209
Ladies Entertainment Ideas, 215
Ladies Lounge, 214
"Ladies Only" Night, 213
Ladies Program—Defraying Costs, 215
Ladies Program—Promotion, 217
Ladies Program—Staffing for, 211
Laugh-In Joke Wall, 112
"Law of Averages—Make It Work for You," 125
Lectures—Ladies, 216
Letter Enclosures for Travel Mailings, 99
Lettering—Hand, 157
Letters from Mailbox, 131
Liquor Consumption Estimating, 221
Liquor Control, 222
Liquor Savings—House Brands, 39
Liquor Service—Types of, 222
Liquors and Wines—Miniature Promotional Bottles, 93
"Listen In On Purchasing" Recording, 64
Listening Teams, 87
Lobby Sign, 175
Local Customs, 192
Local Dishes—Notice of Contents, 195
Local Dishes Publicized, 231
Local Flavor Mailing Ideas, 93
Lucky Key to Treasure Chest, 91
Luggage—Adhesive Strip Room Numbers, 176
Luggage Tags, 174
Luggage Tags—Magic Window, 101
Luncheon—"Learn At" Session, 56
Luncheon Buffet, 229
Luncheon Savings, 41

M

Magic Tricks, 145
Magician—Hospitality Suite, 238
Magnetic Clip Holder, 187
Mailbox—Pull Out Letters from, 131
Mailing Bags, 96, 98
Mailing Ideas—Promotional, 93, 97
Mailing Lists—Sale of, 44
Mailings—Complete Kits, 101
Mailings—Foreign Promotional, 95
Mailings—Travel, 94
Mailings With Fragrances, 100
Manikin—Artist's, 159
Map of Downtown Area, 183
Map of Hotel Locations, 178
Masks, 70
Master Account, 44
Meal Duplication, 229
MEAL FUNCTIONS—HOW TO PLAN, 227
Meal Guarantees, 229, 230
Meal Savings, 40
Meats—Guard Against Cut Meat, 229
Medallion Awards, 116

Meeting Accessories, 115
MEETING FOLLOW-UP, 25
Meeting Follow-Up Ideas, 29
Meeting Opening Communications Test, 119
Meeting Opening Ideas, 112
Meeting Opening Stunt, 139
Meeting Pattern, 56
Meeting Planning Questionnaire, 10
MEETING PROMOTION, 89
Meeting Purpose, 9
Meeting Room Decorations, 5
Meeting Room Prop Checklist, 263
Meeting Rooms—Restaurant, 32
Meeting Theme Art, 96, 169
Meeting Types, 11
Menu—Carved Sandwiches Savings, 37
Menu Imprinted on Balloon, 195
Menu—Local Dish Contents, 195
Menu Savings, 41
Menus—Printed, 231
MENUS AND MEAL FUNCTIONS—HOW TO PLAN AND PREPARE, 227
Message for the Speaker, 125
Message Sign Set, 178
Mexican or Fiesta Party, 203
Mindreading, 128
Miniature Newspaper—Publish a, 93
Minstrels—Wandering, for Cocktail Party, 222
Models—To Change Easel Signs, 127
Models and Bunnies as Greeters, 175
Models Assist in Demonstrations, 128
Moderator's Duties—Panel, 77
Momentos for the Ladies, 215
Money—Big, 142
Money—Fake, 201
Money—Idea, 69
Money—Making Your Own, 142
Money—Names Written on Dollar Bills, 68
Money Envelopes, 98
Money Ideas, 142
Money Theme Welcome Ideas, 187
Money to Be Had, 68
Money Tree, 129
Motion Pictures, 154
Motion Pictures—Using Effectively, 162
Movie Stills—Horror, Mystery, 96
Movie Stills—Slides, 134
Movies—Old Time, 199
Moving Graph Line, 131
Moving People Quickly Out of Room, 114
Mugs—Americana, 208
Mugs—Photo, 186
Multi-Media, 155
Music—Banquet, 195
Music—Do-It-Yourself, 199
Music for Breaks, 142

N

National Park Sites, 53
New Product Introductions, 123
New Product Presentation—Expert Panel, 78
New Salesmen—Making Feel at Home, 112
New Selling Procedure Sent in Advance, 60
News Media Publicity, 108
Newspaper—Special Edition, 129
Newspapers—Gag, 140
Newspapers—Old, 140
Night Club—Take Over for Party, 197
"No Sales Meeting Today" Opening, 112
Nostalgia Theme Supplies, 203
Note Taking Outlines, 82
Novelty Hats, 70

O

Objectives—Evaluating, 27
Objectives of Meeting, 10
Objections—Overcoming, 125
Off-Stage Voice, 59
Old-Time Movie Films, 131
Old-Time Movie Photos in Printed Program, 169
Old-Time Movie Slides, 143
Old-Time Movie Stills, 159
On-The-Spot Drawings, 126
On-Time Attendance Promoting, 138
On-Time Attendance—Special Speaker, 60
Opaque Projectors, 153
Open Bar—Savings, 39
Open House, 58
Opening Ideas—Meeting, 112
Opening Meeting Stunts, 138
Opening Session—Wives, 213
Orange Trees, 94
Orchids from Hawaii, 182
Outdoor Meals, 201, 232
Overhead Projectors—Using Effectively, 163
Overhead Transparencies—Preparing, 157
Overseas Mailings—Promotional, 95
Overtime Charges—Avoiding, 32
Overtime Solutions, 114

P

Packet Boat—New York City, 196
Paging Stunts, 140
Panel Controlling, 77
Panel of Interrogators, 71
Panel Interpreters, 84
Panel Sizes, 77
PANELS—HOW TO MAKE THE MOST EFFECTIVE USE OF, 75
Panels—Planning for, 77
Panels—Types of, 76
Participation—Phases to Use, 84
Participation—Ways to Involve Audience, 67
PARTICIPATION—WAYS TO SECURE, 79
Participation Ideas—Other, 88
Party—Outdoors, 193
Party and Gag Supplies, 205
Party Theme Supplies, 199
Party Themes—Check Hotel, 199
Party—Theme Ideas, 199
Parties—Unusual Locations, 195

Index

Parties Away from Hotel, 195
Passes—Complimentary, 197
Passport Pocket Portfolio, 186
Patriotic and Americana Gifts, 207
Pencil Caddies, 99
Pencils, Tiny, 98
Pennants and Posters—Stock, 117
Personal Promotional Messages, 94
Personalization, 186
Personalized Wine Glasses, 223
Personalizing with Gold Foil, 115
Personalization with Gold Writing Pen, 115
Phonograph Records—Attendance Promotion, 91
Photo—Personal Statuette, 194
Photo Badge, 180
Photo Tracing—Awards Presentation, 117
Photographer—Speculative, 37
Photographs—Stock, 96
Photos of Guest Identity, 183
Pianist, 67
Pill Promotion, 96
Pillowcases—Disposable, 182
Pine Tree Seedlings, 93
Pitchmaker, 128
Placecards—Use of, 60
Placemats for Home, 91
Planetarium—As Meeting Site, 52
Planetarium Meeting, 196
PLANNING A SUCCESSFUL PROGRAM, HOW TO, 7
PLANNING CHECKLISTS, 253
Planning Committee—Program, 8
Planning Forms—Sales, 82
Planning Savings, 46
Plaques—Coins, 207
Plaques—Humorous Sports Award, 247
Pocket Savers, Golf, 247
Pocket Secretaries Containing Program, 185
Pocket Secretaries Containing Printed Program, 169
Policy Evaluation Session, 84
Polynesian Beach Party, 201
Pony Express Mailing, 98
Pool Tables, 198
Poolside Meeting, 113
Pop-Up Mailers, 100
Postcard from Mayor, 93
Postcards—Colors, 100
Postcards—Promotional, 96
Post Conference Questionnaire, 28, 212
POST MEETING EVALUATIONS, 25
Post—Conventional Booklet, 184
Posters, Banners, Lettered, 117
Practical Jokes, 145
Presentation Methods—Types, 13
PRESENTATION SHOWMANSHIP, 121
Pressure Sensitive Stickers, 189
PRINTED PROGRAM—HOW TO ENLIVEN, 167
Printed Program—Savings, 36
Printed Program—Use Odd Starting Times, 113
Printing Savings, 36
Private Meeting Room at Hospitality Suite, 236

Prizes—Golf, 247
Problems Situation from Field, 82
Problem Solving, 59, 83
Product Information Taught by Bingo, 123
Production Aids and Ideas—Promotional, 95
Production Tips—Promotional, 95
PROGRAM STEPS IN PLANNING, 8
Program Contained in Pocket Secretary, 185
PROGRAM PLANNING, 8
Program Planning—Ladies, 211
Program Planning Committee, 8
Program Planning Outline, 8
Program Planning Sources—Ladies Program, 212
PROGRAM PRINTED—HOW TO ENLIVEN, 167
Program Questionnaire, 10
PROGRAM SHOWMANSHIP, 111
PROGRAM THEMES, 21
Projecting—Slides and Films, 160
Projection Pointer, 135
Projection Tips, 160
Promoting Ladies Program, 217
PROMOTING THE MEETING—WAYS TO, 89
Promotion—Planning of Mailings, 90
Promotion of Golf Tournament, 245
Promotional Assistance, 92
Promotional Assistance—Airlines, 102
Promotional Ideas—Local Flavor, 93
Promotional Mailings—Complete Series, 101
Promotional Material Savings, 34
Promotional Production Tips, 97
Prop Checklist, 263
"Proper Mental Attitude" Illustrated, 124
Props—Hotel, 42
Props—Rental, 193
Proverbs and Epigrams—List of, 170
Psychological Stunt, 140
Public Officials as Speakers, 61
Punch for Non-Drinkers, 222
Putting Contest, 193
Publicity—Extra Coverage, 37, 108
Publicity—Hints on Preparing, 109
Publicity—How to Publicize Meeting, 108
Publicity—Ladies Program, 211
Publicity Checklist, 273
Publicity for Honored Salesmen, 108
Publicity Releases—Timing of, 108
Puzzle Mailing, 98
Puzzles, 145

Q

Queens, 42
Question and Answer Session, 82
Question Box, 72
Question Card in Welcome Kit, 69
Questionnaire—Ladies Program, 212
Questionnaire—Post Conference, 28
Questionnaires—Evaluation, 26
Questions—Answers from Audience, 72
Questions—Speakers Ask, 72
Questions—Unanswered Session, 58

Quiz Down, 71
Quiz on Agreement/Disagreement, 71

R

Raffle Ticket Source, 200
Rain Insurance, 232
Raincoats, Bonnets—Plastic, 189
Receipts Timesaver, 177
Reception and Banquet Checklist, 266
Receptions, 190
Reception—"Chip and Dip," 38
Receptions Sponsored by Suppliers, 39
Recorded Music Before Meeting Begins, 112
Recorded Presentations, 154
Recorded Voice—Girls, 58
Recreation—Ladies, 216
Red Carpet for Award Presentations, 115
Refreshments—Theme, 193
Registration—Advance, 90
Registration—Quick, 175
Registration—Chamber of Commerce Help, 46
Registration Checklist, 265
Registration Desk—How to Handle, 176
Registration Desk—Materials for, 177
Registration Fast Service, 178
Rehearsals—Union Savings, 42
Rental Equipment—Savings, 34
Reporter—Inquiring, 68
Representative's Seminar, 86
Resort Social Director, 198
Restaurant Dining Guide, 183
Restaurant Menus—Promotional, 93
Restaurants—Ladies Tour, 216
Reverse Panel, 76
Ribbons—First Aid for, 177
Ribbons with Committee Names, 181
Role Playing, 67, 83
R.O.N. Kits, 186
Room List, 178
Room Name, 56
Room Rates—Complimentary, 31
Room Rates—Taxes, 32
Roster of Attendees, 178
Rulers, 100

S

Salads, 230
Sales and Marketing Clubs—Speaker Source, 62
Sales Literature—Savings, 37
Sales Manual Written by Salesmen, 65
Sales Presentation in Three Minutes, 127
Sales Problem—Overcoming, 129
Sales Promotion "Needs" Session, 85
Sales Psychologist as Speaker, 61
Sales Situation Case Study, 81
Sales Training Film Sources, 72
Salesman Panel, 78
Salesmen Run Own Show, 65

Savings—Transportation, 32
SAVINGS IN COSTS, 31
Screen Size—Choosing, 161
Screens—Types of, 161
Scripts—Audio Visuals, 158
Sears Roebuck Catalog, 186
Secret Message Bullet, 99
Secret Word Game, 67
Security and Identification, 237
Seductive Voice, 128
Self-Questioning Panel, 76
Self-Smoking Cigarettes, 92
Seminar—Representative's, 86
Sergeant at Arms Fines Latecomers, 113
Sheepskin Diplomas, 116
Shipping Tips, 17
Ships—as Meeting Sites, 51
Shoe Shine Packs, 188
Shopping Bags—Plastic, 185
Shower of Money, 142
Showmanship—Panels, 78
SHOWMANSHIP—PRESENTATIONS AND SPEECHES, 121
SHOWMANSHIP—PROGRAM, 111
Sign—Descending, 128
Signs—Identification, Directional, 184
Signs—Pop-Up, 129
Signs of Zodiac Theme, 58
Sightseeing Tours, 42
Silhouettes on Rear—Projection Screen, 130
Site Selection Assistance, 51
Site Selection Checklist, 258
SITE SELECTION TIPS, 49
Sites—Live-in-Inspection, 51
Sites—Types of, 50
Sites, Unusual, 51, 52
Sites, Convention—Questions to Be Answered, 49
Skit—Customer, 67
Skits—Participation, 81
Slap Boards, 152
Slap Boards—Using Effectively, 152
Slide Projector—Kodak, 134
Slides, 154
Slides—Avoiding Upside Down Backwards, 133
Slides—Captioned, Stock, 134
Slides—Girl Title, 143
Slides—Movie Stills, 134
Slides—Projecting, 160
Slides—Stock Art, 158
Slides—Stock Captioned, 159
Slides—Stock for Sales Training, 134
Slides—Using Effectively, 160
Slides—Visual Indicator for Changing, 135
Slides of Attendees, 183
Slipper Socks for Travelers, 102
Smoke—Puff of, Introduction, 123
Smoke Pot, 123
Snack on Your Own, 237
Sound Effects—Circus, Carnival, 202
Sound Effects Records, 133
Sound Rostrum—Portable, 135
Sources of Supply—Local Savings, 34

Index

391

Speaker—Lady, 61
Speaker—Message for, 125
Speaker—Sales Psychologist, 61
Speaker—Special to Get Audience in Early, 60
Speaker Badges, 144
Speaker Biographies, 170
Speaker Agent Savings, 43
Speaker Checklist, 271
Speaker Evaluation, 27
Speaker Materials—Savings, 37
Speaker Savings, 43
Speaker Sources—Ladies, 217
Speaker Tip—Repeat the Question, 84
Speakers—Ask Questions, 72
Speakers—Association Chapters, 61
Speakers—Authors, 61
Speakers—Convention Bureau, 61
Speakers—Customer, Dealer, Distributor, 43
Speakers—Customers, 60
Speakers—Federal Government, 43, 184
Speakers—Government Welcome, 184
Speakers—Humorous, 144
Speakers—Local, 43
Speakers—Local Corporate Branches, 61
Speakers—Professional Speaker's Bureau, 62
Speakers—Public Officials, 61
Speakers—Sales and Marketing Clubs, 62
Speakers—Special Sources, 60
Speakers—Sports, 62
Speakers—Travel Cost Tips, 62
Speakers—Universities, 61
Speaker's Directory, 61, 62
Speaker's Dress, 118
Speaker's Time—Controlling, 114
Specialty Items, 145
Speech Questionnaire, 71
SPEECH SHOWMANSHIP, 121
Speeches—Closed Circuit TV, 59
Speeches—Foreign Language Captions, 126
Speeches—Table Service Suspended, 231
Spinner Coins, 188
Sports Attire as Welcome Gift, 187
Sport's Speakers, 62
Staff Members Identified with Caps, 175
Stage Platforms Close to Audience, 58
Starting on Time Ideas, 113
State Emblems, 118
State Identification Badges, 180
State Tourist Magazine Promotion, 94
Statutettes—Personal Photo, 194
Stick-Ons for Mailings, 100
Stills—Old-Time Movie, 159
Stock Pages for Printed Program, 168
Stopping on Time Ideas, 113
Studio Warm-Up, 138
Stump the Experts, 69
STUNTS AND GAGS TO ENLIVEN THE MEETING, 137, 146
Summons Mailing, 97
Suppliers—Audio Visual, 163
Supplies—Party Theme, 199
Survival Kit, 188

Swizzle Sticks—Sports, 205
Symposium Panel, 76

T

Table Decorations, 232
Table Host for Banquet, 194
Talent Show, 198
Talent—Art and Acting School, 34
Tap Drummer—Start Meeting with, 112
Tape Recorded Announcement Promotion, 91
Tape Recorders—Using Effectively, 163
Tape Recording—Listen in on Purchasing, 64
Techniques—Meeting Conducting, 56
Telegram—Congratulations, 139
Telegram Stunt, 140
Tele-Lecture, Telewriting Service, 57
Telephone—Portable Conference, 57
Telephone Customers from Meeting, 58
Television—Giant Screen, 56
Test Yourself Games, 88
Thank You's Post Conference, 17
Theatre Party, 197
Theatrical Talent—From Universities, 42
Theme Entertainment, 193
Theme—Refreshments, 193
Theme Language, 129
Theme on Hotel Marquee, 175
Theme Party Ideas, 199
Theme Selection, 11, 21
Theme Translated into Foreign Language, 168
THEMES—CONFERENCE, 21
Themes—Wine Party, 225
Three-D Calling Cards, 100
Three Minute Communications Test, 119
Ticket Control—Meals, 231
Time Savings—Budget, 34
Timing of Program, 14
Tin Can Invitation, 99
Tire Gauge, 189
Title Slides—No Developing Required, 133
Tote Bags, 185
Totem Pole Awards, 117
Tour Ideas—Ladies, 215
Tour Packages—Local, 42
Tournaments—For Non-Golfers, 242
Tours—Supplier Sponsored, 46
Towels—Golf, 246
Train Dinner and Ride, 196
Transportation Savings, 32
Travel Agencies, 33
Travel Cost Tips for Speakers, 62
Travel Paks, 187
Travel Planners, 33
Traveling Mike, 126
Triangle and Stopover Fares, 107
Trophy—Golf, 247
"Try for More" Quiz, 71
T-Shirt—Photo on, 70
TV—Live, 155
TV Camera for Small Product Demonstration, 124
Type Faces, 157

U

Umbrellas—Golf, 243
"Unanswered Question Session," 58

V

Vegetables, 230
Vests, 70
Video Tape Sales Presentation, 57
Videotape, 154
VIP Treatment for Top Salesmen, 115
Visual Aids—Types, 152
Visual Build-Up Charts, 131
Visual Presentations—How to Plan, 150
VISUAL PRESENTATIONS, 149
Visual Presentations—Rehearsing, 161
Visual Presentations—Using Effectively, 160
Visuals—Cost Estimates, 159
Visuals—Guideline, 155
Visuals—How to Prepare, 155

W

Waiter—Comic, 192
Walkie Talkies for Staff Members, 178
"We Try Harder Buttons," 70
"We Understand Your Problem" Beginning, 60
WELCOME AND ICEBREAKER IDEAS, 173
Welcome Banner, 175
Welcome Basket, 181
Welcome Gifts, 186
Welcome Ideas, 174
Welcome Ideas for Hotel Room, 181
Welcome Kit—Question Card, 69
What to Wear—Banquet, 195
What to Wear—Notify, 91
Wheel-of-Fortune Game, 69
Wine at Luncheon, 229
Wine Glasses—Personalized, 223, 237
Wine Tasting Parties, 223
Wine Tasting Party—Hospitality Suite, 237
Wine Party Printed Programs, 224
Wine and Drinks at Food Functions, 230
Wines Instead of Cocktails, 39
Winner—Announcing of, 147
Wives at Home—Thoughtfulness for, 17
Wives at Opening Sessions, 213
Wooden Nickels, 142
Woodbook—Convention, 16
Workback to Retain Information, 68
Workshop Session Ideas, 62
Workshop Subjects, 63
Workshops—Source Material, 64
"World's Greatest Salesman" on Badges, 180
World's Greatest Shoeshine, 207
Wretched Mess Gag Gifts, 207
Write in Main Points on Flip Chart, 126
Write on Screen with Overhead Projector, 130

Y

"YCDBSOYC" on Beer Can Tab, 178
Years of Experience, 138
"Years of Experience" Opening, 112
"You Win, You Lose" Spinner Coins, 188
Yo-Yos, 205

Z

Zodiac—Signs of Theme, 58